The Orient Within

THE ORIENT WITHIN

*Muslim Minorities and the
Negotiation of Nationhood in
Modern Bulgaria*

MARY NEUBURGER

Cornell University Press

ITHACA AND LONDON

First published 2004 by Cornell University Press

Printed in the United States of America

Library of Congress Cataloging-in-Publication Data
Neuberger, Mary, 1966–
    The Orient within : Muslim minorities and the negotiation of
nationhood in modern Bulgaria / Mary Neuberger.— 1st ed.
        p. cm.
    Includes bibliographical references and index.
    ISBN 0-8014-4132-3 (alk. paper)
    1. Muslims—Bulgaria. 2. Nationalism—Bulgaria. 3.
Bulgaria—Politics and government—1990–   I. Title.
DR64.2.M8 N48 2004
305.6'97'09499—dc22   2003020155

Cornell University Press strives to use environmentally responsible
suppliers and materials to the fullest extent possible in the publishing
of its books. Such materials include vegetable-based, low-VOC inks
and acid-free papers that are recycled, totally chlorine-free, or partly
composed of nonwood fibers. For further information, visit our
website at www.cornellpress.cornell.edu.

Cloth printing   10 9 8 7 6 5 4 3 2 1

To Donald

For your patience and understanding during my many trips to the Balkans and innumerable hours at the computer.

Contents

Illustrations   ix
Preface   xi
A Note on Transliteration, Translation, and Sources   xv
Introduction   1

1. The Bulgarian Figure in the Ottoman Carpet: Untangling
   Nation from Empire   18
2. Muslim Rebirth: Nationalism, Communism, and the Path
   to 1984   55
3. Under the Fez and the Foreskin: Modernity and the
   Mapping of Muslim Manhood   85
4. The Citizen behind the Veil: National Imperatives and the
   Re-dressing of Muslim Women   116
5. A Muslim by Any "Other" Name: The Power of Naming
   and Renaming   142
6. On What Grounds the Nation?: Parcels of Land and Meaning   169

Conclusion   197
Bibliography   203
Index   217

Illustrations

Figures

1. A Bulgarian family in typical late Ottoman-period dress.   91
2. A scene just prior to the forced conversion of Pomaks during
    the First Balkan War, 1912.   93
3. Scene from the forced conversion of Pomaks during the
    First Balkan War, 1912.   94
4. The leaders of the *Rodina* organization, 1938.   98
5. An illustration from *Yeni Işık* showing Turks participating
    in a parade, 1951.   104
6. A *Yeni Işık* political cartoon depicting a Turkish family in
    caricatured traditional garb.   105
7. A Turkish family in a refugee camp on the Turkish side of the
    Bulgaro-Turkish border, 1953.   106
8. A group of Turkish men in berets in Kirdzhali, 1996.   107
9. A group of Pomak men in berets in Shivachevo, 1996.   108
10. "Veiled" Pomak women, 1996.   137
11. "Veiled" Pomak women represented as a political threat, 1996.   138
12. An elderly Pomak woman in Shivachevo, 1998.   139
13. The author seated between two elderly Pomak women
    near Ribnovo, 2000.   140

Maps

1. The Changing Borders of Bulgaria 1878–1945   20
2. The Distribution of Turks and Pomaks in Postwar Bulgaria   22

Preface

This is an exciting time to be working in the field of Balkan history. My generation of scholars came of age in the late 1980s and 1990s when the world we were studying fell apart and came back together again, however tentatively in places. The fall of Communism in the region opened up unimagined possibilities for research, even as war raged in the former Yugoslavia closing other doors. Many of the difficulties encountered by our senior colleagues have been eliminated, but new challenges have kept our field small. The diminutive size of the field and the countries we study means a scarcity of secondary sources, of historiography to build upon. As a result, Eastern Europeanists, by necessity, are still pioneers in searching out untapped archives and new research directions. Patience and a taste for adventure remain requirements for serious research in many parts of Eastern Europe. And though my patience was often in short supply, I devoted a decade to researching and writing this book, driven above all by a profound passion for Bulgaria and the intricacies of Balkan history. The Balkans as a physical place drew me in by its warmth and color, and the story of Bulgaria's Muslim minorities seemed to tie together all my intellectual interests into a large knot, begging to be unraveled.

But perhaps unraveling the knot was never really my goal. Instead I attempted to hold it up to the light, look at it from new angles, tug at a strand here and there to see where it tightened and where it let loose. I never came close to fully unraveling it, let alone weaving it into a coherent new tapestry. As with all histories, this one is necessarily partial—it is more process than finished product. I hope it inspires thought and discussion and contributes to a growing and exciting field still in its intellectual infancy. I also hope that this book contributes to scholarly debates in the numerous fields that it brushes up against and brings more attention to work in the field of East European history.

Although I take full responsibility for the contents of this book, certain people and institutions deserve special recognition for their roles in making my research possible. I thank the Fulbright commission for funding my research year abroad in Bulgaria (1995–96) along with the other funding sources that contributed to my study of the Bulgarian, Turkish, and Russian languages including the American Council of Learned Societies (ACLS), International Research and Exchanges Board (IREX), and numerous Foreign Language Area Studies (FLAS) grants through the University of Washington. I extend additional credit to IREX for funding two summers of research in Bulgaria in 1998 and 2000; their efforts to support research on this understudied region are commendable. Also, I am sincerely grateful to the National Council for East European and Eurasian Research (NCEER) for funding my research in Bulgaria and writing during the 2000–2001 academic year. Finally, the University of Texas has been more than generous in extending me summer funding and a Dean's Fellowship in 2000–2001.

A number of individuals deserve special recognition for helping to make this book a reality. Special thanks go to the people at the University of Washington who encouraged and coddled me both during and after my graduate program. James Felak helped and inspired me in the early stages of my graduate career; had I not witnessed his witty and informative rendition of "Balkan History Since 1453" in his 1992 course, I would neither have developed my "Balkan obsession" nor written this book. I extend my gratitude to Hillel Kieval whose profound wisdom and creative intellect made a deep imprint on my way of conceptualizing history. In addition, Reşat Kasaba was a veritable rock of support, encouragement, and inspiration throughout my doctoral program. I thank him and all the members of the Turkish Studies Seminar at the University of Washington for offering comments on the manuscript. Thank you Selim Kuru for your help with the Turkish language and suggestions on transliteration for the book. A number of my fellow graduate students at the University of Washington motivated and encouraged me with their comments, suggestions, and personal examples; thank you Melissa Martin, Kate Brown, Paulina Bren, and Ali Iğmen. So many people in Bulgaria and Turkey helped in various phases of this project that I can't possibly name them all but I would like to mention a few. I thank all of the numerous librarians and archivists in Sofia, Plovdiv, Kirdzhali, Smoyan, and Haskovo who helped gather materials for this project in spite of the topic's sensitivity. Thanks also to Kostadin Grozev, Mariana Stamova, Marin Bachvarov, Yulian Konstantinov, and others for all of your help and insights. I extend thanks to the Iğmen family, Turhan Gençoğlu and members of the Balkan Turk Émigré Association for their assistance and hospitality in Bursa. In addition, I express my appreciation to the supportive faculty at the University of Texas who offered useful suggestions on my manuscript or otherwise encouraged me during my years of teaching there. A special thanks to Joan Neuberger, Charters Wynn, and David Crew. Many others commented on the manuscript at various stages and deserve some mention. A warm thank you to Donald Quataert, Maura Hametz, and the reviewers at Cornell University Press for their generous comments and suggestions. Finally, I thank my husband, Donald Wysocki, who has provided the love and support at home so crucial to my completion of this book.

Some of the chapter 4 material on Muslim women and the veil can be found in another form in earlier publications: "Difference Unveiled: Bulgarian National Imperatives and the Re-dressing of Muslim Women in the Communist Period: 1945–89," *Nationalities Papers* 25 (1997): 169–81; and "Pants, Veils, and Matters of Dress: Unraveling the Fabric of Women's Lives in Communist Bulgaria," in *Style and Socialism: Modernity and Material Culture in Post-War Eastern Europe*, edited by D. Crowley and S. Reid (Oxford: Berg Publishing, 2000). I thank both *Nationalities Papers* (http://www.tandf .co.uk) and Berg Publishing for allowing me to reprint this material here.

A Note on Transliteration, Translation, and Sources

In transliterating Bulgarian from the Cyrillic to the Roman alphabet I use the Library of Congress system. I use the same system for Russian, Macedonian, and Serbo-Croatian words and names that appear in the text or bibliography. I made an exception, however, for personal or place names that are already commonly transliterated in another way in English-language historical works or maps. For example, I use Sofia instead of Sofiia, Smolyan instead of Smolian, Alexander Stamboliski instead of Aleksandŭr Stamboliĭski. A handful of Slavic names, especially in the bibliography, also appear in alternative transliteration systems where translated and transliterated by another author. For most modern Turkish words, I use standard modern Turkish and for Ottoman words I use the modern Turkish system of transliteration taken from the Modern Turkish to English Redhouse dictionary. To complicate matters, for a handful of Turkish or Ottoman words with common usage in Bulgarian sources, such as *shalvari*, *feredzhe*, and *teke*, I transliterated straight from the Bulgarian. The names of Turks taken from Bulgarian documents and sources I transliterate straight from Bulgarian to avoid confusion. All translations are mine, except in the rare cases that I cite a source from an English translation.

Archival Sources have been culled from five different archives in Bulgaria: Central Government Historical Archive in Sofia, or Tsentralen Dŭrzhaven Istoricheski Arkhiv (TsDIA); Plovdiv Regional Government Archive, Plovdiv Okrŭzhen Dŭrzhaven Arkhiv (PODA); Haskovo Regional Government Archive, Haskovo Okrŭzhen Dŭrzhaven Arkhiv (HODA); Kirdzhali Regional Government Archive, Kirdzhali Okrŭzhen Dŭrzhaven Arkhiv (KODA); and Smolyan Regional Government Archive, Smolyan Okrŭzhen Dŭrzhaven Arkhiv (SODA). Only the abbreviations for each archive appear in the footnotes as well as the standard Bulgarian style of citation, that is, TsIDA (F-1B, O-5, E-353, L-353: 1958), where F = *fond*, O = *opis*, E = *edinitsa*, and L = *list*. The inclusion of the year is my own variant.

The Orient Within

Introduction

We contact the world only through our boundaries.
—Blaga Dimitrova

The Orient and the Occident are neither places nor civilizations; they are only imagined. Yet they haunt the modern world like overdressed straw men, caricatures of themselves—Western "progress" and Eastern "backwardness." In the cartography of identities "East" and "West" are often the only two points on the compass that are presumed to measure the sum and substance of nations. In spite of scholarly questions about the essence and topography of each, distorted conceptions of East and West still dominate national imaginings around the globe.[1] Particularly on the margins of Europe, questions of the fault lines between East and West have had profound historical resonance. Eastern Europeans have had to confront the agony of their own so-called backwardness in relation to a modern West European norm.[2] Western Europe's condescending eastward gaze, cast upon the Orient as well as on Eastern Europe, has guided imagined geographies, collective soul-searching, and national self-discovery of Eastern Europeans in the modern period.[3] Concepts of East and West, progress and backwardness, along with the concept of "nation" were like stones dropped in a pond whose ripples lapped against the outer edges of Europe. On the margins of imagined continents

[1] A growing body of literature has explored the essentialized concepts of "Orient" and "Occident" and revealed them to be constructs rather than fixed realities. On the question of the East, see Edward Said, *Orientalism* (New York, 1978), and on the West, see James Carrier, ed., *Occidentalism: Images of the West* (Oxford, 1995).

[2] For explorations of backwardness as both an economic phenomenon and a field of cultural debate in Eastern Europe see Andrew Janos, *The Politics of Backwardness in Hungary, 1825–1945* (Princeton, 1982); and Jerzy Jedlicki, *A Suburb of Europe: Nineteenth-Century Polish Approaches to Western Civilization* (Budapest, 1998).

[3] For a discussion of Western perceptions and construction of Eastern Europe as "other" see Larry Wolff, *Inventing Eastern Europe: The Map of Civilization on the Mind of the Enlightenment* (Stanford, 1996). On the Balkans, see Maria Todorova, *Imagining the Balkans* (New York, 1997).

I

and civilizations such concepts assumed new meanings and forms as questions of essence and purity and the clarity of boundaries were confronted with an exceptional vigor. As a result, assertions of Europeanness shared the playing field with various explanations of East European backwardness and political failings. Although ultimately the contagion of progress proved irresistible to Eastern Europeans, the particular path to "Europe" was always a contested one.

In the Balkans, concepts of East and West have had a particular gravity because they inform ongoing Muslim/non-Muslim encounters in the region. Embedded in the newsworthy Balkan conflicts of the 1990s—Croat versus Serb, Serb versus Bosnian-Muslim, and Serb versus Albanian—are questions of elaborated fault lines between East and West.[4] Although these Balkan struggles have attracted ample academic and popular attention because of their bloody outcomes and Western intervention, other Balkan ethnic relationships still remain in the shadows of scholarly attention. This book is a study of one such relationship; it explores Muslim minorities on the geographic and social margins of Bulgaria, a country that is itself on the geographic and conceptual boundaries of Europe. It poses the questions: How did the powerful obsessions of modernity laced with the intoxicating lure of the West shape the Bulgarian encounter with its Muslim minorities? Specifically, how did Bulgarian thinkers and actors, bureaucrats and citizens succumb to the lure and the seeming clarity of Europeanness in the nineteenth and twentieth centuries, even while continually questioning and qualifying their relationship to both East and West? Although my study spans more than a century, from the 1860s until 1989, I focus on the period from the late 1930s through the mid-1980s, years in which the seduction and ambiguities of Western influence were most palpable and had the greatest consequences for the Bulgaro-Muslim relationship. I look in particular at two Muslim groups in Bulgaria: Turkish-speaking Muslims (hereafter called Turks) and Bulgarian-speaking Muslims (hereafter called Pomaks[5]) that today have pop-

---

[4] Although I deal primarily with the "fault lines" between Christian and Muslim in the Balkan context and beyond, in the literature on Eastern Europe numerous other internal fault lines that have even more prevalence in the literature. The cultural fault line between the Catholic and Orthodox Christian portions of the region is routinely used in (and has traditionally pervaded) academic "explanations" of economic and cultural backwardness or failings in the Orthodox World with its "Eastern" orientation and long history (in reference to the Balkans) under Asiatic, Ottoman rule. For an example of such an analysis see Walter Conner, "Europe East and West: Thoughts on History, Culture, and Kosovo," in *Cultures and Nations of Central and Eastern Europe: Essays in Honor of Roman Szporluk*, ed. Zvi Gittlemen, et al. (Cambridge, Mass., 2000).

[5] I am well aware of the debates surrounding the term "Pomak" which has become increasingly "politically incorrect" in historical and contemporary Bulgarian academic parlance for various reasons, such as the apparent lack of use of the term by the Pomaks themselves, and its purported derogatory nature. I prefer the term to "Bulgarian-Muslims" or "Bulgaro-Mohammedans" which imply a kind of essential "Bulgarianness" in the identity of this population, which is far from established. As for the term "Turk," it is anachronistic until at least the 1920s when a sense of "Turkishness" began to spread to local Turkish-speaking Muslims; again, I use the term for the sake of simplicity.

ulations of roughly 800,000 and 200,000 respectively out of Bulgaria's total population of nine million.[6] My central question is: How did Bulgarians map their own national identity and modernity through their relationship to the Muslim minorities within?

The demarcation of the Muslim presence in Bulgaria, I argue, was integral to nineteenth- and twentieth-century Bulgarian efforts to usher in a new era of progress and modernity. Under the influence of such West European intellectual frameworks as nationalism, fascism, and communism, and informed by a subtext of Orientalism, the most powerful voices within Bulgarian nation-building projects attempted to carve a place for Bulgaria in a presumably superior and culturally privileged Europe. Nation building demanded a negation of all that was Eastern within—an explicit rejection of Bulgaria's Ottoman past and its Muslim minority presence. Even during the Communist period when the West was explicitly being rejected and purged from Bulgarian society, modernization and Europeanization still dominated the discourse on social transformation; Bulgaria sought to overtake, and hence out-Europe, Europe. Yet paradoxically, as Bulgarian national discourse sought to reclaim Bulgarian national terrain from its occupation by the Ottoman East, the presence and role of the West were also highly contested from the outset. Bulgarian notions of a national self although intertwined with that of Christian Europe were always tempered by images of the various European powers as foreign, exploitative, and perverting in relation to a mythic, native essence. Purveyors of the national idea had found inspiration in the European "Orientalization" of the Ottoman East, but also were well aware of West European diffidence for the purportedly less civilized "other Europe." In addition, Bulgarian thinkers had always maintained close intellectual contact with Russia, itself "Orientalized" by Western Europeans and grappling with its own position between East and West. The resultant national identity crisis complicated Bulgarian national self-definitions and its imagined geography, as Bulgarians were caught between what were increasingly defined as discreet and distinct civilizations, East and West. At times, political expediency demanded that Bulgarians co-opt Muslims—despite their Oriental attribution—into provisional alliances against other, more odious "foreign" incursions. Hence, the Bulgarian nation building project both accepted and rejected, by turns appropriated and dispossessed both the East and the West in its search for national grounding.

Much of my analysis rests on the body of literature which conceptualizes

---

[6] The Turkish presence in Bulgaria, roughly 10 percent of the population today, is a direct result of the immigration of Turkish-speaking peoples from Asia Minor and the conversion and linguistic assimilation of local Slavs during five centuries of Turco-Ottoman rule. Pomaks, make up roughly 3 percent of the population, and as with Bosnian Muslims, they are the cultural remnants of mass, mostly voluntary conversions that also took place in the Ottoman period. Both Turks and Pomaks live in compactly settled rural enclaves, Pomaks in the remote southern districts of the Rhodope Mountains and Turks along Bulgaria's southern border and in northeastern Bulgaria. Hugh Poulton, *The Balkans: Minorities and States in Conflict* (London, 1991), 111.

how the West came to understand itself through Orientalism, or its invention of the East as an inadequate "other." Orientalism, as defined by Edward Said in 1978, is a body of Western writings and practices that relies on binary categories—East/West, Orient/Occident, backwardness/progress—to define and politically dominate the Orient.[7] Because of its visibility, Said's *Orientalism* has been criticized on various fronts, including methodological inconsistency, overgeneralization, an Anglo-French geographic focus, and its presumed political agenda.[8] The most important critiques argue that Orientalism is linked to modern European colonialism, rather than a timeless phenomenon emanating from Ancient Greece, as Said argues.[9] In the Balkan context, we must understand Orientalism, as well as the concept of the nation itself—as *modern* if we are to grasp Muslim/non-Muslim relations as they unfolded in the post-Ottoman period.[10] We must also complicate the binary categories—East/West, progress/backwardness, self/other—that Said sees as constitutive of Orientalism. Admittedly, dichotomous categories have played an important role in the European definitions of self in relation to the Orient, to colonial "others," and to minority populations within Europe. In the Balkans these categories are exceedingly powerful in coloring and ordering nationalist imaginings. But although the use of such categories should be analyzed and understood, recent studies on nation, empire, and particularly gender—a critical category of analysis in this study—have contextualized and enriched our understanding of Orientalism by illuminating the instability of such categories.[11] Although Said insists that the Orient was, "known in the West as its great complementary opposite," he himself points out that European culture set itself off against the Orient as, "a sort of surrogate or underground self."[12] In his words, "The Orient . . . vacillates between the West's contempt

[7] This process of "elaboration" of Orient and Occident, Said argues, was as much about defining the European self as it was about delimiting and controlling an "unruly" Orient. Said, *Orientalism*, 12.

[8] For example, see Bernard Lewis, *Islam and the West* (Oxford, 1993), 99–118.

[9] See Aijaz Ahmad, *In Theory: Classes, Nations, Literatures* (London, 1992), 159–220; and Mrinalini Sinha, *Colonial Masculinity: The "Manly Englishman" and the "Effeminate Bengali" in the Late Nineteenth Century* (Manchester, 1995), 13–14. Other works have explored Orientalism's application in geographic contexts that Said ignores. On Germany, see Sara Friedrichsmeyer, Sara Lennox, and Susan Zantop, eds., *The Imperialist Imagination: German Colonialism and its Legacy* (Ann Arbor, 1998). On Russia, see Edward Lazzerini, "Defining the Orient: A Nineteenth-Century Russo-Tatar Polemic over Identity and Cultural Representation," in *Muslim Communities Reemerge: Historical Perspectives on Nationality, Politics, and Opposition in the Former Soviet Union and Yugoslavia*, ed. E. Allworth (Durham, 1994), 33–46; and Daniel Brower and Edward Lazzerini, eds., *Russia's Orient: Imperial Borderlands and Peoples, 1700–1917* (Bloomington, 1997).

[10] Recent literature on Muslim/non-Muslim conflicts (as well as Catholic/Orthodox Christian or Croat/Serb conflicts) in the Balkans has rightly insisted on the modernity of such conflicts as opposed to their basis in ancient times. See, for example, Robert Donia and John Fine, *Bosnia and Hercegovina: A Tradition Betrayed* (New York, 1994), and Jasminka Udovièki and James Ridgeway, eds., *Burn This House: The Making and Unmaking of Yugoslavia* (Durham, 1997).

[11] See, for example, the work of Mrinalini Sinha, *Colonial Masculinity*, as well as John Tosh, "Imperial Masculinity and the Flight from Domesticity in Britain, 1880–1914," in *Gender and Colonialism*, ed. Timothy Foley et al. (London, 1995).

[12] In numerous places Said argues, for example, that since the Middle Ages Islam was considered to be a "fraudulent new version of Christianity." See Said, *Orientalism*, 58–59, and 3.

for what is familiar and its shivers of delight in—or fear of—novelty." As Orientalism is reconsidered, it becomes clear that its insistence on binary categories is a symptom of deeper European anxieties about the blurry line between these groupings. It is precisely the cultural alarm provoked by the transgression of boundaries, the volatility of cultural fault lines, and especially hybridity which drives the apparent "certainties" of Orientalism.[13] On the edges of Europe, the prevalence of hybridity and the tangling of cultural boundaries arguably, figure more immediately—and perplexingly—than in Western Europe's more distant colonial encounters with Islam.

With these qualifications, Orientalism holds an untold explanatory context in the Balkans. Not only was the European relationship with Islam replicated on a more complicated historical and cultural terrain, but, as recent scholarship argues, the Balkans were themselves Orientalized or cast as Eastern "other" by Western Europe and later the United States. As a result, Balkan Christians intensified such frameworks as they focused them inward and on Muslim minorities in their midst, a phenomenon that Milica Bakić-Hayden deemed "nesting Orientalisms."[14] But what exactly does "Orientalism" mean in the European-Balkan or Balkan Christian-Muslim context? Assumptions about the European Orientalization of the Balkans, for example, have not gone unchallenged in recent academic writings. Maria Todorova disputes the idea that the Balkans were Orientalized at all, arguing that European observers cast the Balkan peoples as mongrelized or as hybrid, European/Asian half-breeds; not as "other" but as an "incomplete self."[15] Todorova argues that "Balkanism," therefore, is entirely distinct from and much more injurious than Orientalism, in part because it reflects the Western loathing of hybridity. Yet this fear of hybridity itself is an important component of Orientalism. As Europe alternatively Orientalized and hybridized the Balkan Christian peoples, so too were Muslim minorities defined in terms of shifting categories of difference and sameness, that were constructed in response to their perceived in-betweenness. Orientalization and mongrelization of and within the Balkans were not mutually exclusive but rather reinforced each other in discourses that were far from monolithic or consistent.

As Bulgarian theory and practice on Muslims evolved, notions of Muslim difference were always in competition with assumptions about sameness and apprehensions about hybridity. Since the late nineteenth century, writers, thinkers, and especially ethnographers and administrators studied and categorized both Turks and Pomaks. The academic discourse that emerged from

[13] Robert Young argues that such fears go hand in hand with European desires that transgress the boundary between self and other. See Robert Young, *Colonial Desire: Hybridity in Theory, Culture and Race* (London, 1995), 19.

[14] See for example Milica Bakić-Hayden and Robert Hayden, "Orientalist Variations on the Theme 'Balkans': Symbolic Geography in Recent Yugoslav Cultural Politics," *Slavic Review* 51 (1992): 1–16; Milica Bakić-Hayden, "Nesting Orientalisms: The Case of Former Yugoslavia," *Slavic Review* 54 (1995): 917–31; and John Allcock, "Constructing the Balkans," in *Black Lambs and Grey Falcons: Women Travelers in the Balkans*, ed. J. Allcock and A. Young (New York, 1991).

[15] Todorova, *Imagining the Balkans*, 16.

these studies began to construe Muslim difference—all that was presumably not Bulgarian or European—as "foreign" and therefore a defilement of the Bulgarian landscape and Bulgarian bodies. Notions of Bulgarian-Muslim sameness first focused mainly on the Pomak populations, who, because of their shared Bulgarian tongue and other ethnographic markers, were defined as "Islamicized Bulgarians." The same ethnographers and academicians who claimed Pomaks as Bulgarian also began to lay claim to a portion of the Turkish-speaking population, which, they assumed, was also a remnant of an Islamicized, Turkified, Bulgarian population. By the twentieth century, ideas about the essential Bulgarianness of Pomaks captured the imagination of Bulgarians and some Pomaks alike in a dramatic way. The concept of Turks as essentially Bulgarian was definitely more contested, but it too took hold among many Bulgarians and even a handful of Turks by the end of the Communist period. These notions of essential sameness drove the modernizing, Bulgarianizing, assimilation projects of the twentieth century that attempted to integrate Muslims into the Bulgarian nation. Eventually, Bulgarian thinkers and actors began to view concrete differences between Bulgarian and Muslim—as manifested in gender relations, names, clothing, and even religion and language—as inherently superficial. Although many Muslim Turks were driven from Bulgarian soil in this period, for Pomaks and eventually those Turks who remained, these markers of difference became targets for elimination in the name of progress and the greater vision of national, and later socialist, sameness. In cases of Muslim resistance to such changes, the idea that these presumed brothers in Bulgarianness would defy their Bulgarian blood for some half-breed existence was seen as traitorous. The ambiguous interplay of sameness and difference, brother and enemy, flavored the Bulgarian-Muslim as well as the Bulgarian-European encounter throughout. This, I contend, is a critical conceptual axis around which understandings of all Balkan nationalisms and Muslim/non-Muslim relations should revolve.

Getting a firm grip on the ever more slippery concept of nationalism is clearly central to the complex story of Bulgarian Muslim relations. Although Said's work focuses on supranational, that is, European or Western, identity, his ideas have influenced a burgeoning literature on how the construction of an "other" is central to the imaging of nations.[16] In the Bulgarian case, the complicated relationship to Muslim "others" (under direct Russian and West European influence) played a constitutive role in the Bulgarian invention of the national self. In general, I agree with the "modernist" school of thought that posits nations as products of modernity, constructed both by national imaginations and modern bureaucratic states. I embrace the leveling effects of the works of such authors as Benedict Anderson and Ernest Gellner, which

[16] See, for example, Partha Chatterjee, *The Nation and Its Fragments: Colonial and Post-colonial Histories* (Princeton, 1993), and Hommi Bhabha, "Dissemination: Time, Narrative, and the Margins of the Nation," in *Nation and Narration,* ed. Hommi Bhabha (London, 1990).

assert that all nations, in the West as well as the East, were culturally and socially constructed sooner or later in the modern period.[17] In this vein, I object to typical typologies of "Western" nationalisms as "liberal" as opposed to the presumably ferocious "ethnic" nationalisms of the East—often seen as particularly potent in the Balkans. All nationalisms, whether in the United States, Great Britain, France, or elsewhere have been historically about inclusion and exclusion and all have claimed untold victims in the realization of homogenizing impulses.[18] But in emphasizing the similarities and appropriations between European and Bulgarian nationalist ideas, I do not want to imply that Bulgarian nationalism was a mere facsimile or distortion (as many scholars argue) of West European nationalisms. Instead, I agree with Partha Chatterjee's assertion that "latecomer nationalisms" are not just following a "script already written" but are inherently creative projects of individual national imaginations.[19] Furthermore, I argue that not only are all nationalisms inherently gendered, hybrid, and contested but, as Anne McClintock argues, "Nationalisms are invented, performed and consumed in ways that do not follow a blueprint."[20] In this book I only begin to scratch at the surface of the multiple ways in which Bulgarian, and for that matter Turkish nationalisms are devised, consumed, performed, and gendered within the parameters of Bulgaria.

For Bulgarians as for other nations, the path to modernity was far from straight and narrow; it was curvy and meandering, at times an impenetrable maze of meanings. Even in the seemingly monolithic Communist period (1944–89) shifts in destination and direction occurred; nation-building projects were always subject to political constraints, international developments, and local interpretation and response. Both before and during this period, Bulgarian nationalism undoubtedly inherited certain tendencies from its European and particularly Russian and then Soviet "big brothers"; that is, as with all nationalisms, it was informed by Western ideas. I argue, in fact, that it was precisely the ambiguities of these Western frameworks that gave Bulgarian and other Balkan nationalisms their vehemence and aggressive nature, rather than any inherent Balkan "backwardness." Yet, as with any child, Bulgarian nationalism also had its own unique genetic code, a product of its peculiar place on the margins of Europe and its own inverted postcoloniality.

---

[17] See, for example, Benedict Anderson, *Imagined Communities: Reflections on the Origin and Spread of Nationalism* (London, 1983); Ernest Gellner, *Nations and Nationalism* (Ithaca, N.Y., 1983). For a recent survey of debates on the modernity of nations, see Anthony Smith, *Nationalism and Modernism: A Critical Survey of Recent Theories of Nations and Nationalism* (London, 1998).

[18] This assumption pervaded studies on nationalisms until quite recently. See, for example, John Plamenatz, "Two Types of Nationalism," in *Nationalism: The Nature and Evolution of an Idea*, ed. Eugene Kamenka (London, 1976), and Hans Kohn, *The Idea of Nationalism* (New York, 1967).

[19] Chatterjee, *The Nation*, 5.

[20] Anne McClintock, *Imperial Leather: Race, Gender, and Sexuality in the Colonial Conquest* (New York, 1995), 360.

Specifically, Bulgarian national thinkers had to deal with a colonial past in which they, as Europeans, were subject to the rule of a theoretically inferior non-European power, the Ottoman Empire; this only heightened the anxiety of not measuring up to a European ideal. Hence Bulgarians simultaneously discovered and constructed their own Europeanness as they confronted and agonized over their Ottoman colonial past and the continued presence of Islam in their midst. At the same time, the obsessions and ingredients of Bulgarian nationalism were of their own choosing.

Most studies of nationalism and ethnic minorities focus on language or religion as central to national identity and ethnonational relationships. Although both have a place in my study, I look beyond them to what I believe were more important themes of Bulgarian and Muslim identity politics. I do not deny that language and religion were important to identity formation in the Balkans and elsewhere. Bulgarian thinkers and actors confronted and attacked Islam and the Turkish language at times in the course of the nineteenth and twentieth centuries. At the same time, in various periods both the Turkish language and Muslim religious institutions and personnel were sanctioned, co-opted, and used as tools in bigger projects of modernization, westernization, and ultimately Bulgarianization. Still, I argue that Bulgarian national projects and Muslim responses to them were fueled with greater vehemence by material and symbolic vestiges of the Ottoman past. Attempts to reclaim Islamic populations as Bulgarian (or alternatively to expel them as traitors to their true essences) played out primarily in struggles over land holdings, geographic and personal names, dress, and other gendered practices. Bulgarian obsessions centered on Bulgarian territory and what marked the landscape in various ways—who owned or inhabited it, how it and its inhabitants were labeled and named, and how these inhabitants dressed and covered or altered their bodies. In the other words, if the Bulgarian landscape appeared to be Bulgarian, if it was owned by Bulgarians and marked by Bulgarian names and Bulgarian material culture, it would be Bulgarian. In a long and contested process, Bulgarian intellectuals, bureaucrats, and citizens attempted to reconfigure the contours of the Bulgarian landscape and "manscape" (human bodies) into a new image, one that was at once modern and European and somehow particularly Bulgarian.

Although my study spans from the 1860s until 1989, my empirical emphasis is on the Bulgarian Communist period. In this period, pre-1944 ideas and campaigns re-emerge and repeat themselves in telling ways and the rapid drive to modernize propels the most dramatic encounters between Bulgarian and Muslim. This period is at once the most climactic and transformative in Bulgarian history and the most inadequately conceptualized. Now technically a closed chapter in Bulgarian history, it is more than ever an inviting focus for empirical and theoretical work. The most understudied (excepting perhaps Albania) of the former Eastern Bloc, Bulgaria has wrongly been dubbed "most loyal Soviet satellite," the site of least resistance to Moscow or to local Communist hegemony.[21] With the Bulgaro-Muslim relationship as a vehicle, I hope to provide a starting point for new discussions about agency, whether in the form of resistance, cooperation, fulfillment of tradition or individual desire, both before but especially during the thorny Communist period.

In part, this attention to agency is a response to the existing scholarship on the Communist period in Bulgaria and, to a lesser extent, the rest of Eastern Europe in which the so-called totalitarian model remains mostly unchallenged. This model, which remained prevalent in Anglo-American scholarship on the Soviet sphere of influence until the 1970s, posited a monolithic totalitarian state in which society was, at best, whipped into submission by omnipresent coercion, and at worst, absent from the story. Resistance, when present in the "totalitarian" story was overt and dramatic, and always crushed by the all-seeing regime. In studies on the Soviet context, "revisionist" scholars, whose work recognizes that Soviet hegemony was established both through coercion and consent, undermined this model decades ago.[22] Revisionism has met with harried critiques for its lack of recognition of the kinds of oppression that Soviet and (after World War II) East European citizens had to contend with. Still the revisionist approach, unlike the totalitarian model, has proved flexible enough to both recognize the power of coercion and explore the interstices of Soviet power. In a limited way, revisionism has penetrated the field of East European history with discussions of consensus building and diverse paths to legitimacy.[23] Nevertheless, in spite of recognition of both kinds and degrees of complicity, a prevailing tendency has been to focus on Soviet or local Communist domination, in other words, a continued totalitarian paradigm. When resistance is discussed, most commonly under the rubric of organized and formal opposition and dissent, it is presented in rather black and white terms.[24] Certainly, very little scholarship has gone beyond revisionism to explore the "gray zone" between resistance and collaboration (a term coined for the Czech case). Others have discussed

---

[21] At least some of the very spare secondary literature on Communist Bulgaria has dispelled the myth of orthodoxy. See Gerald Creed, *Domesticating Revolution: From Socialist Reform to Ambivalent Transition in a Bulgarian Village* (University Park, Penn., 1998); Robert McIntyre, *Bulgaria: Politics, Economics and Society* (London, 1988); and Edmund Stillman and R. H. Bass, "Bulgaria: A Study in Satellite Non-Conformity," *Problems of Communism* 4 (1955): 26–33.

[22] Here I refer to the body of literature in the revisionist vein that provided a corrective to works such as Zbigniew Brzezinski and Carl Friedrich, *Totalitarian Dictatorship and Autocracy* (Cambridge, Mass., 1965). The earlier works of Sheila Fitzpatrick are the best example of the revisionist school, see Sheila Fitzpatrick, *The Russian Revolution* (Oxford, 1982). Her later works show the flexibility of the revisionist school. See Sheila Fitzpatrick, *Everyday Stalinism: Ordinary Life in Extraordinary Times, Soviet Russia in the 1930s* (New York, 1999).

[23] See, for example, Padraic Kenney, *Rebuilding Poland: Workers and Communists, 1945–1950* (Ithaca, N.Y., 1997).

[24] See, for example, Janusz Bugajski and Maxine Pollack, eds., *East European Faultlines: Dissent Opposition and Social Activism* (Boulder, Colo., 1989), and Rudolf Tökes, ed., *Opposition in Eastern Europe* (Baltimore, 1979).

negotiations of power among Communist regimes and peasants, women, youth, Catholics, and other groups.[25] In spite of such efforts, agency and society are only slowly entering the postwar East European story.

Studies of the Soviet nationalities and minorities of Eastern Europe, in particular, are dominated by traditional notions of domination and resistance. Assumptions of total Soviet domination deny the existence of agency on the part of Soviet nationalities and East European majorities and minorities. Minority populations are often presented as simple victims of majority trepidations, with little discussion of collaboration and only limited conceptualization of resistance. Although the work of Ronald Suny and others in the Soviet history field amply complicate the totalitarian premises behind Soviet nationalities studies, a full exploration of complicity and resistance is only beginning within East European studies.[26] Minority studies, and specifically the sparse works on Muslims in Bulgaria, have yet to consider the texture of resistance and collaboration, both in the relationship of various states to the Soviet Union, and the relationships of minorities to these states.[27] Bulgarian and Muslim submission to the "powers that be" dominates both the literature on Socialist Bulgaria and that on Muslim minorities under Bulgarian socialism. Neither group is seen as having agency, an assumption I intend to challenge.

Outside the Soviet and East European field, agency, resistance, collaboration, and power have been held to more rigorous theoretical scrutiny, particularly in recent decades. In the historiography on West European colonialism and in postcolonial studies, the concepts of power, domination, and resistance have received a very thorough theoretical working over and as a result, more nuanced understandings of these notions have emerged. One important direction in this literature is the attempt to relocate resistance in everyday

[25] For a discussion of the "gray zone" see Jiřiná Šiklova, "The Solidarity of the Culpable," *Social Research* 58 (1991), 765–75. There have been a few recent, notable works in the East European field in peasant studies. See, for example, Gerald Creed, *Domesticating Revolution* and Melissa Bokovoy, *Peasants and Communists: Politics and Ideology in the Yugoslav Countryside, 1941–1953* (Pittsburgh, 1998). On women and resistance in Ceausescu's Romania, see Gail Kligman, *The Politics of Duplicity: Controlling Reproduction in Ceausescu's Romania* (Berkeley, 1998). See also Jan Kubik's discussion of the negotiations of power between hegemonic and counterhegemonic discourses in his *The Power of Symbols against the Symbols of Power: The Rise of Solidarity and the Fall of State Socialism in Poland* (University Park, Penn., 1994).

[26] See also Ronald Suny, *Revenge of the Past: Nationalism, Revolution, and the Collapse of the Soviet Union* (Stanford, 1993).

[27] Until recently, the literature on Muslims in Bulgaria was exceedingly sparse and partisan; little archival work was done on the subject and most of that tended to take a Turkish or a Bulgarian point of view. See, for example, Bilâl Şimşir, *Bulgaristan Türkleri: 1878–1985* (Ankara, 1986); E. Misirkova, *Turetskoe Menshinstvo v Narodnoe Respublike Bolgarii* (Sofia, 1951); or Atanas Primorski, *Bŭlgarite Mokhamedani v Nashata Narodnostha Obshtnost* (Sofia, 1940). For more balanced recent political surveys see Ali Eminov, *Turkish and Other Muslim Minorities of Bulgaria* (New York, 1997) or Valeri Stoianov, *Turskoto Naselenie v Bŭlgariia Mezhdu Poliusite na Etnicheskata Politika* (Sofia, 1998). For new and noteworthy anthropological work see, for example, Gulbrand Alhaug and Yulian Konstantinov, *Names, Ethnicity and Politics: Islamic Names in Bulgaria 1912–1992* (Oslo, 1995).

acts, in the trivial, mundane, and uncoordinated.[28] Although the academic romance with resistance admittedly can go to extremes, I believe that broadening the concept of resistance is of vital importance in understanding postwar Eastern Europe. Equally vital is the need to question the very idea of resistance and domination as oppositional, binary categories. Scholars such as Saba Mahmood have rightly problematized resistance by recognizing motivations, desires, and goals that are not necessarily driven by a longing for "liberation." This is especially true in the case of women and minorities who, she argues, may have other prevailing ties and incentives, such as religious piety or ethnic survival.[29] Unfortunately, it is not always possible to uncover such forms of intent, leaving our understandings of them necessarily partial. Still, it is important not to overdetermine (or underdetermine) power as we uncover its myriad forms and what McClintock calls the "diverse politics of agency" made up of a "dense web of relations between coercion, negotiation, complicity, refusal, dissembling, mimicry, compromise, affiliation, and revolt."[30] This broader view offers a fertile ground for exploring the complex entanglements between power and agency, domination and resistance in postwar Eastern Europe.

Without question the Soviet Union and Bulgarian Communist Party (BCP) played key roles in directing and even dominating domestic developments in Bulgaria—but neither were monoliths. In this book I explore Bulgarian deviation from the Soviet model as well as overt and everyday Muslim resistance, and other forms of agency, in the face of Bulgarian Communist dictates. Despite apparent loyalty to the Soviet Bloc, the BCP had its own approach to dealing with Muslim minorities that varied from the Soviet model in important ways. Ultimately, the BCP went much further in the attempt to fully assimilate their Muslim minorities than did seemingly similar Soviet projects in the Caucasus, Central Asia, and even the non-Muslim Slavic republics. The integrating impetus of Sovietization and "Russification" were always tempered by local autonomies inherent in the federal model. In fact, as Ronald Suny, Yuri Slezkine, and others have shown, the Soviet Union actually created more nations than it destroyed.[31] In Bulgaria the initial Leninist policy of "national in form, Socialist in content" did provide for the mass development of Turkish presses and educational and cultural institutions that con-

[28] James Scott, *Weapons of the Weak: Everyday Forms of Peasant Resistance* (New Haven, Conn., 1985). This approach has drawn some criticism because of its alleged overestimation of the scope and intent of "subversive acts," for example, locating resistance in such endeavors as "breaking wind when the king goes by." See "Entanglements of Power: Geographies of Domination/Resistance," *in Entanglements of Power: Geographies of Domination/Resistance*, ed. Joanne Sharp, et al. (London, 2000), 3.
[29] Saba Mahmood, "Feminist Theory, Embodiment, and the Docile Agent: Some Reflections on the Egyptian Islamic Revival," *Cultural Anthropology* 16 (2001): 202–36, 208.
[30] McClintock, *Imperial Leather*, 15.
[31] See, for example, Yuri Slezkine, "The USSR as a Communal Apartment, or How a Socialist State Promoted Ethnic Particularism," *Slavic Review* 53 (1994): 414–53.

tributed to the diffusion of modern Turkishness to otherwise illiterate, prena-
tional Muslim masses. But by the 1960s the Party was aggressively eliminating Turkish institutions, and Turco-Muslim autonomy was deemed dangerous and undesirable. In Bulgaria, a self-proclaimed uninational socialist
state, Pomaks were never granted any kind of autonomy or separate cultural
development and the development of modern Turkishness, it seems, was only
a pit stop on the way to integration into the "socialist nation." Furthermore,
even though the BCP model for modernizing the "backward" Muslim
provinces did resemble Soviet campaigns in its Muslim provinces, Bulgarian
campaigns were built on presocialist foundations. The Communist-inspired
"brotherhood of the toiling masses of Bulgarians and Turks" eventually was
replaced by old concepts of sameness and difference based on blood and soil.
Sameness became intertwined with a blood definition of Bulgarianness in
which Pomaks, and eventually Turks, were claimed as true Bulgarians. Although the Soviet Union planned for the eventual *sblizheniie* (coming together) of its nationalities, it never assumed the essential "Russianness" of
the far-flung and diverse peoples within the federation. In concept and practice the BCP both followed and deviated from that of the Soviets, responding
to Bulgarian voices from the past and the present, merging Marxist categories with Bulgarian national ones in a surprisingly comfortable working relationship.

When possible, discussion of Muslim agency in its diverse forms also en-
ters into this book. First and foremost, I do not wish to create false di-
chotomies of Bulgarian perpetrator versus Muslim victim, Bulgarian domination versus Muslim resistance, or even Bulgarian modernizer versus Muslim
traditionalist. Admittedly, Turks and Pomaks were at times victims or
guardians of tradition in the face of the Bulgarian modernization and assimilation programs. In many cases, Muslim tradition was often retained or reinvented, not as an indication of some sort of essential backwardness, but
rather as a response to the dislocation that modernity generated. At times,
however, Muslims enter the story as navigators of modernity on their own
terms. Muslims in Bulgaria, as in neighboring Turkey (which provided one
model among others), felt the momentum of modernization and willingly altered or eradicated traditions. Although not all Muslims were "modernizing"
per se, neither were all Bulgarians. Kernels of modernizing elite had existed
among the Muslim population since the nineteenth century and only grew in
strength by the twentieth century. At times such modernizers as the Pomak
Rodina (homeland) movement in the 1930s, and some modernizing Turks
(or Kemalists) after 1944 built alliances with Bulgarian political and cultural
elites or even fringe political parties with their own agendas. Often, these and
other Muslims cooperated with Bulgarian government programs even at the
expense of Muslim collective interests. Muslim "collaboration," or willingness to participate in Bulgarian programs whatever the motivation or intent,
seems to have gone unnoticed in the existing literature. As a rule these studies focus on Muslim victimization or overt and episodic forms of Muslim

resistance, such as demonstrations, violent clashes, and organized opposition. In fact, there was a spectrum of Muslim responses to Bulgarian assaults on local practices, including collaboration, passivity, overt resistance, and the more mundane forms of agency that often fall under the rubric "everyday resistance."[32] Not only were both resistance and cooperation operative and important, but the line between Muslim cooperation and obstruction was shifting and blurred, and at times, I argue, almost indiscernible. A major task of this book is to examine the inherently hazy perimeter or "gray zone" between Muslim collaboration and resistance.

Muslim agency is an integral part of the story of the Bulgarian-Muslim encounter, which I relate in bold outline in the first two chapters of the book. Here I take a general chronological and conceptual approach, sketching the topography of Bulgarian nationalism, its primary compass and obsessions, the ideas that drove it, and the cultural and social transformations it propelled. I trace how their imagined geographies of East and West influenced Bulgarian thinkers and actors as they mapped and remapped the parameters of the "Bulgarian lands." Quite literally, they had to define the territorial and ethnographic parameters of Bulgaria out of the complexity of the Balkan morass. Once the Bulgarian lands were defined, the people and places that comprised them had to be redefined, sorted, and either appropriated as "native" or confronted as "foreign." Consequently, "illegitimate" pieces of the Ottoman past—material and symbolic culture—which had been left behind to defile the landscape and manscape were to be discarded or expunged. Once stripped of these "vestiges," Bulgaria and Bulgarians could emerge in their essential purity. As a rule, intensive campaigns to eliminate the vestiges of the past and integrate first Pomaks and then Turks into the Bulgarian nation surfaced at times of great societal mobilization, but only when domestic politics and favorable international alliances allowed. Hence vigorous campaigns against markers of Muslim difference occurred during the First Balkan War (1912), World War II, and the Communist period (especially after 1956), but with necessary reversals during the Second Balkan War and World War I, as well as during the early Communist period. It was in the context of these periods of mobilization and political reversals that Turkish and Pomak difference and sameness were delimited and the plethora of Muslim responses germinated.

The book's remaining chapters are thematic, focusing on the specific national motifs most central to Bulgarian national projects and Muslim responses. In chapters 3 and 4, I explore how Bulgarian thinkers and actors constructed Muslim difference and sameness around gendered concepts of the nation. These chapters are informed by a growing literature on the links between "gender" and "nation" as well as works on gendered constructions

---

[32] James Scott asserts that mundane everyday forms of resistance can have a greater long-term effect on the erosion of state power than the more dramatic cataclysmic kinds of resistance that receive more attention in the literature. See Scott, *Weapons of the Weak*.

of the East.[33] Gender as a category has only recently been introduced into analyses of other Balkan nationalisms and interethnic relations, and the Bulgarian case remains a glaring exception.[34] In fact, gender pervades the Bulgarian-Muslim encounter from the outset, as Bulgarians constructed and stabilized their own notions of manhood, womanhood, and nationhood precisely through encounters with Muslim manhood and womanhood. In addition, the influential and pervasive categories of East and West have important gender connotations that play out in the Bulgarian context. The notions of West as male and East as female are appropriated from the European-colonial encounters along with their inherent complications and contradictions. As in Western "civilizing missions" the liberation of the colonized female—in this case Muslim women—from her veil, became an oft-stated rationale for far-reaching attempts to destabilize and penetrate local power structures and autonomies.[35] In Bulgaria nation builders reproduced the "colonial gaze" with its focus on the veil when constructing concepts of Muslim otherness. Western notions about the veil and assumptions of Muslim women's oppression were appropriated wholesale into the Bulgarian context even though local practices generally did not include a heavy or oppressive veil, only a Balkan headscarf, as well as other draping garments. The presumed symbol of the oppression of Muslim women by Muslim men, the veil was ultimately thought to hide and disfigure the essential sameness (Bulgarianness) of Muslim women. As we will see in chapter 4, the veil and its accompanying accoutrements became a central issue around which Muslim "backwardness" was confronted and Muslim responses cohered.

Bulgarian nationalist discourse conceived Muslim gender relations as intolerably backward and degenerate, an affront to "Bulgarianness" and progress. As a result, the foci of Bulgarian actions were the symbol-laden material expressions of Muslim womanhood and manhood—for women the "veil" and "Oriental" baggy pants or *shalvari*, for the men the fez, turban, and circumcision. As a rule, the fez and turban, constructed as particularly male symbols of backwardness and the Ottoman past, proved far less tenacious than the accoutrements of Muslim women. Circumcision, which became a focus of Bulgarian modernizing efforts by the 1960s touched a far more tender cultural nerve, however. As in other campaigns, the "backwardness" of the practice was highlighted, but here, also, concern was raised about its "deformative"

[33] Although most works in the canon of theoretical writings on nationalism summarily ignore gender, an expanding body of empirical and theoretical work explores the very integral connections between these categories of analysis. As Yuval-Davis points out, "constructions of nationhood involve specific notions of both manhood and womanhood." Nira Yuval-Davis, *Gender and Nation* (London, 1997), 1.

[34] Much work has been inspired by the recent wars in Bosnia and Kosovo. See, for example, Wendy Bracewell, "Rape in Kosovo: Masculinity and Serbian Nationalism," *Nations and Nationalism* 6 (2000): 563–90; and Wendy Bracewell, "Women, Motherhood and Contemporary Serbian Nationalism," *Women's Studies International Forum* 19 (1996): 25–33.

[35] This echoes the argument made by McClintock who in turn elaborates on Fanon. See McClintock, *Imperial Leather*, 364, and Franz Fanon, *A Dying Colonialism* (New York, 1965), 37–38.

outcome. In spite of other stated rationales, anticircumcision campaigns seemed to be guided by the idea that the practice disfigured the essentially Bulgarian maleness of Muslim men in the same way that baggy Turkish pants and draping veils hid or misshaped the Bulgarian essence of Muslim women. And although Bulgarian authorities went to extreme lengths to ensure that the foreskin of the nation would remain intact, so too did its removal, by definition, become a "performative" act of resistance.[36]

Names and the practice of naming, the central theme of chapter five, similarly became the focus of Bulgarianization campaigns and multifarious Muslim response.[37] The practice of naming and the question of the relationship between names and the named have increasingly occupied a growing place in scholarship influenced by the "linguistic turn." From Michel Foucault's ideas on knowledge, power, and representation to Pierre Bourdieu's more elaborated theoretical work on the tectonics of naming, the power of the name has made a place for itself in the pantheon of academic concerns. For Bourdieu, naming is wrapped intimately in the "alchemy of representation" and processes of making or contesting identities, both as a creative process and as an act of "symbolic violence."[38] David Kertzer, in his reading and apt elaboration of Bourdieu (and Foucault) explores how naming can be a part of "symbolic struggles" over identity and meaning. He asserts that renaming can both create and destroy, as it "not only calls upon people to take up a new name and hence a new identity, but beseeches them to abandon their old name and with it their previous identity."[39] The key issues in the works of Bourdieu, Foucault, Kertzer and others are: Who has the power to name? How is meaning imposed through naming? How are names received and negotiated? Many levels of categorization and naming in the Bulgarian context speak to these questions, at times in dramatic ways. In this chapter I briefly discuss, for example, toponyms and the very deliberate state campaigns to Bulgarianize the map. I also touch on the "Turk" and "Pomak" ethnonyms that categorized, labeled, and systematized Muslim difference before it could be questioned and eradicated. The chapter's primary focus is Muslim personal names and the recurrent campaigns for Pomaks and Turks to discard their Turco-Arabic first names and surnames in favor of Slavo-Bulgarian names. Although name-changing campaigns began before 1945, they were far more dramatic in the Communist period. In donning or rejecting names, the "difference" or

[36] I rely here on Judith Butler's concept of "performativity" as elaborated in various other works on resistance. I agree that agency—resistant or otherwise—is actualized through creative acts or repeated, ritualized, and often mundane kinds of "performance." Judith Butler, *Gender Trouble: Feminism and the Subversion of Identity* (New York, 1990), 139–40. See also Mahmood, "Feminist Theory, Embodiment," 210.

[37] In chapter 5, I won't revisit in-depth the topic of the "Balkan" nomen and its meaning for Bulgarian concepts of "self," as this is more than adequately elaborated by Todorova, *Imagining the Balkans*, 32–33.

[38] Pierre Bourdieu, *Language and Symbolic Power* (Cambridge Mass., 1982), 68.

[39] David Kertzer, *Politics and Symbols: The Italian Communist Party and the Fall of Communism* (New Haven, 1996), 67.

"sameness" of Pomaks and Turks was ultimately encoded for all to see on every state document and in every public greeting, as names identified cultural affiliation and political loyalty. Muslim responses, both dramatic and deliberate, or more subtle and everyday are charted. In many instances Muslims demonstrated in the streets, and for decades after the official changes, most maintained unofficial Muslim names for home use. In other instances they voluntarily took on Bulgarian names and even played leading roles in forcing name changes among their coreligionists. Names became one of the key battlegrounds for the negotiation of the parameters of Bulgarian and Muslim identities, as well as both political and cultural loyalties.

My final thematic chapter is on land—how land was encoded with national meanings, thereby providing a subtext to national desires and actions. Land, I argue, is central to both local concerns and national imperatives in the Bulgarian context. Bulgaria was primarily a peasant society before World War II and Muslim minorities are still overwhelmingly rural today. Land provided the livelihood and sustenance of both the Muslim and non-Muslim peasants, and it was the soil in which Bulgarian nationalists imagined and rooted their essential Bulgarianness. From the very beginnings of the Bulgarian national projects, nation builders reclaimed "Bulgarian lands" from perceived foreignness—both outside and within—in the name of the Bulgarian peasant, the presumed embodiment of the nation, local and uncontaminated. As nationalist thinkers began to imagine the limits of the Bulgarian territorial expanse, the peasant masses were like vessels of ethnographic "truths" spread across the Balkan landscape, sculpting a Bulgarian manscape. On the one hand, the discovery of Pomak, and later Turkish, "sameness" provided "scientific" justification for extending Bulgaria's national frontiers or consolidating power on Bulgaria's geographic margins. On the other hand, lingering questions about Turkish "difference" predicated waves of expulsion from the Bulgarian State that lasted well into the Communist period. At the same time, Turks in particular had to assert or reclaim their own dominions, both individual and collective (that is, *vakf* or religiously endowed properties), in a milieu of national redefinition. Turks either rooted their presence and emergent sense of Turkishness in ancestral Turkish lands now subsumed by the new Bulgarian state, or uprooted and resettled in the Ottoman Empire and its political successor, Turkey. At times, shared territoriality was employed in Bulgarian and Muslim discourses on sameness, on shared fates, on brotherhoods of place and experience. Even in the Communist period, land was laden with national meaning as all of Bulgaria's land and private property was made *obshtonardono* (all national) and thereby rescued from encroaching "foreign" interlopers. Significantly, almost all forms of "foreign" ownership, both Western and Muslim, were liquidated by the Communist regime. Property and place emerge as tropes both of difference and division as well as unity and sameness, as evolving perceptions of territory and land taken and lost, occupied and absconded, were important factors in the growing rift between Bulgarian and Muslim.

There can be little doubt that intensification of Bulgaro-Muslim antipathy was one of the unfortunate results of the Bulgarian appropriation of European modernity. Trails furrowed by the plow of modernity permanently broke the soil of Bulgaro-Turkish and Bulgaro-Pomak relations. Once planted in Bulgarian soil, notions of East/West, Europe/Asia, progress/backwardness—not to mention the very concept of "nation"—could not help but damage Muslim/non-Muslim relations. Exclusive and excluding, national ideas chafed against the local coexistence of Muslim and non-Muslim, leaving behind a palpable residue of Bulgarian anti-Turkishness and Muslim anti-Bulgarianness. So strong are these legacies that many observers have ventured that the presumed "ancient enmities" of the Balkans also hold explosive potential in Bulgaria. This book seeks to demonstrate that there is nothing inherent, inevitable, or specifically "Balkan" about Bulgarian antagonism toward local Muslim populations. Rather, Bulgaro-Muslim encounters evolved in the shadow of Western social and political ideologies that facilitated a radical transformation of Bulgarian national soil and society. For Bulgarians, Turks, and Pomaks, their land, names, dress, and bodies remain sites for these conflicts, which have taken on new forms after 1989. But contrary to my initial assumption that projects of modernity had only served to divide Bulgarian from Muslim after centuries of coexistence, I have concluded that these projects served alternately to divide and to integrate. Nationalism and modernity did drive a wedge between Bulgarians and Muslims on the local and national levels. At the same time, the process was fraught with ambiguities which allowed room for "modern" coexistence and cooperation. In spite of ethnic tensions, Bulgaria has a functioning democracy with active Muslim political participation; to date, Bulgaria is not another Bosnia or Kosovo.

I *The Bulgarian Figure in the Ottoman Carpet: Untangling Nation from Empire*

It is only when one steps back from those small things which are knitted together in the narrative that one can see, as Henry James said, "the figure in the carpet."
—MICHAEL ONDAATJE

At the margins of maps, one inevitably finds conceivable centers for "others." By the nineteenth century, Balkan intellectuals had begun to explore the edges of Ottoman and European maps and draft schema for their own vast and overlapping national territories. The politically charged observations and ethnographic "discoveries" of European scholars and travelers in the region ignited Balkan national visions and ambitions. Self-proclaimed "Bulgarian" thinkers, as with other Balkan men of letters, began to seek the clarity of a Bulgarian national figure in the cultural complexity of the Ottoman tapestry. This search for a Bulgarian national self was often characterized by disentanglement from the Ottoman realm and the search for a geographic and conceptual grounding in Europe and the West. At the same time, Bulgarian acceptance of West European authority was never absolute. Bulgarian intellectuals inherited the modern European sense of superiority and self-critique which they aimed both westward and inward. Furthermore, they came of age under the influence of Russian and Ottoman ideas and practices, societies struggling with their own positions on the margins of Europe, who both emulated and rejected European presences in their midst. Hence Bulgarian nationalist thinkers began to look both literally and figuratively for the contours of the Bulgarian national figure in the thick of this tangled web, between the overlapping and conflicting realms of this imagined East and West.

As the Bulgarian national idea emerged out of the Ottoman morass its purveyors sought to clarify and impose conceptual and physical "legibility" on the intricate and unruly Balkan terrain.[1] Both before and after gaining autonomy in 1878, influential Bulgarians attempted to rethink and then reorder the surrounding landscape with its maze of people and their cultural attributes. Bulgarians occupied the new center of this rewoven Balkan carpet, spread out over their imagined ethnographic expanse. This had important consequences for minorities left behind in the post-1878 Bulgarian principality, including Muslims but also Greeks, Jews, Gypsies, and others. Admittedly the Bulgarian state was relatively tolerant toward all minorities from 1878 to 1945, based on inherited Ottoman practices and European-inspired constitutional provisions. But ultimately, historical and contemporary bases for autonomy or tolerance were exceedingly pliable and somewhat fragile. It eventually became clear that minorities would occupy a marginal if not tenuous place in the new Bulgarian nation-state, with predictable consequences. For Greeks and Jews, for example, their numbers would be severely depleted in the course of the post-Ottoman period as a result of population exchanges, deportations, and voluntary or coerced emigration.[2] But significantly, anti-Greek and anti-Semitic sentiments, to the extent that they existed, were primarily grounded in accusations of Greek-Ottoman and Jewish-Ottoman complicity. Furthermore, as both carried some stigma as traitors by association, neither group had a visible "Oriental" presence to offend Bulgarian national sensibilities by hindering their quest for European modernity. Turks and Pomaks left behind in the Ottoman wake, however, were a critical part of the Bulgarian reclamation of the past and present from the Ottoman Asiatic presence, recast as barbaric and antithetical to a Bulgarian future. They were, perhaps inescapably, perceived as living representatives or vestiges of the Ottoman past by virtue of their visible (and sometimes hidden) Turco-Arabic cultural markers. Hence they would play a special, if not central, role in constructions of modern Bulgarian nationhood and the administrative remodeling of the nation and its territory.

Significant populations of Turks and Pomaks were inherited by the fledgling Bulgarian principality, which was established in 1878 and officially granted independence in 1908. The relative numbers of both groups have dwindled significantly since 1878 due to migration and death in various wars, but both have maintained a tangible presence and a somewhat constant

[1] I borrow the term "legibility" from Timothy Mitchell, *Colonizing Egypt* (Berkeley, 1988); 33–94, and James Scott, *Seeing Like a State*, 9–53. Both use the term to describe how modern states impose order and so render segments of society "legible" or "available to political and economic calculation." Mitchell, *Colonizing Egypt*, 33.

[2] Bulgaria lost much of its Greek population when the Greco-Turkish population exchanges accompanying the 1923 Treaty of Lausanne were extended to include Bulgaria. See Stephen Ladas, *The Exchange of Minorities: Bulgaria, Greece and Turkey* (New York, 1932). Bulgaria's Jews were deported during World War II (from Bulgaria's occupied territories) or emigrated in the immediate postwar period because of a special agreement with Israel; only a small community remains. See Vicki Tamir, *Bulgaria and Her Jews*. In addition to Turks and Pomaks, Gypsies are the only minority that has maintained a significant presence in Bulgaria after 1945.

Map 1. The Changing Borders of Bulgaria 1878–1945

percentage of the population since about the 1930s, approximately 10 percent for Turks and 3 percent for Pomaks. As of 1992, there were approximately 822,253 Turks and 286,971 Pomaks out of the 8,487,317 total population of Bulgaria.[3] The origins of both Turks and Pomaks are disputed especially within the region itself, but there is somewhat of a consensus outside the region (and many sources within) that Pomaks are descendants of Slavic Christians who converted to Islam in the seventeenth century.[4] As far

[3] Statistical data on the number of Turks and especially Pomaks in Bulgaria are generally unreliable and a matter of some dispute. These figures for Bulgarians and Turks are based on the 1992 census. The numbers for Pomaks—a category not included on the 1992 census—are based on estimates. Ali Eminov, *Turkish and Other Muslim Minorities*, 81, 100.

[4] One can find sources written by virtually all of Bulgaria's Balkan neighbors claiming Pomaks as their own. For Turkish sources which claim Pomaks as Turks see Halim Çavuşoğlu, *Balkanlar'da Pomak Türkleri: Tarih ve Sosyu-Kültürel Yapı* (Ankara, 1993); and Hüseyin Memişoğlu, *Pages of the History of Pomac Turks* (Ankara, 1991). An example of a Serbian source that claims the "Muslims of the South" as Serbian is Dragişe Lapčević, *O Naşim Muslimanima: Socioloşke i Etnografske Beleşke* (Belgrade, 1925). For a Macedonian source, which asserts that "Torbeshi" (Pomaks) are Macedonians see Hijazi Limanoski, *Izlamskata Religija and Izlamiziranite Makedontsi* (Skopje, 1989). Also see Poulton, *The Balkans*, for some discussion of national claims on Pomaks in Albania, *Balkans*, 201–3, and Greece, 175–76.

as Turks are concerned, most non-Bulgarian (and many Bulgarian) scholars agree Turks are the progeny of Islamic, Turkic-speaking migrants from Anatolia, who came to the region beginning in the fourteenth century and whose numbers were bolstered by some admixture of local converted Slavs.[5] Concerning the conversion of Slavs to Islam, a preponderance of Bulgarian sources view any and all conversions as the product of coercive "assimilationist" Ottoman policies. In contrast, outside, as well as some newer Bulgarian, sources tend to focus on conversion as the product of gradual and voluntary intermarriage, or mass voluntary conversion in the case of the Pomaks.[6] In reference to the latter, Antonina Zheliaskova and others have convincingly argued that the presumed proof of the forcible nature of Pomak conversions was based on documents falsified by Bulgarians in the nineteenth and twentieth centuries.[7] Debates about conversion and origin have always been integral to the evolution of the Bulgaro-Muslim relationship in the modern period, as shifting boundaries between Bulgarian and Turk, Bulgarian and Pomak, as well as Europe and Asia, have fluctuated and solidified. The assertion that many (and later all) of Bulgaria's Muslims were really converted Bulgarians or a violated and deluded "self," continually complicated constructions of Muslim as "other." Hence far from representing a simple obstacle on the Bulgarian "path to Europe," Muslims in Bulgaria were part and parcel of a complex and contested process of material and conceptual disentanglement from the Ottomans and the East more broadly.[8]

Of course Bulgarian constructions of Muslims as "other"—as Eastern, barbaric, and antithetical to progress—existed, persisted, and became central in Bulgarian campaigns to eradicate Muslim difference on Bulgarian soil. Bulgarian nationalism emerged in an era dominated by the European tendency to draw and reinforce borders between peoples and places, in particular, between the so-defined East and West. In fact, no body of scholarship and practice was more formative to Bulgarian nationalism than the "imaginative geography" of what Said terms "Orientalism." As Said argues, it was through defining the Orient as "other" that Europe discovered and invented itself, presumably immersed in progress and civilization as opposed to Orien-

---

[5] Eminov, *Turkish and Other Muslim Minorities*, 39.

[6] Most Bulgarian sources still adhere to the forced conversion thesis with notable exceptions such as Antonina Zheliaskova. "The Problem of the Authenticity of Some Domestic Sources on the Islamization of the Rhodopes, Deeply Rooted in Bulgarian Historiography," *Etudes Balkaniques* 4 (1990): 105–11. For an outside source that accepts the notion of forced conversion see Peter Sugar, *Southeastern Europe under Ottoman Rule 1354–1804* (Seattle, 1977), 52.

[7] See, for example, Zheliaskova, "Problem of the Authenticity," 105–11 and Eminov, *Turkish and Other Muslim Minorities*, 36–38.

[8] I use the phrase "path to Europe" here with some irony because it has become a post-1989 catch phrase in which a renunciation of Communism and Bloc loyalties in Bulgaria and elsewhere have been linked to a presumed "return to Europe" (another such catch phrase). The "path to Europe" seems also apropos for the nineteenth-century projects under discussion. For a discussion of the contemporary usage of the phrase in Bulgaria see Anna Krasteva, "The Vision of the Open Cultural Identity: The Idea of Europe in the Mirror of Bulgarian Cultural Identity," in *Bulgaria Facing Cultural Diversity*, ed. Goedele de Keersmaeker and Plamen Makeriev (Sofia, 1999).

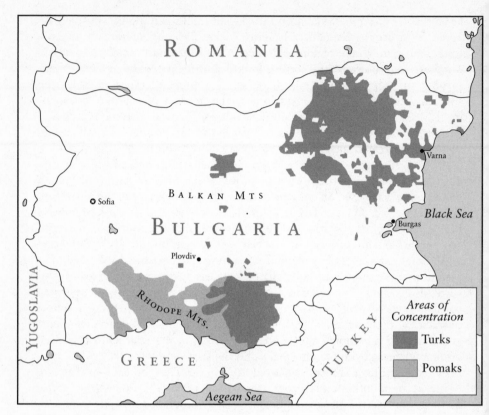

Map 2. The Distribution of Turks and Pomaks in Postwar Bulgaria

tal backwardness and barbarism. The construction of such a contrast was used as justification for European conquest and domination of its "Oriental" colonies, a process that reached its apogee in the nineteenth-century age of imperialism.[9] This is precisely the period in which Bulgarian nationalism came of age. The binaries inherent in Orientalism provided a powerful foundation for Bulgarians to assert their own Europeanness and contrast themselves to Ottoman, and later local Muslim, "Asianness" and all that implied. Such notions gave Bulgarian nationalism self-assurance, placing it on a firm European foundation, thereby providing justification for the domination of Muslim populations in the post-Ottoman period. Still, European influence and the grafting of Orientalist binaries onto the Balkan context were not without complications.

Local conditions necessitated a "domestication" of European ideas and practices, including Orientalism and nationalism—concepts and practices with their own inherent instabilities. First and foremost, the peoples of the Balkans were not impervious to the fact that they themselves were "Oriental-

[9] Said, *Orientalism*, 1–27.

ized" to a large degree by European observers. In recording and interpreting direct encounters with Balkan peoples, West European observers often described Balkan Christians as backward and Oriental, or at least semi-Oriental, the presumed result of prolonged contact and contamination by the neighboring Ottoman East.[10] As Todorova argues, Europe cast the Balkans as hybrid, as an "incomplete self."[11] This was similar to the designation assigned to Asia as a whole, whose "otherness" was also always grounded in concepts of a deficient self.[12] But for the Bulgarians, as with other aspiring European nations, more was at stake; their very place in Europe was rendered tentative. Bulgarians looking to Europe could not help but internalize such formulations that emphasized their own Oriental entanglements. As a result they agonized over their colonial (and later postcolonial) condition—they were, after all, "Europeans" who had been subject to five centuries of Ottoman, "Asiatic" rule.[13] Such a legacy burdened the Bulgarian national psyche with an intermittent inferiority complex and even self-Orientalization, that paradoxically stimulated an overcompensatory superiority complex. The distinct dynamic of the Bulgaro-Muslim relationship could not help but be driven by these fixations as well as the historical reality of direct geographic proximity and prolonged, intimate contact. The latter magnified anxieties about Bulgaro-Muslim hybridity and ultimately provoked claims of ethnic sameness, based on presumptions of shared origins. Hence, though armed with a conceptual arsenal gleaned from European colonial encounters, the Bulgarian Muslim encounter required a new recipe for meanings, (mis-) understandings, and underlying obsessions.

The Ottoman Legacy

Ottoman history, as with the history of all dead empires, is frequently read as a eulogy of an ill-fated and doomed dinosaur. More often than not, Ottoman last rites are replaced by an autopsy report, an enumeration of the cause of death, rather than a commemoration of the Empire's long life. Deaths, after all, are more significant than lives to the trustees of a will or those who can claim the status of victor on history's battlefield. With this in mind, Ottoman history is generally understood as backward by those who are attempting to live forward. Significantly, it was only at the end of the Ot-

[10] For a more complete discussion of "Orientalization" of the Balkans see Bakić-Hayden and Hayden, "Orientalist Variations," and Allcock and Young, eds., "Constructing the Balkans," 170–91.

[11] Todorova, *Imagining the Balkans*, 16. See Introduction for a discussion of how Todorova's views on Orientalism and the Balkans differ from those of Bakić-Hayden and Hayden, Allcock and Young, and the author.

[12] See, for example, Said, *Orientalism*, 58–59.

[13] Todorova rejects notions of Bulgarian postcoloniality via Europe claiming that the Bulgarian "sensibility of victimization is much less acute" (than former colonies of Europe). Todorova, *Imagining the Balkans*, 16–17.

toman period, in the late eighteenth and early nineteenth centuries, that self-proclaimed Bulgarian voices began to reconstruct their place in Ottoman history. With visions of the future in mind, Bulgarian thinkers deposited layers of meaning on the landscape of Ottoman Bulgaria. Such visions were not conjured from Ottoman documents or even local experience. Rather, they were guided and supplemented, if not invented, by European notions of Ottoman, and more generally, "Asiatic" depravity and barbarism. Hence modern Bulgarian thinkers imposed a conceptual clarity on an Ottoman reality—past and present—that was complex and replete with hybridity in terms of local cultural practices and meanings. Without question, the imposition of legibility on the Ottoman past was Bulgaria's first step in mapping its national present and future.

European, and in particular Russian, understandings of the East were seminal if not critical in Bulgarian reconstructions of the past. Significantly, Europe's most direct and immediate encounter with the Orient was with the Ottoman Empire itself, first as "the present terror of the world," but by the nineteenth century as the weak and decadent "sick man of Europe."[14] Since the eighteenth century, European military victories—in particular Austrian and Russian—and the resultant Ottoman loss of territories had confirmed the growing European sense of cultural preeminence. By the nineteenth century, the more fluid Enlightenment interest and respect for cultural difference had given way to a more categorical rejection of Eastern culture as irrefutably savage and base.[15] Although the European model became increasingly attractive to Bulgarian observers, they could not help but notice that notions of European supremacy did not embrace the Balkan peoples within their cultural parameters. Conveniently, Russian academics, with whom the early Bulgarian nationalist thinkers had close contacts, provided a conceptual antidote to this European condescension. Western Europeans had long considered Russia, like the Balkans, as only semi-European at best, spurring Russian debates about their own place in Europe.[16] Perhaps most influential from this body of writings was the very useful Russian concept of the "Tatar yoke," which posited that Russian backwardness was a direct result of over two centuries of Mongolian-Tatar rule. According to this paradigm, not only had the Mongols held Russia back from the general path of "Western civilization," but Russia had actually saved Europe by holding back the Mongol hordes.[17] Not coincidentally, the concept of the "Turkish" or "Ottoman yoke," which came to dominate Bulgarian and other Balkan historiographies, reproduced the Russo-Tatar formulation in form and content. The "Turkish

[14] Lewis, *Islam and the West*, 15.

[15] See, for example, Maxime Rodinson, *Europe and the Mystique of Islam* (Seattle, 1987), 59.

[16] See, for example, Iver Neumann, *Russia and the Idea of Europe: A Study in Identity and International Relations* (New York, 1996).

[17] For a discussion of the myth of the "Tatar yoke" see Charles Halperin, *Russia and the Golden Horde: The Mongol Impact on Medieval Russian History* (Bloomington, 1987).

yoke" concept was similarly grounded in the assumption that Bulgaria had been held back from the general course of European history by five centuries of Ottoman Turkish barbarism and that Bulgarians "saved" Europe from the same fate. Hence, with a selective hand, Bulgarian thinkers pulled devices for understanding their past from the European conceptual toolbox.

With the Turkish yoke in mind, by the nineteenth century a portion of the Bulgarian elite had begun to understand the Ottoman period in rather black-and-white terms, with political goals shaping historical interpretation. Such understandings were limited to a handful of mostly European-educated nationalist thinkers and organizers, who presumed that only by the shirking of the Asiatic yoke could the Bulgarian nation truly flourish. As Georgi Rakovski mused in his famous poem, "The Forest Traveler," published in the Bulgarian émigré press in 1866:

> The Turkish yoke, four centuries endured
> Let us smash heroically.
> Our dear, beloved homeland,
> Let us bravely free
> So that our nation may be reborn.[18]

The Turkish yoke concept implied that the Bulgarian nation was rooted in European soil underneath an onerous Oriental cloud cover. As Rakovski lamented elsewhere, "twelve million Christians live in Europe under the savage rule of this bestial people."[19] Only European enlightenment and progress could cause this latent national seed to germinate and flower and the nation to be "reborn." From the onset Bulgarian nationalist thinkers wrapped appeals for "liberation" of Bulgarian territory in Orientalist garb, interweaving the desire for "progress" and civilization with a presumed eternal battle between the cross and the crescent.

Constructs of Europe as paragon of progress and Christendom as opposed to Turco-Muslim barbarism furthered Bulgarian expectations of European support for national liberation. Consequently, Bulgarian intellectuals were disillusioned by Europe's relative inaction and seeming hypocrisy in relation to the Balkans, especially in Bulgaria prior to 1878. As the great Bulgarian nationalist, Liuben Karavelov, expressed, "Don't raise your head so high holy Europe, don't be so proud of your civilization and your Christianity when you don't have a pure heart or a clear conscience."[20] Rakovski, as other Bulgarian nationalists, censured Europe for its lack of action in alleviating perceived Balkan oppression, "This very educated Christian Europe without shame prevents nations, which endlessly suffer under the Muslim yoke . . .

[18] Mari Firkatian, *The Forest Traveler: Georgi Rakovski and Bulgarian Nationalism* (New York, 1996), 113.
[19] Ibid., 162.
[20] Ivan Indzhiev and Stoian Bozhkov, eds., *Publitsistika na Liuben Karavelov: Do Izlizaneto na Vestnik "Svoboda" 1860–1869* (Sofia, 1957), 101.

from eliminating the thievery of their masters, the Turks, and from restoring national rights and freedom to our ravished native land."[21] Early on it was clear that in spite of rhetoric about European-Christian unity, Europeans were never united in their concern for Balkan fates, but rather, competed for spheres of influence in the Balkans as elsewhere. It was the fractious diplomacy of the "Eastern Question" and the general abhorrence for revolution in the wake of the Napoleonic Wars that lay behind the European inability, prior to 1878, to deliver liberation to the newly defined Bulgarian nation. This necessarily soured the Bulgaro-European relationship, even as Bulgarian nationalists were employing European intellectual authority against the Ottoman presence. In fact, the rising cacophony of Bulgarian voices often saw in Europe a threat as great as the Ottoman one; they saw a patron that was both condescending and controlling. Bulgarian thinkers were not blind to the discrepancies between European theories and practices, between liberation and expansion, between the spread of "civilization" and domination.[22] Paradoxically, Europe became both the goal and the ubiquitous anathema of Bulgarian nationalist projects both before and after liberation. In spite of this ambivalence, Bulgarian nationalist ideas and later practices endeavored to impose a European-influenced modern intelligibility onto the ambiguous and flexible reality of the Ottoman milieu.

A closer look at the Ottoman period reveals—for historians now as then—the dilemma of imposing clear boundaries and categories onto a society where East and West were often indistinguishable, woven together into a pattern of continuous and intermingled difference. Surprisingly, it is only recently that scholarship on the Ottoman Empire has begun to challenge the dichotomous analyses that, as with Bulgarian historiography, present Ottoman history in terms of a grand clash of religions or national cultures. Numerous contemporary sources have revealed that from its inception the Ottoman polity emerged from a synthesis of peoples, cultural influences, and legacies, Roman-Byzantine as well as Islamic.[23] Cemal Kafadar, for example, explores how the complex Ottoman experience had the profound effect of creating a deep cultural synthesis that marked the Ottoman ethnoscape with alliances, interactions, coexistence, and a symbiosis that was "both possible and common."[24] The emergence of such a synthesis resulted in part from porous and flexible Ottoman administrative practices on the local level that left behind a tangle of cultures and dominions, often without clear boundaries. These

---

[21] Georgi Rakovski, *Izbrani Săchineniia* (Sofia, 1946), 66.

[22] In fact, a critique of Western concepts and practices was imbedded in European influence itself. The writings of self-reflective Russian intellectuals such as Herzen, Bakunin, and Chernishevskii, in particular, held sway over Bulgarian nationalist-revolutionary thought. Marin Pundeff, "Bulgarian Nationalism," in *Nationalism in Eastern Europe*, ed. Peter Sugar and Ivo Lederer (Seattle, 1994), 111.

[23] See Donald Quataert, *The Ottoman Empire, 1700–1922* (Cambridge, U.K., 2000), 3–4; and Cemal Kafadar, *Between Two Worlds: The Construction of the Ottoman State* (Berkeley, 1995), 19.

[24] Kafadar, *Between Two Worlds*, 19.

practices also left a considerable imprint on the territories and peoples that later would come under Bulgarian authority. The conceptual and territorial untangling of Bulgaria from the Ottoman polity must be viewed against this backdrop, namely the intricate landscape of the "Bulgarian lands."

In the Ottoman period, mass migrations and conversions transformed the already complicated human geography of the provinces that are now part of modern Bulgaria. Ottoman administrators, military, and cultural leaders brought their temporary presence into the "Bulgarian lands" and many became permanently fixed into the fabric of Balkan life. In addition, Turkic-speaking migrants, who came en masse from Asia Minor, made a permanent home in the plains and mountains of Bulgaria. Some estimate that the Muslim descendants of these peasants, artisans, herdsmen, and those who intermixed with them comprised 40 to 50 percent of the population of the Bulgarian principality at the time of liberation.[25] Without question interaction, coexistence, intermarriage, and cultural mixing occurred among Turkic and Slavic populations in these areas. Furthermore, mass conversions to Islam in the seventeenth century by Slavic-speaking peasants and herdsmen in the Rhodope Mountains brought another cultural variant to the region—Slavic Muslims, or Pomaks. As a rule, Ottoman officials in the Balkans did not actively promote mass conversion to Islam among Balkan Christian peasants; instead Christians and Jews under Ottoman rule became protected "people of the pact" and were granted ample religious tolerance. Forced conversions although not unheard of were uncommon and generally were carried out only in connection with the *devşirme* system, which entailed a Christian "child levy" whereby Ottoman officials periodically gathered the best and brightest Christian boys, who were converted and educated in Istanbul. They then filled its elite slave ranks, such as the famous janissary corps, and high administrative posts. In the Ottoman Golden Age they were a gelded bureaucracy, who owed their status and position to the Ottoman palace. The children of the *devşirme* lost their families and connections to their native locales, but also gained power and status and literally ran the Empire for many centuries.[26] Consequently, both on the local level and among the Ottoman elite, symbiosis, cultural convergence, and hybridized coexistence were characteristic of Ottoman society.

By the end of the Ottoman period, the Bulgarian lands were home to a spectrum of cultural variants. Although these territories were populated primarily by Bulgarian-speaking Orthodox Christians and Turkish-speaking Muslims, they were also were settled with Pomaks, Gagauz (Turkish-speaking Christians), Greeks, Sephardic Jews, Gypsies, Armenians, Vlachs, and others. Muslims settled in both urban and rural areas, but Slavs were primarily a rural population until the nineteenth century when they began to mi-

---

[25] Kemal Karpat, *Ottoman Population, 1830–1914: Demographic and Social Characteristics* (Madison, 1985), 56.
[26] Sugar, *Southeastern Europe*, 58.

grate into growing towns and cities. The urban centers of the Bulgarian lands were historically a mix of non-Bulgarian elements: Turks, Greeks, Armenians, Gypsies, and Jews, although after 1878 the new capital of Bulgaria, Sofia, was gradually Bulgarianized as urban Turks and other ethnic elements gradually emigrated and Bulgarians urbanized. In Balkan cities and villages it was generally apparent who was a Christian, who was a Jew, and who was a Muslim; people usually lived in religion-based communities or quarters within the same village or town. Differences in language, too, were surely encountered in everyday interactions. At the same time, bilingualism, intermarriage, and syncretic religious practices were common and a blurring of cultural lines was also integral to Balkan life. In the Balkans, as elsewhere in the Empire, neither Muslim nor Christian beliefs and rites were necessarily brought into strict conformity with the dogmas and rituals of established religious authorities. Islamic peasants in the Balkans practiced what is best characterized as folk-Islam, often incorporating the use of Christian icons, recognition of saints' days, and other non-Muslim features. A variety of local pagan and folk customs colored the spectrum of local practices, obscuring the distinction between Islam and Christianity during the long centuries of coexistence.[27] Thus, although religion was a key defining feature of status within Ottoman society as so many scholars have emphasized, distinctions between cultures and peoples were often blurred on the local level. For the most part, Muslims and non-Muslims coexisted or periodically came into conflict as intimate neighbors with shared local identities and knowledge. In spite of later Balkan histories that speak to the contrary, there is no evidence of the widespread existence of "national" consciousness, feelings of national oppression, or pervasive Muslim/non-Muslim conflict until the very end of the Ottoman period.

The incredible longevity of the Ottoman system can be attributed in large part to the flexible reality of Ottoman administrative practices in relation to its many non-Muslim peoples. These practices are generally referred to as the "*millet* system," a kind of extra-territorial local self-rule through non-Muslim confessional institutions. Although Muslims of the Ottoman Empire were subject to the Şeriat (Islamic law), non-Muslims were for all intents and purposes under the civil and religious jurisdiction of their respective *millets*. These *millets* were divided along confessional lines, originally into Jewish, Orthodox Christian, and Armenian, with the later additions of Catholic (1830), and Protestant (1860) *millets*. In spite of its label as a "system," the *millet* practice was actually a flexible, porous, and ad hoc Ottoman strategy for granting self-rule to non-Muslims. Daniel Goffman, in line with other recent scholarship on *millets*, has argued that *millet* authority was not centralized until the late Ottoman period.[28] In fact, the term *millet* (which translates

[27] Sugar even advances the notion that the similarity between Christian and Islamic folk forms explains the mass conversions of Balkan peasants to Islam in the Ottoman period. Ibid., 52.
[28] Daniel Goffman, "Ottoman Millets in the Early Seventeenth Century," *New Perspectives on Turkey* 11 (1994): 135–59.

as "nation" in modern Turkish) was not in widespread use within the Empire until the nineteenth century, precisely when cultural boundaries of various kinds were being reconfigured and consolidated.[29] Although the term itself is often misunderstood, non-Muslims within the Ottoman domain did enjoy widespread local confessional autonomy, and therefore certain rights and privileges, in a time when religious tolerance was scarce on the European continent. This relative confessional tolerance might help explain the fact that Bulgarian extrication from Ottoman rule began only in the nineteenth century.

As with culture, the flexibility of Ottoman economic practices also most certainly contributed to the longevity of Ottoman rule in Bulgaria. Throughout the Ottoman period, the economy in the Bulgarian provinces was based on small-scale agriculture and animal husbandry carried out by Muslims and non-Muslims and loosely administered by Muslim elite. As a rule the Ottoman economic system has been mistakenly labeled as "feudal" or guided by highly centralized "Oriental despotism." Such characterizations, emerging out of nineteenth-century European critiques of the Empire as backward and "oppressive" to Christian peasantry, have remained surprisingly static. In recent years, however, a whole literature has undermined the notion that the Ottoman land regime was feudal in either a classical European or an "Oriental despotic" sense. Instead, research has revealed the amazing diversity and flexibility of the system.[30] In fact, as far as agriculture is concerned, the system was designed to protect the Muslim and non-Muslim peasantry, who—as the only taxpayers—were the fiscal base of the Empire. Although peasants had de facto hereditary usufruct rights to plots of land, Muslim landlords were given only nonhereditary privileges to administer lands based on service and merit in a system meant to minimize the building of local power bases and abuses of the peasantry. In practice, local centers of power and abuses did exist, especially periods when Ottoman provincial control diminished. But because peasants were not serfs in the traditional European sense, many were able to avoid such abuses through migration to adjacent or distant lands or by direct appeal to Ottoman officials. As Amy Singer asserts, unlike serfs, Ottoman peasants were "tied to the land practically and not absolutely."[31] In spite of this, nineteenth-century Bulgarian nationalists inspired by European writings were quick to impose a rigid interpretation of Muslim feudal oppression onto the flexible reality of the Ottoman economy.

Although life in Ottoman Bulgaria was never ideal, it was only in the nine-

[29] Benjamin Braude, "Foundation Myths of the *Millet* System," in *Christians and Jews in the Ottoman Empire: The Functioning of a Plural Society*, ed. Benjamin Braude and Bernard Lewis (New York, 1982), 73.

[30] See, for example, Halil Inalcik and Donald Quataert, eds., *An Economic and Social History of the Ottoman Empire, 1300–1913* (Cambridge, U.K., 1994); Sevket Pamuk, *The Ottoman Empire and European Capitalism, 1820–1913: Trade, Investment and Production* (Cambridge, U.K., 1987); and Bruce McGowan, *Economic Life in the Ottoman Empire: Taxation Trade and the Struggle for Land 1600–1800* (Cambridge, U.K., 1981).

[31] Amy Singer, *Palestinian Peasants and Ottoman Officials: Rural Administration around Sixteenth Century Jerusalem* (Cambridge, U.K., 1994), 12.

teenth century that European and Bulgarian writings began to produce the most damning critiques of the Ottoman period as a whole. Such writings had multiple political and cultural agendas, written as they were in a period when Europeans were penetrating and subjugating large parts of the non-Western world. For Bulgarian thinkers, Ottoman inferiority and the presumably barbaric and oppressive nature of their system provided justification for European intervention and Bulgarian political independence. Ironically, Bulgarians rewrote the Ottoman past in order to move forward in a period when the Ottoman Empire was reforming and reinventing itself. Ottoman military defeats at the hands of the Habsburg and Russian Empires had resulted in a ceding of Ottoman territories in 1699, 1718, and 1774, provoking new directions in Ottoman reform. Paradoxically, it was the transformation to a modern administrative system rather than Ottoman "backwardness" that proved the biggest liability to Ottoman survival. In the midst of attempts to solidify the formerly flexible boundaries in economy and culture, new boundaries emerged which were ultimately antithetical to Ottoman integration. Although reform began somewhat earlier, the reform period known as the Tanzimat was officially proclaimed by Mahmud II in 1839 as an attempt to foster Ottoman fiscal health—necessary for military success—and to seek new avenues of legitimacy and order. The Tanzimat proclamation, the Hatt-ı Şerif of Gülhane of 1839, offered a theoretical political equality to all of the citizens of the Empire. Reinforced in the Hatt-ı Hümayun of 1856, Sultan Abdülaziz extended "to all the subjects of my Empire, without distinction of class or religion . . . security of their persons and their property."[32] The reforms associated with the Tanzimat reflected attempts to integrate the increasingly disparate loyalties of the peoples of the Empire through the concept of *Osmanlılık* (Ottomanism) or political loyalty to the Ottoman fatherland. Ottomanism remained a rather malleable concept, one that still allowed for the existence of non-Muslim collective identities.

In fact, the Ottomans encouraged the transformation of local autonomies into consolidated *millets* as part of an attempt to offer concessions to disgruntled non-Muslim elites and hence foster cultural and administrative integration. Although cultural integration did occur in various ways, in other ways *millets* were detrimental to the greater project of Ottomanism.[33] *Millet* centralization was first instituted in the eighteenth century, when the Greek Orthodox hierarchy was given unprecedented power over the Orthodox peoples of the so-called Rum (Roman or Orthodox Christian) *millet*. Although this may have served to bolster Greek elite loyalties in the short term, in the long term it provoked non-Greek Orthodox resentment. For example, whereas in the ad hoc local practices of earlier Ottoman times, Old Church Slavonic was used in the Orthodox churches of the Bulgarian lands, by the

---

[32] Bernard Lewis, *The Emergence of Modern Turkey* (Oxford, 1961), 116.
[33] Kemal Karpat, *An Inquiry into the Social Foundations of Nationalism in the Ottoman State: From Social Estates to Classes from Millets to Nations* (Princeton, 1973).

early eighteenth and late nineteenth centuries liturgical Greek had encroached on the local Slavic Orthodox ceremonies.[34] By the late eighteenth century the "church question" began to enter into Bulgarian Orthodox clergy writings. In fact, the first voices of dissatisfaction with the status of the Bulgarian inhabitants of the Empire were raised not in opposition to Ottoman rule, but against the domination of the Greek Orthodox Patriarchate over the Orthodox *millet*. The well-known tract of Paisiĭ Khilendarski which appeared in 1762, *Slavianobŭlgarska Istoriia*, first articulated the need for Bulgarians to reclaim their past, their homeland, and their language from the foreign "Greek" presence.[35] Interestingly, Bulgarian collective cultural rights in the form of demands for a separate Bulgarian Orthodox Exarchate were first asserted in the context of, not in opposition to, Ottoman institutions. The final granting of the Exarchate by *ferman* (imperial edict) of the Sultan in 1870 amounted to a separate *millet* status for the so-proclaimed "Bulgarian" churches within the Empire, separating them from the ecclesiastical control of Orthodox Greeks. Ironically, this *ferman* was the first official act from any state that gave official recognition to the Bulgarian nation as an entity and hence is recognized even by Bulgarian sources as a defining moment in the struggle for national independence.

Although *millets* and the Bulgarian Exarchate were religion-based organizations, language played a critical role at this stage of Bulgarian cultural development. It was, after all, the Bulgarian tongue that separated Bulgarian from Greek in the church dispute. At the same time, the Exarchate was granted jurisdiction over any eparchy (church administrative district) in which two-thirds of the Christian inhabitants decided by a "peoples' vote" to be subordinate to the Bulgarian church rather than the Greek Church. As a result of this provision, a battle between Greek and Bulgarian Orthodox churches over territorial jurisdiction ensued in which language played a secondary role. Both Greeks and Bulgarians claimed the Orthodox populations of Macedonia and Thrace, with each side maintaining that the latter group had linguistically assimilated, in other words Hellenized or Slavicized, local populations. As a result, each claimed the locally population as ethnically Bulgarian or Greek respectively regardless of language, provoking a long-term territorial battle over souls in these regions. With the prevalent bilingualism and mixing of Orthodox populations of these areas, local populations often claimed cultural affinities based on the shifting winds of political changes, in many cases families were even divided by such ethnic proclamations.[36] In the nineteenth century, *millet*ism within Ottoman parameters was

[34] Barbara Jelavich, *History of the Balkans: Eighteenth and Nineteenth Centuries* (Cambridge, U.K., 1983), 337.

[35] Paisiĭ Khilendarski, *Slavianobŭlgarska Istoriia* (Sofia, 1989).

[36] For two recent studies on the historical and contemporary complexity of cultural affiliation in Macedonia see Anastasia Karakasidou, *Fields of Wheat, Hills of Blood: Passages to Nationhood in Greek Macedonia, 1870–1990* (Chicago, 1997); and Loring Danforth, *The Macedonian Conflict: Ethnic Nationalism in a Transitional World* (Princeton, 1995).

hence transformed from an extra-territorial into a territorial concept causing tensions within the Orthodox *millet* in particular.

And although the Exarchate arguably established a basis for Bulgarian separatism it also created the potential for Bulgarian loyalty to flourish within the Ottoman context. In spite of the more radical demands of certain Bulgarian nationalists, perhaps a greater number of Bulgarians in the 1860s–70s still adhered to the premise that Bulgarian interests could best be served within the confines of the Empire. The Ottoman Empire still held a large piece of Balkan territory, with an intractable mix of peoples, including Slavs; the untangling of this morass was still unthinkable to most elites. In addition, the bulk of the Bulgaro-Slavic population in this period was peasants who tended to have primarily local identities and were generally anti-revolutionary by nature, if not openly loyal to the sultan.[37] Furthermore, the vast majority of Bulgarian elite in Istanbul, which housed the greatest urban concentration of Bulgarians anywhere in the nineteenth century, were Ottoman-loyal. In articles in such Bulgarian publications as *Tsarigradski Vestnik*, *Turtsiia*, and *Makedoniia*, published in the 1860s and 1870s in Istanbul, numerous authors even advanced the abortive idea of a dual monarchy based on the Habsburg model, with the Turks and Bulgarian as leading nations.[38]

Allegiance to the *millet* idea on the part of many Ottoman Bulgarians may have been in part a shared Ottoman-Bulgarian reaction to the eminent challenge of European economic and political dominance. At times, Bulgarian voices in the Ottoman capital were raised in anger against Russian and other European intrigues in the Balkans. They censured, for example, Russian attempts to thwart the positive effects of Ottoman reform efforts, in particular the far-reaching pilot reform projects of Midhat Pasha (himself a Pomak) in the Danubian *vilâyet* (northeastern Bulgaria).[39] They were keenly aware that by the nineteenth century European penetration of the Ottoman economy had ruined Bulgarian artisans in the newly burgeoning towns of Ottoman Bulgaria. Even the newly prosperous Bulgarian merchants of the nineteenth century were not unequivocally pro-Europe and anti-Ottoman, as is so often assumed.[40] Many had made their fortune not from trade with Europe but from supplying wool and other provisions to the Ottoman government and,

[37] Inalcik, for example, posits that the Vidin uprisings of 1841 and 1850 were inspired by social rather than national grievances and that the local Slavic peasantry looked to the sultan for aid against local incursions. See Halil Inalcik, *Tanzimat ve Bulgar Meselesi* (Ankara, 1992).

[38] In this period the largest center for the publishing of books and other materials in modern literary Bulgarian was Istanbul, which by the nineteenth century housed the largest concentration of self-proclaimed Bulgarians anywhere. Viktoria Tileva, *Bŭlgarsko Pechatarsko Druzhestvo "Promishlenie" v Tsarigrad: 1870–85* (Sofia, 1985).

[39] See, for example, *Makedoniia* (Istanbul), 3 December 1868, 2. For a discussion of Midhat Pasha's reforms see Georgi Pletinov, *Midkhat Pasha i Upravlenieto na Dunavskiia Vilaiet* (Veliko Tŭrnovo, 1994).

[40] Until recently Stoianovich's assumption that the prosperous Orthodox merchants were closely allied with European interests held sway. See Traian Stoianovich, "The Conquering Balkan Orthodox Merchants," *Journal of Economic History* 20 (1960): 234–313.

as Reşat Kasaba points out, non-Muslim merchants were often in direct competition with European merchants or imperialist interests.[41] In addition, a perceived encroachment on Ottoman territories by Russia and Austro-Hungary in particular represented a potential fragmentation of the vast realm of internal Ottoman trade. Finally, as beneficiaries of Ottoman rule, the so-called *çorbacı*—local elders, traders, or notables that by the nineteenth century had become representatives of Ottoman fiscal authorities—were also, in general, strong opponents of political independence. Hence, among numerous social groups within the Empire, there was a strong movement to seek internal solutions, to recast and strengthen the Bulgarian place in Ottoman society, often in opposition to Europe.

In spite of its integrative potential, *millet*ism eventually was the ground on which non-Muslim identities would grow, divide, separate and burgeon. Although *millet* leaders themselves remained essentially Ottoman-loyal, the *millet* established a basis for rights based on lines of language and religion. Ottoman reform held the potential for Bulgarian integration but also cultural and political extrication as the Bulgarian figure began to emerge from the Ottoman carpet. For Bulgarians the slow process of untangling the web of Ottoman mutuality had begun. It was not necessarily inevitable that Ottomanism or *millet*ism would fail, that the apple would fall far from the tree. But although some found new moorings in the reconstituted modes of Ottoman legitimacy, others sought a place for Bulgaria on a separate map and a separate continent. The articulate voices of Bulgarian revolutionaries eventually found a ready audience outside the Empire, when their visions melded with the interests and paradigms of the European powers.

Breaking the Yoke

Ultimately it was Russian military invasion, and not nationalist visions or power, which brought about the territorial separation of Bulgaria from Ottoman Europe. After the Ottoman defeat in the Russo-Turkish war of 1877–78, Bulgarian territorial autonomy was secured and the search for the Bulgarian national self continued with renewed fervor. More voices entered the project of depicting, defining, and delimiting the outer limits and the inner sanctum of the national domain. At its core, this contested process sought to delineate the Bulgarian nation in relation to East and West, to untangle and extricate the foreign threads from the native tapestry. As Bulgarian bureaucrats and intellectuals began to negotiate the new parameters of the nation inside their autonomous territories, a discourse of reclamation of the Bulgarian lands from an illegitimate, "foreign" occupation gained in strength. Postliberation culture venerated the revolutionary few who had re-

---

[41] Reşat Kasaba, *The Ottoman Empire and the World Economy: The Nineteenth Century* (Albany, 1988), 50–56.

jected and fought the Ottoman presence and played a role in liberation from the Turkish yoke, even as ambivalence toward the West never abated. Bulgarian heroes were made from historians, poets, and revolutionaries who had rendered the local landscape Bulgarian and set out to free it from alien presences, although such determinations were inescapably complicated. The fate of Muslim minorities that remained in the new Bulgarian state was intimately intertwined with this process.

The circumstances under which Bulgaria gained autonomy in 1878 were a harbinger of things to come, including a new era for Bulgaro-Muslim relations. The European powers, who by this time had already secured Greek independence (1830) as well as Serbian (1830) and Romanian (1856) autonomies, had thus far proceeded slowly when it came to the "Bulgarian question." In part this had been dictated by the complicated diplomatic game of the "Eastern question" and the European balance of power.[42] Heretofore, the assumption that an independent Bulgaria would be a mere extension of Russian power in the Balkans had kept the British, French, and Austrians from openly supporting any Bulgarian bid for independence. In fact, after each major territorial revision of the Balkans, the status quo again became a common European cause. The Bulgarian elite itself was split on the issue of independence, whereas the general population was mostly indifferent or uninvolved. Nevertheless, the April Uprisings of 1876, organized by a handful of Bulgarian revolutionaries, set in motion a momentous change in the political life of the Bulgarian provinces. In conjunction with the uprising, local revolutionary committees staged a massacre of Muslim civilians, provoking intense Ottoman reprisals carried out by irregular troops, Circassians, and Başıbozuks, who slaughtered an estimated 12,000 to 15,000 local Christians.[43] Although the uprising itself secured local Bulgarian sovereignty for only a short time, the reprisals that followed turned the eyes of Europe to the long-ignored Bulgarian situation. William Gladstone, a prominent nineteenth-century British prime minister, helped raise public indignation over the "Turkish atrocities" against Bulgarians with images of the "Turkish infidel" lording over "European Christians." Along with other outpourings of support for the "Bulgarian cause" in the European press, Gladstone advocated action: "I have great faith in the power of opinion, of the opinion of civilized and Christian Europe. It can remove mountains."[44] Soon after Gladstone's impassioned appeals, the Russian tsar Alexander II, with the tacit support of the West European powers, confronted and ultimately invaded

[42] On the Eastern question see A. L. Macfie, *The Eastern Question, 1774–1923* (London, 1996), and Marion Kent, ed., *The Great Powers and the End of the Ottoman Empire* (London, 1984).

[43] Jelavich, *History of the Balkans*,347. For a Bulgarian memoir that recounts the events of the uprisings see Zakhari Stoianov, Iz "Zapiski po Bŭlgarskite Vŭstaniia" (Sofia, 1972), which has been translated into English, Zahari Stoyanov, *Extracts from Notes on the Bulgarian Uprisings* (Sofia, 1976).

[44] William Gladstone, *Lessons in Massacre; or, The Conduct of the Turkish Government in and about Bulgaria since May, 1876* (London, 1877), 5–6.

Ottoman Bulgaria, defeating the Ottomans in the 1877–78 Russo-Turkish War. During the war itself, an estimated 200,000 to 300,000 Muslims were massacred and a significant number fled their homes, following the retreating Ottoman forces.[45] Many Bulgarians joined the Russian forces and many Bulgarians were pitted against Muslims in a Russian-led crusade of the cross against the crescent—the first modern Christian-Muslim conflict of significance in this region.[46]

It is no coincidence that this disruption in Bulgaro-Muslim relations occurred just as Russia gained a new measure of prestige in the eyes of Bulgarian leaders. Russian prestige was enhanced by their victory in the Russo-Turkish war and subsequent sponsorship of the 1878 San Stefano settlement that created an autonomous Bulgarian polity with a very large expanse of land including the coveted territories of Macedonia and Thrace. As a result, the myth of the Russian Christian protector "Diado Ivan" (Grandpa Ivan) as liberator from the Ottoman overlords was popularized, and Tsar Alexander II—whose equestrian statue would later grace the center of the Bulgarian capital, Sofia—would be forever remembered in national histories as "Tsar Liberator." In contrast to Russia's new stature, a growing sense of West European betrayal occurred as a result of the revision of the San Stefano borders in the subsequent Treaty of Berlin (1878). The new Bulgarian principality would be much smaller in reach, mostly because of Great Power suspicions that Bulgaria would become a Russian client in the Balkans. Bulgarian nationalist thinkers would never forget the truncation of territory that resulted from the adjustment of these so-called natural borders.

In the newly autonomous Bulgarian principality a Russian provisional government and troops helped establish a new, European-style order, albeit one constrained by the Treaty of Berlin. Because there were no remaining survivors of the Bulgarian royal family, the Treaty of Berlin stipulated that the new king of Bulgaria would be culled from European royalty but would not be of Russian descent. As a result, Alexander of Battenburg, a prince from the German lands, took the Bulgarian political helm and reigned under the mandate of a European-inspired, liberal constitution, complete with European-dictated minority treaties. Paradoxically, Europe bestowed the new Bulgarian polity with the cultural foundation for belittlement and hatred of Muslims, as well as the political structures to institutionalize tolerance.

The Bulgarian principality always gave ample lip-service to constitutional tolerance of minorities, but in practice it relied on Ottoman-inspired methods of minority administration. After all, in spite of its new European pedigree, postliberation Bulgaria was still, in many ways, entangled conceptually and territorially with its Ottoman neighbor. Many Muslims had fled the new principality, both from the rapidly Bulgarianizing cities and the rural areas,

[45] Karpat, *Ottoman Population*, 49.
[46] Mary Neuburger, "The Russo-Turkish War and the 'Eastern Jewish Question': Encounters between Victims and Victors in Ottoman Bulgaria, 1877–8," *East European Jewish Affairs* 26 (1996): 53–66.

where it was difficult for many to reclaim or hold onto properties, especially those abandoned by necessity during the war. But the continued presence of large numbers of Muslims on Bulgarian soil (and Bulgarians on Ottoman soil) was central to the Bulgaro-Ottoman entanglement. As of 1881, even after the mass exodus of Muslims precipitated by the Russo-Turkish War, an estimated 578,000 Muslims still lived in Bulgaria—28.8 percent of the total population.[47] By 1885, the unilateral territorial merger of Bulgaria with Eastern Rumelia (another autonomous principality created by the Treaty of Berlin) brought an even larger number of Muslims—Turks and Pomaks—under the direct administration of the Bulgarian principality. This again caused significant emigrations, but the overall number of Muslims in Bulgaria nevertheless had increased to 676,215 by 1888, though the overall percentage of the population had dropped to 21.4 percent.[48] Though Bulgarians and Muslims traded places as rulers and ruled, Muslims were granted a special administrative place in the new state. In a hybrid of the *millet* system of the late Ottoman period, Muslims were granted fairly far-reaching autonomy under the umbrella of local Muslim Confessional Organizations (MCOs), controlled by the Head Muftiship in Sofia. Though theoretically answerable to the *Şeyhülislam* (the head of the religious establishment in the Ottoman Empire) in Istanbul, for all practical purposes Bulgaria now had its own Muslim hierarchy. As with Christian *millets* in the Ottoman period, Muslim subjects retained their own courts under the *Şeriat*, their own private schools, and, for the most part, administered communal affairs through local self-governing institutions. These institutions were funded by the extensive MCO-administered *vakf* properties that remained from the Ottoman period. This state of affairs sanctioned by treaty with the Ottomans, proved an effective Bulgarian strategy for internal management of disparate populations.[49] Muslims were separated and contained as the fledgling state and society grappled to define and establish itself. At the same time, the granting of Muslim autonomy was, in part, predicated on the need to insure the continued *millet* rights of Bulgarian populations and institutions spread over the remaining "Bulgarian lands" under Ottoman rule. The seat of the Bulgarian Exarchate was still located in Istanbul and continued to function and even expand its influence and activities in Thrace and Macedonia.[50] Ottoman models of extraterritorial autonomy were often more useful than European-inspired Bulgarian constitutional structures in dealing with Muslims within and especially in maintaining and spreading Bulgarian influence outside its borders. In many ways, this reliance on Muslim and Ottoman forms com-

[47] Eminov, *Turkish and Other Muslim Minorities*, 71.

[48] Ibid., 71.

[49] Huey Kostanick, *Turkish Resettlement of Bulgarian Turks: 1950–1953* (Berkeley, 1957), 20.

[50] See, for example, Iliia Galev, *Zdravno-Sotsialnata Deĭnost na Bŭlgarskata Ekzarkhiia v Makedoniia i Trakiia, 1870–1913* (Sofia, 1994).

promised Bulgarian efforts to carve and expand its place in Europe, to re-claim Bulgarian land and peoples from the Ottoman milieu.

As state and society were Bulgarianized on various fronts, other complications abounded. Underlying romantic notions of liberation and deliverance of an idealized Bulgarian nation collided with the ugly particulars of state-craft and the economic and political realities of independence. In spite of some economic successes, the severing of Bulgaria from the Ottoman territories and markets which was completed with independence in 1908, did not bode well for merchants, local craftsmen, or peasants. Certain sectors of the Bulgarian economy were nearly devastated by the influx of cheap European goods, and new taxes and payments expected for lands acquired from re-treating Muslims further impoverished the peasantry. A famous peasant adage—*Prez tursko zhiveekhme po dobre* (In Turkish times we lived bet-ter)—became a well-known epithet.[51] The disillusionment was also felt among the new Bulgarian elite. By the turn of the twentieth century, various Socialist movements appeared that were critical of "foreign exploitation" and intent on "liberating" the toiling masses from bourgeoisie and Euro-pean/capitalist exploitation. Nativist outlooks increased; politicians and in-dustrialists espoused economic protectionism and expressed distrust of for-eigners "from whom we have more to fear than an epidemic" and encroachments of European and Russian influences in Bulgarian politics.[52] At times, the Muslims of Bulgaria and even the Ottoman Empire itself be-came provisional allies in Bulgarian projects, whether subversive or official, to ward off other foreign—namely Russian and European—political incur-sions.[53]

As postliberation euphoria gave way to disillusionment among Bulgarian intellectuals, the artificial divide between Orient and Occident was further complicated, even as it continued to provide a framework for understanding Bulgarian history. The elaboration and popularization of the Turkish yoke—and other Orientalist-inspired—explanatory constructs proceeded within the Bulgarian literary, historical, and other academic fields as they became estab-lished and professionalized. This is illustrated in particular by the work of the father of modern Bulgarian literature, Ivan Vazov. His famous novel *Pod Igoto* (*Under the Yoke*), published in 1889–90, in many ways is one of the most seminal texts in the elaboration of Bulgarian national sentiment. It

[51] See, for example, Ivan Elenkov, "Versii za Bŭlgarskata Identichnost v Modernata Epokha," in *Zashto Sme Takiva? V Tŭrsene na Bŭlgarskata Kulturna Identichnost*, ed. I. Elenkov and R. Daskalov (Sofia: Izdatelstvo "Prosveta," 1994), 14.

[52] John Lampe, *The Bulgarian Economy in the Twentieth Century* (London, 1986), 39.

[53] This was clearly the case when Prime Minister Stephan Stambolov replaced Alexander of Battenburg with Ferdinand of Saxe-Coburg in 1887 without Great Power sanctions and in direct opposition to Russian demands. Stambolov turned to the Ottoman Empire which was the first to recognize the new regime, heralding a new trend of favorable Bulgaro-Ottoman relations. On the Stambolov era see Duncan Perry, *Stefan Stambolov and the Emergence of Modern Bulgaria, 1870–1895* (Durham, N.C., 1996).

paints a picture of preliberation Bulgaria as a society crushed under the weight of an oppressive and arbitrary yoke of Oriental Ottoman despotism. Vazov's image of the Turk is that of an unequivocally cruel, if not bestial, alien interloper, occupying and preying on essentially "Bulgarian" cultural and material belongings. Vazov's paradigm, which draws on the revolutionary ideas and figures of the preliberation era, is rife with nationalist anti-Turkish content, but significantly, is also critical of Bulgarian culpability. In the period leading up to the Balkan Wars, anti-Turkish images and sentiment, although seminal to the process of national redefinition, were complicated by various counterimages, as well as Bulgarian self-doubt and blame. Although Vazov's anti-Turkishness is unmistakable, he also has numerous negative Bulgarian characters who are condemned as harmful and traitorous to the Bulgarian national cause. Tellingly, Vazov's Bulgarian antagonists are under "foreign" influence of some kind, such as the loathsome *çorbacı* (local officials) who side with the Turkish authorities. He also lampoons many of the dandified, Europeanized Bulgarian characters who tend to hobnob with the *çorbacı* instead of seeking out true connection with the Bulgarian people and their plight. Significantly, it is these hybridized traitors, as well as the barbaric Turk, that *Under the Yoke* vilifies.

Although the cultural and political imperatives of this period demanded that Bulgarian be divided from Turk, the reality of historical and contemporary cultural hybridity and the ambiguous European presence required more nuanced untanglings. In *Staroplaninski Legendi* (*Legends of Stara Planina*), prominent literary figure Iordan Iovkov intermittently painted positive images of the wise or kind Turkish villager as an integral part of the Bulgarian village landscape. Here the local Turk was conceptualized as a dying breed rather than as a symbol of a hated past, with a note of nostalgia for a time of cultural richness and interaction that was still alive in the Balkan village.[54] At the same time, Bulgarian writer and political commentator Aleko Konstantinov created what became a popular archetype of Bulgarian backwardness in his character Baĭ Gano (from a book by the same name), that was indicative of a deeper identification with the "Oriental" within the Bulgarian national self.[55] *Baĭ Gano* is a collection of stories about a Bulgarian traveling salesman who travels throughout Europe and even visits the United States, revealing his own bumbling and uncouth "Oriental" manners in relation to the "civilized" worlds he encounters. In reading and interpreting *Baĭ Gano* since its publication in 1894–95, Bulgarians were willing to laugh, as well as agonize, over their own backwardness and apparent hybridity; the Bulgarian national self was at once European and semi-Oriental.[56] It was perhaps this type of

---

[54] Iordan Iovkov, *Staroplaninski Legendi* (Sofia: Bulgarski Pisatel, 1980).

[55] For a contemporary Bulgarian analysis of the multiple meanings of Baĭ Gano see Boian Penev, "Prevrŭshtaniiato na Baĭ Gano," in *Zashto Sme Takiva? V Tŭrsene na Bŭlgarskata Kulturna Identichnost*, ed. Ivan Elenkov and R. Daskalov (Sofia, 1994), 121–31,

[56] The meaning of Baĭ Gano as a literary archetype is often debated in Bulgarian literary criticism and cultural history. Generally, the arguments revolve around its meaning as either a na-

self-aversion of the Orientalized, or more accurately, hybridized national self that ultimately drove twentieth-century projects to clarify borders between Bulgarian and Turk. Even as writings such as *Baĭ Gano* complicated simplified binaries of civilized Bulgarian and barbaric Muslim, they may have also inspired or encouraged impulses to eradicate visible marks of hybridity both on the Bulgarian self and on the ever-present Muslim populations.

Although Bulgarian literature provided crucial soul-searching, ethnography was always at the heart of efforts to determine and clarify ethnic boundaries via the alleged markings of Bulgarianness on the landscape. Since before liberation, the ethnographic-historical work of the Russo-Ukrainian Slavicist, Iuri Venelin, among others, had spawned a wave of amateur Bulgarian ethnographic endeavors which supported Bulgarian claims for territorial independence and later expansion.[57] As Catherine Clay asserts in the case of Russia, ethnography was "grounded in imperial expansion" as a way for the Empire, or in this case the nation, to consolidate and extend its power.[58] Amateur ethnography was integral to the early writings of Bulgarian nationalists as well as foreign enthusiasts, who began to chart the borders of the Bulgarian mental map. By the early twentieth century, Bulgarian ethnography had gained momentum and was increasingly professionalized and politicized. As in other fledgling Balkan nations, Bulgarians began to embark on ethnographic ventures that drew "scientific" conclusions about the ethnicity or race of the populations in question. Proving the "Bulgarianness" of Thracian and Macedonian Slavs was the most central element of Bulgarian attempts to redraw the ethnographic map of the Balkans in their own territorial favor. Since the 1870s Macedonia had become the primary stage of a battle for territorial claims waged on multiple fronts among Balkan pretenders—Greek, Serbian, and Bulgarian—with the backing of various and shifting Great Power patrons.[59] The ethnographic map more often than not was the weapon used to assert these claims on the basis of ethnic affiliation, claims which inevitably involved the Muslim populations of these provinces.

---

tional/ethnic symbol—"the average Bulgarian," or as a socio-historical type—as one type of Bulgarian in this time period, a representative of the new bourgeoisie. Compelling arguments have been made on both readings of the work since its publication, including Todorova's socio-historical interpretation of Baĭ Gano as representative of a *nouveau riche* subtype of Europeanness. Todorova, *Imagining the Balkans*, 39–42. But in spite of the nuances of Todorova's interpretation, in both historical and contemporary interpretations and popular readings of the work, Baĭ Gano is at least as often, if not more often, understood as a backward and self-Orientalized "Bulgarian" figure in relation to European civility. For a recent article supporting this interpretation see Roumen Daskalov, "Modern Bulgarian Society and Culture through the Mirror of Bai Ganio," *Slavic Review* 60 (2001): 530–49.

[57] For a discussion of foreign and Bulgarian ethnography during the pre-1878 period see Delcho Todorov, *Bŭlgarskata Etnografiia pres Vŭzrazhdaneto* (Sofia, 1989).

[58] Catherine Clay, "Russian Ethnographers in the Service of the Empire," *Slavic Review* 54 (1995): 45–62.

[59] For a thorough discussion of Balkan and Great Power pretensions and the use of ethnographic maps in regional power politics see Henry Wilkinson, *Maps and Politics: A Review of the Ethnographic Cartography of Macedonia* (Liverpool, 1951); and Elizabeth Barker, *Macedonia: Its Place in Balkan Power Politics* (London, 1950).

In the midst of ethnographic discovery, the endlessly mutable criteria for ethnonational affiliation left scholars a broad canvas on which they could reconfigure and elaborate national claims. Although language and religion were important aspects of determining where to draw ethnographic lines, they also could easily be discarded in favor of other measures of belonging that were more supportive of any given ethnographic assertion. Early on this opened the door for Bulgarian ethnographic claims to extend beyond Orthodox Christian Slavs and into the villages of Slavic and even Turkish-speaking Muslim populations. Islam (unlike Judaism, for example) continued to be conceptualized as a false and illegitimate presence, brutally imposed by Ottoman overlords on essentially Bulgarian souls. The well-known ethnographer Stoiu Shishkov and other ethnographers assumed the "illegitimacy" of Islam among Pomak populations and also among a portion of Turks, or "Turkified" Bulgarians. Religion was thus seen as a vestige of imposed "foreign" culture on native souls rather than as a proof for ethnic belonging. Linguistic analysis was often central to these academic projects (in Bulgaria and the Balkans generally) and to subsequent territorial claims, nevertheless ethnographers could similarly conceive language as a secondary layer or an "imposed" cultural sediment. Language and other non-Bulgarian ethnic characteristics were presumably forced on populations in the distant past and left to occupy bodies that were essentially of another national ilk. As Shishkov claimed, "The picture drawn today in [Bulgarian] history in comparison with other nations is as rare as it is tragic. Hellenized Bulgarians to the South, Romanianized in the North, Serbified in the West, and Turkified in all districts which fall within the ethnographic reach of the Bulgarian tribe."[60] Here Shishkov asserts that Turks within the Bulgarian lands are linguistically "Turkified" Bulgarians. Language is thus only honored as an objective criterion for the Bulgarian national expanse insofar as it supports the outer limits of national claims. Although non-Bulgarian speakers were seen as proof of assimilation and historical injustice, the Bulgarian tongues of Pomak populations were, in contrast, taken as proof of the Bulgarianness of these populations and hence justification of future projects to reclaim them as an integral part of the Bulgarian nation.

Proving the essential Bulgarianness of Pomaks became the express focus of the work of Shishkov and an expanding number of early twentieth-century ethnographers. According to Shishkov, the geographically contiguous "Turks," like the Pomaks, were the product of "Ottoman assimilation politics" who had irretrievably lost their Bulgarian heritage.[61] Pomaks, on the other hand, whom Shishkov insisted should be called "Bulgaro-Mohammedans," "spoke the most pure dialect of old-Slavic" and so were Bul-

[60] Stoiu Shishkov, *Pomatsi v Trite Bŭlgarski Oblasti: Trakiia, Makedoniia i Miziia* (Plovdiv, 1914), 3.
[61] See Shishkov, *Pomatsi;* and Stoiu Shishkov, *Bŭlgaro-Mokhamedani: Istoriko-Zemepisen i Narodouchen Pregled c Obrazi* (Plovdiv, 1936).

garians in the "purest" sense.[62] Although Shishkov paid close academic attention to the Bulgarian nature of the Pomaks' Slavic dialect, more of his work was devoted to other markers of Bulgarianness in Pomak tradition and material culture. When these markers coincided with presumed Bulgarian attributes, Shishkov assumed they were solid proof of Pomak Bulgarianness. When outward signs of ethnicity did not coincide with Bulgarian traits, Shishkov lamented the persistence of these "imposed" foreign remnants of the Ottoman past. In particular, Shishkov pointed out and polemicized against the persistence of Turco-Arabic clothes and names as outward signs of the brutal imposition of the Ottoman yoke. These visible and audible signs of difference—even more than language and religion—were to play a central role in future campaigns to impose Bulgarian clarity on the hybridized and complicated Balkan landscape. Once the borders of modern Bulgaria had been imagined, it was up to ethnographers, historians, and other academicians to fill in the lines. Territory, it seems was the only constant; wherever there was Bulgarian soil, the bodies and souls that peppered it must be Bulgarian.

Imposing Clarity

The relevance and influence of the work of Shishkov and others became clear after the eruption of the First Balkan War in 1912, when official actions reified academic notions. In what amounted to a modern crusade of the cross against the crescent, Bulgaria, Serbia, Greece, and Montenegro invaded the Ottoman Empire in an attempt to divide and conquer its remaining European territories. As Bulgarian troops, themselves occupiers, euphorically "liberated" the "Bulgarian lands" from Ottoman occupation, they were accompanied by Orthodox priests who forcibly converted some 200,000 Pomaks from Islam to Christianity in hundreds of villages in Thrace, Macedonia, and the Rhodope Mountains. Conceived of and presented to locals as "liberation" from the vestiges of the Ottoman past, Bulgarian officials took extreme measures to eradicate the outward signs of Turco-Islamic difference among Pomak populations. The occupying authorities forced Pomaks to take Bulgarian first names and surnames, and the "foreign" fez, the turban, and the so-called veil were replaced with Bulgarian hats and scarves.[63] Religious and administrative crusaders requested supplies—bibles, crosses, hats, and scarves—so that Muslim heads and homes could be covered, marked, and filled with national meaning.[64] The hope was that icons would make churches out of mosques, and hats, kerchiefs, and Slavo-Christian names

---

[62] See Shishkov, *Pomatsi*; and Shishkov, *Bŭlgaro-Mokhamedani*.
[63] Velichko Georgiev and Staiko Trifinov, *Pokrŭstvaneto na Bŭlgarite Mokhamedani, 1912–1913: Dokumenti* (Sofia, 1995), 8.
[64] Ibid., 60, 101, 163.

would make Bulgarians out of Pomaks. Beginning with the First Balkan War, Pomaks became the express targets of dramatic campaigns to purge them of overt signs of difference and integrate them into the Bulgarian nation whereas Turks remained mostly unscathed within the confines of their autonomous institutions until the end of World War II.

The mobilization of the First Balkan War drove radical Bulgarian experimentation, however temporary, in terms of an assault on overt markers of Islam. Brewing for decades in academic theory, the violence and momentum of war drove Bulgarian projects to radically unearth hybridized markers from Bulgarian soil, to attempt to idealize and unify the complicated and compromised project of national regeneration. But the imposition of Christianity and Slavic names and clothing, as it turned out, was a short-lived experiment. After the First Balkan War ended in military disaster and the Second Balkan War flared in the summer of 1913 over the spoils of Ottoman defeat, Bulgaria quickly shelved its radical program. By the fall of 1913, the interim regime of Vasil Radoslavov announced that the Pomaks would be allowed to convert back to Islam, and reclaim their former names and clothes. This reversal in policy was a strategic effort to win favor with the Ottoman Empire and the quickly coalescing Austro-German Central Powers as well as to earn Muslim votes in the upcoming elections. As a result of the policy reversal, Pomaks immediately reclaimed their hats, veils, names, and mosques, often in very public and demonstrative ways.

The Pomak reaction made it clear that such efforts to liberate them had not been welcome in the remote Pomak provinces. The cataclysmic incursions of military and religious authorities into the intimate recesses of Pomak material and symbolic culture went beyond any past confrontations, giving rise to a wave of Pomak resentment and resistance. The mass migration of Pomaks out of Bulgarian territories both during and after the Balkan Wars was by far the most momentous of these responses. To abandon territories that these Slavic populations had inhabited for more than a thousand years was a clear sign that they could find no place in Bulgarian society. Those Pomaks who held firm to the land and remained promptly returned to everyday local practices when given the opportunity. Any gradual integration that might have been possible under the modernizing conditions of the twentieth century was ironically and immeasurably slowed by the heavy-handed forced assimilation and conversion campaigns of the First Balkan War which proved to be some of the most erosive events in Bulgarian history in terms of Bulgaro-Pomak relations.

The beginning of World War I in 1914 dictated a decided truce on the Bulgaro-Muslim front, since the regime needed Muslims as provisional allies in its more critical drive for territorial aggrandizement. The Bulgarian government pursued an alliance with the Austro-German Central Powers, including the Ottoman Empire, in order to gain the "lost" territories of the Treaty of San Stefano. In contrast to the First Balkan War, Muslims were not the special target of wartime campaigns and endeavors and, in fact, Muslims supported the war effort alongside Bulgarians. While the major battles of World War I were fought on the Western front and the Russo-Habsburg frontier, Bulgaria expanded deep into Thrace, Macedonia, and Dobrudzha, helping to establish the Central Powers' control in the Balkans for much of the war. Muslims were left to their own devices while the regime pursued an active Bulgarianization of Christian populations under its control. Schools were built, newspapers were printed and the cultural parameters of Greater Bulgaria were secured. Teams of ethnographers fanned out across the occupied territories to study the cultural practices of local populations, Muslim and non-Muslim alike, looking for scientific justification for annexation.[65] As in the past, such endeavors focused on "proving" the essential Bulgarianness of local populations. In Bulgarian-occupied coveted territories discovery, invention, and, in some cases, imposition of true Bulgarianness was a wartime priority. However, when the war ended in the Central Powers' defeat in 1918, Bulgaria resumed its pre-War territorial parameters and such projects ceased.

In the first years of the interwar period, Bulgarians looked for allies—not enemies—within, in hopes of national regeneration. The wars had furrowed deep rifts between Bulgaria and her Balkan neighbors and had exacerbated social tensions. As the war came to a close in 1918, the Bulgarian peasantry was radicalized: they had fought at the front and suffered immense loss of life—the military dead alone numbered one-fifth of the adult male population.[66] To avert revolutionary upheaval, the postwar regime invited Alexander Stamboliski of the popular antiwar Bulgarian Agrarian National Union (BANU) to form a coalition cabinet, which was confirmed in the elections of August 1919.[67] Stamboliski's government made every effort to alleviate international and regional tensions by signing the Treaty of Neuilly, even though it saddled Bulgaria with heavy indemnities and reparations in addition to limits on military buildup and burdensome territorial losses. He not only accepted the territorial severance of Macedonia, Thrace, and the Dobrudzha but openly denounced Bulgarian irredentists. In addition, he extended promises to Western Europe and the United States that his social programs would present a barrier to the rising specter of Bolshevism to the East.[68]

While pursuing rapprochement with Balkan neighbors and their patrons, Stamboliiski also turned his efforts inward to establish what Joseph Rothschild termed the "dictatorship of the village" over the cities.[69] Stamboliski himself refused to live in the state capital of Sofia due to his abhorrence for what he considered a foreign, contaminated, and corrupt urban milieu, in-

---

[65] For one such ethnographic expedition see Khristo Petrov, ed., *Nauchna Ekspeditsiia v Makedoniia i Pomoravieto, 1916* (Sofia: 1993).

[66] Joseph Rothschild, *East Central Europe Between the Two World Wars* (Seattle, 1974), 325.

[67] Ibid., 335.

[68] Joseph Rothschild, *The Communist Party of Bulgaria: Origins and Development* (New York, 1959), 112.

[69] Rothschild, *East Central Europe*, 334.

stead choosing to live in a rural area outside the city.[70] His anti-urban sentiments clearly echoed past and contemporary ponderings on the "foreignness" of the city; as Naĭden Sheĭmanov, reflecting the tone of other interwar intellectuals, ventured, "Countless paths have led us to the corrupted City, where we are transformed by the dynamic cultures of Europe."[71] It was therefore natural that Stamboliski should turn to the peasant village for the imposition of his national designs. He based his convictions on the simple belief that the peasantry was "the noblest and wisest of God's children in whose interests Bulgaria . . . must be governed."[72] Stamboliski's approach to the peasant question in Bulgaria was explicitly internationalist and also extended to local Muslim populations, who were never excluded from Stamboliski's vision of Bulgaria as a peasant state. In fact, most sources laud Stamboliski as one of the most tolerant (pre-1989) Bulgarian leaders of the twentieth century in his policies toward Muslims.[73] In spite of Stamboliski's popularity among the peasant masses—Muslim and Christian—he was unable to contend effectively with his adversaries and was assassinated in 1923.

Throughout the rest of the interwar period, various regimes were forced to confront Muslim and other potential sources of perceived "foreign" influence and threat. The Muslim question was by no means the focus of national wrath; the Bulgarian government tended to consider the Muslim masses to be "inert," and conservatively "loyal," as opposed to being a radical or decisive political factor. Actually, the threats of the Bulgarian Communist Party, politicized refugees from Thrace and Macedonia, and the related thirst for territory and scarcity of land most plagued the regimes that followed Stamboliski. By the 1930s, leading Bulgarians began to see the emigration of Muslims as part of the solution to the Bulgarian land problems. Many Muslims themselves sought emigration to Turkey as a solution to their mounting sense of insecurity on Bulgarian soil. The Turco-Muslim communities that remained in Bulgaria divided and transmuted in this period both in reaction to Bulgarian national projects and to the establishment of the Turkish republic in 1923. By the 1920s Turks were split between conservative "Old Turks," by far the vast majority of the population, and Kemalists, who were promodernizing reformers along the lines of the new leader of Turkey, Kemal Atatürk. Similarly, the majority of Pomaks were conservative and pro-Old Turk, while a small but vocal group formed the *Rodina* (homeland) association that advocated modernization of Muslim tradition, along with the inculcation of a Bulgarian national consciousness. Far from being impervious to these developments, the Bulgarian government took an active interest in

[70] John Bell, *Peasants in Power: Alexander Stamboliski and the Bulgarian Agrarian Union, 1899–1923* (Princeton, 1977), 155.

[71] Naĭden Sheĭmanov, "Preobrazhenie na Bŭlgariia," in *Zasto Sme Takiva? V Tŭrsene na Bŭlgarskata Kulturna Identichnost*, ed. I. Elenkov, and R. Daskalov (Sofia, 1994), 267.

[72] Rothschild, *Communist Party of Bulgaria*, 85.

[73] See, for example, Eminov, *Turkish and Other Muslim Minorities*, 126.

quelling, supporting, or directing such change within the Muslim communities in the name of perceived national interest.

In bold outline, until 1944 the Bulgarian administration supported the primacy of the conservative Old Turks in the Islamic hierarchy and their local personnel, muftis, imams, and *hocas* (teachers), including anti-Kemalist emigrants from the new Republic of Turkey. On one hand, the Bulgarian government tended to view Muslim conservatism among Turks as the best way to keep the Turkish masses inert and loyal to the state. On the other hand, Bulgarian statesmen viewed politically potent Kemalism as a potential threat to Bulgarian territorial integrity. They feared the implications of a Turco-Islamic community amassed on Bulgaria's southern border, identifying itself with the Turkish republic. In addition, it was often wrongly assumed that Kemalists were also Communists and so linked to a foreign Bolshevik threat. On the local level, known Kemalists in administrative positions were replaced with conservative Muslims under the direction of the Head Muftiship in Sofia.[74] In this way, the regime sought to contain the sinister potential of assertive secular Turkishness within the confines of conservative Islam. This coincided with the interests of the Old Turks themselves who sought to preserve Muslim tradition—even as it evolved within Bulgaria—safe from the consequences of Atatürkian modernization. In the Turkish republic, *Şeriat* courts had been eliminated since the late 1920s, Muslim *vakf* properties were appropriated, and national campaigns were launched for the eradication of the Muslim fez and veil. In contrast, in Bulgaria, Muslims held onto their courts, their properties, and their head gear. The Bulgarian Head Muftiship and its local representatives did selectively invoke "Turkish" sentiments in claiming its inheritance on Ottoman-Muslim properties, but otherwise every effort was made to keep the modernizing Kemalist-type reforms out of Bulgarian territory. In fact, an outspoken opponent of Kemalist reforms, Osman Nuri Bei, mimicked Bulgarian suspicions that Turkey was under the direct influence of the Soviet Union. In a letter to the Head Mufti, he charged that Turkey had cast out not only the *Şeriat* courts but also all that is religious and moral, "like today in Bolshevik Russia." He drew an explicit connection between the conservatism of Bulgarian Muslims and their lack of "foreign" influence, concluding that, "Bulgaria should not tolerate material or nationalist ties with a foreign country."[75] In a similar vein, the Head Mufti and other top Muslim officials also posited the "foreignness" of Turkish-language reform, specifically the transition from the Arabic script to the Latin alphabet: "We don't want a foreign alphabet and we don't want to become a weapon of foreign interests and dogmatism. We want to live peacefully and modestly in our homeland and serve its interests."[76]

[74] KODA (F-14K, O-1, E-85, L-214: 1934).
[75] TsIDA (F-471, O-2, E-8, L-2: 1934).
[76] KODA (F-14k, O-2, E-12, L-29: 1938).

In contrast to the state's harmonious relationship with Old Turks, Bulgarian officials observed, rooted out, and even incarcerated Kemalist Turks throughout the country. Like the Old Turks, Kemalists tried to assert a commonality of interest with Bulgarians but without the same response. Kemalist papers such as *Halk Sesi* (The People's Voice) advocated Bulgaro-Turkish friendship and cooperation in numerous articles and exposés, which stressed modernization and progress as cornerstones of mutual interests and visions. But Bulgarian statesmen tended to distrust such self-proclaimed Turkish voices that sought to confirm and reshape the Turkish presence in Bulgaria. By the mid-1930s the local police in Muslim districts put virtually all influential Turks under observation with an explicit focus on Kemalists, who were also suspected Communists.[77] The adherents of Kemalist ideas in Bulgaria became increasingly organized under the umbrella of *Turan*, a Turkish cultural-educational association formed in 1927. Bulgarian Police reports from the 1930s detail the activities of Turkish teachers and intellectuals who were "missionaries of *Turanism*" and so "oppose the interests of the Bulgarian nation and government."[78] Local reports of isolated incidents of Turks singing Kemalist songs and raising Turkish flags were widely circulated and further raised the concerns of Bulgarian authorities.[79] Finally, the Ministry of Foreign Affairs disbanded *Turan* in 1936 after declaring the association to be "against the laws of the country" and "dangerous for the social order and security."[80] In the face of *Turan*, Bulgarian statesmen saw the specter of the Turkish nation rise out of the heretofore indistinct Muslim masses and pose a potential threat.

Whereas Turkish modernism was shunned and suppressed, Pomaks, in contrast, were encouraged to seek radical new answers to questions of identity, as long as they were pro-Bulgarian. Pomaks, as with the conservative and loyal Old Turks had been perceived by the regime as "the best of citizens, great tax payers, good soldiers, and honest government servants."[81] Bulgarian academicians continued to expand on assumptions about the essential Bulgarianness of the Pomak population, building on prewar ethnographic conclusions. They continued to explore the ethnic peculiarities of Pomak men and women by conceptually sorting their Bulgarian characteristics from the "foreign" traits, presumably imposed by the Ottoman occupiers. Exonerated from their roles as presumed Ottoman collaborators, they were considered to be victims of Ottoman crimes and hence worthy of liberation. On a linguistic and "racial" basis Pomaks were welcomed into the Bulgarian national fold while their foreign names and clothes were lamented. Hence when a small but vocal modernist Bulgarian-nationalist movement emerged mostly from within the Pomak community itself, it was welcomed

[77] KODA (F-14–K, O-1, E-96, L-73,135,514: 1936).
[78] KODA (F-14K, O-1, E-85, L-62: 1934).
[79] KODA (F-14K, O-1, E-89, L-10: 1935).
[80] TsIDA (F-264, O-1, E-44, L-1: 1937).
[81] TsIDA (F-264, O-1, E-439, L-2: 1934).

by a multitude of Bulgarian scholars and statesmen. The Bulgarian government supported the reformist modernizing thrust of this group, *Rodina*, although such an orientation was explicitly rejected for Turks.

Significantly, one of the primary founders of the *Rodina* movement was not a Pomak but a Bulgarian ethnographer, Petŭr Marinov. Marinov, along with a handful of Pomak reformist-Islamic thinkers founded *Rodina* in Smolyan, the regional capital of the central Rhodope region in 1937. Marinov's ethnographic agenda—proving the ethnic "Bulgarianness" of Rhodope Pomaks—melded well with the zealous Bulgarian nationalism of *Rodina's* Pomak founders, themselves primarily products of Bulgarian military training and experience. *Rodina* was established initially as a cultural movement, with the stated goal of diffusing "Bulgarianness" to the country's "misguided [Pomak] brothers and sisters."[82] Since Marinov was the self-avowed intellectual heir of Stoiu Shishkov and his ethnographic tradition, he deemed the term "Bulgaro-Mohammedan" most appropriate as a label for the Pomak population. The *Sbornik Rodina*, a collection of writings on the association's aims and activities, detailed the organization's quest to "uproot all that is un-Bulgarian in the spirit and life of Bulgaro-Mohammedans" while "drawing them closer together to Bulgarians."[83] In the words of *Rodina* leaders, "Our social obligation which falls not only on our group but on all of our brothers, Bulgaro-Mohammedans, young and old, is to leave behind our formerly stagnant lives and move ahead on the path of culture and progress, the path which our tribesmen have already set out upon and gone far ahead."[84] As with Kemalism *Rodina* accepted much of the modernizing impetus of reformist Islam, but instead of embracing Turkishness laid a Bulgarian path to the Bulgaro-Mohammedan national future.

Furthermore, like other modernizing Muslims, *Rodina* members—many of them employees of Muslim institutions—did not explicitly reject Islam. Instead, they advanced a language-based kinship to the Bulgarian nation and embraced the premise of the inherently progressive nature of Bulgarianness as opposed to Turkishness, "The time has come for our Muslim coreligionists to recognize their Bulgarian nationality, to break with this darkness and ignorance, to have a clear comprehension and consciousness, that we are Bulgarians by nationality and this does not interfere with our practice of the Muslim religion."[85] Interestingly, the Pomak inability to recognize his Bulgarianness is here connected to "darkness and ignorance" whereas Islam itself is held exempt. In fact, *Rodina* leaders went to great lengths to refute the claims of elderly Pomaks who opposed the association based on the belief that it "weakened the faith and led the youth into an atheistic understanding."[86] *Rodina* countered accusations that its members were "infidels" and

---

[82] Petŭr Marinov, ed., *Sbornik Rodina* (Sofia, 1942), 4: 55.
[83] SODA (F-26K, O-1, E-2, L-8–9: 1939).
[84] Marinov, ed., *Sbornik Rodina*, 2: 20.
[85] Ibid., 13.
[86] SODA (F-26K, O-1, E-29, L-1: 1937).

even "Communists" with the assertion that "on the contrary one of the goals of the association is to care for the correct fulfillment of Muslim traditions."[87] *Rodina* even justified its work as crucial to restoring a fading Muslim faith to Pomaks, who "if left alone, will be led to total atheism."[88] They claimed that this was because religion was taught in a "completely unknown, incomprehensible language, in still more unknown letters."[89] As a remedy to this perceived crisis, *Rodina* developed initiatives for the translation of the Kur'an (Koran) and Muslim prayers into Bulgarian.[90] *Rodina* members, in line with Bulgarian academic thinking at the time, stressed the *language* connection between Pomaks and Bulgarians while allowing for the existence of religious difference within the modern Bulgarian nation-state. But although language was important in establishing the ethno-racial link between Bulgarian and Pomak, it did not constitute a central issue or problem for *Rodina* writings and discussion.

Instead in the various writings and actions of the *Rodina* movement, the central focus is clearly on the eradication of Turco-Arabic personal names and clothes—such as the fez, turban, and veil—aspects of everyday culture that marked and separated Pomaks from the Bulgarian national core. *Rodina*, deeply rooted in Marinov's scholarly writings, conceived ethnographic names and garments as remnants of foreign occupation, which "separate and hinder the common merging, unity, and brotherhood between Bulgaro-Mohammedans and Bulgarian Christians."[91] The modernization of Pomak clothing was the first and most urgent of *Rodina* programs that endeavored to rid Pomak men of the turban and fez, and women of the so-called veil, all presumed signs of backwardness and the barbaric past. In the first few years of *Rodina*'s founding, the leaders of the organization tried to set personal examples for modern dress by shedding their own fezzes and sending out printed appeals to Pomak villages. The wives of *Rodina* leaders also shed their veils and adopted modern, Bulgarian modes of dress. But it was not until the eruption of World War II that *Rodina* with Bulgarian state support, subjected Pomak men and women to more active campaigns targeting their ethnic garments.

In Bulgaria, as elsewhere in Europe, World War II was a war fought on multiple fronts from the battlefield to the home. The Bulgarian entrance into war on the Axis side in 1941 brought clarity of purpose to Bulgarian leaders. Bulgaria was never home to an overtly Fascist mass movement or dictator akin to other Axis powers, but wartime Bulgaria was still the scene of mass mobilization, as the expanded Bulgarian state extended its power and programs into new territories and arenas of action. The primary and openly

[87] Maria Stoianova, "Kŭm Istoriiata na Dvizhenieto "Rodina" v Istochni Rodopi," *Izvestiia na Muzeite ot Iuzhna Bŭlgariia* 16 (1990): 244; SODA (F-26K, O-1, E-29, L-1: 1937).

[88] SODA (F-26k, O-1, E-31, L-3: 1938).

[89] SODA (F-26k, O-1, E-31, L-3: 1938).

[90] Marinov, ed., *Sbornik Rodina*, 2: 19, and SODA (F-26k, O-1, E-31, L-1: 1938).

[91] Marinov, ed., *Sbornik Rodina*, 2: 34.

stated goal of the wartime Bulgarian government was "to create and preserve the conditions for the peaceful development and progress of *Bŭlgarshtina* (all that is Bulgarian) in the name of the Bulgarian people, the Bulgarian nation, and every Bulgarian, wherever he is."[92] The regime necessarily focused these nation-building projects on the margins of the national domain, the "newly liberated territories" of Dobrudzha, Thrace, and Macedonia. The very scope of the regime's action required it to forge provisional alliances, in particular with select Muslim leaders, against new sources of foreign incursion perceived as more dangerous to national interests. Conservative Turco-Muslim and modernizing Bulgaro-Muslim elites (Pomaks in *Rodina*) remained allies of the wartime regime, gaining new spheres of influence among Muslim populations in the expanded Bulgarian state.

World War II brought intensified state campaigns against "foreign propaganda" and influence, in which all that was Allied, Communist, Jewish, or Turkish nationalist tended to be blurred into a monolith of presumed anti-Bulgarian conspiracy.[93] In reality, only select Turks were suspect as the regime recognized that their links to the Communist Party, which by far represented the greatest threat, were tenuous. As in the interwar period, when Communist partisans organized armed resistance, they did not look primarily to Turks and Pomaks as the seedbeds of revolutionary potential. Rather, their perceived conservative backwardness and loyalty to the regime turned the focus of Communist efforts elsewhere. Unlike in many other East European countries, it was Bulgarian nationals rather than disgruntled minorities who made up the core of the Bulgarian Communist Party (BCP). There is evidence of only isolated efforts on the part of the BCP to bring Muslim minorities into their rather scanty wartime resistance efforts, although Communist sources later lauded the "mass participation" of Pomaks and Turks in the "Peoples Front against Capitalism and Fascism."[94] Although Bulgarian authorities recognized that local Muslim populations were not hotbeds of Communist activity, it was not uncommon for influential Kemalist Turks to be interned based on local police or Old Turk suspicions that they fostered connections with Turkey or the BCP. The Mufti of Kirdzhali, for example,

[92] TsIDA (F-264, O-1, E-160, L-15: 1941).
[93] The mostly Sephardic Jews of Bulgaria were relatively insignificant numerically (about 50,000 or .8 percent of the population in 1934) and anti-Semitism arguably was not deeply rooted in Bulgarian society. Nevertheless, even before Bulgaria was fully committed to the Axis cause, anti-Jewish legislation had proved Bulgaria's loyalty to the German vision of a reordered Europe. As with the Nazis, the Bulgarian regime stripped Jews of their dignity, humanity, and property. The fact that Bulgaria did ultimately save its Jews from total deportation and annihilation has been emphasized in much of the Bulgarian and non-Bulgarian literature on World War II. Yet the historical record contradicts this literature, showing that Jews were deported en masse from the "newly liberated" territories and that mobilization for deportation within Bulgaria proper was underway. On Bulgarian Jews see Frederick Chary, *The Bulgarian Jews and the Final Solution* (Pittsburgh, 1972), and Tamir, *Bulgaria and Her Jews*.
[94] On Pomaks see Nikolai Branchev, *Bŭlgari-Mokhamedani (Pomatsi): Zemepisnite Predeli* (Sofia, 1948), 52. On Turks see Iusein Memishev, *Uchastieto na Bŭlgarskite Turtsi v Borbata Protiv Kapitalizŭm i Fashizŭm 1919–1944* (Sofia, 1977), 109–219; and Misirkova, *Turetskoe*, 9.

reportedly "fired all active and enthusiastic Turks" who were accused and interned as presumed Communists, Kemalists, and "saboteurs of the fatherland."[95] In spite of this phenomenon, it was more common for local Bulgarian administrators to report on the loyalty of Turks in their districts.[96] In one case, the Kirdzhali police even reported that the district clearly had no Communists "because the population was Turkish" and so "had no ideological leanings."[97]

As in Bulgaria proper, the regime identified a spectrum of conspiring forces in the occupied territories.[98] Officials from the Ohrid district in Macedonia, for example, sent a report to Bulgarian authorities about the potential for local conspiracy stating, "The problem is difficult here because there is a crossing of interests; English propaganda, Serbophilism, Albanophilism, Ohrid Turks and Communism." They feared that, "the adherents of all this will enter into an unnatural alliance. Keeping in mind the alliance of Bolshevik Russia and plutocratic England, anything is possible."[99] Significantly, a new ethnic frontier had opened on the Bulgarian horizon, as enclaves of Albanian Muslims (and some Albanians who were not Muslim) were subsumed in the Bulgarian territorial advance. In the abstract, the Albanians had always bounded the Bulgarian nation—assuming the Slavs of Macedonia are Bulgarian—at its furthest theoretical stretch into Western Macedonia. As early as 1902, a well-known Bulgarian diplomat noted, "We have our longest ethnographic border with the Albanians."[100] Under the conditions of World War II occupation and national reorganization, the Albanian element in Macedonia, as well as "Bulgarian" populations in the newly expanded Albania, became a major concern of the Bulgarian occupying forces. Bulgarian officials openly expressed concern that Albanian "terror" against the "300,000 Bulgarians behind the demarcation line" was perpetrated in spite of their new Italian masters, wartime allies of Bulgaria. Albanian actions were linked conceptually in many cases with the Ottoman past; one official noted, "history repeats itself . . . again the wild Ghegs and Tosks [the two tribal divisions of the Albanian nation] commit outrages against the Bulgarians."[101] Loyal Old Turks from the Bulgarian kingdom, though also representatives of the Ottoman past, became nevertheless valuable in the task of taming and controlling the "wild" and "tribal" Albanians.

The Turco-Muslim administrative hierarchy proved useful allies in this and other tasks associated with the Bulgarian quest for a new order in their now-vast lands. The interwar alliance between the Bulgarian regime and Old

95 KODA (F-24K, O-1, E-4, L-9: 1944).
96 KODA (F-14K, O-2, E-1, L-2–6: 1943).
97 KODA (F-14K, O-1, E-12, L-115: 1942).
98 TsIDA (F-264, O-1, E-143, L-124: 1941).
99 TsIDA (F-264, O-1, E-151, L-1: 1941).
100 Bobi Botev, "Sŭotnoshenie Mezhdu Pozitivnoto i Negativnoto v Predstavite na Bŭlgariia za Albantsite," in *Vrŭzki na Sŭvmestimost i Nesŭvmestimost Mezhdu Khristiiani i Miusiulmani v Bŭlgariia*, ed. A. Zheliaskova (Sofia, 1994), 243.
101 TsIDA (F-264, O-1, E-396, L-2: 1943).

Turks was now extended as the regime granted the Turco-Muslim hierarchy considerable autonomy, tolerance, and even an extension of its influence in exchange for continued loyalty to the regime.[102] Specifically, Turco-Muslim institutions assumed direct jurisdiction over all non-Pomak Muslim communities in the occupied territories. Although the extension of Turco-Muslim power over other Turks in these territories was less problematic, the change of administration in Albanian districts in Macedonia in particular, incited protest both from local Albanians and from the Italian patrons of occupied Greater Albania.[103] In response, the Bulgarian government granted only minor concessions, such as replacing several recently appointed Turkish Muftis with Albanians in the most compactly settled Albanian districts.[104] Continued Italian and Albanian complaints served to heighten Bulgarian suspicions that both were trying to integrate the whole Muslim population into "Albanianness."[105] According to local reports, Albanians, with the help of the Italian consulate, were handing out maps of greater Albania extending all the way to the Vardar River, deep into Bulgarian-occupied territory.[106] Bulgaro-Italian tensions over the Albanian question continued until the capitulation of Italy in 1943 and the withdrawal of Italian troops and consulates from the region.[107] In essence, the Bulgarian alliance with Turkish elements remained unshaken even at the expense of inter-Axis relationships.

In exchange for the Head Muftiship's loyalty in carrying out these and other domestic policies, Turks generally were tolerated as loyal citizens during the trying war years. Although isolated incidents of persecution of Turks occurred during the war, generally only Kemalists or suspected Kemalists faced blatant maltreatment. The authorities in Sofia discouraged anti-Turkish policies on the local level, balancing their desire to Bulgarianize the new territories with their need for good relations with the Muftiship and the Turkish consulate, and the maintenance of order in the provinces. The regime, however, did call on Turkish-Muslim institutions to help block any Jewish escape from anti-Semitic legislation or deportations. It placed considerable pressure on the Head Muftiship, for example, to help enforce the "Law of the Purity of the Nation" passed in 1940, which prohibited mixed marriages between citizens of "Bulgarian" and "non-Bulgarian" descent. Thereafter, Turks were not allowed to marry Bulgarians or Pomaks (who were considered to be of Bulgarian descent). It is noteworthy that this law also applied to Turkish-

[102] This domestic Bulgaro-Turkish alliance was similar to the Croatian Ustaša (the Nazi puppet government) alliance with the Bosnian Muslim establishment, which was organized against Serbs, Communists, and other disloyal local elements. On Yugoslavia see Pedro Ramet, *Nationalism and Federalism in Yugoslavia: 1963–83* (Bloomington, 1984), 7.

[103] TsIDA (F-264, O-1, E-297, L-245: 1942).

[104] TsIDA (F-264, O-1, E-297, L-247: 1942).

[105] Although some local Turks did indeed complain about Albano-Italian propaganda, others seemed more receptive. The Turks of Bitola, for example, were reportedly divided into pro-Albanian and anti-Albanian. TsIDA (F-264, O-1, E-494, L-193: 1942).

[106] TsIDA (F-264, O-1, E-297, L-246: 1942).

[107] TsIDA (F-370, O-6, E-1882, L-6: 1944).

Jewish intermarriage, which had apparently been used as a way for Jews to hide their origins from the authorities.[108] But although Jewish-Turkish intermarriage was relatively rare in this period, Pomak-Turkish intermarriage was relatively common. Clearly, the Turkish establishment was enlisted to enforce the cultural border between Turks and Pomaks—which was relatively fluid—as the price for their extended influence in the provinces.

In the Pomak case, *Rodina* became partner to the wartime regime and supported all of the regime's key legislation, including the "Law for the Purity of the Nation."[109] The association embraced Bulgarian expansion, and sent out broad appeals to Pomaks in the new territories, condemning the Ottoman legacy and embracing a Bulgarian national future:

> Brother Bulgarians,
> With this appeal we, organized in the revival movement of Bulgaro-Mohammedans, raise a loud voice in front of society and the world, as we sincerely and openly declare our Bulgarian nationality. We know that the bloody sword and merciless ruling hand [of the Ottomans] cut us off from our historical past and mercilessly nailed us to the wall for eternal suffering of uncertainty, delusion, and blindness. As illiterates, backward and lost, the centuries threw us against the rocky shores. Dejected, we endured slavery and a heavy yoke . . . which bifurcated our souls. Every recess, every hillock, every rock from our mother mountains is steeped in tears. Every cliff, every valley and crossroads attests to unheard of humiliation and violation.[110]

In every nook and cranny of the Pomaks' Rhodope realm *Rodina* uncovered the signs of foreign injustice and the resultant bifurcation of souls. The only remedy to Ottoman injustice was the eradication of the hybrid residue of Ottoman occupation in favor of a presumed Bulgarian cultural purity.

Bulgarian statesmen were never in full agreement as to the pace and extent of such a program. The most radical stance on the Pomak question went beyond the parameters of *Rodina* visions and called for the mass conversion of Pomaks to Christianity, reminiscent of the action taken during the First Balkan War. The parliamentary representative from Zlatovgrad, Sirko Stanchev, for example, asserted that, "the liquidation of the painful Bulgaro-Mohammedan question in Bulgaria can only happen with the total baptism of all Bulgaro-Mohammedans."[111] According to Stanchev and others, the very souls of Pomaks would have to be liberated from "foreign" occupation for the barriers between Bulgarian and Pomak to disappear. Despite the views of these statesmen, in practice the state supported *Rodina*'s approach toward integration in the old and new provinces of Bulgaria. The decision to tread softly on religion may have been, in part, a strategic one as both the re-

[108] TsIDA (F-471, O-1, E-426, L-13: 1939), TsIDA (F-264, O-1, E-440, L-9: 1941).
[109] Marinov, ed., *Sbornik Rodina*, 4: 13.
[110] Ibid., 15.
[111] TsIDA (F-264, O-1, E-440, L-13: 1941).

gime and *Rodina* directly utilized Islam in their modernizing Bulgarianization campaigns. By 1942, Pomak Muftis were appointed directly by the Bulgarian Ministry of Internal Affairs rather than the Turkish Head Mufti in Sofia.[112] When a new Muftiship was established in Ksanti, the key city of occupied Greek Thrace, the prestigious position of Mufti was immediately bestowed to Arif Beĭski, one of the founding members of *Rodina*.[113] The regime sanctioned the expansion of the *Rodina* movement into the new territories by insuring that all Muftis and clerics in Bulgaro-Mohammedan districts were pro-*Rodina* Pomaks and not "Turks" or Pomaks with Turkish leanings.[114] In this way the regime assured that "no foreigner" would be "the spiritual representative of the Bulgarian population."[115]

Thus installed in power, *Rodina* lorded over the constellation of reform measures that sought to reorder Pomak everyday culture. Only through the uprooting of so-called foreign names, clothes, and household habits could *Rodina* reroot Pomaks in healthy Bulgarian soil. *Rodina* officials were proud of the isolated prewar "progress" they had made in de-veiling Pomak women and de-fezzing Pomak men, and were ready to expand their arena for action into the "newly liberated" (occupied) territories. By 1943, the wartime regime had passed the "law on clothes" which codified the ban on the turban, fez, and veil-like clothing.[116] Before the war, *Rodina* had made very limited progress in their efforts to convince Pomak populations within Bulgarian territory to shed their Turco-Arabic names."[117] By the summer of 1942, *Rodina* intensified its name-changing drive, bolstered by a new law passed in the Bulgarian National Assembly for the "Bulgarianization of the Mohammedan names of Bulgaro-Mohammedans" which led to the rapid forced name-changes of some 60,000 Pomaks.[118] Finally, *Rodina* reform efforts focused on the actual form and content of Muslim homes. The local police in the new territories were called on to enforce measures aimed at the de-Turkification of the Bulgaro-Mohammedan home."[119] This "reform" of Pomak residences included the prohibition of *kafes* (lattice windows) and other Turkish-style household forms.[120] Pomaks were called on to reorder their homes and home life, to improve their "dark and unhygienic" living conditions.[121] These measures were not as widespread or as thoroughly enforced as the changing of Pomak names and clothes. Nevertheless, they were indicative of the wartime thrust of national imperatives across the threshold of the Pomak home,

---

[112] TsIDA (F-142, O-2, E-128, L-82: 1944).
[113] TsIDA (F-471, O-1, E-1084, L-4: 1942).
[114] TsIDA (F-142, O-2, E-128, L-85: 1944).
[115] TsIDA (F-370, O-1, E-1165, L-2: 1942).
[116] SODA (F-26K, O-1, E-31, L-1?: 1942).
[117] SODA (F-42K, O-15, E-10, L-319: 1942).
[118] Khristo Khristov, *Iz Minoloto na Bŭlgarite Mokhamedani v Rodopite* (Sofia, 1958), 136, 144.
[119] TsIDA (F-264, O-1, E-308, L-16: 1942).
[120] TsIDA (F-264, O-1, E-308, L-16: 1942).
[121] SODA (F-26K, O-1, E-31, L-4: 1942).

where it was assumed the essential Bulgarian dwelled behind a foreign facade.

Conclusion

By the nineteenth century a handful of Bulgarian elite began to step back and see the Bulgarian figure in the Ottoman carpet. They discovered the Bulgarian national self intricately embedded in the Ottoman morass, in need of untangling and clarifying. Under profound European intellectual influence, the Bulgarian national self was defined as essentially European and hence enjoyed the same essential superiority to the Ottoman East that Western Europe and Russia had claimed. True, the Europeanness of Bulgaria—as of the rest of the Balkans, Russia, and other parts of Eastern Europe—was in question by many. But this did not impede the authority which Europeanness and its attendant modernity was allotted in post-Ottoman Bulgarian nation-building projects. In fact, it was the abhorrence of the hybrid and Oriental within which drove dramatic attempts to cleanse the Bulgarian landscape of hated vestiges of the Ottoman past. By the twentieth century, Muslim minorities became central to the Bulgarian drive to remake their society in a modern, European image. The visible and audible signs of hybridity became central to Bulgarian campaigns to eradicate and remodel the landscape in a new national Bulgarian image. The most far-reaching efforts were undertaken against Pomak populations in times of war, namely the First Balkan War and World War II, with heightened vigilance against "foreign" threats and euphoric crusades to root out hybrid vestiges of a hated "Oriental" past. During these times the Bulgarian state began to unwittingly plant seeds of conflict between Bulgarian and Muslim even as other bases of alliance with the Muslim populations were cultivated. By World War II, the complicated nature of the Bulgaro-Muslim relationship was playing itself out through various policies, alliances, and campaigns that typified the potential both for conflict and commonality. Bulgaro-Muslim relations swung from ethno-cultural and political alliance to open conflict, as Muslims began to navigate the perilous terrain of resistance and collaboration. In the extreme conditions of the postwar period, alliances, tensions, and bases of resistance would evolve and magnify in a period of rapid and astonishing transformation.

2 Muslim Rebirth: Nationalism, Communism, and the Path to 1984

"Enemy Mania" acted like a powerful bellows fanning into a blaze
fiendish feelings and ambitions that otherwise would have remained
locked in the cold silence of an untapped human coal seam. If,
throughout the centuries, men have felt a need for the existence of
God, king or leader, in our time many people felt the need for an
enemy.

—GEORGI MARKOV

In the wake of World War II, East and West took on new meanings in Bulgaria as elsewhere along with Cold War reconfigurations of power. In conjunction with the Red Army advance, the Bulgarian Communist Party (BCP) staged a "peoples' revolution" on September 9, 1944, seizing power as part of a nominal coalition, the so-called Fatherland Front (FF). As the Soviet sphere spread west, the concept of "Eastern Europe" and the "Eastern Bloc" solidified in opposition to the newly constituted "West," namely Western Europe and the United States.[1] Although part of the new Bloc's raison d'être was military and ideological opposition to the capitalist West, this did not imply a civilizational identification with the East. Bulgaria, like the rest of the Bloc, paid extensive lip service to Marxist internationalism and spreading

---

[1] This is not to say that "Eastern Europe" was solely a postwar construct, though it did solidify in a new way behind the Iron Curtain. As Larry Wolff maintains, Eastern Europe as an intellectual construct and a European divide had existed since the Enlightenment. See Wolff, *Inventing Eastern Europe*, 356. Since the 1980s and especially after 1989 a rather labored attempt on the part of self-ascribed East Central Europeans pointed to the falseness of Eastern Europe as a Cold War invention. See Timothy Garton-Ash's discussion of this in *The Uses of Adversity: Essays on the Fate of Central Europe* (New York, 1990), 179–213. But as Maria Todorova correctly asserts, "East Central Europe" is also fictive, invented partly by self-proclaimed East Central Europeans to distinguish themselves from the vilified Balkans. See Todorova, *Imagining the Balkans*, 140–60.

Communism to the colonized East, but with a subtext of assumed superiority of the more developed "European" cultures within and outside the Bloc. Though the term "West" became tainted by its imperialist-Fascist connotations, the term "Europe" remained unsullied. In Bulgaria, as in the Soviet Union, Europeanness—in opposition to Eastern or Oriental backwardness—retained its semiotic significance, even as East and West as places and cultural concepts were ostensibly set loose from their traditional moorings. Hence, the paradigms that had anchored Bulgarian national identity in the past were not discarded; the terms and categories were merely recast. In practice, Bulgaria, like its Soviet patron, endeavored to overtake the West and Europe through a revolutionary remaking of society that called for a war against Eastern backwardness within.

Ironically, the BCP rationalized this war on Muslim difference or Bulgaro-Muslim hybridity, even more so than in the past, by assertions of Muslim sameness—although now on a class as well as blood basis. Admittedly there was a brief period at the end of World War II when Muslim difference was recognized and tolerated—if not begrudgingly embraced when the Party-led coalition replaced "bourgeois-Fascist" measures with rhetoric about a "new era" of Marxist internationalist tolerance toward Muslims. In theory, the BCP stressed the *class* unity of the Bulgarian and Muslim "toiling masses" as the basis of the "socialist nation." Since the bulk of Turks and Pomaks were rural "laborers," they were embraced as "brother" populations that had been oppressed and exploited by the "bourgeois Fascists," as well as the Ottoman "feudal" overlords. In fact, because their oppression under the post-Ottoman Bulgarian regimes was twofold—social and national—Muslims and especially Muslim women held a privileged place in the Bulgarian-Marxist hierarchy of oppression.[2] With their status as victims secured, in the early postwar years Turks were given state-sponsored resources for their own "national" development, albeit at the expense of pre-1944 autonomous institutions. Indeed, such institutions arguably played a major role in consolidating a Turkish national identity among the largely illiterate Turkish-speaking masses. As in the Soviet Union, the Bulgarian Communist Party, perhaps inadvertently, far from simply suppressing nationalism actually played a role in nation-building—in this case among Turks.[3] For Pomaks, on the other hand, their difference was never fostered. The victim status was firmly grounded in prewar assertions that they were Bulgarians by blood, forcibly Islamicized and Turkified in the Ottoman period. Prewar assumptions about Pomak blood ties were elaborated by academicians—ethnographers, historians, lin-

---

[2] Muslim women were defined as the "ultimate proletariat," oppressed in terms of social, national, and gender relations. I am indebted to Massell for his conceptualization of this hierarchy in the Soviet context. See Gregory Massell, *The Surrogate Proletariat: Moslem Women and Revolutionary Strategies in Soviet Central Asia, 1919–1929* (Princeton, 1974).

[3] Although Bulgaria hardly had what Slezine calls the "ethnophilia" of the Soviet Union, it was at least initially as Suny deems the Soviet Union, "a state making nations." Slezkine, "The USSR," 415; Suny, *Revenge of the Past*, 160.

guists, and others—who used newly culled ethnographic and historical "evidence." Gradually, such assumptions were extended to Bulgaria's Turkish population, who were also first partially and then wholly claimed as "blood brothers," presumably Islamicized and also Turkified in the Ottoman period. Hence, as both Turks and Pomaks were ultimately conceived as class and blood-brothers, as victims of historical injustices, it was both warranted and necessary to rectify Ottoman misdeeds, both for the sake of the nation and for progress itself.

This rectification took the form of Communist campaigns to eliminate the palpable remnants of the Ottoman past on the Bulgarian map and Muslim bodies. Before 1944 this had taken the form of seizing lands, encouraging emigration, changing place names, and, in times of war, unleashing campaigns against Turco-Arabic personal names and clothes. In the Communist period the state targeted the same kinds of everyday markers of Turco-Ottoman occupation, but with new ideological and practical tools of implementation; the BCP had inherited from their Soviet patrons a system of police terror and surveillance, as well as the political gumption to mobilize against newly defined enemies at the altars of modernization and "national integration." Although all minorities were sucked into the current of integration to some degree, the Party viewed Muslims in particular as obstacles to Communist progress. Jews and Armenians, for example, maintained some autonomous cultural institutions throughout the period.[4] They never represented the visible Oriental affront to Bulgaria's modernity, nor were they viewed as "traitorous" or "deluded," as Muslims were, by virtue of their presumed Bulgarian origins. The BCP's newly developed academic machine went to great lengths to prove these origins along with espousing and justifying various measures for advancing toward Communism. As elaborated in both popular and academic writings, "vestiges" of the Ottoman past were considered to be a major obstacle to Communist progress, incompatible with the development of a new socialist consciousness.[5]

As never before, material culture became the focus of Bulgarian Communist projects that tackled the Muslim question. Marxism, after all, was at core a material ideology based on the idea that material conditions (the base) determine consciousness (the superstructure) on history's unilinear march from "savagery" to "civilization."[6] One of the key features of the Soviet and East European socialist experiments was the total restructuring of the macroeconomy, that is, the nationalization of property and collectivization of agri-

[4] Greeks were not granted such institutions, perhaps because only 8,241 remained by 1965. Gypsies are a rather special case, but Muslim Gypsies were subject to many of the same measures as Turks and Pomaks. Poulton, *Balkans*, 116–18.

[5] Buchli presents an excellent summary and analysis of Soviet perceptions and debates on *perezhitki* (vestiges) of the pre-Revolutionary past. Victor Buchli, *An Archeology of Socialism* (New York, 1999), 24–25.

[6] See Buchli's discussion of the influence of the mid-nineteenth-century ethnographic work of Lewis Henry Morgan on Marx and Engels' formulations on materialism. Buchli, *Archeology of Socialism*, 5.

culture. In Bulgaria, as with other nations in the Bloc, these projects were conceived as the reclaiming of foreign-held and hence exploited land and property in the name of the people or nation. With this semantic twist in mind, these were always nationalist as well as socialist projects from their inception. Even more pointedly, in Bulgaria as in the Soviet Union the foreign and Asiatic material culture of Muslims—closer as it was to savagery—came under particularly close scrutiny.

Aspects of Muslim "*bit*" or *byt* in Russian (daily life or way of life) were fundamental to the Communist confrontations with the Muslim provinces. Muslim *bit*, as Bulgarian *bit*, was the academic stomping ground of ethnographers who led the charge for the integration of Bulgaria's Muslims. The BCP advocated a revolutionary transformation of *bit* into a nebulous form of socialist *bit* for all citizens of Bulgaria, but the war on Bulgarian *bit* was always comparably feeble in relation to the war on Muslim *bit*. In fact, ethnographers often extolled the virtues of the Bulgarian way of life and material culture as progressive. In contrast, the BCP employed fastidious albeit sporadic measures to transform Muslim *bit*. The Party spearheaded measures, for example, that were much more far-reaching than *Rodina*'s war-time measures to transform the Muslim household into a "European" one. They were ultimately highly successful in the widespread introduction of European-style windows at the expense of *kafes* (lattice screens), as well as beds, tables, and radios into Muslim village life. However, by far the most intensive and contested efforts were Party campaigns against gendered Turco-Arabic attire—in particular the fez, the so-defined veil, and the *shalvari* (baggy Turco-Arabic pants). If *bit* determined consciousness as the Communists espoused, Turks and Pomaks would only become good Communists if they were wearing "modern European" clothes. The Communist obsession with materiality pervaded these attempts to transform Muslims into Communists and Bulgarians.

The BCP also had an interrelated fixation on names, particularly personal and familial names. Name-changing campaigns, admittedly, were also a thing of the past, i.e. the forced Bulgarianization of Pomak names during the First Balkan War and World War II. In this period, however, name-changing crusades were carried out with a new meaning and force that was tantamount to Muslim "rebirth" into both the "socialist nation" and the Bulgarian one. These campaigns, centered on Party-directed measures to change Muslims' Turco-Arabic names to Bulgarian ones, climaxed during their respective "Rebirth (or Revival) Processes" (*vŭzroditelen protses* in Bulgarian) from 1968–75 for Pomaks and 1984–85 for Turks. The BCP conceived and justified these actions both in terms of socialist progress and integration as well as a continuation of the Bulgarian national revival. In Bulgarian academic and popular parlance the nineteenth century had been labeled the period of *vŭzrazhdane,* literally the national renaissance or "revival" from the verb *vŭzrazhdam* (from the same root as the adjectival *vŭzroditelen*)—to regenerate or breathe new life into. As Bulgarians had been "reborn" through their national awakening in the nineteenth century, so too, according to the Communist Party, were Muslims now "reborn" as Bulgarians. In academic writings of the period the Rebirth Processes were described as part of a "nat-ural, hundred-year process" which enjoyed particularly fertile conditions under the special conditions of Communist rule.[7] The fertile conditions in-cluded the widespread use of force and novel theoretical justification. As elaborated by Bulgarian academics, names, as with clothes and other mate-rial markers, actually shaped or determined the consciousness and hence the form of their bearers. A handbook printed during the Pomak name-change campaigns, for example, asserted that "Oriental names left the deepest stamp of Mohammedanization" and so "play a harmful role in the formation of Bulgarian national consciousness."[8] Clearly, transformations in Muslim eco-nomic life and material culture did not suffice; Muslims also had to bear the label of progress, a Bulgarian name.

But Muslims did not bear the imposition of names, as clothes, without ri-poste. The intensity of Muslim minority resistance and collaboration, as well as the murky space in between, is integral to the unfolding of Bulgaro-Mus-lim negotiations of power. Since the beginning of the Communist period at least a minority of Turks and Pomaks openly cooperated with the Commu-nist regime. Many at least initially shared some common interests with the Communists because they came from various modernizing Muslim move-ments, such as Turkish Kemalists and *Rodina* Pomaks. Although Muslim membership in the BCP was admittedly low, many Turks and Pomaks jumped on the Communist bandwagon and reaped the benefits of the politi-cal association. Numerous Muslim functionaries helped to carry out BCP policies in the 1970s and 1980s, while other Turks and Pomaks were co-opted in humdrum everyday ways. Co-optation was an insidious part of daily life in the Muslim provinces; it was a critical part of Muslim minority survival and advancement strategies that is often overlooked in studies of their experience under Communism. At the same time it was in the rural set-ting of the Muslim village, I argue, that everyday forms of Muslim resistance were most palpable. Within their rural enclaves, outside of the direct gaze of the Sofia authorities, various kinds of exploits were more possible. Here Muslims could and did wear Turco-Muslim clothes and used their birth names even after they had been discouraged or banned. Such lack of con-formity—or rather conformity to a customary norm—was neither entirely consistent nor part of any grand design. Instead it was mundane and haphaz-ard. Individuals maintained or reinvented tradition as was possible and com-fortable for survival within the context of their local communities. Various faces—and clothes and names—were worn for various officials, visitors, friends, and neighbors. In this way, complicated entanglements of power emerged on the Bulgarian periphery in which Muslim minorities were caught in perpetual motion, negotiating a place between resistance and cooperation.

Significantly, the BCP itself had to negotiate its own place within the larger

[7] See, for example, Boncho Asenov, *Vŭzroditelniiat Protses i Dŭrzhavna Sigurnost* (Sofia, 1996), 8.
[8] A. Spasov, ed. *Sbornik v Pomosht na Uchiteli ot Rodopskite Raĭoni* (Sofia, 1961), 8.

web of Soviet power, with regard to its handling of the Muslim minority issue. The Bulgarian Communists naturally paid more than ample homage to the Soviet model of modernization in Muslim Central Asia and the Caucuses. At the same time clear continuities with the pre-Communist past emerged and BCP theory and practice ultimately went much further with its attempts at total assimilation of Turks and Pomaks than the Soviets. In the Soviet context Russification did proceed but the USSR's federal structure always provided for some form of "national" autonomies for Muslims. Although the Soviets advocated *sblizhenie* or the "coming together" of the Soviet nationalities, they never advocated total integration of Muslims on the basis of shared blood, only on the basis of class unity. The Bulgarian Communists recognized that their Muslim question was unique and required different, and ultimately much more radical, measures. Unlike the Soviet multinational federal model, the Bulgarian Communists were working within a uninational context, albeit with recognized minorities. Furthermore, Bulgaria was a small nation, bordering a powerful NATO-allied Turkey. With much of its own Muslim minority population concentrated on its southern border, Bulgaria had a heightened sense of national insecurity.

Since the inception of its bid for power and influence in Bulgaria, the BCP dressed Bulgarian national claims and promises in a Marxist-Leninist cloak, while coloring its Marxism with nationalism. In gathering political power, the BCP sincerely endeavored to command local loyalties on a mass scale through claiming to be the ultimate, true voice of the people and the nation, merged in one Bulgarian word, *narod*. The Muslim question presented one of the biggest challenges to this larger project of Communist nation building. In practice, issues of national security and national integration came into direct conflict with the principles of "socialist brotherhood" in relation to Muslim minorities. How could the Party tolerate the ongoing presence of cultural practices which were considered the epitome of the backwardness and foreignness that were anathema to both socialist and national interests? As the Communist period progressed, the Party's use of nationalism became more and more blatant and it became increasingly clear that Communism was not moving beyond nationalism at all. Instead nationalism would become the tool with which Communism could pave Bulgaria's new "road to modernization." Ultimately this road penetrated the remote Muslim provinces of the Bulgarian periphery, creating havoc and provoking conflict, but also ironically bearing new vehicles for cooperation and alliance.

Nationalism in Communist Garb

In spite of the very real changes in postwar theory and practice, a strong nationalist undertow always flowed under the apparently smooth Marxist surface of Bulgarian Communist politics and policy. Admittedly, in the immediate postwar period, there was an apparent caesura in nationalist discourse.[9] Consistent with Party policy, the BCP censured Bulgarian nationalism as "bourgeois" and "Fascist" and, with much fanfare, reversed all of the wartime measures that had impinged on Muslim cultural practices such as the wearing of the fez and veil, and the use of Turco-Arabic names. The new regime, it seemed, had set out on a new course in which past "mistakes" would be replaced by a Bulgaro-Muslim unity of the "toiling masses." In theory, the door was opened for new kinds of Bulgarian/Muslim alliances with a new, seemingly idealistic harmony of interests. In practice, though, new foundations for cooperation between Bulgarians and Muslims were built over old and freshly gaping fault lines. On one hand, the BCP rejection of Bulgarian nationalism was largely fictional from the outset in spite of the Party's verbose rhetoric to the contrary. On the other hand, the Party was far more unswerving in its attendant repudiation of Turkish nationalism, which was seen as a far greater threat to the territorial integrity of the Bulgarian socialist republic. Although the new state was nominally internationalist, there was never a doubt that the "progressive" Bulgarian nation was at the helm and that the Muslim presence was viewed as an obstacle to its survival and success.

Of course, the fickle Marxist-Leninist-Stalinist approach to the national question complicated Party strategies and practices toward Bulgarian and Muslim populations alike. Much of the problem was rooted in the contradictions and shortcomings of Marx's writings as a formula for dealing with the phenomena of nationalism, national minorities, and the nation-state in a systematic theoretical way. Marx's famous exhortation in the *Communist Manifesto*, "the worker has no country," and his assumption that regional and national particularisms would disappear after the coming of a global worker's revolution made nationalism a supposed moot point in the postcapitalist world. According to Marx, nationalism was by definition bourgeois and hence part of the capitalist stage of development, sure to "whither away" along with the state and other capitalist forms. In Marx's post-1848 journalistic writings, however, he does pass judgment on particular nationalisms, opening the door for future Marxist interpretation. In these works, Marx supports, for example, the consolidation of states into larger territorial units—such as the unification of Italy and Germany—as progressive historical developments. At the same time, however, he opposes the "Balkanization" of territory, for example the Habsburg and Ottoman Empires, by little "reactionary" nationalisms.[10] Both Marx and Engels had looked with particular contempt on the "nonhistoric" South Slav "lilliput nationalities" that they described as, "pastoral pig keeping tribes without urban life" as well as,

---

[9] This was the case for all of the new East European satellites. See Maria Todorova, "Ethnicity, Nationalism, and the Communist Legacy in Eastern Europe," in *The Social Legacy of Communism*, ed. S. Wolchik and J. Millar (Cambridge, 1994), 100.

[10] Shlomo Averini, "Marxism and Nationalism," *Journal of Contemporary History* 26 (1991): 641–43.

"abject dogs, Gypsies, and Slavonic beasts of animal idiocy."[11] But Marx actually supported the progressive Polish national movement as a protective buffer that would shield progressive European movements from reactionary Russian nationalism. In spite of Marx's clear denunciation of Russian and Balkan nationalisms, his writings left the theoretical door open for his followers to denounce "bourgeoisie reactionary nationalisms" as counterrevolutionary, while still applauding revolutionary "anti-imperialist" nationalisms as progressive. This loophole allowed the BCP, to extol the "progressive" essence of the Bulgarian nation throughout the Communist period. Perhaps of greater importance the BCP was attuned to Marx's preference for consolidated, as opposed to "Balkanized" nations, which justified their own projects of national integration. And although the Soviets too sought to integrate their Union of Soviet Socialist Republics, the BCP went two steps beyond in ultimately attempting to enforce a complete ethnonational amalgamation of the citizens on Bulgarian soil.

In short, the BCP consistently repudiated nationalism as an ideology, but not at the expense of the Bulgarian nation. With clever semantic smoke and mirrors the Party embraced the Bulgarian "people" or "nation," conveniently encapsulated in one Bulgarian word—*narod*. The Bulgarian *narod*, they argued, was the inherently progressive foundation on which the socialist nation would be built. In fact, the Communist Party's stellar success at the ballot box at the end of World War I had been in large part due to its opposition to that war, which was such a disaster for Bulgarian national interests.[12] The Party—crushed, exiled, and underground since its abortive revolt in Bulgaria in 1923—had the political savvy to continue appealing to national as well as social sensibilities in its rather paltry bid for influence through the end of World War II. Since its assumption of power in 1944, the BCP asserted its role as the new ruler of Bulgaria based on its ousting of the foreign enemies of the Bulgarian nation, including Axis troops and the Germanic Bulgarian royal family. Furthermore, from its first years in power the regime embraced and published the works if selectively of nineteenth-century Bulgarian revolutionary nationalists while seeking legitimacy and continuity in their "progressive" tradition. Far from wholly rejecting the Bulgarian nationalist past, the BCP threw out nationalism in name only rather than in sum or substance.

The Bulgarian nationalism of the immediate postwar period, however, was in some senses heavily repressed when it came to the Muslim question. Openly anti-Turkish expressions of Bulgarian nationalism became decidedly politically incorrect, given Muslims' special status as the "ultimate proletariat" along with the myth of the active participation of Bulgarian-Turks and Pomaks in the "peoples' front against capitalism and Fascism."[13] Initially, Turks in particular became major beneficiaries of the Party's Leninist line of "socialist in form, national in content," which necessitated Turkish

[11] As cited in Jacob Talmon, *The Myth of the Nation and the Vision of Revolution* (Berkeley, 1981), 43–44, 55.

[12] Rothschild, *Communist Party of Bulgaria*, 96.

[13] On Turks see Memishev, *Uchastieto*, 109–219; on Pomaks see Khristov, *Iz Minoloto*.

national development as a vehicle for mobilization, modernization, and Communist indoctrination. The Party heavily invested funds and rapidly built an impressive number of secular Turkish schools and printing presses for Turkish-language periodicals, as well as theatres and other secular cultural institutions.[14] The institutions inadvertently contributed to the spread of a modern Turkish national consciousness in Bulgaria among the largely illiterate Turkish-speaking populations, many of whom had only a Muslim identity previously. But it was never in the Party plan to build a base for Turco-Muslim separatism on its soil. Although Turkish but not Pomak difference was recognized and fostered as a base for Communist propaganda, such measures were seen as temporary from the outset; as in the Soviet Union, national cultures were used as vehicles for advancing Communist modernization.

Also on the Soviet model, the BCP needed to woo Muslim cohorts to ensure order and compliance with government programs in the far-flung Muslim provinces. In building political alliances the BCP was, at least in theory, selective and so presumably "Fascist" Turks and Pomaks were not welcomed into the fold. As far as Pomaks are concerned, the regime considered *Rodina* Fascist because of its cooperation with past regimes, in spite of its pro-Bulgarian promodernizing stance.[15] *Rodina* members themselves tried to assuage these fears with a sudden turn to a pro-Communist stance as World War II came to a close. The organization's key members, many of whom joined the Communist Party in 1944–45, were initially enthusiastic about the new regime with the assumption that the progress-oriented Communists would support their cause. By 1947 however, as the BCP consolidated power in Sofia, most *Rodina* leaders were expelled from the Party and from positions of responsibility after being accused of carrying out Fascist forced name-changes and clothing-reform measures during World War II. Ironically, Pomaks who had once been considered too conservative to enter *Rodina*'s ranks were considered more appropriate for Party recruitment. In the Turkish case, the regime had an unfavorable view of so-called Old Turks, anti-Kemalists who had cooperated with the former regime in return for support of their traditionalist stance on Muslim practice. The BCP turned instead to the modernizing "Young Turks," Kemalist faction of the Turkish intelligentsia, which in principle supported many of their social and economic programs. The Party held a Turkish national conference in 1944, which unanimously approved measures to purge the Head Muftiship and other Muslim-Turkish institutions of Fascist elements and put in new elements loyal to the regime.[16] Hence in its attempt to repudiate the Fascist past the Party attempted to reverse all

[14] Many sources look with favor on the contribution to Turkish literacy made by the Communist education system, although it came at a price. See, for example, Eminov, *Turkish and other Muslim Minorities*, 131–33. For an overall study of the Turks of Bulgaria with the most detailed attention to education see Bilâl Şimşir, *Bulgaristan Türkleri*, which has also been translated into English as *Bulgarian Turks: 1878–1895* (London, 1988).

[15] TsIDA (F-28, O-1, E-399, L-76: 1946).

[16] HODA (F-182K, O-1, E-92, L-1: 1944).

past government–Muslim alliances and start anew—regardless of ideological incongruencies.

In practice, the BCP was compelled to pursue ad hoc measures to activate and co-opt any potentially useful and loyal Muslim elements. In fact, the unbridled enthusiasm of certain reform-minded Kemalist Turks to participate in Communist programs provoked suspicions in the higher circles of the BCP. The BCP often interpreted their enrollment and filling of local administrative posts in the Party as a way for Turks to infiltrate and "keep out Bulgarian officials." As one official noted, "The Turanists are working among the Turks and have adapted well to the new situation," allowing "Turkish reconnaissance to flourish unfettered."[17] The Party was, in many ways, more secure in its dealings with the Islamic establishment, although necessarily purged of unfriendly elements. The BCP, as with Communist parties elsewhere, unequivocally considered religion as the "opiate of the masses" and accordingly waged open attacks against Islam (as well as Christianity) in Bulgaria. Still, Muslim religious institutions, historically loyal to the Bulgarian state, were left intact as a needed supplement to the meager and not fully trusted new Turkish recruits to the Bulgarian Communist Party cause. The Head Muftiship, its sixteen regional Muftiships, and its local religious servants—imams (congregational leaders) and hocas (preachers or teachers)—were seen as more likely to be effective in administering Party programs and penetrating the consciousness of the Muslim masses. The separation of Pomak religious institutions from Turkish ones that had been instituted during World War II was continued and finalized by 1948 so that Islamic institutions could no longer serve as a base of common loyalty and identity for the two Muslim groups.[18] Instead, every religious leader was expected to be an agitator for the BCP and "activate the Turkish population and awaken interest and love toward the homeland and national ideals."[19]

In spite of suspicions and fears about Turkish nationalism, the BCP also did attempt to build a Party-loyal Muslim secular elite. One of the first acts of the Party in 1945 was to implement Turkish-language alphabet reform by replacing the Arabic with the Latin alphabet, as had been implemented in the Turkish republic in 1928. The Party regularly published *Yeni Işık* (New Light), *Yeni Hayat* (New Life), and other Turkish-language newspapers in the Latin script as a vehicle for spreading, explaining, and popularizing Party doctrine to Turks. Education in modern Turkish was fundamental to efforts to inculcate the general Muslim population with Communist ideas and lay the foundation for a beholden and cooperative Muslim elite. In a kind of affirmative action, the Party began to offer Turkish and Pomak children places in new regional secondary-level boarding schools and easy entrance to Bulgarian institutions of higher education without the odious exams that Bul-

[17] TsIDA (F-1B, O-6, E-34, L-7: 1945).

[18] SODA (F-42K, O-6, E-2, L-57: 1949); and TsIDA (F-168, O-3, E-61, L-63: 1948).

[19] TsIDA (F-165, O-3, E-840, L-10: 1948); See also HODA (F-182K, O-1, E-93, L-91: 1948).

garian students had to pass.[20] By 1947 "*Niuvab*," the private Muslim seminary school in Shumen, had been converted into a secular Turkish gymnasium and pedagogical institute, renamed Nazim Hikmet after the Communist
poet from Turkey. Its purpose was to prepare Turkish cadres for administration of Turkish districts and teaching in the new Turkish-language schools.
These new Turkish Communist cadres, 99 percent of whom were drawn
from rural areas, were required to participate in the new "agitator brigades"
which went from village to village in Turkish-speaking areas spreading information on the various Bulgarian five-year economic plans and explaining the
progressive character of the new peoples' democracy.[21] Although the Party
always complained of a shortage of Turkish cadres, the BCP nevertheless
found sufficient recruits willing to partake of the free education at Nazim
Hikmet and move up into the higher ranks of the new elite.

A significant number of Pomaks also took advantage of this new social
mobility. Because the Communist regime considered Pomaks to be Bulgarians it was actually against the law for them to enroll in Turkish schools or
seminaries, even though it had been the practice for centuries.[22] As a transitional measure, a separate "Bulgaro-Mohammedan" Islamic Seminary was
established in Plovdiv in 1947 as a conduit for bringing new Pomak cadres
into Party ranks and inculcating Bulgarian national consciousness.[23] The
school was named Mehmed Sinap after a renowned local Pomak warlord
who, in Bulgarian historical lore, had opposed Ottoman authority in the
eighteenth century and so presumably asserted his "Bulgarianness." Pomak
students were enticed to come to Mehmed Sinap from the countryside to
room and board in Plovdiv, the largest city in southern Bulgaria, to help facilitate "the fast merging of Bulgaro-Mohammedans and Bulgarian Christians."[24] Within three years however, the BCP had already decided that the
"fast merging" of Pomaks and Bulgarians was best accomplished by the elimination of Mehmed Sinap. As one Party official argued, "The existence of a
Bulgaro-Mohammedan preparatory school isn't justified. On the contrary,
not only would its future existence impinge on the government budget, but it
would be an injurious influence on the consciousness of Bulgaro-Mohammedans. The existence of a special school for them upholds the mistaken
conviction that they are some kind of a minority and something separate
from Bulgarians.[25] As of academic year 1950–51 the school was closed. In
contrast, pedagogical institute Nazim Hikmet remained justified in the eyes
of the commission because of its "ideological, political role."[26]

[20] TsIDA (F-747, O-1, E-15, L-21: 1948).
[21] TsIDA (F-747, O-1, E-28, L-65: 1947).
[22] TsIDA (F-747, O-1, E-30, L-33: 1948); TsIDA (F-142, O-4, E-94, L-53: 1947).
[23] The term "Bulgaro-Mohammedan" was used for only a brief period by Bulgarian Communists for lack of any better way to discuss this population without highlighting its difference
from "Bulgarian." By the 1950s the terms "Bulgarians of Muslim faith," or "Bulgarian-Muslims" were more common.
[24] TsIDA (F-84B, O-1, E-121, L-21: 1947).
[25] TsIDA (F-165, O-3, E-307, L-7: 1950).
[26] TsIDA (F-165, O-3, E-307, L-8: 1950).

As a rule the process of bringing secular and religious Muslims into the Bulgarian administration was not without obstacles, in part from Bulgarians themselves. Many Bulgarian Communist functionaries blocked the intensified drive to include Muslims in the new administration in the Communist-inspired "affirmative action." The new social mobility for Muslims, after all, would mean the sharing of traditionally "Bulgarian" political positions, administrative jobs, and university positions with ambitious young Muslim recruits. In Smolyan, for example, a local Bulgarian complained that, "in Turkish times the mayor wasn't a Muslim and now we will elect a Mohammedan . . . the mayor should be a Bulgarian, regardless of what government is in power."[27] In reality, although there were a significant number of Muslims in the Party administration, the percentage of Muslims that occupied positions of responsibility in the government was much lower than for Bulgarians in terms of percentage of the population. An estimated .12 percent of the Turkish population held state positions of responsibility compared to .55 percent of the Bulgarian population. Furthermore, Turks tended to hold the lower rank Party posts and only a select few made it into the upper ruling circles of the Party; of ninety-seven members in the 1954 Central Committee of the Bulgarian Communist Party only one was Turkish, and there were no Turks in the nine-member Politburo.[28] In spite of this discrepancy, there was a pervasive Bulgarian assumption that Muslims were given an unfair advantage at their expense.

In addition to the tensions engendered by limited power sharing, Muslims were generally deemed suspect by the regime because of important changes in the international state of affairs. The breakdown of Soviet relations with the United States and Britain and the intensification of Cold War divisions were key factors in rampant BCP national insecurities. Uncertainty was aggravated by the raging civil war between Anglo-American-supported Royalists and Soviet-Yugoslav-supported Greek Communists in bordering Greece. Rumors reportedly circulated in the Muslim countryside that Anglo-American troops were just across the border ready to invade and reclaim land in southern Bulgaria for Turkey if the Communists lost the various elections, staged from 1945–47.[29] The prevalence of these hostile rumors increased suspicions about Turkish and Pomak loyalties. The BCP could not help but harbor concern, for example, over a letter allegedly sent by a group of Pomaks to the U.S., British, and Greek governments against the tyranny of the Bulgarian yoke. The letter contended that Pomaks are "racially Turkish" and therefore wish to immigrate to Turkey via Greece and avoid imminent "Bulgarianization."[30] This letter heightened BCP fears that the bulk of the Pomak population "considered themselves to be Turkish."[31] Suspicions of Turkish duplicity

---

[27] TsIDA (F-28, O-5, E-55, L-52: 1949).
[28] *Prava i Svobodi*, February 25—March 3, 1991, 8.
[29] TsIDA (F-1B, O-12, E-222, L-81: 1946).
[30] TsIDA (F-165, O—1, E—38, L-1: 1946).
[31] TsIDA (F-146, O-5, E-605, L-1: 1945).

became more prevalent in Party discussions. As the Minister of Foreign Affairs cautioned in 1945, "We cannot sacrifice the interests of Bulgarian democracy for one Turkish minority. . . . If we give rights to various reactionary people then we will make a weapon out of them."[32] Along these same lines, in 1947, one Party official described Turkish propaganda as an "ulcer" in the Bulgarian body politic, warning that the enemies of the Bulgarian nation might at any minute "plunge a knife into the back of Bulgaria."[33]

By 1947, as the BCP consolidated political power domestically and Cold War lines were drawn though the Balkan map, the war on external and internal enemies escalated. The pledge of direct U.S. support in 1947 for Greece and Turkey in the Truman Doctrine demarcated the boundaries of U.S. commitment to "containment" of Communism in the region and brought the capitalist threat to Bulgaria's backyard. The new Cold War sense of Greek and Turkish threats melded well with prewar formulations in Bulgarian national historiography about Bulgaria's "double yoke" of Greek Orthodox cultural and Ottoman-Turkish political and economic oppression. In spite of its self-proclaimed internationalism, the BCP began to express suspicion about internal vestiges of anything Greek, and especially, Turkish because of presumed historical and contemporary peril to Bulgarian national autonomy: "These two governments have enslaved us politically and spiritually and we need to be freed from them. They even now are preparing to enslave us and we need to liquidate everything Turkish and Greek without distinction of historical or economic circumstances."[34] But although vestiges of the Greek past were limited in scope by this period, the Turkish presence was seen as a greater menace.

In fact, the fear of Turkish nationalism and the general perception of Turks as obstacles to BCP programs prompted the famous "expulsion" of Turks in 1950–51. Although the reasons for what was tantamount to an eviction of some 140,000 Turks from Bulgarian territory is still disputed, there seems to have been both domestic and foreign policy rationale. On the domestic front the mass exodus "cleansed" the countryside of large numbers of potentially disloyal Turks, while opening up vast amounts of agricultural lands for collectivization. At the same time, the timing of the expulsion seems to indicate that there was a desired effect of destabilization of Bulgaria's southern neighbor, Turkey. Although Turkey didn't join NATO until 1952, the Turkish government showed its commitment to Anglo-American foreign policy goals by dispatching a Turkish brigade in 1950 to participate in the Korean War. Significantly, many Pomaks tried to join the wave of Turkish emigrants but were categorically denied exit visas, because they were officially defined as "Bulgarians." Whatever the primary rationale, the 1950–51 expulsion was indicative of the deep ambivalence and contradiction that characterized the

[32] TsIDA (F-214B, O-1, E-81, L-8–9, 21: 1945).
[33] TsIDA (F-214B, O-1, E-716, L-19: 1947).
[34] TsIDA (F-142, O-5, E-67, L-2: 1948).

BCP approach to the Turkish minority. Even as Turks were actively courted and integrated, they were also seen as potential enemies and so actively removed from Bulgarian territory.

While Turco-Bulgarian sameness was being brokered only on class grounds in this period, the new regime unequivocally assumed and declared Pomaks as an inseparable, nonnegotiable part of the Bulgarian nation. In spite of grave reservations about the loyalty of both, the BCP accepted Pomaks into the parameters of the Bulgarian nation and offered Turks a partnership of compliance and prestige. But both Turks and Pomaks were subject to BCP demands for political, social, and cultural conformity, demands that became more pointed as BCP power penetrated deeper into the Muslim countryside. In the wake of the Turkish exodus, the BCP came to realize that it needed to increase and improve work with Muslim minorities in Bulgaria. A new series of measures were introduced beginning at the Party plenum in 1951 for the further integration of Turks and Pomaks into Bulgarian society. In the period that followed, the Party would truly begin to pursue its ultimate objectives in work with Muslims with vigor and pragmatism, the inculcation of a new "socialist consciousness," the creation of "new people" and "a new life."[35]

The Great Leap Forward and Beyond

By the late-1950s heightened Bulgarian nationalism—albeit still in a Communist guise—and an aggressive approach to a socialist "merging of nations" increasingly colored Bulgarian policies toward its Muslim minorities. Todor Zhivkov, who came to power in 1956 and ruled until 1989, laid the path for the remainder of the Communist period with his optimistic vision of the approach of "ripe Communism." The 1956 April Plenum ushered in the Zhivkov era and the assertion of the so-called April Line which meant, above all, a quickened pace toward progress in all realms of Communist development. In the Muslim provinces, the ability of local Party operatives to eliminate the visible vestiges of the Ottoman past was increasingly used as a litmus test to determine the degree of progress along the path to a utopian future. When such vestiges persisted, the Party interpreted them as modes of resistance to the multifaceted Party drive to socialist integration. Along with the persistence and even resurgence of local Islamic practices, the changing international climate intensified Bulgarian fears of the Islamic threat within. These factors, coupled with the growing demographic imbalance between Bulgarian and Muslim populations, brought more radical approaches to the Muslim question to the fore.

After only a few years in power, the Zhivkov regime launched a set of measures that involved the far-reaching economic and cultural transformation of

---

[35] HODA (F-675, O-1, E-112, L-4: 1951).

Muslim-inhabited rural districts of southern and northeastern Bulgaria. In a direct emulation of Communist projects in China, the BCP announced the "Great Leap Forward" and the accompanying "Cultural Revolution" that were carried out from 1958 to 1960. In line with Communist philosophy, the BCP assumed that radical change in the material lives of Turks and Pomaks would create a new socialist consciousness. The main thrust of the BCP approach to eradicating the cultural backwardness of Muslim minority districts centered on economic integration of Muslims into the new socialist economy. Since assuming power in 1944 the Party had tried to lure Muslims into the expanding collective farms in the Bulgarian countryside. Muslims, like Bulgarians, were resistant to collectivization because of their long history of small-scale independent farming. Though the Party called on Muslim secular and religious cadres to enter collectives and set an example, a very small percentage had collectivized by the end of 1940s.[36] The mass expulsion of Turks from the Dobrudzha region in 1951 certainly abetted the state's collectivization efforts by partially cleansing this agricultural region of resistant inhabitants. By the 1950s, coercive measures brought increasing numbers of Muslims into the collectives. Still, by 1958, 70 percent of Turks were collectivized compared to 92 percent of the population as a whole.[37] Finally, from 1958 to 1960, the remotest of Muslim districts were targeted and the remaining Muslims were brought into state-run collective farms.[38]

From its inception the BCP imposition of agricultural collectivization had more than an economic agenda. The Party clearly harbored expectations about the Cultural Revolution that would accompany it. For example, within the new collective farms Muslim minorities were expected to do their part in the raising of pigs. Although the rearing of pigs and consumption of pork was historically anathema to Muslims, local officials began to send reports to Sofia, boasting that "almost every Turkish family is raising pigs." Reports from the Turkish-inhabited provinces gave details of the new presumed Turkish affinities for pig husbandry as if it were a sure sign of progress by way of integration into the socialist economy, "The attitude of laboring Turks toward pigs and pig farming has changed. Until recently they couldn't even speak of such a thing and now it is part of their economic activities. . . . Even Turkish women are working in the pig farms."[39] Clearly the focus on pork production in such commentary was less about the regime's economic imperatives and more about cultural conformity, with an increasingly clear gender dimension.

In the same period that Turks were forced to become part of local agricultural collectives, Turkish women were being reeducated on the details of "household culture." Committees for work with Muslim women organized

[36] SODA (F-42K, O-6, E-2, L-33), 1949.
[37] TsIDA (F-1B, O-5, E-353, L-448: 1958); and TsIDA (F-1B, O-5, E-353, L-457: 1958).
[38] TsIDA (F-1B, O-5, E-353, L-390: 1958).
[39] TsIDA (F-1B, O-509, E-5, L-51: 1962).

classes on "putting the household in order."[40] Party officials impressed on Muslim women in the new collectives the need to buy tables, chairs, beds, and all that is needed for a beautiful home.[41] The revolution in household culture was described in the Turkish-language organ of the Party, *Yeni Işık,* in the following way, "The tumble-down huts smeared with manure and grasses were replaced by sunny homes with radios, needed beds, and furniture which entered into the way of life for Turks in the cooperatives."[42] As part of the Cultural Revolution, female Bulgarian Party members actually went door to door telling Turkish women how they were supposed to keep house.[43] In addition, Turkish women often were recruited to offer testimonials on the benefits of the "transition in household culture." One Turkish woman, for example, after having embraced the BCP Cultural Revolution in matters of the home, is reported to have proclaimed, "I feel that now I began to live as a person. I bought a radio, a bed, an oven, and now we are preparing to build a house and so I feel that everything in our home is in order, and in no way is different from those of our Bulgarian women comrades."[44] Undoubtedly, the Party expected that Muslim women needed to put into practice changes in household material culture that, in turn, could provide a foundation on which order and socialist sameness could be built. Campaigns for the "voluntary" shirking of Muslim headgear and dress in favor of modern, European garb also began in earnest during these early years of Cultural Revolution. The fez and the turban were mostly phased out in this period, when Muslim men, in particular, were pressured to conform to socialist standards. But increasingly coercive crusades against the so-defined veil and *shalvari,* as worn by Muslim women, also spread to the Muslim countryside. These women's garments, however, seemed to have much greater staying power as campaigns against them continued into the decades that followed.[45] As a result, Muslim women attracted increasing attention as the presumed guardians of Muslim tradition and the hidden, and hence menacing, realm of the Muslim home.

Throughout the period, the Muslim religion itself came under direct attack, even as the Party contradictorily continued to employ its institutions and leaders for its own ends. In Party discussions about Islam, its backward and barbaric practices were observed and condemned as they persisted not just among the toiling masses but also among Muslim Party members. In one such discussion, a Party official related an incident in the village of Smir-

---

[40] KODA (F-50, O-1, E-27, L-4: 1956); and TsIDA (F-28, O-16, E-49, L-15: 1959).
[41] KODA (F-50, O-1, E-27, L-36: 1958).
[42] TsIDA (F-1B, O-5, E-353, L-353: 1958).
[43] TsIDA (F-1B, O-509, E-5, L-31: 1962).
[44] TsIDA (F-28, O-16, E-49, L-108: 1960).
[45] See Mary Neuburger, "Difference Unveiled: Bulgarian National Imperatives and the Redressing of Muslim Women in the Communist Period: 1945–89," *Nationalities Papers* 25 (1997): 169–81; and Mary Neuburger "Pants, Veils, and Matters of Dress: Unraveling the Fabric of Women's Lives in Communist Bulgaria," in *Style and Socialism: Modernity and Material Culture in Post-War Eastern Europe,* ed. D. Crowley and S. Reid (Oxford, 2000).

nenik, where a hoca had put a hair in a bottle and started the rumor that it was a "hair of Mohammed." Villagers allegedly offered gifts to the hoca in return for showing the hair to villagers.[46] This story and others were alarming to Party officials who saw local manifestations of Islam as both backward and out of their control. Perhaps because of such anxieties, the Party continued to work with official Muslim elites throughout the Communist period who were a welcome alternative to unofficial Muslim leaders that proliferated in the Muslim provinces. According to one local Party official, there were 1,860 "official" hocas in Bulgaria, but an army of thousands of "unofficial" hocas were roaming the country, interfering daily in Party programs."[47] Still the Party never stopped its official war on Islam, carried out, in part, through public lectures with clearly anti-Islamic messages such as, "Islam: the obstruction to the building of socialism in our country."[48]

In the decades that followed, the perceived Muslim threat had an increased gravity as the Cultural Revolution faltered and international developments presaged a new era of Turkish and Islamic potency. Beginning in the 1960s and peaking with the 1975 partition, the Cyprus affair raised a red flag about presumed Turkish support of irredentist ambitions. Fears that the "Turkish nationals want a Cypriot variation in our country" brought a further acceleration in "integrationist" policy.[49] With Cyprus in mind, Bulgarian Communist officials feared that local Turks would also want territorial autonomy under Turkish tutelage.[50] By the late 1960s, reports from the Muslim provinces began to note the "rise of unhealthy phenomena" and the proliferation of illegal organizations, which had a new and reportedly pervasive sway among "influential" Muslims in Bulgaria, including Party members.[51] Party discussions abounded with fears not only of "reactionary Turkish nationalism," but after the 1979 Iranian revolution, "Islamic fundamentalism." The fact that the Yugoslav Communists incarcerated numerous supposed "Islamic fundamentalists" was not lost on the Bulgarian establishment. By the 1980s Islamic fundamentalism became the new bogeyman in Communist nightmares.

BCP perceptions of Turkish elites as potential threats to both national security and Bulgarian national development continued and deepened in this period. As early as 1958, a delegate at a Party plenum counseled that reactionary spies among the Turkish intelligentsia in the provinces are like a "Trojan horse" in our socialist motherland.[52] Along these lines, Party members began to question the wisdom of drawing Turkish cadres into the ranks of the Communist elite, "We are investing a lot of resources into the educa-

[46] TsIDA (F-1B, O-5, E-353, L-358: 1958).
[47] TsIDA (F-1B, O-5, E-353, L-356: 1958).
[48] TsIDA (F-28, O-16, E-49, L-103: 1960).
[49] Stoian Mikhailov, *Vŭzrozhdenskiat Protses v Bŭlgariia* (Sofia, 1992), 93.
[50] TsIDA (F-1B, O-509, E-5, L-131: 1962).
[51] TsIDA (F-1B, O-6, E-5371, L-148: 1968).
[52] TsIDA (F-1B, O-5, E-353, L-383: 1958).

tion of the Turkish population for the creation of an intelligentsia among them, but whom will they serve: the Peoples Republic of Bulgaria or reactionary Turkey? . . . Many with higher educations who became teachers are painfully nationalistic, part of the 'fifth column of Ankara.' "[53] The creation of a Turkish intelligentsia via the Turkish education system was increasingly viewed as a liability. As Pencho Kubadinski, a top-ranking Communist official expressed, "Our biggest mistake is that during the past few years we created a Turkish intelligentsia, which became the carrier of Turkish nationalism among the Turkish population."[54] As a result of the perceived failure of Turkish schools in planting a healthy socialist consciousness in Turkish children, in 1958–60 Turkish and Bulgarian elementary schools were merged as part of a "decisive stage" in the integration of Turks into Bulgarian society.[55] By 1959 Turkish-language pages in regional papers, such as *Savaş* (War) in Shumen, had been eliminated.[56] In 1960–61 Turkish high schools were closed or transformed into Bulgarian schools as part of a set of "school reforms" that aimed at ensuring that Turks could go on to a higher education "without a disadvantage."[57] Although Turks were part of a general plan of "socialist" but not ethnonational integration in this period, many Turks already felt that ongoing campaigns against their educational institutions, religion, dress, and other practices were tantamount to assimilation. At a Party plenum in 1962, for example, a delegate from northeast Bulgaria reported that local Turks had pointedly asked, "Why are you making Bulgarians out of us?" But such complaints were hardly a deterrent. By 1974–75 all Turkish schools had been closed and most Turkish language newspapers and journals had been terminated or were issued only or mostly in Bulgarian.[58] Significantly, the Turkish language in this period did not come under direct assault, as had other Muslim everyday practices. Instead, the institutions that supported it were merely Bulgarianized or phased out once sufficient Turks were conversant in Bulgarian. Bilingualism flourished, perhaps more than ever, but without educational support it was hoped that the Turkish language would eventually die out.

Far from dying out, the Turkish language persisted as did other vestiges of the Ottoman past, a state of affairs made more menacing by the rising demographic imbalance. In the postwar period, a large percentage of the Bulgarian population had flocked to Sofia and other urban areas, with an attendant dramatic decrease in birth rates. Muslims, in contrast, remained primarily rural in this period and so their birth rates stayed high.[59] As Pomak, and es-

---

[53] TsIDA (F-1B, O-5, E-353, L-353–5: 1958).
[54] TsIDA (F-1B, O-6, E-6952, L-65: 1967).
[55] TsIDA (F-28, O-16, E-49, L-12: 1959).
[56] Valeri Stoianov, 130.
[57] TsIDA (F-28, O-16, E-49, L-141: 1960).
[58] Kemal Karpat, "Introduction: Bulgaria's Methods of Nation Building—the Annihilation of Minorities," *International Journal of Turkish Studies* 4 (1989): 7.
[59] Turks still comprised only 9 percent of the population according to the 1965 census, but they were 10.4 percent of the "new" population and therefore were seen as a looming threat. In

pecially Turkish, population growth began to far outstrip the scant Bulgarian population increase in the 1960s and 1970s, it provoked new national concerns about the Muslim minority presence. As a result emigration was again considered as part of a potential solution to the growing Turkish problem. After various official visits to Turkey, an agreement was signed in 1968, which allowed emigration of Turks whose family members had departed in 1950–51. By 1977, 53,392 had taken advantage of the new policy, although many more waited for permission. Significantly, only months after the agreement the Bulgarian Politburo announced a decision about the "acceleration of the natural process of overcoming ethnic differentiation."[60] Clearly, the lack of a prolific rural Bulgarian population and the presence of a demographically vital Muslim one made the need for a socialist merging of nations ever more critical. If the Bulgarian peasant, elevated to progressive symbol of the nation in both the prewar and postwar periods, was to become extinct, wasn't the best course of action to uncover and enforce the Bulgarian essence of the Muslim peasant?

Even more so than in the past, *bit* was central to the discussion and implementation of the socialist and ultimately Bulgaro-Muslim ethnonational merger. Ethnographic writings from this period are riddled with vague discussions about *bit* and its role in "socialist progress."[61] Khristo Gandev and other ethnographers wrote theoretical articles about the primacy of questions concerning everyday life and culture and the role of ethnography in studying and directing the life and culture of the national masses. Although Gandev is vague about what exactly he has in mind, he does assert that the primary task at hand is the elimination of negative "vestiges of the past."[62] As in the past ethnographers were employed in recording and sorting progressive-Bulgarian and backward-Muslim cultural artifacts and practices in the provinces. In fact, by the mid-1970s, the BCP had created a special commission in the Bulgarian Academy of Sciences whose primary task was to study "ethnic differentiation" among the Muslim population and to untangle the native from the foreign in the Bulgarian provinces.[63] While virtually all aspects of Turco-Arabic Muslim culture were considered undesirable vestiges of the Ottoman past, ethnographers were trying desperately to record and preserve progressive Bulgarian folk culture, endangered by the rapid urbanization of Bulgarian populations. At the same time, ethnographers, along with historians and other academicians, were increasingly obligated to supply "scientific proof"

addition, a 1972 prognosis for demographic growth put Turks above 10 percent of the population by the year 2000. Valeri Stoianov, *Turskoto,* 139, 147.

[60] Ibid., 141.

[61] In the literature on the Soviet Union, many scholars have recognized the critical role of *bit* in the socialist transformation. See, for example, Buchli, *Archeology of Socialism,* 23, and Fitzpatrick, *Everyday Stalinism,* 11.

[62] Khristo Gandev, "Za Sŭvremena Marksistko-Leninska Metodologiia i Problematika na Bŭlgarskata Etnografiia," *Izvestiia na Etnografskiia Institut i Muzeĭ* 8 (1965): 26.

[63] Eminov, *Turkish and Other Muslim Minorities,* 105.

about the Bulgarianness of large portions and eventually all of the Muslim population.

The idea of blood-based sameness of Bulgarians and Muslims increasingly seeped into the discourse and political action of the Zhivkov regime. As academics set out to "uncover" the essential Bulgarianness of Muslims in this period, political operatives began to enforce it on the ground. Although Turkish "ethnic" difference was officially recognized until 1984, in this period, Party rhetoric about "unification" or "merging" was slowly infiltrated by formulations about Bulgaro-Turkish blood-based sameness and secret calls for "assimilation," generally a taboo term in Communist parlance. Communist functionaries had long alluded to Turks and Bulgarians as, "people belonging to one and the same nation, to one homeland . . . with the same Communist ideals."[64] By the 1970s, however, Party discussions, although still no official pronouncements, made it clear that at least a portion of Party higher-ups considered Turks to be ethnically Bulgarian. By 1970, discussions in the Central Committee of the Politburo on national integration, for example, hold such assertions as, "according to certain historical documents, in Bulgaria there has remained primarily Turks who are of Bulgarian decent . . . it is a delicate question, but historical truth is on our side."[65] In general, academic writings in this period increasingly supported the idea that a significant portion of the Turkish population was actually Bulgarian—more specifically, were descendants of Janissaries or mixed marriages that resulted from Ottoman soldiers and officials who intermarried with Bulgarian women.[66] Slowly a "scientific" case was built for national integration that was advanced in increasingly bold statements, "Whether we call it unification or assimilation, this population [Turks] should become part of the Bulgarian nation."[67]

In the same period the BCP attempted to finalize the Pomak-Bulgarian merger. Since 1945, the Party had duly recognized that under Ottoman rule the Pomaks had lost their "national background" and lamented that now in their closed conservative world, "they think they are Turks."[68] Since the beginning of the period, the Party had high hopes for the social and cultural integration of Pomaks because of the "special care" they had extended for the economic and cultural "uplifting" of their Rhodope districts. Since the beginning of the Cultural Revolution, Bulgarian Communist cadres had canvassed villages spreading atheism, patriotism, and socialist consciousness to Pomak households.[69] They too had been subject to collectivization and campaigns to modernize apparel and household material culture. Still, the Party continu-

---

[64] TsIDA (F-1B, O-5, E-420, L-22: 1960).

[65] TsIDA (F-417, O-4, E-58, L-74: 1970).

[66] Valeri Stoianov, *Turskoto*, 135.

[67] TsIDA (F-1B, O-6, E-6952, L-63: 1967). Eminov also notes that according to the prominent academician Nikolai Todorov, discussions of assimilation of Turks began as early as the 1960s. Eminov, *Turkish and Other Muslim Minorities*, 85.

[68] TsIDA (F-146, O-5, E-605, L-1: 1945).

[69] HODA (F-675, O-1, E-113, L-5: 1958).

ally noted Pomak affinity for Turkishness and Islam and by the 1960s began an intensified drive to popularize the "truth" about the "origins and cultural characteristics of Bulgaro-Mohammedans." Academics such as Nikolai Branchev extolled the "essence" of Pomaks, which he concluded was "more Slavic than Bulgarian Christians." He called them the "truest offspring of their homeland," attributing this to their historical antipathy towards migration and urbanization, the very things that have stripped Bulgarians of many age-old traditions.[70] With this in mind, the persistence of vestiges of the Ottoman past among Pomaks—the embodiment of Turco-Bulgarian hybridity and the quintessential national prodigal sons—was veritable salt in the wound of Bulgarian backwardness. For the Bulgarian Communists the elimination of these vestiges was an important hurdle in the race toward a "bright future."

By the 1960s and 1970s Pomak names took center stage. Work continued on elimination of other remnants of the Ottoman past, including the "veil" and *shalvari* of Pomak women. But the Party began to target Turco-Arabic names as one of the most formidable obstacles to socialist progress and national integration. Could Pomaks be truly Bulgarian if they carried Muslim names? By the 1960s the Party began to mull over this question and a series of "voluntary" name-changing campaigns were slowly introduced in Pomak districts, targeting Pomak Party members and school children, the presumed vanguards of revolutionary change. By 1964 a list of "acceptable" Bulgarian names had been prepared by the Bulgarian Academy of Sciences and distributed to local teachers and others in positions of authority.[71] In the Pomak districts of the Blagoevgrad prefecture in southwest Bulgaria, unlike elsewhere, these efforts were implemented with force.[72] In these districts many Pomaks took to the hills and large-scale, often violent protests erupted, most notably in the village of Ribnovo. The extent of the resistance took local and national officials by surprise, igniting fear and alarm in Party circles. As a result, the forced name-changes were temporarily reversed and the issue was shelved until 1970 when it, again, emerged on the Party agenda. From 1970–74 the Party carried out mostly forced name-changes among all of the Pomaks in the country.[73] Again, the measures met with resistance on an immense scale, but this time no reversals occurred. All official documents, gravestones, and other places where Pomaks' birth names were present were now destroyed or altered. No stone was left unturned in what was meant to be the final stage in the absorption of Pomaks into the Bulgarian national body.

By the 1960s and 1970s, the Bulgarian Communist Party had fully em-

[70] Nikolai Branchev, *Bŭlgari-Mokhamedani (Pomatsi): Zemepisnite Predeli* (Sofia, 1948), 24–25.
[71] Valeri Stoianov, *Turskoto*, 135.
[72] For an eyewitness account of these events by a Bulgarian Communist official see Petŭr Diulgerov, *Razpnati Dushi: Moiata Istinata Vŭzroditelniia Protses Sred Bulgaro-Mokhamedani* (Sofia, 1996).
[73] Gulbrand Alhaug and Yulian Konstantinov, *Names, Ethnicity and Politics: Islamic Names in Bulgaria 1912–1992* (Oslo, 1995), 31.

braced and even surpassed the methods and formulations of pre-Communist Bulgarian nationalists in its approach to the Muslim minority question. Since the rise of Zhivkov to power and the articulation of the "April Line," the Party pursued an aggressive approach to national integration. The total collectivization of agriculture and the cultural revolution that accompanied it focused on the material base which theoretically determined the superstructure of Muslim consciousness. Every material thing that Muslims touched, wore, ate from, and slept on—as well as the names that labeled and defined them—had to embody socialist advancement in order for progress to permeate their consciousness. Increasingly, modernity, Europeanness, and socialist progress became synonymous with Bulgarianness. In this way, what one recent Bulgarian analyst has dubbed the "Path to 1984" was laid brick by brick.[74]

There Are No Turks in Bulgaria

As it turns out, the Pomak Rebirth Process foreshadowed projects that endeavored to finally and totally eliminate the Turkish presence on Bulgarian soil. In a move both bold and unprecedented across the Bloc, the Party attempted to decisively finalize a complete Bulgarian-Turkish ethnonational merger in 1984–85. Earlier efforts to socially or materially integrate Muslims into Bulgarian national life had met with only partial success; Turco-Muslim material culture had persisted, resurfaced or, at times, been reinvented under the new Communist conditions. With Pomaks theoretically assimilated by the 1970s only Turks continued to sully Bulgaria's European self-image, as a living reminder of the Ottoman past and an embodiment of Turco-Bulgarian hybridity. Using various scientific discoveries of the period as rationale, the total assimilation of Turks became official BCP policy with the announcement of the second so-called *vŭzroditelen protses* (Rebirth or Revival Process) in 1984. With this announcement, Turks, as with Pomaks before them, were officially stripped of their "Turkish origins" and redefined as Bulgarians who had been forcibly "Islamicized and Turkified" under the "Ottoman yoke."[75] Like Pomaks, Turks were considered an indelible part of the Bulgarian nation that had been cut off for centuries by Ottoman assimilation practices, later compounded by bourgeois "mistakes" and Turkish nationalist propaganda. Only historical truths could reunite the deluded Turks with their Bulgarian brethren, as socialist (class-based) and nationalist (blood-based) sameness fused in official discourse. Cultural vestiges of the Ottoman past were defined as false and ephemeral, whereas Bulgaro-Muslim ethnic sameness was defined as permanent and essential. All remaining material ves-

[74] See K. Kunchev, "The Path to 1984," *Prava i Svobodi*, February 25–March 3, 1991, 8.

[75] Kemal Karpat, "Introduction: Bulgaria's Methods of Nation Building and the Turkish Minority," in *The Turks of Bulgaria: The History, Culture, and Political Fate of a Minority*, ed. K. Karpat (Istanbul, 1990), 5.

tiges came under fire, but, as in the Pomaks' case, the cornerstone of the Rebirth Process was the forcible change of Turkish names into Bulgarian ones.[76] Todor Zhivkov's famous statement of 1985—after the completion of the name-changes—was the last official word on the Turkish question; "There are no Turks in Bulgaria."[77]

Government campaigns against Turkish names and virtually all manifestations of Turkishness began in southeastern Bulgaria in the winter of 1984 and moved to Turkish enclaves in the northeast by the following spring. In the interim, northeastern Turks were told that such campaigns would only affect the southern Turks because the Turks in the north were the only "true Turks" in Bulgaria.[78] Within months, though, they too had their villages surrounded by tanks and police with roads out of villages blocked and phone lines cut off. In many cases, Turks were then assembled in the town square to hear speeches about their true Bulgarian origins and then forced, sometimes literally at gunpoint, to "volunteer" to change their Turco-Arabic names to Bulgarian ones.[79] In other cases Party officials went door-to-door, confiscating old passports and documents with Turco-Arabic names, providing a list of appropriate Bulgarian names to choose from and new passports. In larger cities, name-changes took place in the work place or in government offices, where Turks went to collect pay or pension checks. Basically, without taking on Bulgarian names, Turks were noncitizens in Bulgaria. Old documents with Turco-Arabic names on them were destroyed as were scores of graveyards, large numbers of Turkish books and other artifacts.[80] The use of the Turkish language in public became a punishable offense and state-sponsored newspapers were no longer published in Turkish or featured Turkish-language columns. Distinctive Turkish clothing was often confiscated and destroyed, and wearing such garments—especially the veil and *shalvari* for Turkish women—in public was expressly outlawed.[81]

Islam itself, unlike other "vestiges of the past," was never actually outlawed (as it was in Albania in 1967, for example). After the process was completed in 1985 all "former" Turks, as Pomaks, were henceforth referred to as "Bulgarian Muslims." More commonly, however, Turks—when there was a need to report on their progress—were referred to as "reborn Bulgarians," "Islamicized Bulgarians" or "citizens with restored names."[82] Admittedly, many mosques were closed during the Rebirth Process but the Party also utilized the Muslim establishment in carrying out the assimilation decrees. Muslim functionaries who obliged, were granted pay raises and other incentives prompting widespread cooperation in propagating and enforcing the tenets

[76] For complete discussion see Karpat, "Bulgaria's Methods," and Ali Eminov, "There Are No Turks in Bulgaria," *International Journal of Turkish Studies* 4 (1989): 203–22.
[77] Eminov, "There are No Turks," 217.
[78] Eminov, *Turkish and Other Muslim Minorities*, 86.
[79] Poulton, *Balkans*, 132.
[80] Eminov, *Turkish and Other Muslim Minorities*, 89.
[81] Valeri Stoianov, *Turskoto*, 180.
[82] TsIDA (F-1B, O-63, E-9, L-3: 1988).

of the Rebirth Process and the continued praise of "religious freedom" in Bulgaria for international consumption.[83] The Head Mufti at the time, Nedim Gendev—later called the "Red Mufti" by critics—was intimately involved in carrying out the name-changes on the local level.[84]

A portion of the secular Turkish elite was also complicit in the Rebirth Process. Shukri Takhirov, for example, who enthusiastically changed his name to the Bulgarian "Orlin Zagorov" had been actively writing about the need for Turks to integrate into the socialist nation and shed the vestiges of the past since the early 1980s.[85] He and others, out of enthusiasm, fear, or opportunism came forward and voluntarily changed their names and embraced a Bulgarian national identity. Not only did they embrace Bulgarianness, they led the charge in implementing forced assimilation of other Turks.

But Turks also resisted the Rebirth Process on a massive scale. While the Rebirth Process was being carried out violent clashes erupted throughout the country.[86] Crowds gathered, town halls were stormed and, in one case in the village of Yablonovo in northern Bulgaria, a three-day siege was necessary to bring the town under government control. Demonstrations were widespread and scores were killed, with estimates ranging from the hundreds to thousands, and thousands were arrested and interned.[87] As in the past, many Turks also resisted by fleeing to the mountains or over Bulgaria's borders during the onslaught and in the years that followed.[88] As with collaboration, the extent of Turkish resistance and other kinds of Turkish agency has been mostly overlooked, especially in broader studies of resistance and collaboration in the Bloc. And though Turkish agency was clearly possible and present in many forms, it still inevitably raises questions. In cases of rather overt resistance, the intent of Turkish actors is quite clear. But the questions of collaboration and more mundane forms of nonconformity are inevitably murkier. In fact, very few Turks fell into the neat categories of active resisters or collaborators and even those who did most certainly vacillated from year to year, day to day, and perhaps even hour to hour. Most were somewhere in-between.

The Rebirth Process inevitably provokes many other questions, such as "why did the BCP stage such a bold maneuver and why at precisely this time?" Virtually all sources agree that there was a definite element of surprise in the seemingly sudden announcement of the name-changing and other related policies in the winter of 1984.[89] Even at the highest levels, in spite of all foreshadowing, the Rebirth Process was beyond imagination and expectation (both inside and outside Bulgaria) in 1984. In hindsight the timing and scope

---

[83] Poulton, *Balkans*, 133.
[84] *Prava i Svobodi*, August 9, 1991, 3.
[85] Valeri Stoianov, *Turskoto*, 147.
[86] See Valeri Stoianov, *Turskoto*, 164, and Poulton, *Balkans*, 139 for details.
[87] Eminov, *Turkish and Other Muslim Minorities*, 90.
[88] *Prava i Svobodi*, March 11–17, 1991, 3. See also Valeri Stoianov, 197.
[89] Valeri Stoianov, *Turskoto*, 161.

of the undertaking have ample explanation. The Cyprus affair and the international rise of Islamic fundamentalism had provoked fears of Turkish or Muslim fundamentalist threat since the 1970s and early 1980s.[90] Assumptions about continued Turkish and Pomak affinities to Turkey and Islam—presumed threats to Communist progress and national security—made the larger goal of integration even more urgent. These fears were exacerbated by developments in neighboring Socialist Yugoslavia, including rising the Kosovar riots of 1981 and rising Muslim/non-Muslim tensions. Throughout the 1970s and 1980s illegal Turco-Islamic organizations increased within Bulgaria's borders. And although the frequent BCP labeling of such Balkan Muslim groups as "fundamentalist" or "terrorist" was certainly erroneous, several bombing incidents in public places—for example, in the train stations of Plovdiv and Varna in August of 1984—occurred just prior to the implementation of the Rebirth Process.[91]

Most scholars also agree that demographics was a critical factor.[92] Although, as Eminov points out, birthrates for Turks had also slowed in this period, the fact remains that for the primarily rural Turks and Pomaks, birthrates were dramatically higher than for Bulgarians.[93] Formerly Bulgarian villages tended to be inhabited only by the elderly, whereas in Turkish and Pomak villages there was an abundance of children. In the cramped living quarters of Bulgarian cities, most young couples were having only one or, at most, two children. By the late Communist period, the population in Turkish districts was growing two times faster than in Bulgarian areas. Many speculate that the 1975 census, which was never published, held sobering statistics about the imbalance in Bulgarian and Muslim population growth.[94] Emigration, while used in the past to keep the Turkish percentage of the population low, was not put forward as a viable option in 1984, probably because of valid fears of labor drain and economic ruin, especially as Turks were concentrated in the critical agricultural regions of the northeast and south.[95] Instead of expelling these populations, the problem of their presence was to be solved via their total incorporation. As the viable and fertile Bulgarian peasant had become an endangered species, the Bulgarianization of the Muslim peasant reincarnated the genus and solved the demographic problem in one fell swoop.

At its very core the Rebirth Process followed the logic of many decades of pre-Communist and Communist formulations about the Bulgaro-Muslim relationship and Bulgarian national development itself. In fact, in many of the writings and pronouncements about the "rebirth" (also translated as revival) process it is seen as akin to and an extension of the Bulgarian national "re-

[90] Eminov, *Turkish and Other Muslim Minorities*, 96.
[91] Valeri Stoianov, 164.
[92] Ibid., 153.
[93] Eminov, *Turkish and Other Muslim Minorities*, 95.
[94] Ibid., 96.
[95] Ibid., 95.

vival" of the nineteenth century. The core assumption of the Rebirth Process was, after all, that Turks really were Bulgarians, who had not experienced the Bulgarian national revival. As explained in a Politburo discussion, "There isn't and never was a Turkish minority in Bulgaria. . . . It is well known that Bulgaria was under Ottoman slavery for five centuries. The struggle for national survival was brutal and bloody. Hundreds and thousands of Bulgarians were brutally Islamicized and Turkified. But in the memory of this generation, the forcible denationalization did not erase the Bulgarian national origin and character of the majority of the local population."[96] These "Bulgarian Muslims," in the official view, did not participate in the Bulgarian national revival process because it was so closely tied to the Orthodox Christian Church.[97] Following the BCP logic, Bulgarian bourgeois governments, in their assumption that all Muslims in Bulgaria were Turkish, had only solidified the differences between Bulgarian and Turk. Since the 1944 "revolution" the Communist regime had been working to eliminate the falsely imposed differences between Bulgarian and Muslim and hence rectify historical injustices perpetrated by both the Ottoman and Bulgarian bourgeois governments. Pomaks had been privy to the "benefits" of national revival since the 1930s, under the now "re-habilitated" *Rodina* movement and even more so after 1944. Now this process was very belatedly extended to Turks. According to BCP formulations, all those "Bulgarian Muslims" who were actually Turkish had left either in 1877–78, 1912–13 or in the 1950–51 or 1968–78 waves of emigration. All those who remained were "true" Bulgarians who would voluntarily "restore" their Bulgarian names and accept the truth about history and their origins.[98]

It is telling that such a radical Communist program was initiated at the tail end of a period of Soviet political instability and just as the young Mikhail Gorbachev came to power. Some scholars speculate that the Soviet Union actually ordered the policy to be carried out as a testing ground for finding answers to their own Muslim question.[99] But such a proposition seems unlikely given the weakness of the Kremlin at the time, the reformist direction of Soviet policy in the years that followed, and the utter impossibility of such a scenario ever working in the Soviet case.[100] In fact, considerable tension between the Soviets and Bulgarians resulted over the launching of the radical program and its repercussions for Soviet foreign policy in the late 1980s. At a time when Gorbachev sought rapprochement with the West, the assimilation drive aggravated Cold War tensions as Turkey and its U.S. patron condemned Bulgaria's flagrant human rights abuses. Perhaps as a token ideological gesture, BCP leaders actually claimed that the Rebirth Process

[96] TsIDA (F-1B, O-63, E-4, L-1: 1988).
[97] Asenov, *Vŭzroditelniiat Protses*, 8.
[98] TsIDA (F-1B, O-63, E-4, L-1: 1988).
[99] See Alexander Bennigsen and Chantal Lemercier-Quelquejay, *Islam in the Soviet Union* (New York, 1967).
[100] Valeri Stoianov, *Turskoto*, 158.

contributed to Gorbachev-inspired reform in the Bulgarian context, "In the situation of deep and comprehensive revolutionary *perestroĭstvo* [the Bulgarian equivalent of Soviet *perestroika*] in Bulgaria, of the democratization of our society . . . the further strengthening of the unity of the Bulgarian Socialist Nation is one of the primary factors in the transformation of Bulgaria into a highly developed and cultural country."[101] But the Rebirth Process clearly went against the substance and intent of Gorbachev's turn in domestic and foreign policy. All existing sources agree that the responsibility for the decision seems to be limited to a few top people in the BCP establishment; no Party in Bulgaria has pointed the finger of blame in the Soviet direction since the fall of Communism in 1989 and no smoking gun has emerged. Although the Soviet Union had pursued its own version of "merging of nations," Soviet Muslims actually had more, not less, autonomy in the late Communist period and by 1986 there was an explosion of new mosques being built in the Muslim republics.[102]

In Bulgaria the Rebirth Process and its repercussions, including Turkish (and Bulgarian) responses to it, extended throughout the 1980s. Party officials carried out the administrative end of the name-changes in a relatively short time, but attempts to implement prohibitions on the use of the Turkish language, Turco-Arabic names, dress, circumcision, Muslim burial, and other rites continued until 1989. BCP attempts to police everyday culture were countered by the persistence of these practices on the local level. It is clear that many kinds of negotiations of power became part of daily survival in post-1985 Bulgaria. As reported in discussions in the Bulgarian Politburo, many Turks frequently still spoke Turkish (some didn't even know Bulgarian), used their birth names, and wore Turkic clothing both at home and in public places.[103] This everyday resistance was neither consistent nor systematic but intermittent and haphazard, interspersed with periods of passive cooperation and occasional active collusion. Turks might resist in the morning and cooperate in the afternoon. It was all in the name of survival in two senses—individual survival within an authoritarian system, and collective—ethnic survival. By the end of the 1980s, Turkish objections to the imposition of "rebirth" conditions began to mount. A number of Turks interned in the infamous Belene Prison launched prolonged hunger strikes in 1987.[104] By May of 1989, public demonstrations that began in the Turkish districts of northeast Bulgaria and spread throughout the country were brutally repressed and many Turkish leaders were expelled. Clearly, the Rebirth Process had not been even remotely successful. Within months this was made abundantly clear.

One week after the May demonstrations had flared and been crushed

---

[101] TsIDA (F-1B, O-63, E-84, L-1: March, 1989).
[102] Mark Saroyan, *Minorities, Mullahs, and Modernity: Reshaping Community in the Former Soviet Union* (Berkeley, 1997), 91.
[103] TsIDA (F-1B, O-63, E-9, L-3: 1988).
[104] Poulton, *Balkans*, 139.

Todor Zhivkov made his famous announcement that was broadcast and distributed on Bulgarian TV, radio, and in the press. He called for all "Bulgarian Muslims" who thought they were of Turkish origin and wanted to "visit" Turkey to apply for exit visas and leave the country as soon as possible.[105] The implications of the announcement were clear. The BCP now wanted to free the country of Muslim undesirables. In fact the announcement came directly on the heels of a Politburo decision for the "further unification of the Bulgarian Socialist nation." In reference to the announcement, which was tantamount to a call for emigration, Zhivkov was reported to have said, "We've got to get rid of at least 200,000 Muslims or else in several years Bulgaria will be another Cyprus."[106] This last act of the Zhivkov-led BCP was indicative of one side of the dual message of integration and expulsion that had colored Bulgaro-Turkish relations throughout the Communist period. Bulgarian propaganda, which had spent the last decade convincing its citizens of the "Bulgarianness" of local Turks, had suddenly launched a massive campaign, asserting that Turks "are infidel to the Bulgarian state and should leave forever."[107] Significantly, hundreds of Pomaks had also applied for visas to travel to Turkey, since they too were officially defined as "Bulgarian Muslims." They were denied visas, however, with the vague explanation that they were "another category of people."[108] As a result of the mass distribution of tourist visas to Turks the biggest mass exodus in Europe since World War II ensued: from June to August 1989, 350,000 Turks crossed the border into Turkey.[109] In many ways this mass exodus was reminiscent of the 1950–51 emigration: hurried, unorganized, and destructive both for the Turkish community and the Bulgarian economy. Almost one half of Bulgaria's 900,000 Turks left the country within a few months, in what euphemistically became known as the "Grand Excursion."

The "excursion" was a major contributing factor to the fall of Communism in Bulgaria on November 10, 1989. There are certainly many others, some totally unrelated to the Muslim issue, such as the fall of Communism elsewhere in Eastern Europe, the stimulus of Gorbachev's reform program, the challenge of the West, and the erosion of legitimacy across the Bloc. But in the Bulgarian case the Turkish question loomed large among factors contributing to the collapse. The excursion itself had caused severe economic dislocation in Bulgaria. Because Turks were concentrated in the important agricultural sector—wheat in the north and tobacco in the south—their mass exodus caused panic as Bulgarians were called from the cities to do their patriotic duty and help in the late summer and fall harvest.

More importantly the exodus of Turks was indicative of their general lack

[105] Eminov, *Turkish and Other Muslim Minorities,* 97.

[106] Valeri Stoianov, *Turskoto,* 204.

[107] Darina Vasileva, "Bulgarian Turkish Emigration and Return," *International Migration Review* 26 (1992): 349.

[108] Eminov, *Turkish and Other Muslim Minorities,* 106.

[109] Ibid., 97.

of support for BCP's integrative measures that had played a role in eroding the façade of BCP legitimacy. Furthermore, the radical nature of the Rebirth Process had been distasteful not only to Turks, but many Bulgarians, who began to question or more openly question the legitimacy of their regime. In 1988–89 Bulgarian intellectuals began to organize in open dissent of the Communist regime. Initially named the "Club for Support of Glasnost and Perestroika," this club called for, among other things, the reversal of the Rebirth Process and the general respect for Muslim human rights.[110] This opposition group became the core of what came to be known as the Union for Democratic Forces, which played a key role in toppling the regime. In the post-Communist period, the reversal of the Rebirth Process was one of the first items on the political agenda. By early 1990, legislation had been passed reversing both Pomak and Turkish Rebirth Processes.

Conclusion

Since the early years of Communist power, the Communist Party asserted its own power and legitimacy in the name of the nation, using nationalism selectively—even while condemning it. The BCP intertwined Communist and nationalist terms and categories—sometimes awkwardly but often quite conveniently—to bolster nationalist imperatives. Although internationalist in name, the Bulgarian Communist approach to Turks and Pomaks ultimately extended pre-Communist nationalist projects aimed at integrating the Muslim periphery. Central to this project was the nationalization of properties and the collectivization of agriculture, economic transformations that were expected to bring about a revolution in consciousness. But accompanying or following such economic changes, the BCP initiated campaigns to replace other kinds of backward everyday culture, such as Turco-Arabic clothes and names, into modern Bulgarian forms. These became centerpieces in BCP campaigns to rectify history and eliminate these markers of Bulgaro-Muslim hybridity in favor of Bulgaro-Communist sameness, and hence progress. Such projects reached their highest pitch in the 1970s and 1980s given an intensified fear of Islamic fundamentalism and imbalance between the higher birthrates of rural Muslims in relation to urban Bulgarians. According to official proclamations Pomaks had been fully integrated into the Bulgarian nation by 1975 and Turks by 1985. Both had presumably realized the truth about their own past; namely that they were truly and essentially Bulgarian.

In reality, however, the heavy-handed methods of the Communist Party and its representatives alienated most Turks and Pomaks from the Communist cause and in many cases, from Bulgarian society and soil. Numerous Turks and Pomaks resisted in various ways and faced the wrath of the Communist authorities. Such resistance was undoubtedly complicated by inter-

110 Valeri Stoianov, *Turskoto*, 204.

mittent collaboration and other myriad forms of local agency. Muslims entered the Communist Party, joined collective farms, studied in Bulgarian schools, read Communist newspapers, and a large percentage lost their Muslim religiosity and outer expressions of this identity. The Muslim masses were educated and integrated in ways unimaginable in the pre-1944 period, resulting in a large degree of real integration. In some respects sameness did triumph under the bulldozer of modernization, while in other ways difference reinvented itself and proved more resilient than assumed. The tensions and divisions that were the legacy of the Communist period still haunt Bulgarians, Turks and Pomaks since the pluralization of Bulgarian society after 1989. At the same time, the real social transformations of the period laid the groundwork for new kinds of "modern" alliances and bases for coexistence.

3 Under the Fez and the Foreskin: Modernity and the Mapping of Muslim Manhood

> Gentlemen, it was necessary to abolish the fez, which sat on the heads of our nation as an emblem of ignorance, negligence, fanaticism, and hatred of progress and civilization, to accept in its place the hat, the headgear used by the whole civilized world, and in this way to demonstrate that the Turkish nation, in its mentality and as in other respects, in no way diverges from civilized social life.
>
> —KEMAL ATATÜRK

Manhood and its accoutrements were central fixations in the process of the divination of the modern Bulgarian nation, dangling, as it were, between East and West. Although ultimately it was Bulgarian manhood and Europeanness that were at issue, Bulgarian scrutiny and confrontation of Muslim manhood were critical to this contested process. Bulgarian writings that defined the nation as modern and European invariably represented Muslim men as backward, barbaric, and relentlessly virile, a threat at once political, cultural, and demographic.[1] The notion of Muslim men as dangerous, however, was subverted by academic formulations positing the essential Bulgarianness of a portion—and eventually all—of the Muslim minority population. Were Muslim men culturally the same or different? Were they victims or perpetrators? Were they blood brothers or an enemy threat? Most disturbingly, did they

---

[1] Bracewell makes a similar argument when she links the assertion of Serbian nationalism in relation to Albanians as part of a Serbian "crisis of masculinity," caused by the "emasculation" of historical submission to Yugoslavism, and the fact that Serbia was "losing" to Albanians in the "demographic race" in Kosovo. Bracewell, "Rape in Kosovo: Masculinity and Serbian Nationalism," *Nations and Nationalism* 6 (2000), 577.

occupy a place in-between? Bulgarian writings and practices since the nineteenth century had associated the fez, turban, and the practice of circumcision—symbols of Muslim manhood—with domination, betrayal, and cultural transgression. Bulgarian anxieties about Muslim manhood and the instability of cultural and political boundaries ultimately drove twentieth-century campaigns to eliminate these markers of manhood. In essence these were efforts to both emasculate and then "re-masculate," to subordinate and then assimilate Muslim men.

A growing literature on European manhood and masculinity has elucidated the constitutive role of cultural constructs of manhood in the defining and controlling of nations, societies, and civilization.[2] Integral to much of this literature is the notion that concepts of manhood tend to evolve in opposition to the manhood of an "other." George Mosse asserts, for example, that in the process of the consolidation of European maleness, "the imagined presence of a countertype reinforced and further clarified the manly ideal."[3] Although Mosse posits Jews as the internal "other" for his "countertype," a compelling body of work has explored how European identities and manhoods were constituted and enacted in opposition to colonial others.[4] This work has clearly been inspired by, and at times represents a poignant corrective to Edward Said's *Orientalism*. In particular, the growing literature on gender and empire has revealed that gender is one of the terrains on which the clarity of dichotomous categories such as masculine/feminine and East/West have been destabilized. The gender of empire is far more complex than the traditionally ascribed "masculine ethos of empire" and consequent feminization of the penetrated "Orient."[5] When gender analysis is brought to bear, the categories of self and other, masculine and feminine, civilization and barbarity become disorderly and blurred, even as Orientalism's dichotomous categories still hold sway. European men might have feminized certain colonial men, such as the "Bengali babu," but they also had anxieties about their own "lost" masculinity, which appeared to be more vibrant in the "martial races."[6]

In theory and practice Bulgarian intellectuals and statesmen tended to ap-

---

[2] See, for example, George Mosse, *The Image of Man: The Creation of Modern Masculinity* (Oxford, 1996); Michael Roper and John Tosh, eds. *Manful Assertions: Masculinities in Britain since 1800* (London, 1991); and Gail Bedermen, *Manliness and Civilization: A Cultural History of Gender and Race in the United States, 1880–1917* (Chicago, 1995).

[3] Mosse, *Image of Man*, 77.

[4] See McClintock, *Imperial Leather;* Sinha, *Colonial Masculinity;* and Tosh, "Imperial Masculinity."

[5] Said, *Orientalism*, 6. Said has been criticized by numerous scholars for his lack of attention to gender in his overall analysis, and for his use of gender only in a metaphoric sense. For a more contextualized and complex exploration of the "masculine ethos of empire" see John Tosh, "What Should Historians Do with Masculinity? Reflections on Nineteenth Century Britain," in *Gender and History in Western Europe*, ed. Robert Shoemaker and Mary Vincent (London, 1998).

[6] See Sinha, *Colonial Masculinity*, on the Bengali babu. On "lost masculinity" see Tosh, "What Should Historians Do?" 80.

propriate European colonial discourse in conquering their Muslim provinces. Bulgarian disdain for Muslim backwardness and anxiety about Muslim virility are strikingly similar to European writings about male colonial subjects. Influenced by European writings on the "East," Muslim men were often feminized as irrational, phlegmatic, weak, and unworthy of ruling over a European Christian people. Muslim "femininity" helped explain their presumed essential inferiority, but it seemed to contradict the historical and contemporary reality of Muslim political and demographic vitality? With this in mind, the masculinized Islamic iconography present in popular European literary and newspaper depictions of lascivious Ottoman Muslim men raping the Balkan Christian women were even more influential. Hence Todorova's argument that the Ottomans were feminized by Western Europeans whereas the Balkans were masculinized, does not fully epitomize the mutable barrage of gendered European images of both the Ottomans and Balkans.[7] In Bulgarian writings, Muslims more often than not represented a barbarically *male* Muslim threat to Bulgarian national survival. The magnitude of this Muslim maleness provided a ready explanation for Bulgarian political impotence in the face of an imputed cultural inferior.

It also elucidated the relative demographic weakness of Bulgarians on the European continent. In defining the difference and sameness of Muslim populations in relation to Bulgarians, accusations of Turco-Muslim sexual assault and virility were central. Muslim rape of Bulgarian women is a prominent theme in Bulgarian writings about nineteenth-century uprisings against the Turks, clearly mimicking depictions in contemporary European publications. Bulgarian images of Muslim men raping, abducting, and intermarrying with Bulgarian women continued to be popularized in twentieth-century literature and film. At the same time such images were "rationalized" in the "scientific" canon of Bulgarian historical, ethnographic, and other academic writings of the postliberation and especially the Communist period. Bulgarian academic works were increasingly focused on proving that Muslim men had both violated the Bulgarian national body and thinned and diluted the Bulgarian demographic presence in the historic Bulgarian lands. Bulgarian ethnographers and historians bemoaned the prevalence of Turkish-Pomak intermarriage characteristic of both the Ottoman and the post-Ottoman periods. Once Pomaks were defined as ethnically Bulgarian, intermarriage was seen as violating Bulgarian-Turkish ethnic boundaries and increasing the number of Turks at the expense of Bulgarians. In the postwar period, diminished birth rates among Bulgarian Christians and high birth rates among the Muslims of Bulgaria further sharpened trepidations about the majority-minority demographic balance.

Significantly, Muslims simultaneously engaged in the process of re-mapping their own manhood in relation to Bulgarian political power. Muslims weighed their options and opportunities as members of minority populations

---

[7] Todorova, *Imagining the Balkans*, 15.

that lived on the political, social, and geographic margins of Bulgaria and Europe. They assessed the promise and price of modernity for the Muslim community and themselves as men. By the 1930s, a growing minority of Muslims appropriated Bulgarian or other modernizing discourses. Vocal splinter groups of Turks and Pomaks enthusiastically shed the turban and the fez and bared their heads or sought the shelter of European hats in hopes of a brighter future. But most Muslims in Bulgaria, at least until after World War II, clung to their hats along with other local practices. In any event, the wearing of fez or turban, along with the practice of circumcision, were "performative" acts through which Muslim manhood was both constituted and enacted.[8] By suppressing or redirecting such practices, Bulgarians and Muslims attempted to construct, dismantle, or remodel Muslim manhood. For Muslim men, manhood could prevail only in their ability to cover or uncover their heads on their own terms.

Out from Under the Fez

In a nineteenth-century account of the famous 1876 April Uprising against Ottoman rule, the fez and the turban were central characters in a drama of lust and violence in Pangiurishte, Batak, and other towns in the central Balkan Mountains. That April a marauding band of Bulgarian revolutionaries took control, if only fleetingly, of a cluster of villages with the intent of setting up a local, and then national, revolutionary government. Zakhari Stoianov, an eyewitness, recounted the tale of local Bulgarian men joining the revolutionaries: "They rushed out to meet us bareheaded, tearing their fezzes to pieces and throwing them down in the mud."[9] According to Stoianov, Bulgarian revolutionaries threw off the hated fez (also worn by Christians in the late Ottoman period) in favor of the Bulgarian peasant *kalpak* (sheepskin hat). When *kalpaks* were unavailable they went bareheaded. As Stoianov ventured, "it just would not do to rush out into the streets rebelling against the Turks with the fez's tassel dangling on your head." Stoianov related scenes of Turkish reprisal in a montage of turbans, fezzes, and sheepskin hats, assuming that national and political loyalties were clearly conveyed by the shape of one's hat. In the chaos of the ensuing violence replete with rape and other atrocities against Bulgarians, it was the hat that identified the enemy. As Stoianov recounted, "There was a young mother kissing the handle of a bloody knife begging for the life of her infant, but the inhuman turbans . . . cut down the mothers and infants indiscriminately.[10] Similarly the fez appeared in the dramatic scene of Ottoman soldiers storming a Bulgarian

---

[8] Butler, *Gender Trouble*, 139–40.
[9] Zakhari Stoianov, "Iz 'Zapiski,'" 76.
[10] Ibid., 114.

church in which a group of villagers had barricaded themselves. In a moment of high revolutionary tragedy the Bulgarian men killed their own families and themselves when "the red fezzes and the loose Turkish trousers appeared in that holy shrine of Bulgaria's freedom."[11]

As newly idealized visions of Bulgarian manhood emerged in the nineteenth century, Muslim men were seen as the primary threat to the realization of these ideals. Bulgarian nationalist writings were rife with swagger and machismo as Bulgarian men sought to reassert their right to rule as European Christian men. The assertion of Bulgarian manhood took the form of secret revolutionary organizations, small-scale uprisings, and brigandage—a show of strength to both Ottomans and Europeans. If Europeans had any question as to the right to rule of this "non-historic" nation the Bulgarians would quell such doubt with a declaration their political manhood. Bulgarians asserted an ideal of Balkan manhood that stressed bravery, honor, and the right to self-rule. On the one hand, Bulgarian nationalist writers feminized both the Ottomans and Europeans, the former as Oriental and irrational, the latter as dandified, restrained, and cunning. On the other hand, both were depicted as barbarically male in their penetration and domination of the Balkans. Out of this complex picture of gendered understandings of East, West, and national self, Bulgarians lashed out against hybridity and sought clarity in the assertion of a purely Bulgarian manhood.

As in Western Europe, Bulgarian men were the first affected by a revolution in dress as a reflection and indicator of larger economic and social changes, and of shifting concepts of "manhood."[12] Long before women's clothing held such political meaning, Bulgarian men were aware of the cultural and political implications of dressing *ala franga* (in the manner of the French). With the influx of European fashions into the Ottoman Empire in the nineteenth century, men from the ranks of the Muslim and non-Muslim elite began to be influenced by European fashion. In spite of its popularity for some Bulgarian male elites, dressing *ala franga* also came to represent affinities for, if not selling out to, the encroaching West. The Europeanization of men's dress was viewed askance by some Bulgarian thinkers, who questioned the penetration of European influence in clothing as in other areas of Bulgarian life.[13] Petko Slaveĭkov, for example, leveled a penetrating critique at Bulgarians who had "silly pretensions . . . in words and in clothes."[14] Slaveĭkov reproached the Bulgarian middle class who imitated European ways and therefore didn't "look like the nation in their appearance. . . . The clothes of

[11] Ibid., 134.

[12] See Anne Hollander, *Sex and Suits* (New York, 1994), 45; David Kuchta, "The Making of the Self-Made Man: Class Clothing and English Masculinity, 1688–1832," in *The Sex of Things: Gender and Consumption in Historical Perspective*, ed. Victoria DeGrazia and Ellen Furlough (Berkeley, 1996), 54–79.

[13] Lamenting the erosion of national dress in favor of European dress was surely common on Europe's margins. Jedlicki describes a similar phenomenon in Poland. Jedlicki, *Suburb of Europe*, 27.

[14] Petko Slaveĭkov, *Sŭchinenie*, vol. 7 (Sofia, 1989), 201.

these people is of the latest fashion, but their lives are an imitation of European life." Imitation, according to Slaveĭkov, was tantamount to spiritual impoverishment and denial of national belonging, and hence it was traitorous to the nation. The evils of the East and West blur together in Slaveĭkov's indictment of the "*çorbacı-modnitsi*" (the fashionable *çorbacı*, or notables) and "Europeanism."[15] As in other Bulgarian nationalist writings, the focus on the people (*narod*) was infused with a critique of the Bulgarian upper classes, who were seen as exploiters by virtue of collaboration with their Ottoman overlords or the encroaching Europeans.

Along these lines, wearing of the fez by Bulgarian men was also stigmatized—at least by a vocal nationalist minority—as a symbol of ethnic loyalty and hence collaboration with the Ottoman state. The fez, far from being a time-honored Ottoman hat, had only been introduced by decree of Sultan Mahmud II in 1829. His goal was to replace the common Muslim-identified turban with a more integrative hat to be worn by Ottoman elites irrespective of religion, hence inculcating Ottomanism.[16] As in Western Europe before the French Revolution, dress in the Ottoman Empire had always been an arbiter of status and headwear in particular had been a repository of allegiance and social station.[17] The introduction of the fez provoked intense resistance on the part of Ottoman Muslims, many of whom continued to wear the turban (often under the fez) for generations. Among non-Muslims only the upper and middle classes, local administrators, merchants, and the *çorbacı*—ironically, many of the same people who began to dress *ala franga*—adopted the new Ottoman hat.[18] (see fig. 1) Since Bulgarian peasants generally did not wear the fez, it actually became synonymous with the *çorbacı* who were demonized and lampooned in Bulgarian émigré revolutionary presses. Essentially hybrid, the fez donned the head of the westernizing Turk and the politically "Turkified" Bulgarian. Though the turban also emerged as an unadulterated emblem of Ottoman barbarity, the fez in particular was indicative of what was considered the loathsome Bulgaro-Turkish and Turco-European mongrel.

After Bulgaria gained its autonomy from the Ottomans following the 1877–78 Russo-Turkish war, the fez quickly fell out of fashion for Bulgarian male elites. In this early phase of nation building, Bulgarian thinkers began to

---

[15] Ibid., 201.

[16] Donald Quataert, "Clothing Laws, State, and Society in the Ottoman Empire, 1720–1829," *International Journal of Middle Eastern Studies* 29 (1997): 403–25.

[17] For more details on the story of the fez in the Ottoman context see Quataert, "Clothing Laws"; and Patricia Baker, "The Fez in Turkey: A Symbol of Modernization?" *Costume: Journal of the Costume Society* 20 (1986): 72–86.

[18] Negative images and analyses of the *çorbacı* as "enemy to their own tribe" have tended to dominate both popular representations and academic analyses of this "class" since the nineteenth century. At the same time, some academics have recognized the positive role of some *çorbacı*s in the Bulgarian national revival. Similarly, in Ivan Vazov's famous novel *Pod Igoto* (Under the Yoke), one good *çorbacı* character, Baĭ Marko, distinguishes himself from the preponderant bad *çorbacı* (Sofia, 1956). For a recent discussion of Bulgarian historiography on the *çorbacı* see Mikhail Gruncharov, *Chorbadzhiĭstvoto i Bŭlgarskoto Obshtestvo Prez Vŭzrazhdaneto* (Sofia, 1999).

Fig. 1. A Bulgarian family in typical late Ottoman-period dress, that is, traditional with some French-style elements. Note the man's fez and the head covering of the woman on the far right similar to the Muslim veil. University of Sofia Cyril and Methodius Library, photo collection.

delve into and assimilate European clothing as part of fashioning a national identity on the ruins of an Ottoman past, now more widely understood as a five-hundred-year Ottoman yoke that held Bulgaria back from the general currents of European experience.[19] The fez was rejected as tied to the Bulgarian *çorbacı* who "donned the fez" instead of fighting for Bulgarian indepen-

---

[19] Interestingly, by the 1870s the fez began to be questioned by the Ottoman Muslim modernizing elite, who also saw the hat as outmoded and retrograde. Baker, "Fez in Turkey," 77.

dence.[20] The image of the hybrid and traitorous *çorbacı* was popularized, even while it was subtlety complicated, in Ivan Vazov's *Pod Igoto* (Under the Yoke). In this famous and widely read Bulgarian novel, the most hated characters are clearly embodiments of both Ottoman-Bulgarian and European-Bulgarian hybridity. The duplicitous villains of the book are the unsavory wearers of the fez, such as Çorbacı Iordan, and the rather clumsily dandified characters Kiriak Stefchov and (the appropriately named) Mikhaliki Alafranga, who dress in "outdated European clothes" but were "*çorbacı* in both spirit and background."[21] Vazov depicts the in-betweenness of the hated Stefchov and *çorbacı*, as is apparent in their apparel, as particularly reprehensible. But although European fashion was increasingly accepted with less ambiguity in the post-Ottoman period, the fez was another matter.

By the twentieth century the assault on Turco-Muslim maleness and specifically the visible symbols of Bulgaro-Muslim hybridity within Bulgaria's borders could proceed. Having thrown off the fez, an emblem of their own hybridity, Bulgarians looked to politically subordinate and then impose Bulgarian purity on the Pomak population, in part through the elimination of the fez and turban. After the eruption of the First Balkan War in 1912, mass forced conversions of Pomaks in the occupied territories were accompanied by the forced replacement of the fez and turban (along with the veil) with Bulgarian hats (and scarves).[22] (see fig. 2) For the first time Pomak men were forced to bare their heads and proclaim their loyalty to the Bulgarian authorities. Their political impotence at the hands of the Christian forces was literally exposed as they surrendered the fez in the midst of mass baptismal ceremonies. (see fig. 3) The change in hats was seen as integral to the re-Christianization of these populations which was carried out with much fanfare. Local Bulgarian priests who were dispatched to carry out the conversion of Pomaks in their remote districts requested that the central authorities send not only Bibles and crosses, but also hats for their missionary work. As one Orthodox priest explained, "for the newly baptized we urgently need the corresponding number of hats . . . because we can't tell who has been baptized and who hasn't."[23] These priests clearly assumed that Christianity, only in combination with so-defined Bulgarian hats, would make Bulgarians out of Pomaks. This first experiment in Pomak de-fezzing, however, was almost as short lived as Bulgarian military successes. Changes in diplomatic direction after the Second Balkan War in 1913 and the need for Pomak votes in the June 1914 elections prompted the Bulgarian government to issue a manifesto, allowing Pomaks to return to Islam and resume wearing the fez.

By the fall of 1913 local reactions to the manifesto by both Pomaks and local Bulgarians made clear the extent to which the Balkan Wars had rendered the fez an even more powerful symbol in the local imagination. Large

[20] See, for example, the polemics against the *çorbacı* in Rakovski, *Izbrani Sŭchineniia*, 67.
[21] Ivan Vazov, *Pod Igoto*, 59.
[22] Georgiev and Trifinov, *Pokrŭstvaneto*, 8.
[23] Ibid., 219.

Fig. 2. Prior to the forced conversion of Pomaks during the First Balkan War (1912), Pomak men appear in turbans while Pomak women still wear the so-called veil. PODA, 959k—photo collection.

numbers of Pomak men spontaneously donned the fez and turban in celebratory public displays after receiving word of the manifesto. Priests who witnessed these events sent numerous reports to the Holy Synod of the Bulgarian Orthodox Church in these months, expressing dismay and even fear about the "tragic" re-donning of the fez. As Father Atanas Zlatkov reported from the village of Baniia, for example, "the newly baptized Pomaks . . . yesterday demonstrated along the streets and in the cafes with fezzes and turbans, like the socialists, who celebrate the first of May."[24] Such demonstrations provoked alarm among priests who described "throngs" of Pomak men appearing brazenly on the streets and in cafes with their fezzes and turbans.[25] In several locales, incidents of public re-fezzing provoked violent reactions on the part of local Bulgarians, as one administrator reported "several provocative [Pomak] elements demonstrated by putting on the fez . . . provoking religious fanaticism among the local Christian population, which began to rip off the fezzes and as a result there were clashes."[26] In spite of these manifestations of

[24] Ibid., 443.
[25] Ibid., 405, 475,
[26] Ibid., 444, 458.

Fig. 3. Scene from the First Balkan War (1912). The Pomak who is bent over bares his head for baptism by an Orthodox Christian priest. Pomak men in the background, presumably all baptized, appear bareheaded while the still "veiled" Pomak women wait their turn. PODA, 959k—photo collection.

Bulgarian animosity for the return of the fez, it is also clear that at this juncture Pomaks were not yet universally accepted as Bulgarian. In one case a Bulgarian military officer was described as traveling from village to village, apparently enforcing the "re-Islamicization" manifesto. The Bulgarian was said to have forced fezzes onto the heads of Pomaks with the words, "You are all Turks, throw off your [Bulgarian] hats."[27]

In the confusion of war and its aftermath the line between Pomak and Bulgarian was erased and then redrawn as the Pomak fez was pulled off and then back on. After the first real state-driven attempt to erase Bulgaro-Muslim hybridity and impose sameness, difference emerged triumphant. Not only was the Bulgarian nationalist project itself contested and constrained but Pomaks made their own choices, and ultimately asserted themselves as Muslims and as men. In many ways the violence and coercion of the act of de-fezzing created tensions between Pomak and Bulgarian that would not soon be forgotten. On the other hand, in the period that followed many Muslims themselves began to throw off the fez—some in cooperation with Bulgarian

[27] Ibid., 475.

thinkers and authorities—as they looked to recast their manhood along modern, European lines.

Rodina, Kemalism, and the Fez

By the interwar period, the presence of modernizing Muslims among both Turks and Pomaks in the Bulgarian lands complicated the place of the fez on and off the Muslim head. By the late 1920s events in Turkey provoked the very limited development of Kemalism within Bulgaria. Advocates of this modernizing Turkish nationalist movement called for shedding of visible signs of Muslim backwardness, including the fez, turban, and veil. At the same time the modernizing association *Rodina* crystallized among Pomaks, who also called for the throwing off of the fez and the veil, but in favor of "Bulgarian hats and scarves." Both movements, I argue, sought to recast Muslim men as modern and European and, in a sense, to reinvigorate their manhood and nationhood. And although both represented only a minority of the Turkish and Pomak populations respectively, their divergent fates within the Bulgarian state were telling. Consistent with the growing Bulgarian compulsion to eradicate Pomak hybridity, the state supported and embraced *Rodina*'s modernizing program. In contrast, Kemalism was seen as a political threat and actively suppressed. By keeping the fez on the Turkish head while de-fezzing Pomaks, Bulgarian authorities made it clear that Muslim manhood would be recast only within closely prescribed parameters.

Though the immediate postwar years were a time of tolerance for the Turkish minority, by the 1930s various regimes began to erode the autonomy of Turco-Islamic institutions. In asserting state control, the authorities ensured that the so-called Old Turks, or conservative Islamic elements that opposed dress reform or other Kemalist ideas, would control Turco-Islamic institutions. In fact, by the 1930s the Bulgarian government actively observed and incarcerated Kemalists, whose visibility was greatly enhanced because many of them "wore hats."[28] By the 1930s the shedding of the fez became a powerful political statement, denoting both an affinity for the Turks of Turkey and readiness for social change. But the Bulgarian authorities did not want Turks to remake their manhood in a new and improved, modern, powerful, and capable image. Instead the Bulgarian state (as did the Old Turk establishment) wanted the fez to stay on the Turkish head.

Fortuitously, the bulk of the Turkish population was in agreement. Kemalism in Bulgaria was weak at best and the majority of Muslim men had no desire to shed the fez. Surprisingly, even among Kemalists the fez was not universally rejected. In Kemalist newspapers such as *Turan* and *Halk Sesi* (Voice of the People) images of fez-less men were comfortably interspersed with men

---

[28] In 1938 forty-six local Kemalist organizations had an estimated 10,000 members. TsIDA (F-370, O-6, E-422, L-5: 1938).

still wearing the fez, long after the fez had been made illegal in the Turkish Republic in 1925.[29] In contrast to Turkey, even Kemalist Turks saw the importance of the fez and turban, which differentiated Turks from the Bulgarian majority population. In his memoirs, Osman Kiliç, a Turkish teacher from Shumen, explains such attitudes about the fez and turban:

> The turban on the head of the Deliorman [northeastern Bulgarian] Turk always has played a very positive role . . . above all, as our national costume, it reminds us of our identity and our Turkishness. The idea of opposition to Atatürk's clothing revolution never even entered our minds. As a matter of fact, if a Turk obtains a passport for emigration, before doing anything else he goes and buys a hat and puts it on his head. But as we live in Bulgaria in these dreadful days [1930s], far from our motherland, where all our ties are cut and we are left as orphans, our national clothes remain our rock of salvation.[30]

As Kiliç points out, Turks were more resistant to a revolution in hats outside the context of Turkey, because the fez and turban assumed a role as visible marker of Turkishness. Significantly, the fez and turban as presumed markers of "Turkish" identity obscured the fact that these types of headgear were also worn by Pomaks. As Turkish nationalism gained a foothold in Bulgaria, this and other Islamic symbols were appropriated as "Turkish." This stands in sharp contrast to Turkey proper, where the fez, the turban, and other Islamic markers were actively attacked in this period as part and parcel of a backward past.

Ironically, although the Bulgarian state officially opposed Kemalism, the fez and the turban continued to be construed as hated symbols of the Ottoman period. They were a constant reminder of Bulgaria's past political impotency. In many cases such attitudes were acutely felt on the local level. For example, Kiliç describes an incident where he and a fellow Turk, garbed in fez and turban, encounter a Bulgarian policeman on a quiet street in Shumen. Kiliç interprets the policeman's reaction to the head coverings in the following way:

> How could he [the Bulgarian policeman] swallow the reality that two Turkish intellectuals with fezzes and turbans on their heads were walking freely in a district where he had jurisdiction? He is one of the rulers of this country and Turks are the subjugated. They [Turks] are second-class citizens. They need to kowtow to him and greet him with respect. It is his [the policeman's] national responsibility to avenge the hardships and cruelties that his ancestors had to endure in Turkish times. Bulgarians think this way . . . that the fez and the turban are a symbol of Turkishness, a symbol of Ottoman rule.[31]

[29] For a discussion of de-fezzing in Turkey, see Baker, "Fez in Turkey," 81. The fez also came under fire in Iran in this period, see Houchang Chehabi, "Staging the Emperor's New Clothes: Dress Codes and Nation-Building under Reza Shah," *Iranian Studies* 26 (1993): 209–33.
[30] Osman Kiliç, *Kader Kurbanı* (Ankara, 1989), 81.
[31] Ibid., 128–29.

Attitudes such as these made the fez and the turban into a dilemma for Bulgarian policy makers. In one case, for example, a Bulgarian police inspector from the town of Novi Pazar in the Shumen district launched his own "special mission to force Turks to take off their turbans." In line with official policy, he was reprimanded and punished for publicly beating Turks in turbans, igniting a turban on a public square, and telling Turks that such acts were ordained by the government.[32] In spite of local vigilantism, the Bulgarian government still viewed the Turk without the turban or fez as the bigger political problem. As a later source would report, "many Turks were put in prison as harmful elements toward the homeland just because they wore hats."[33]

In contrast, Bulgarian thinkers and statesmen, along with a contingency of Pomaks, began to increasingly encourage Pomak men to take off the fez in favor of a "Bulgarian" hat. The modernizing *Rodina* movement was at the center of efforts to remake the Pomak community in the Bulgarian image via a process that was deeply connected to an assault on Muslim gender practices and norms. From the beginning, one of the primary goals of *Rodina* was to mobilize Muslim women both to shed their Islamic covering garments and to enter into Bulgarian public space. They strove to accomplish this by encouraging Pomak women to attend plays, meetings, excursions, and other *Rodina* events. Pomak men who opposed such changes in Pomak women's behavior were demonized in *Rodina* writings as "reactionary Turcophiles." Bulgarianness was the purported antidote to the affliction of the Muslim patriarchy. *Sbornik Rodina*, a collection of writings published by the movement, stressed the importance of uprooting the "purely foreign borrowings in laws, traditions, customs, clothes, language, and way of life, which separates and hinders the common merging, unity, and brotherhood between Bulgaro-Mohammedans and Bulgarian Christians."[34] For *Rodina* the re-dressing of both Muslim men and women was intertwined but the change in hats for men was deemed paramount. After all, how could a man in a fez allow his wife to de-veil? In other words, a revolution in men's dress and, consequently, in consciousness was seen as integral to the process of Bulgarianization. (see fig. 4)

By 1938, *Rodina* sent out a printed appeal to Pomak districts, promoting the conviction "that they are Bulgarians by nationality and should throw off the red fez, a symbol of foreignness, which offends our Muslim religious sentiments."[35] The widely distributed appeal called for Pomak men to "immediately throw off forever the foreign hat—the fez, and replace it with a Bulgarian national hat."[36] But unlike during the Balkan Wars where de-fezzing had accompanied forced conversions, *Rodina* first attempted to inspire a volun-

[32] TsIDA (F-370, O-6, E-415, L-8: 1934).
[33] KODA (F-2K, O-1, E-4, L-9: 1944).
[34] Petŭr Marinov, ed. *Sbornik Rodina*, 2: 34.
[35] SODA (F-26K, O-1, E-2, L-6: 1939).
[36] Ibid., 18.

Fig. 4. Leaders of the *Rodina* organization with modern hats, or bareheaded, and their families. Although some women are de-veiled, others wear traditional head coverings (1938). PODA, 959k—photo collection.

tary change in hats and make the separation of religion and nationality—and hence dress practices—explicit. In writings on the subject, they explained that "religion has nothing in common with clothes and hats."[37] But the almost total failure of the appeal to achieve the desired results prompted spontaneous violent incidents of de-fezzing. In *Rodina* writings one such incident in Smolyan in 1940 is described in detail:

> On the last day of Bairam the most active members of the association *Rodina* organized and gathered around forty people and without any kind of previous plan went to the upper end of the city, a neighborhood which is completely Mohammedan in order to "pluck off fezzes." They dispersed along the streets, blocked exits and took up the task of taking all "fezzes" from their owners! The president of *Rodina*, Arif Beĭski, stood on a hillock on the edge of the neighborhood and gave orders from on high. The whole neighborhood broke into laughter, rumors, and outcries. One could hear jokes and protest.
> —Oh . . . hold on to your fez!
> —Down with the red fez![38]

[37] Marinov, ed., *Sbornik Rodina*, 2: 19.
[38] Ibid., 20.

Apparently, Pomak responses varied from laughter to horror as *Rodina* enthusiasts waited at the entrances of Pomak homes to pull off the fezzes from
Pomak men and uncover the Bulgarian beneath. But generally such efforts
were in vain and the majority of Pomaks continued to wear the fez in spite of
appeals and more active campaigns.

It wasn't until the outbreak of World War II that *Rodina* programs began
to be enforced by law and a change in hats became unavoidable. During the
war years the Bulgarian government openly supported *Rodina* programs in
Bulgaria proper and in the "newly liberated" provinces of Thrace and Macedonia. By 1941 *Rodina* members proudly boasted that when the German
troops passed through Smolyan they hadn't realized that the population was
of a different faith because of the people's "lack of Oriental clothes."[39] But
Rodina leaders also emphasized to the representatives of the regime that
"there is a significant number of Bulgarians of Mohammedan faith who are
still not touched by this movement. The men still wear fezzes and make their
women wear veils."[40] They claimed that decisive measures were needed to
"establish general order" and to make the population feel "its attachment to
the motherland"; *Rodina* proposed that it was in the nation's best interest to
finally de-fez Bulgaro-Mohammedans, replacing the Oriental garments with
Bulgarian national hats and clothes.[41]

By 1943 the Bulgarian government had passed a Law on Clothes which
legislated a ban on "foreign" clothing for so-defined "Bulgarians."[42] Because
Turks were not classified as Bulgarians the legislation did not apply to them,
rather, the authority of the conservative Old Turks was maintained and expanded to the provinces. Pomaks, in contrast, were ordered to toss away the
fez, knitted caps, and other head coverings that "look like fez."[43] As the ban
was implemented *Rodina* writings were often euphoric with the results and
their historical significance. *Rodina* founder, Petŭr Marinov, elaborated in
his diary: "The casting off of the fez was an important change in the appearance of the Bulgaro-Mohammedans. It happened as a result of the advance
preparation and agitation that had convinced people that for this moment
it—this un-Bulgarian hat—had outlived its time, and had served only in the
delusion of simple and naive Bulgaro-Mohammedans, and had lead them—
with the wearing of it—to think that they were not Bulgarians."[44] According
to Marinov, the very wearing of the fez was felt to have infected the Pomak
mind with "lies" about their own identity. Although Marinov asserts that Pomaks were ready for such a change, there is also ample discussion in *Rodina*
writings about resistance to these measures. Marinov mentions numerous
written complaints and questions from local Muslims about whether this de-

[39] Marinov, ed., *Sbornik Rodina*, 4: 11.
[40] TsIDA (F-264, O-1, E-440, L-6: 1941).
[41] TsIDA (F-264, O-1, E-440, L-6: 1941).
[42] TsIDA (F-264, O-1, E-440, L-9: 1941).
[43] SODA (F-26K, O-1, E-31, L-13: 1942).
[44] SODA (F-959K, O-1, E-110, L-66: 1958).

fezzing law came from the government or *Rodina* itself. Some opponents of the de-fezzing movement even consulted lawyers. One, for example, brought a suit against *Rodina* for having destroyed his fez. The plaintiff demanded only the cost of the fez itself, but the suit was never heard in court.[45] But perhaps the best indication of Pomak attitudes toward the de-fezzing was the rapid move to bring back the fez when the wartime regime was overthrown, as had happened after the Balkan Wars. As World War II came to a close, the Communist-controlled Fatherland Front took power and reversed the Law on Clothes; Pomaks again quickly reclaimed their fezzes and turbans.

Throughout this period, Muslim manhood was subject to dramatic expectations of change, from the Bulgarian government and from Muslim men themselves. The fez, turban, or hat were worn and changed along with shifting political loyalties and ethnonational orientations. A handful of Turks began to take off the fez, only to be discouraged by the Muslim establishment supported by the Bulgarian government. For Turks, the wearing of the fez paradoxically represented both an assertion of ethnic and religious difference and a sign of loyalty to the powers that be. Pomaks, on the other hand, displayed political and national loyalty to the Bulgarian regime by baring their heads or covering them with a "Bulgarian hat." Clearly, in this period Pomak manhood via the fez and turban was subject to the most dramatic expectations of change. In the postwar period, Turks, too, would be expected to become new men.

Taking the Snake by the Head

Under Communism the rationale for remaking Muslim manhood was magnified and deepened. The Bulgarian Communist regime sought to politically subordinate the entire population of Bulgaria, majority and minority, to an unprecedented extent. The Party attacked the Muslim patriarchy much more ardently than any preceding Bulgarian regime. The reining in of Muslim masculinity and the Muslim threat more generally, was part of the broader Communist drive for political and cultural control. The apparent aim was to rid Bulgaria once and for all of the hated signs of the Turco-Ottoman past that marked and hybridized Muslims as political and cultural traitors and half-breeds. Communist and nationalist priorities melted into a powerful alloy of rhetoric and practice that eventually sought to remake all Muslim men in a modern Bulgarian image. Bulgarian Communists demanded that Muslims shirk the signs of Muslim masculinity so that the new "socialist man" could emerge in his purely Bulgarian form.

In the course of the Communist period, Muslim manhood met with sustained and relentless attack as Muslim men and "their" women were visibly transformed. The Muslim patriarchy, always an object of some derision, was

[45] SODA (F-959K, O-1, E-110, L-67: 1958).

now denounced as the very source of backwardness and oppression that impeded the "building of socialism." In part, this was connected to the larger goal of the emancipation of women articulated by virtually all Communist governments.[46] In fact, Communist attempts to truly undermine and challenge the patriarchy were mostly abandoned in Soviet Russia by the 1930s.[47] By the time Communism spread to Eastern Europe in the 1940s, what remained was primarily lip service to a true "revolution in consciousness," although women's education and employment were still priorities.[48] Still, Islamic women in Bulgaria, as well as in the Soviet Union, were a special case since they represented the "ultimate proletariat" under the presumably more onerous Muslim patriarchy. As one Soviet source claimed, Islamic women were the "slaves of Muslim men" who could be liberated only through de-veiling and inclusion in "socialist production."[49] Discussions of the veil are almost always tied to accusations against reactionary Muslim men who "force" their wives to wear it.[50] For both the Soviets and Bulgarians, this "liberation" of Muslim women served to politically subordinate Muslim men as well as free up labor for the socialist economy and facilitate the visible modernization of their respective societies.

As in the past, the revolution in hats for men was seen by many as a prerequisite for the much more difficult problem of the veil. Although the two often went hand in hand with such slogans as "Down with the Veil and Turban!" the change of hats for men was the first priority.[51] As Ibrakhim Fakhredinov, a Turkish speaker at a 1945 conference on the Turkish question, explained: "We first and foremost concluded that we didn't need to de-veil but first to take off the turban and fez . . . with the idea that when the men changed their clothes that we would approach the issue of the veil."[52] The assumption was that a change in hats would bring about a change in consciousness and that only a man without an Oriental hat would allow his wife and daughters to de-veil. In other words, the Muslim patriarchy had to be undermined before women could enter socialist society, a major theme in Communist writings on both Muslim men and women.

[46] The reality of emancipation of women under these regimes is another, more controversial matter. See for example Lalith deSilva, "Women's Emancipation under Communism: A Re-Evaluation," *East European Quarterly* 27 (1993): 301–13.

[47] For the best analysis of the Soviet case see Wendy Goldman, *Women, the State and Revolution: Soviet Family Policy and Social Life, 1917–1936* (Cambridge, 1993).

[48] See, for example, Chris Corrin, "Introduction," in *Superwomen and the Double Burden*, ed. C. Corrin (London, 1992); and Sabrina Ramet, "In Tito's Time," in *Gender Politics in the Western Balkans: Women and Society in Yugoslavia and the Yugoslav Successor States*, ed. S. Ramet (University Park, Penn., 1999).

[49] Bibi Palvanova, *Emansipatsiia Musulmani: Opit Paskreposhcheniia Zhenshchini Sovetskogo Vostoka* (Moscow, 1982), 15. For other Soviet sources see Dilorom Alimova, *Reshenie Zhenskogo Voprosa v Uzbekistane: 1917–1941gg* (Tashkent, 1987); Zhanetta Tatybekova, *Velikii Oktiabr i Zhenshchiny Kyrgzistana* (Frunze, 1975); and Rohat Nabieva, *Zhenshchiny Tadzhikistana v Borbe za Sotsializm* (Dushanbe, 1975).

[50] HODA (F-675, O-1, E-113, L-16: 1951).

[51] TsIDA (F-28, O-16, E-49, L-226: 1959).

[52] TsIDA (F-1B, O-25, E-66, L-65: 1945).

A Communist-led transition in hats was initially postponed in light of short-term political expediency. Through the remainder of the 1940s, the Bulgarian Communists made a conscious choice to tread softly on the fez and turban issue in order to garner support among Turkish and Pomak populations who were opposed or at best indifferent to the new regime. While Bulgarian Communist officials, in contrast to the pre-1944 regimes, celebrated Kemalism and its drive to get rid of the fez as progressive, in the face of potential opposition they decided to initially leave the fez and turban on the Turkish head.[53] As one Communist official's report on work with the Turkish minority proclaimed, "we will meet with difficulty if we recklessly attack the turban."[54] In fact, the newly Communist-loyal Muslim officials were allowed, if not encouraged, to make public appearances in Muslim districts wearing the turban. In Osman Kiliç's memoirs he describes one such episode: "In the early years he [a Turkish People's Deputy] used to come and go from the Peoples Assembly in a turban. This, of course, was Communist demagoguery and deception. He acted as if he was a representative of the Turkish people. In other words, I would doubt the sincerity of a man who would wear a white turban in a Communist Assembly. I said that this was demagoguery because a Communist has to be really brave to be able to wear the turban, a symbol of Islam. . . . It's all a game, mere window dressing."[55] In response to such doubts Party representatives explained their position to Turkish Communist recruits at a national conference in the following way: "We should not take off the turban by force. That is not necessary. Let us first put something under the hats and into the heads of people and they will take off the fez themselves. There is no need to take off the turban by force."[56] The hope was that a revolution in consciousness, or a focus on the head and not the hat, would bring about the desired changes in Muslim culture.

Pomaks also enjoyed this period of toleration, with a bizarre twist. A political changing of the guard spurred an actual imposition of the fez in certain cases. Pomaks had re-donned the fez en masse at the end of the war after clothing-reform measures were summarily reversed. As Marinov related in his diary: "Everyone was incredibly astonished when the rumors began that they were going to restore the fez . . . exactly as was the wish of our opponents and which completely coincided with the Ankara Turkish politics for the preservation of the old ways and backwardness and encouragement of the Turkish outward appearance of the Rhodope Bulgaro-Mohammedan."[57] What Marinov failed to recognize was that the return of the fez was part of a BCP attempt to gain the support of the Pomak masses who still had affinities for the Islamic headgear. In addition, the BCP also brought back the fez, in some cases by force, to politically subordinate *Rodina*, which was suspect be-

53 TsIDA (F-214B, O-1, E-189, L-27: 1947).
54 TsIDA (F-1B, O-25, E-66, L-59: 1945).
55 Kiliç, 367.
56 TsIDA (F-1B, O-25, E-66, L-101: 1945).
57 PODA (F-959K, O-1, E-110, L-85: 1958).

cause of its ties to the former regime. Marinov himself described one such telling incident after the change of political power: "in a demonstration of force fezzes . . . were pulled onto the heads of *Rodina* members and in the village of Turun they put an armed guard—a Bulgaro-Mohammedan with a fez—on the arrested *Rodina* officials."[58]

In spite of the political motivation behind the initial return and even imposition of the fez, the spirit and form of most other *Rodina* campaigns would be revisited by the BCP and also applied to Turkish populations in the context of socialist progress and integration. After 1950, the pages of *Yeni Işık* bore images of the new socialist Turk, either bare-headed or in a European-style cap juxtaposed with the Turk in the turban or fez, an object of ridicule. (see figs. 5 and 6) By the late 1950s, more aggressive campaigns against the fez and turban were being carried out on the local level by Bulgarian and Muslim Communist functionaries and representatives of the Communist-loyal Muslim establishment. Communist conferences on the Muslim minority question frequently reported on the success of these efforts as an important measure of socialist success and political compliance in the provinces. The anti-fez and anti-turban measures climaxed during the 1958–60 Cultural Revolution, during which turban- and fez-wearers were coerced into discarding these accoutrements. In virtually every district with a Muslim population there was discussion of intensified attempts to "liquidate the turban and fez."[59] As a Bulgarian Party official from Shumen succinctly stated, "Socialism can not be built from behind a veil and underneath a turban."[60]

In many ways campaigns against Muslim headgear were separate from the concurrent Communist assault on Islam. In fact, the regime-loyal Muslim establishment lent its support to these campaigns by professing that there was nothing in the Koran about the necessity of the fez or turban. In practice, though, local hocas continued to wear the fez or turban in their remote villages, far from the view of Sofia. In some cases, it was hocas who became the express targets of anti-turban campaigns carried out, in part, by local Turkish Communist elites. As religious figures, hocas were seen as leaders, respected by local populations. As one Bulgarian official noted: "We knew that the population in this region [Shumen] is plagued by the remnants of Islamic religious influence and that we needed to take the snake by the head. Therefore we convinced the hocas from the village of Khasovo and Timarevo to take off their turbans.[61] "Taking the snake by the head" was an apt metaphor for the de-fezzing of hocas and Muslim men in general. Bulgarian Communists assumed that Muslim men and particularly local Muslim leaders, many of whom had more credibility than the regime-loyal Muslim officials in Sofia, were the "head" of Muslim community. Only by uncovering its head could the unruly snake be brought under control.

58 PODA (F-959K, O-1, E-110, L-85: 1958).
59 TsIDA (F-28, O-16, E-49, L-114: 1959).
60 TsIDA (F-28, O-16, E-49, L-34: 1959).
61 TsIDA (F-28, O-16, E-49, L-12: 1959).

9 Eylûl zaferi ve Türk halkının kazançları

Fig. 5. Illustration from *Yeni Işık* showing Turks participating in a parade celebrating the Communist "peoples' revolution" of 9 September 1951. Note that the Turkish woman wears a traditional head covering whereas the men wear modern hats or are bareheaded. *Yeni Işık* (Sofia), 9 September 1951, 1.

Campaigns for de-fezzing and elimination of the turban met with startling success in the first decades of the Communist period. (see fig. 7) By the late 1960s the fez and the turban were mentioned only in isolated cases and were worn only on the heads of elderly men in remote Muslim villages; both rather quietly disappeared off the official radar. This anticlimactic end to such a dramatic story can be explained in various ways. The fact that the fez and turban were no longer acceptable in Turkey itself must have had an impact. Contacts with the Turks of Turkey were severely curtailed by the dropping of the Iron Curtain but the success of Atatürk's reforms was known to the Muslim population at large. In addition, for most Muslim men the risk of wearing the fez and turban was just too great, so submission to these directives became the rule. Finally, another factor in the change according to Petŭr Marinov, a keen observer of these events, was that the fez simply was unavailable to Muslims by 1960.[62] Since they were no longer manufactured or sold in Bulgaria many Muslim men switched to the beret, which still distinguished them from non-Muslims. (see figs. 8 and 9) Some began to wear other distinguishing caps or went bareheaded.

[62] PODA (F-959K, O-1, E-225, L-242: 1975).

Fig. 6. A political cartoon from *Yeni Işık* showing a Turkish family that immigrated to Turkey as part of the 1950–51 exodus. They are depicted in caricatured traditional garb. The caption reads: "An interview with emigrants in Turkey.—Did they rob you in Bulgaria?—They certainly did.—Who?—The Turkish consulate." *Yeni Işık* (Sofia), 13 April 1951, 4.

Though the "problem" of the turban and fez was solved by the early 1960s, both continued to color the popular imagination. In the mid-1960s through mid-1970s the Bulgaria Communist regime initiated the Rebirth Process among the Pomak population during which all signs of Turco-Muslim belonging came under attack, including the mostly absent fez and turban. In the midst of one of the most dramatic cases of Pomak resistance in this period the fez and turban made an appearance as a symbol of opposition to the Bulgarian authorities. In a violent revolt against name changes that rocked the village of Ribnovo in 1964, locals took control of the village for several days and openly confronted the military detachments that had been dispatched from Gotse Delchev, the regional capital. According to an eyewitness, Pomak insurgents caught and disarmed several Bulgarian soldiers and reportedly "put fezzes on them and wrapped turbans around their heads."[63] Obviously for both Bulgarians and Muslims, the fez and turban were still

[63] Diulgerov, *Razpnati Dushi*, 27.

Fig. 7. A Turkish family in a refugee camp on the Turkish side of the Bulgaro-Turkish border after the 1950–51 mass expulsion. Huey Kostanick, *Turkish Resettlement of Bulgarian Turks: 1950–1953* (Berkeley: University of California Press, 1957), 161.

tools of power and receptacles of "symbolic capital," to utilize Pierre Bourdieu's term, even after their practical demise.[64]

One of the primary goals of the period of the Rebirth Process was to popularize among both Bulgarians and Pomaks the historical assertion that Pomaks were forcibly Islamicized in the seventeenth century, so justifying their return to Bulgarianness. Anton Donchev's *Vreme Rasdeleno* (A Time of Parting), first published in 1964 as a historical novel and later made into a motion picture, relates in gruesome detail the mythic forced conversion of Pomaks. Much as Vazov before him had popularized the image of the *çorbacı* as a hated Bulgaro-Ottoman hybrid, Donchev deepened public awareness of the hated janissary who carried out the presumably forced conversions.[65] The figure of the janissary was deplored in Bulgarian historiography as the most ferocious of the Ottoman military elite and the product of the much-deplored *devşirme*—also known to Bulgarians as "the blood tax." According to the canon of Bulgarian historiography these elite Ottomans were in essence abducted, turbaned, and circumcised Bulgarians, hated hybrid figures who

[64] Pierre Bourdieu, *Outline of a Theory of Practice* (Cambridge, 1977).
[65] Anton Donchev, *Vreme Razdeleno* (Sofia, 1971).

Fig. 8. Turkish men in berets gathered near the market in Kirdzhali, 1996. Author's photograph.

haunted the Bulgarian collective memory. Donchev's janissary villain, Karaibrakhim, and his Turkish retinue descend on their Bulgarian victims and began to forcibly convert the population with much bloodshed. In the midst of the violence and chaos, Donchev's hero, Manol, proclaims, "It is not our children that they want to make into janissaries but all of us."[66] Hence the novel popularizes the image of the Pomak as a kind of latter-day janissary, as both a perpetrator in need of punishment and a victim in need of liberation.

The fez and the turban play an important symbolic role in Donchev's story as the conversion process is accompanied by the command, "pour ashes on your

[66] Ibid., 68.

Fig. 9. Pomak men in berets in front of the mosque in the village of Shivachevo in the Balkan Mountains, 1998. Author's photograph.

heads and let each of you place one of those fezzes and turbans on the ashes."[67] In a show of resistance, a Bulgarian man from Manol's village proclaimed, "I do not want a turban, I want a fur cap."[68] The fez and the turban are important tropes in the novel and the Bulgarian collective imagination, even after their virtual elimination from Pomak heads. As the visible signs of Muslim male difference faded from sight, the final and hidden marker of Muslim maleness and the Muslim male body itself became a target of Bulgarian state intrusion.

Modern Janissaries

In the latter decades of the Communist period a clear shift in emphasis occurred from visible to hidden signs of Muslim manhood, from the fez and tur-

[67] Ibid., 199.
[68] Ibid., 96.

ban to the practice of circumcision. Circumcision not only marked Muslim male bodies as different, it was the ceremony that signified the Muslim male's coming of age. In the Balkan Muslim tradition, this ritual surgery was performed generally on boys between the ages of five and seven, who only after circumcision were invited to enter the mosque and pray among men. From about 1968–89, the Bulgarian state attempted to bring the act of circumcision under state control and eventually eliminate it as a Muslim practice. It was no coincidence that these measures took place precisely when apprehensions about Muslim virility and political threats were growing. Various reasons were given for Communist objections to the circumcision of Muslim boys in the course of these decades, but the primary reason was increasingly clear. That is, circumcision was seen as a mutilation of essentially "Bulgarian" bodies. The circumcision of "Bulgarian" boys marked them as hated hybrids, as modern janissaries, and holy warriors for anti-Bulgarian politics. Only in leaving the foreskin uncut could true Bulgaro-Muslim sameness be achieved and mongrelization (and the Muslim threat) finally eliminated.

It is difficult to know to what extent, if any, Bulgarians were influenced by European discourse on circumcision. Nevertheless, there are important parallels in the meanings that Bulgarians imposed on the practice of cutting the male prepuce. Since the Age of Discovery, European explorers and geographers had surveyed and mapped the practice of circumcision from Australia to North America as a practice of savage "circumcised races."[69] By the nineteenth century, such ideas about circumcision were redirected and used most commonly in polemics against Jews on the European continent. Medical and historical writings on the subject deplored this practice of Jews, which seemed to prove that they were both out of place (in Europe) and time (they belonged to the past).[70] In various writings of the period the practice was linked not only to Jewish "barbarity" but also to Jewish danger and impurity. Even more significantly, circumcision marked Jews with an alternative loyalty, as a danger to the nation-states of nineteenth-century Western Europe. Jews as an infectious presence in Europe, very literally, became part of a medical polemic against the syphilitic, diseased Jew whose "Jewishness (as well as his disease) was inscribed on his penis."[71] Only in the Anglo-American world did circumcision as a "clean" practice which eliminated smegma and hence disease, gain credence and become standard practice among non-Jews by the turn of the twentieth century.[72] On the European continent circumcision remained a strictly Jewish and Muslim practice.

In Bulgaria the all-out assault on circumcision had only shallow roots in the pre-Communist period. Before World War II, circumcision was viewed as

[69] David Gollaher, *Circumcision: A History of the World's Most Controversial Surgery* (New York, 2000), 38.
[70] The best discussion of these writings is in Sander Gilman, *The Jew's Body* (New York, 1991), 90–96.
[71] Ibid., 96.
[72] Gollaher, *Circumcision*, 102–8.

a strictly Muslim (and Jewish) affair. It was not until the 1930s that it is mentioned in *Rodina* writings, which accuse "imams, muftis, hocas, and *sünnetçis* (circumcisers)" of holding the Pomak masses in ignorance about their presumed Bulgarian origins.[73] Anti-circumcision campaigns had only a minor place in *Rodina's* public writings and appeals. Perhaps because of the sensitivity of the issue it was subordinated to the more dramatic campaigns focused on Pomak dress. Still, the practice is openly discouraged in a 1941 *Rodina* article on circumcision:

> Health is not only a personal matter, it is social. . . . Today medicine has moved significantly ahead. The achievements are great and they are moving forward with the new times. But here in the Rhodopes there exist practices that are centuries behind, for example, circumcision of Bulgarians of Mohammedan faith. It is performed by people who are from another epoch. They do it in a very simple and dangerous manner. . . . If circumcision must be done, why not do it with a doctor? . . . The darkness and vestiges of the centuries-long yoke must be destroyed.[74]

In general, *sünnetçis* were listed as among the enemies of enlightenment, and the practice was apparently prohibited during World War II when *Rodina* was at its peak of power.[75] As Marinov lamented in his diary after the war, the Pomak population, "immediately carried out circumcisions on all the uncircumcised children who had accumulated in the past few years, and this in an especially celebratory setting."[76] Ironically, this rash of ritual circumcisions among Pomaks ushered in the strongly anti-circumcision Communist period.

The practice was quietly tolerated for the early Communist years until campaigns against circumcision began in the late 1950s accompanying the Cultural Revolution in the Muslim provinces. By December 1959, the Bulgarian Ministry of Health criminalized private or ritual circumcision among Muslims as well as Jews. Legally, circumcision could only be performed by doctors, generally Bulgarian doctors in Bulgarian hospitals; an altogether unacceptable setting for the ritual from the point of view of the Muslims of Bulgaria in this period.[77] The primary justification for these anti-circumcision measures was a general concern with "hygiene" and "contamination." Warnings were sent to local health institutions, claiming that circumcision among Turks and Pomaks were performed in a "primitive manner" by "self-pro-

---

[73] Marinov, *Bulgarite Mokhamedani*, 34.
[74] Marinov, ed., *Sbornik Rodina*, 3: 108–9.
[75] Maria Todorova, "Identity (Trans)formation Among Pomaks in Bulgaria," In *Beyond Borders: Remaking Cultural Identities in the New East and Central Europe*, ed. L. Kürti and J. Langman (New York, 1997), 65.
[76] SODA (F-959K, O-1, E-110, L-86: 1958).
[77] Nikolai Mizov, *Istinata i Neistinata za Obriazvanieto* (Sofia, 1964), 24–25; and TsIDA (F-747, O-1, E-8, L-13: 1960).

claimed surgeons."[78] The Ministry of Health rationalized its stand on circumcision to the Islamic establishment as a reaction to a purported increase of "reports and complaints of doctors from hospitals and health institutions in the country about fatal incidents . . . after the circumcision of Turkish boys."[79] In the same document, the Ministry declared that "from the medical point of view in our climate and way of life," circumcision is "unnecessary and unjustified."[80] In 1964 a short monograph by Nikolai Mizov, *Istinata i Neistinata za Obriazvanieto* (The Truth and Untruth about Circumcision), was published, offering a more detailed critique of the practice. The book is filled with horror stories, such as an elaborate tale of the death of a Pomak boy as a result of his "unhygienic circumcision."[81] Mizov specifies the "barbaric" conditions under which the *sünnetçi* operated: "Most *sünnetçi* were rural barbers, hocas, or their sons or friends who used a razor or an ordinary pocketknife. They worked in unsanitary conditions and without anesthesia . . . normally *sünnetçi* performed group circumcisions in which they used the same instrument for all the children without disinfecting it."[82] Mizov describes a particular circumcision scenario almost as a brutal rape carried out by two strong men, who drag a struggling Pomak boy into a separate room and hold his legs down while the damage is done.[83] The language of backwardness and infection was prevalent in official discussions of the practice and Muslims who were willing to give their sons over "into the dirty hands of the ignorant *sünnetçis*" were admonished as barbaric and retrograde.[84] But were these writings really about bacterial or cultural contamination?

There was also a purported class dimension of circumcision related activities. In a directive to local institutions the Ministry of Health decried the fact that "*sünnetçi* demand high fees and hence rob the population . . . hiding their profit."[85] The fact that the practice was both exploitative and "hidden" enhanced the sense of political threat. According to Mizov, even though the ritual was technically illegal, hocas, and *sünnetçis* secretly performed it in order to make money.[86] In class terms, he explains, "circumcision hinders the class unification of workers, and instead unifies workers with their exploiters and oppressors." Just as the *sünnetçis* were depicted as exploiters, so too were the Muslim masses reprimanded for the "wasteful, lavish feasts" that they held in connection with the circumcisions.[87] Such feasts did not stay within the parameters of socialist propriety. Circumcision and its attendant

---

[78] TsIDA (F-747, O-1, E-8, L-14: 1957).
[79] TsIDA (F-747, O-1, E-8, L-10: 1959).
[80] TsIDA (F-747, O-1, E-8, L-14: 1957).
[81] Mizov, *Istinata i Neistinata*, 3.
[82] Ibid., 20
[83] Ibid., 22.
[84] Ismail Dzhambazov, *Religioznite Praznitsi i Obredi v Islama* (Sofia, 1964), 61.
[85] TsIDA (F-747, O-1, E-8, L-14: 1957).
[86] Mizov, *Istinata i Neistinata*, 24–25.
[87] Ibid., 28–29.

festivities were seen as a diversion from building socialism, a "waste of time" that took workers away from factories and collective farms.[88]

The ethnic and religious dimensions of circumcision were also explicitly addressed in academic writings bent on persuading Muslims to give up the barbaric practice. In a monograph on religious holidays and traditions of Islam, for example, Ismail Dzhambazov chastised Muslims who circumcised on religious grounds pointing out that "circumcision is not in the Koran."[89] With the practice thus disassociated from Islam, Dzhambazov also criticized the fact that even "progressive" Communist Turks circumcise themselves and their sons "as a sign of national belonging." He questioned the logic of such Turks who purportedly claimed that, "We are not Muslims, we don't believe in Islam or its prophet. But we are Turks and therefore we circumcise our sons.'"[90] In response, Dzhambazov pointed out that Arabs also circumcise and Muslim Gypsies don't, and therefore circumcision should not be equated with Turkishness. Following Dzhambazov's logic, therefore, it was still possible to be a Muslim or a Turk and not circumcise.

Although official discourse focused on the physical and social threat to Muslim bodies, the Bulgarian body politic was clearly of the highest concern. Although rarely articulated, connections between concerns about circumcision and Muslim virility are expressed in occasional references to circumcision as connected historically with the "holiness of the penis" and the "cult of fertility."[91] Anxieties about demographic imbalance were heightened by a sense of the potential for a return of Muslim political virility. Would the "fallen masters" rise again like their brothers in Turkey or the newly politicized Muslims of the Middle East? The persistence of local large-scale circumcision ceremonies struck fear, alarm, and dismay into the hearts of Bulgarian administrators. According to a report from the Korovo district in the Rhodope Mountains, some 50,000 Pomaks gathered for the circumcision of 130 children in 1964. Pomak celebrants were said to have flown the Turkish flag, a "manifestation of Turkism" indicative of both political and ethnic disloyalty, that is, Pomak affinities for Turks and capitalist Turkey.[92] Displays such as this may have contributed to the aggressive turn in policy toward Pomaks and the initiation of the Rebirth Process soon after. It is no coincidence that the ritual became highly politicized in the 1970s and 1980s, when the perceived Muslim threat was heightened. In 1970, the Central Committee of the Communist Party made the decision to carry out widespread propaganda against the circumcision of Muslim boys and intensify efforts to incarcerate *sünnetçis* and the parents of the circumcised.[93] The escalation of such campaigns was in response to continued reports and concerns about the "wide-

[88] Ibid., 29; and TsIDA (F-28, O-16, E-49, L-22: 1960).
[89] Dzhambazov, *Religioznite Praznitsi*, 47.
[90] Ibid., 57.
[91] Ibid., 47.
[92] SODA (F-957k-O-217, E-2, L-1: 1964).
[93] TsIDA (F-417, O-4, E-59, L-5: 1970).

spread practice of the illegal circumcision of boys."[94] As Takhir Aga, a *sün-netçi* from the town of Kirdzhali, related in his "memories from prison": "I circumcised hundreds of our boys . . . they fined me many times and finally I ended up here [in prison]. Especially in our region, even a mention of the word "sünnet" (circumcision) was dangerous. The local police did checks on the boys playing on the streets and if they found out that they were circumcised, there were bitter circumstances for their parents and *sünnetçis*."[95] Aga's discussion of spot checks by the local police is especially chilling in that it hearkens back to Nazi practices in occupied Poland and elsewhere, in which men suspected of being Jews were subject to public penile inspection.[96] In Bulgaria by the 1970s circumcision became by definition an act of opposition. As a practice it came to represent a threat, not only to the body politic but to the "Bulgarian" body itself.

It is no coincidence that the dénouement of the anti-circumcision story took place as a part of the more comprehensive assimilation campaigns of the 1970s and 1980s. In the case of both Turks and Pomaks, anti-circumcision campaigns had the most impetus precisely when claims of blood-based sameness proved most decisive. Evidently, it was the disfigurement and infection of the "Bulgarian" body—and by extension the Bulgarian nation—that was at stake. Circumcision, after all, was intimately linked to the conversion of Bulgarians to Islam and hence the very historical injustices that the Party wished to rectify. Circumcision, as Mizov claims for the Pomak case, always accompanied conversion and this "mark of the prophet" was used to "assimilate" and separate Muslims from the "uncut infidels."[97] As Bulgarian projects of integration proceeded, especially when justified by assertions of blood ties, this mark of separation had to be eliminated. Hence the total integration of Pomaks into the Bulgarian nation during the 1970s Rebirth Process was accompanied by intensified anti-circumcision propaganda and harsh punishments: the disfigurement of "Bulgarian" bodies would not go unpunished.

From 1984 to 1989, the ban on circumcision although already in effect for all Muslims was even more strictly enforced among the Turkish population. Efforts to convince Turks to abandon the practice were stepped up and Turkish parents were forced to sign a form with the following disclosure: "With this declaration, I promise not to have my son___ circumcised, because it is playing with the life and health of my son."[98] The Party used various rationales for the renewed focus on circumcision, but the primacy of the Bulgaro-Turkish national merger was apparent. In conjunction with the assimilation decrees, this all-out indictment of circumcision appeared in the *Yeni Işık*

---

[94] TsIDA (F-417, O-4, E-59, L-7: 1970).
[95] *Musulmani* (Sofia), April 1993, 2.
[96] Lenore Weizman, "Living on the Aryan Side in Poland: Gender, Passing, and the Nature of Resistance," in *Women in the Holocaust*, ed. D. Ofer and L. Weizman (New Haven, 1998), 202–3.
[97] Mizov, *Istinata i Neistinata*, 14.
[98] Eminov, *Turkish and Other Muslim Minorities*, 182.

(now appearing exclusively under the Bulgarian name *Nova Svetlina*): "Circumcision is nothing more than a means of delusion for the masses under the ideological veil of Islam. This mark of ignorance and backwardness serves to preserve the ethnic isolation of a portion of the working classes in our country, and hinders friendship and understanding between working people in their socialist homeland, it also destroys their moral-political unity . . . and hampers progress on the path to Communism."[99] Among the high crimes of circumcision, it seems, were its preservation of "ethnic isolation," and destruction of "moral and political unity," both required for socialist progress. Even more so than in the past, health officials made regular visits to Turkish households and schools to monitor the ban by means of physical checks of boys.[100] *Sünnetçis* and the parents of circumcised boys were more uncompromisingly punished as "enemies of the people."[101] Significantly, the commonly imposed five-year sentence for circumcision was justified through accusations of "bodily harm" (*telecna povreda*).[102] By 1984 the essentially "Bulgarian" bodies of Turks, as Pomaks before them, came under the close supervision of the state.

In spite of these measures, 1986 discussions at the highest level of the Communist government were still concerned with the need to "lead a decisive battle against circumcision of young children." Initiatives included mostly ideological and educational work but the incarceration of offenders was still common. Communists and other government cadres were asked to set a personal example and unwaveringly carry out the policy of "the liquidation of circumcision practices."[103] It was not until 1987, however, that official sources claimed the circumcision problem to be "solved."[104] The battle against circumcision was fought almost to the bitter end of the Communist period.

Conclusion

Anxieties about Muslim male political and sexual power drove twentieth-century campaigns against visible and hidden signs of Muslim maleness, first targeting Pomaks and later Turks. In the midst of the Bulgaro-Muslim encounter, manhood was constantly being reinvented, by both Bulgarians and Muslims. First the fez and turban and later circumcision became the foci of criticism and assault. The nineteenth-century Europeanization of Bulgarian men's apparel provided an antecedent for twentieth-century projects that attempted to Bulgarianize and hence neutralize the threat of Muslim men. By

[99] *Yeni Işık* (Sofia), 3 November, 1984, 4.
[100] Eminov, *Turkish and Other Muslim Minorities*, 182.
[101] *Prava i Svobodi* (Sofia), 24 January, 1992, 2.
[102] Valeri Stoianov, *Turskoto*, 181.
[103] TsIDA (F-1B, O-63, E-1, L-5: 1986).
[104] TsIDA (F-1B, O-63, E-2, L-53: 1987).

the twentieth century Bulgarians and, at times, modernizing Muslims launched ongoing and ultimately successful campaigns to "Europeanize" the headgear of the Muslim male population of Bulgaria. Campaigns against circumcision were slower in developing, but eventually the foreskin, too, came under the supervision of the Bulgarian state. By the late 1950s, the Muslim "coming of age" ritual was tantamount to a political protest, and by the 1970s a political crime. Significantly, these campaigns were predicated not on Muslim difference but on sameness, or the presumed essential Bulgarianness of these populations. Muslim men were simultaneously emasculated and "re-masculated"; they were stripped of traditional bases of patriarchal power and invited to share newly constructed Bulgarian ones. In taking away Muslim markers and passages to manhood, the Bulgarians intended to provide a conduit to becoming a Bulgarian man.

Very few Muslims embraced Bulgarian manhood for very long. Many, of course, accepted Bulgarianness, if only officially, during the Communist period and even took part in enforcing the ban on the fez, turban, and practice of circumcision. In fact, there was a spectrum of responses among the Muslims of Bulgaria to Communist programs, from collaboration to overt resistance. The responses were also never absolute. In practice, Muslim men might "resist" in the morning and cooperate in the afternoon; they might show their loyalty via their hats but hide their opposition in their pants.

In post-Communist Bulgaria, circumcision has reemerged in force, although it was not until 1998 that circumcision ceremonies were officially sanctioned.[105] The fez and turban, however, have not reappeared with the death of Communism, except as still highly politicized symbols. In 1995, for example, the ruling Union of Democratic Forces was accused of "pulling on the fez" when it entered into a coalition with the Turkish-minority-controlled Movement for Rights and Freedoms (MRF).[106] These markers of manhood, it seems, will continue to capture Bulgarian and Muslim imaginations and play a role in political and cultural negotiations of manhood and nationhood in post-Communist Bulgaria.

---

[105] Significantly, the Albanians of Kosovo were unable to circumcise during the ten-year Serbian occupation from 1989–99. Symbolically, mass circumcisions were performed by Turkish mobile units after NATO occupation.

[106] *Zemiia* (Sofia), 11 September 1995, 4.

4 *The Citizen behind the Veil: National Imperatives and the Re-dressing of Muslim Women*

> Unveiling this woman is revealing her beauty; it is baring her secret, breaking her resistance, making her available for adventure. Hiding the face is also disguising a secret; it is also creating a world of mystery, of the hidden.
>
> —FRANZ FANON

By the modern period the woman behind the "veil" in Bulgaria had become the object of national desire. Nineteenth-century Bulgarian critiques of the veil translated into twentieth-century campaigns to de-veil Muslim minority women. Both theory and deed were very clearly the result of the appropriation of West European assumptions about veiling as an oppressive and barbaric practice. As with European colonialists, in the Bulgarian case the veil was seen not only as culturally retrograde but politically dangerous. It shrouded Muslim women from state surveillance and marked her (and her man's) resistance to cultural modernization.[1] As in the West European case, Bulgarians saw de-veiling as liberation of Muslim women, integral to the civilizing mission that accompanied their imposition of control over Muslim populations. European influence on Bulgarian conceptualization and action toward the veil is unmistakable. But differences also abound. European cri-

---

[1] A similar argument is made by Yeğenoğlu about the veil in the French-Algerian case. She posits that the French colonizers, prompted by political imperatives, attempted to extend a "Lacanian gaze" to veiled women who could see but not be seen. Meyda Yeğenoğlu, *Colonial Fantasies: Towards a Feminist Reading of Orientalism* (Cambridge, 1998), 43. Yeğenoğlu draws heavily on the Foucauldian notion of power, as constituted and imposed through a system of surveillance and visibility. Michel Foucault, *Discipline and Punishment: The Birth of the Prison* (New York, 1979).

tiques of the veil were directed toward the "other," distant or subject *foreign* Muslim women. In contrast, Bulgarian campaigns against the veil were carried out on their immediate periphery among Muslims that were ultimately claimed as blood Bulgarians. Bulgarian de-veiling, therefore, was tantamount to reclaiming an abducted, violated, and lost self, covered and hybridized by Turco-Arabic garments. How could Bulgaria be truly European when it was partially obscured by a draping veil?

In the context of the European (and later the U.S.) encounter with the Muslim world, the veil was and continues to operate as the most powerful symbol of difference and presumed Islamic backwardness. As the image of the "pious mother" became key to Western national self-images, it was the counterimage of the women of the harem—veiled, oppressed, and mysterious—that typified representations of Eastern barbarism.[2] The dress and gendered practices of elite Muslims were not only misunderstood, but conflated with practices across the Islamic world.[3] The veil was assumed to be a uniform phenomenon that oppressed all Muslim women and rendered them (and their men) uncivilized. As a result the liberation of Islamic women via removal of the dreaded veil became central to Western civilizing missions, even as putting clothes on scantily clad African women was key to their civilization.[4] Ironically, the same European men that preached liberation in the colonies—what Leila Ahmed calls "colonial feminism"—did not necessarily support suffrage or equal rights for women at home.[5] Just as Western women needed to be kept in check, so too did the irrational "veiled" Orient need Western penetration and taming.[6]

The consistency and timelessness of European (including Bulgarian) and U.S. assumptions about the veil are striking, especially considering that the very term "veil" is so dubious. In its English-language usage, "veil" can denote a variety of coverings for the hair, face, and body, or signify the general

---

[2] On the "pious mother" see George Mosse, *Nationalism and Sexuality: Middle Class Morality and Sexual Norms in Modern Europe* (Madison, 1985) 23; For discussions of the centrality of the image of veiled women see, for example, Yeğenoğlu, *Colonial Fantasies*, 1–4, and Mohja Kahf, *Western Representations of the Muslim Woman: From Termagant to Odalisque* (Austin, 1998), 1–9.

[3] The colonial woman was the hidden object of desire in elaborate fantasies about veiled women of the harem and their supposed orgiastic revelry. In the Ottoman Empire only elite Muslim households had harems; the term "harem" technically means "women's quarters." The harem was generally a place of tight sexual regulation rather than a place of sexual license. For the most recent and nuanced book on the Ottoman harem see Leslie Pierce, *The Imperial Harem: Women and Sovereignty in the Ottoman Empire* (New York, 1993).

[4] McClintock, *Imperial Leather*, 31.

[5] Leila Ahmed, *Women and Gender in Islam: Historical Roots of a Modern Debate* (New Haven, 1992), 151–52. Ahmed characterizes Lord Cromer as a prime example of someone who hypocritically used feminism abroad in Egypt and was decidedly antisuffrage at home in Britain.

[6] Numerous sources elaborate on the image of the Orient as female. See for example Mark Alloula, *The Colonial Harem* (Minneapolis, 1986); Todorova, *Imagining the Balkans*, 14–15; and Yeğenoğlu, *Colonial Fantasies*, 11. In fact "Oriental" and Balkan men were intermittently feminized and hypermasculinized, each image emerging when convenient and appropriate to sway European public opinion.

practice of seclusion of women from the public sphere.[7] In other words the word "veil" is most often used out of context, without recognition of the diversity of both garments and practices in Islamic communities. Significantly, there is no single word for "veil" in Arabic or Turkish, because there are a number of articles that are subsumed under the very general and imprecise English term.[8] The Bulgarian language, as with Turkish and Arabic, has a variety of terms for "veil" including *feredzhe*, *yashmak*, *bulo*, and *zabradka*—the first two having Turkish and Arabic roots, the latter two Slavic roots. In Bulgarian writings on the practice, however, the terms are used interchangeably, without concern for the differences between them or variances in practice either within Bulgaria or between Bulgaria and the Near and Middle East. In addition to the terminology problems "veiling" as a monolithic practice and essential symbol of Islam is at odds with recent findings on the historical origins of the practice. Ironically, recent scholarship has placed the origins of the veil in ancient Greece, the purported cradle of "Western Civilization."[9] Other sources identify the veil's origins as Byzantine Christian, but, again, both views stress that it was a general near-Eastern practice, rather than an originally Islamic one.[10] Others have refuted the idea that the veil is dictated by the Koran, finding only scant reference to it, and certainly no clear decree about covering or seclusion.[11] Instead, these sources argue that the practice of veiling is a result of regional tradition in combination with various interpretations of Islam across time and space and, as a result, the "oppressive" nature of veiling is frequently called into question. Face and body covering in many times and places were a sign of status. In some contexts Muslim men also covered or were segregated to denote their social separation from the general population.[12] Generally, veiling was historically an urban elite phenomenon, which in some locales might have increased to a more widespread phenomenon only during the colonial period because of the intrusive presence of Westerners.[13]

This scholarship has important implications for the Balkan context. Bulgarian assumptions dating from the nineteenth century about the barbaric and oppressive nature of the veil are based mostly on suppositions from outside the local context. In the Balkans there is no evidence that heavy veiling, especially of the entire face, was ever a significant practice among a large sector of the Muslim population. Although urban and some rural elites most

---

[7] Beth Baron, "Unveiling in Early Twentieth Century Egypt: Practical and Symbolic Considerations," *Middle Eastern Studies* 25 (1989): 370–86.

[8] See Fadwa El Guindi, *Veil: Modesty, Privacy and Resistance* (Oxford, 1999), xi.

[9] See, for example, Ahmed, *Women and Gender;* El Guindi, *Veil;* and Nilüfer Göle, *The Forbidden Modern: Civilization and Veiling* (Ann Arbor, 1996).

[10] Juan Cole, "Gender, Tradition, and History," in *Reconstructing Gender in the Middle East: Tradition, Identity, Power,* ed. F. Göcek and S. Balaghi (New York, 1994), 26.

[11] See Fatma Mernissa, *Beyond the Veil: Male-Female Dynamics in a Modern Muslim Society* (Bloomington, 1987), 7.

[12] El Guindi, *Veil,* 14.

[13] Cole, "Gender, Tradition," 24.

probably covered their faces and bodies in the Ottoman period, by the twentieth century such elites had been severely depleted by migration back into the Ottoman confines. In fact, by the time Bulgarian campaigns against the veil had emerged, the Muslim population of Bulgaria was primarily rural. As a result, in many cases, the veil referred to little more than a Muslim peasant headscarf that perhaps differed in color or size from the Bulgarian version or was draped across the chin instead of tied in the back. With this in mind the "oppressive" nature of these garments is called into question. As in the European case, from the very beginning of Bulgarian musings on the veil an inordinate focus was placed on the so-called oppression of Muslim women and their need for liberation. This reached its pinnacle in the Communist period when Muslim women were conceptualized as the "ultimate proletariat," hidden under seemingly infinite layers of oppression—feudal, bourgeois, and patriarchal.[14] But in all periods under discussion, Bulgarian rhetoric about oppression masked the true concern with the "Oriental" backward appearance of Muslim women that differentiated them from Bulgarian women. Oriental garments not only obscured the shape of "Bulgarian" bodies, but they were a visible blot on Bulgarian Europeanness, and hence a perceived barrier to national progress. With this in mind, the Bulgarian anti-veil campaigns have much in common with what Ayşe Kadıoğlu labeled the "state feminism" of Atatürk's Turkey and Reza Shah's Iran.[15] There, as in the latter-day colonial feminism of the Soviet Union, women assumed an important role within nation-state building projects—not just as producers and reproducers, but also as visible displays of national progress. As Kadıoğlu points out, "Women were burdened with the difficult task of defining the boundaries between tradition and modernity since the initiation of modernization projects from above."[16]

But de-veiling projects in Bulgaria, as elsewhere, were not always instigated from above. As Bulgarian invective against the veil gained momentum in the twentieth century, internal Muslim debates about the veil also developed. Although such debates were less developed in Bulgaria than elsewhere in the Muslim world, local Muslims also initiated and carried out de-veiling projects on their own terms and with their own motives. An active minority of Muslim men and women played an important role in de-veiling movements that began in the 1930s among Kemalist Turks and *Rodina* Pomaks. In the Communist period, many modernizing Muslims actively participated in the state-directed campaigns against the veil and also the *shalvari* which were similarly conceived as backward and oppressive. Muslim men and women participated in such campaigns, and Muslim women intermittently shed and re-donned their veils and *shalvari*, whether out of modernist affini-

---

[14] I am indebted to Massell for his seminal work on de-veiling in the Soviet Union. Massell, *The Surrogate Proletariat*.

[15] Ayşe Kadıoğlu, "Women's Subordination in Turkey: Is Islam Really the Villain?" *Middle East Journal* 48 (1994): 651.

[16] Ibid., 646.

ties or as a survival strategy. Others resisted, openly, sporadically, inconspic-
uously, and often inconsistently. As in the contemporary Middle East, the
veil, at times, became a collective weapon against the heavy-handed imposition and penetration of Western influence.[17] It also became a mirror in which
Muslim identity changes and survival strategies were reflected. In the course
of the twentieth century, Muslim women's garment choice, by definition, became politicized, a mark of loyalty to or defiance of the community, the state,
and the nation, whether Bulgarian or Turkish. In short, the veil became a battleground upon which Muslim identity and modernity was negotiated both
with the Bulgarian state and among Muslims themselves.

Veiled Difference or Sameness?

Difference in dress has been a fact of life in the cities, towns, and villages of
the Balkans since before the Ottoman period. A dizzying array of traditional
dress—of color, drape, and style—differentiated individuals and groups by
gender, class, social status, and regional origin. On the local level, dress practices tended to distinguish non-Muslim from Muslim, perhaps solidified to
some degree by Ottoman sartorial restrictions for non-Muslims, though
these were rarely enforced. At the same time, before modern influences penetrated the countryside vast regional differences in Bulgarian dress may have
been as dramatic as that between Bulgarian and Muslim. In some regions
Bulgarian women were covered as fully as Muslim women, and their head
coverings were very similar to what would later be called the veil on their
Muslim counterparts. (see fig. 1) But ultimately women's dress was part of
the mosaic of local identities and meanings that were sorted and recast in the
European categories and terms that guided nineteenth-century Bulgarian nationalism.

Initially the veil appeared on the Bulgarian cultural radar as part of the historical, ethnographic travelogue genre of the mid-to-late nineteenth century.
From Konstanin Irichek to Ivan Vazov, foreign and native travelers sojourned
to the remote recesses of the country and made amateur ethnographic observations about the local culture, including dress. Not surprisingly, those populations defined as Bulgarian tended to be celebrated for their colorful and
diverse dress. The dress practices of Muslims, on the other hand, were seen as
fundamentally backward, a foreign import to the "Bulgarian lands." The
wearing of "Oriental" covering or draping garments by Pomak women, in
particular, was a curiosity that seemed to fascinate and horrify. In the Pomak

---

[17] The more recent resurgence of veiling, or re-veiling, in the Middle East and elsewhere,
therefore, is not a return to tradition but a modern phenomenon, in many cases a sign of resistance to the penetration of Western influence. For a discussion of veiling, de-veiling and re-veiling in Iran see Nahid Yeganeh, "Women, Nationalism, and Islam in Contemporary Political Discourse in Iran," *Feminist Review* 44 (1993): 3–18. For a discussion of the same issue in Turkey
see Kadıoğlu, "Women's Subordination."

case, the veil marked difference, but difference that had been illegitimately imposed by Ottoman overlords.

Writings about Pomak women and their Oriental accoutrements gained momentum from 1878 through the early twentieth century precisely as Western influence grew in the newly formed Bulgarian state. The imperatives of national consolidation gained urgency during this period, including the search for the "native" as the basis for this consolidation. Ironically, the beginnings of the urbanization of Bulgarian populations and their continued Europeanization in the urban context threatened this very "native" essence before it had time to be defined and consolidated. In many ways dress was the most obvious and visible way that urban Bulgarians were being subsumed into a generalized European material culture and fashion norm.[18] As a result, Western fashion was embraced but also subject to criticism for its "superficiality" and "empty materialism" that polluted the assumed purity of Bulgarian culture.[19] This ambivalence toward the West was responsible, in part, for driving exploration and codification of the native, or *Bŭlgarskoto* (Bulgarianness), in the Bulgarian countryside. It was in these rural areas that the scattered remnants of the Ottoman past—perhaps the most politically charged among them being the veil—were discovered, repudiated, and eventually assailed.

The most famous Bulgarian observer of the Pomak veil in the immediate postliberation period was undoubtedly Ivan Vazov, who describes his journey through southern Bulgaria in *Great Rila Wilderness*. His observations of Pomak men and women, like others of this period, tend to be vague and sometimes contradictory but still infused with generalized assumptions about veiling as a retrograde practice. In one breath Vazov deplores the covering practices of Pomaks as unusually zealous, "As is typical of the renegade, the Pomaks were more ardent Muslims than the Turks. Turkish women were not so zealous in hiding from Bulgarian eyes as were the Pomak women."[20] But in another passage he describes the unusually "liberal" covering practices of Pomak women from a particular Rhodope village: "On the path through the hazel grove I . . . was passed by hosts of Pomak women carrying bundles, wearing blue tunics braided at the side; they were probably returning from the baths and the majority was young and pretty. To do them justice, I should say that they did not cover their faces as strictly as their sisters from other Chepino villages. Later I gathered that these Chepino beauties were famous for their liberal manners, which made this very romantic spot a popular one for visitors."[21] Vazov observes a wide variety of covering practices

---

[18] For a discussion of the Europeanization of Bulgarian dress see Maria Veleva, "Za Periodizatsiata v Razvitieto na Bŭlgarskite Narodni Nosii," *Izvestiia na Etnografskiia Institut i Muzeĭ* 15 (1974): 5–53.

[19] In Peiu Slaveĭkov's journal for women printed in 1868–69, he engages in polemics against European fashion, which he claims "distracts and exploits" Bulgarian women. See *Ruzhitsa* (Istanbul), 15 January, 1868, 5.

[20] Ivan Vazov, *Velika Rilska Gora* (Sofia, 1954), 146.

[21] Ibid., 138.

among Muslim women of the region, none of which is characterized as full veiling. In an incongruous twist, Vazov assumes that the less-covered Pomak women are morally "loose," even while portraying the more-covered women as "zealous." Vazov's undue focus on the harem and "the baths" in his writings on Pomak women mimics European obsessions with Oriental women as hidden and erotic. With an air of voyeurism, Vazov imagines Pomak women frolicking naked in groups in their Turkish baths and harems, hidden from the Bulgarian gaze.[22]

In his historical reflections, Vazov's encodes and popularizes the idea that Pomak women are the remnant of a female Bulgarian population taken into Muslim harems after the massacre of their men. During his visit to Batak, one of the sites of the famous April Uprising, Vazov reflects on the loss of Bulgarian men as a great tragedy that resulted from the ill-fated uprising. But it is the violation of women and their Islamicization in the context of Muslim harems that Vazov bemoans as the greatest of historical injustices: "There had been attempts to rape the prettier women, for example, at the house of Bogdan. . . . But then these women, who were like sluggish lambs waiting their turn on the block, became lionesses and fought the evil-doers desperately until they were cut down and only their dead bodies were left. But not all of young women were so fortunate. . . . Many were killed after being raped . . . And many beautiful young women and girls were taken to the harems."[23] Vazov portrays women as the most tragic of victims, but also the unsung heroes of the event, especially those who martyred themselves rather than enter the Muslim harem. The observations of Bulgarians such as Vazov were the beginning of the larger project of seeing, recording, and conceptualizing Pomak women in the postliberation period. Turkish women, as a rule, were not subject to similar scrutiny; it was the search for the native behind the Pomak veil that inspired ethnographic commentary.

By the early twentieth century increasingly professionalized ethnographers began to undertake elaborate expeditions, mapping the regional variations in Bulgarian folk costumes and their national meaning.[24] Every thread of Bulgarian (and Pomak) women's dress was counted, recorded, mapped, and analyzed, in part because of the recognition of cultural change and the threat of irreversible loss of Bulgarian folk culture. The issue of the covering practices of Bulgarian Christian women was duly noted by prominent ethnographers such as Dimitur Marinov who asserted that in Bulgarian villages, "A bareheaded woman is synonymous with a naked woman," especially after marriage when only her husband can see her hair."[25] In many cases such cover-

---

[22] For an excellent discussion of European desire and "voyeurism" in relation to Muslim women see Alloula, *Colonial Harem*.

[23] Ibid., 192.

[24] For a useful overview of Bulgarian ethnography see Khristo Vakarelski, *Etnografiia na Bŭlgariia* (Sofia, 1974).

[25] Dimitŭr Marinov, "Narodna Viara i Religiozni Narodni Obichai," *Sbornik za Narodni Umotvorenie i Narodnopisi* 28 (1914): 146.

ings were virtually identical to rural Pomak and Turkish coverings and were even labeled with the same terms, *bulo, zabradka,* and *yashmak.* As Stoiu Shishkov asserted: "Before the 1870s and 1880s in such mixed villages the Bulgarian Christians also wore a kind of head covering—a *yashmak* on their heads—outside their homes. And now in many villages Bulgaro-Mohammedan women do not cover their faces . . . [their] clothes are the same, especially further from the cities where the influence of the Turk colonizer is less apparent."[26] Even though many recognized the prevalence of Christian covering, it was never equated with the essentially "foreign veil" in spite of similarities. In fact, Shishkov assumes that in the cases when Bulgarian women wore the *yashmak* it was because of their contact with Pomak women, who were in turn infected by proximity to the Turkish colonizer. Alternatively, in cases where Pomaks did not cover their faces it was because of their contact with Bulgarian women and distance from Ottoman cities.

In writings on the Ottoman period, the Turkish city and/or garrison was often conceptualized as the center of a penetrating and contaminating foreign culture that polluted the purity of the Bulgarian lands. Shishkov, for example, assumes that the pure Bulgarian character of the area had been polluted in the Ottoman period via the bodies of Bulgarian women. Along the same lines as Vazov, Shishkov claimed that Bulgarian men had been killed wholesale and Bulgarian women taken into the harems of the Ottoman soldiers, some Turkified, others only Islamicized. Hence he defined all Pomak and at least a portion of Turkish women as coming from Bulgarian stock. The further from the Ottoman garrisons the "purer" and more "virginal" the Bulgarian—and Bulgaro-Mohammedan—population was presumed to be.[27] The presence of the veil on the heads of Pomak, and in theory also Turkish, women was therefore illegitimate and *chuzhdo* (foreign) as opposed to *narodno* (native). It was the ultimate mark of "impurity," literally a result of miscegenation.[28] But though the veil marked Pomak women as impure hybrids, it also was their badge of victimization that exonerated them from Ottoman crimes and deemed them worthy of liberation.

It was in this context of Pomak-as-victim that liberation was first contemplated. With the outbreak of the First Balkan War in 1912, the gravity of Bulgarian assumptions about Pomak clothes prompted extreme measures. With the euphoria of wartime mobilization, the liberation of Pomaks from foreign occupation was accompanied by an assault on material vestiges of the past, the veil being a primary target. During the mass forced conversions of Pomaks during the First Balkan War the veil was replaced with what was considered appropriate Christian headgear, in this case "Bulgarian scarves."[29] (see figs. 2 and 3) According to Bulgarian sources, this change from veil to Bulgarian scarves was voluntary and carried out with a minimum of violence.

[26] Shishkov, *Bŭlgaro-Mokhamedani,* 85.
[27] Ibid., 64.
[28] Ibid., 65.
[29] Georgiev and Trifinov, *Pokrŭstvaneto,* 8.

And while there is no evidence of a violent reaction on the part of Pomaks, reports of mass migrations of Pomaks across the Ottoman border attest to strong reactions to the wartime measures. Interestingly, an Orthodox Christian priest from one district reported that Pomaks were puzzled by the dress policy, not because the garments had any religious significance, but rather for practical reasons: "In the village Buknush, after the baptism an old woman asked me why are they doing away with the *feredzhe* [body-covering cloak] because now it is already cold (March 20) and outer clothes are necessary for warmth."[30] Clearly the various meanings of Pomak garments—be they religious, ethnic, moralistic, or simply practical—are impossible to precisely ascertain. Perhaps this woman, while appealing to the Bulgarian priest on practical grounds, also had deeper religious objections to the shedding of her garments. At any rate, Pomak women objected to their forcible re-dressing and practical considerations should not be discounted.

Perhaps the clearest indication of the Pomak reaction to de-veiling was the prompt re-veiling by the fall of 1913. With the end of the Second Balkan War and a change in political regime rumors began to circulate about a reversal of the conversion and dress policy toward the Pomak populations. In response, Pomak women publicly reclaimed their veils. As one local Bulgarian official reported, "The women are now dressed in the newest *feredzhe* and covering their heads in the kind of *bulo* which they didn't even wear in Turkish times, in a word, now everything has come to the worst end."[31] Other reports echoed this concern that the veiling practices of Pomak women were not only being resumed but had taken on a new form, "The women now are veiling, you could say, one hundred times more than in Turkish times."[32] As in the case of re-fezzing, public re-veiling by Pomak women provoked concern not only among local priests and administrators but also other local Christians. In the Chepinsko district, for example, numerous Pomaks complained that Christians had assaulted them on the streets and ripped off their veils. In other cases priests reportedly ignored the change in policy and continued to force Pomaks to go to church, while not "allowing" Pomak men to "cover their women."[33] In the midst of this chaos, cultural fault lines seemingly deepened precisely at a time when the church and state had attempted to erase them.

With Bulgarian and Muslim identities in flux, by the 1930s the Bulgarian government had taken an active interest in controlling and directing de-veiling movements that had emerged with Muslim minority communities themselves. The government openly discouraged Bulgaria's Turks from adopting the Kemalist modernizing model, including its emphasis on the de-veiling of Muslim women. The de-veiled Turkish woman, more so than her veiled counterpart, represented a potential political threat as she visibly

[30] Ibid., 468.
[31] Ibid., 405.
[32] Ibid., 415.
[33] Ibid., 458.

bared her affinities for modernizing Turkey. Indeed, as policy, the administration supported the conservative Old Turk line of the Islamic hierarchy
within Bulgaria on veiling and other issues, in order to cut off local Turks
from outside Turkish influence. Turkishness, therefore could be contained
behind the veil in an inert and loyal Muslim population. In fact, without
much government prompting de-veiling movements didn't take hold among
the largely illiterate Turkish masses. For Pomaks, in contrast, the government
supported the modernist *Rodina* movement with its inordinate focus on dress
reform. Without her veil the Pomak woman could be fully integrated into the
Bulgarian nation and separated, by draping cloth, from her Turkish sisters.

Since its founding in 1937, *Rodina* launched de-veiling (and de-fezzing)
campaigns that were entirely "voluntary," executed through the mass distribution of appeals. By 1939 leaflets were widely circulated, which demand
that: "Women shall cast aside once and for all the *feredzhe, bula, yashmak*
and other such reshaping articles as these. They shall exchange them with
Bulgarian costumes—a regular dress, and scarves, which are tied behind the
head."[34] From this quote and photographs from the organization's published
writings, the recommended changes in costume were often as inconsequential
as tying a scarf behind instead of in front of the head, but any garment that
deformed the shape of Pomak women was seen as distorting her Bulgarian
essence. More often than not the targets of de-veiling appeals were Pomak
men who presumably controlled their wives' covering practices: "Uncover
their faces so they will see the light and all of its beauty in the same way that
we see it. . . . In order to prove that you are true followers of the Koran and
free citizens of the country and that in truth you are moving toward culture
and progress, free your wives, mothers, and daughters from their black veil,
the symbol of slavery. Then, freed they will be confident that they will become better mothers and that they will have better children, fit for life."[35]
Men were implored to let their wives see "light" and "beauty," but the
change was ultimately justified in terms of their own "culture and progress,"
citizenship, and true adherence to the Koran. The *Rodina* amalgamation of
Islam with progress was typical of modernist Islamic movements which appealed to men's own sense of self and vanity alongside but primary to concerns with the rights or choice of women.

Although the majority of Pomaks were opposed to *Rodina* and its de-
veiling program, state support ensured that pro-*Rodina* Muslims held an increasingly large measure of local control. The Smolyan archives attest to the
fact that local Islamic institutions were largely staffed by pro-*Rodina* officials
as early as 1938.[36] In *Rodina* documents from that year, members of the society express surprise when one of their "appeals to Bulgaro-Mohammedan
women" was ripped down off the walls of the Muftiship, whose own printed

---

[34] SODA (F-26k-O-1, E-2, L-7: 1939).
[35] Strasimir Dimitrov, ed. *Rodopski Sbornik*, vol. 7 (Sofia, 1995), 207.
[36] SODA (F-42k, O-15, E-2, L-142: 1938).

order had also urged the shedding of the garments of "black slavery."[37] With the outbreak of World War II, intensified state backing ensured that *Rodina* influence and campaigns were rapidly expanded into the occupied territories of Thrace and Macedonia. By 1943 the government had passed the Law on Clothes which codified the shirking of the veil and required that Pomak women tie their scarves behind their heads and remove the *feredzhe*.[38] From persuasion to legislation the *Rodina* program was realized, but only for a short time. As World War II came to a close and the Communist-led Fatherland Front coalition came to power, the Law on Clothes was reversed and Pomak women duly re-veiled.

The Nation Unveiled

Before 1945 Bulgarian thinkers and statesmen had increasingly defined the veil as fundamentally foreign to Bulgaria, an obstacle to its cultural Europeanization. In the Communist period, the presence of veiling in the Bulgarian countryside became even more laden with meaning in light of the ever-intensifying state modernization drive. The veil—and a number of other backward Muslim garments—were conceived as a barrier to national integration and Communist progress. De-veiling became the measure of success in the drive toward socialism and the building of a homogeneous nation. Dress became highly politicized in an era when the transformation of everyday material culture was deemed critical to a revolution in consciousness. At the same time, dress choice was a powerful vehicle through which Muslim women expressed loyalty and identity. The wearing of the veil and other Oriental garments was a way of asserting nonconformity and hence a degree of resistance to Communist directives on the local level.

In the immediate postwar period, Soviet supremacy demanded a dramatic reconceptualization of the role of women and especially Muslim women in Bulgarian society. Along these lines the new Communist regime touted the emancipation of all women in conformity with the Soviet interpretation of Marxist-Leninism. At the same time (as with the Soviets), Muslim women were constructed as the "ultimate proletariat"—victims of feudal and bourgeois pasts and a patriarchal present in the Muslim countryside. According to Soviet sources, Muslim women, mostly concentrated in Central Asia and the Caucasus, were among the most oppressed segments of the population from the pre-Communist period: "Inequality of women was one of the defining features of pre-Revolutionary Russia. The situation of women in the Tsarist frontiers, in Central Asia and especially in Turkmenistan, was the most humiliating and unequal. The patriarchal way of life and Islam reigned; the woman was enslaved in the literal meaning of the word . . . darkness, igno-

---

[37] SODA (F-42k, O-15, E-10, L-142: 1942).
[38] TsIDA (F-264, O-1, E-440, L-9: 1941).

rance, domestic slavery, and slave-like subordination to men were the fundamental characteristics of life."[39] The Soviets, while vilifying the Tsarist past and Muslim patriarchy alike, attempted to rectify the situation by bringing Muslim women into Soviet collective farms and industry, and freeing them from their "enslaving clothes."[40] The Soviet de-veiling campaigns that were at their most intense from the 1920s to 1940s were held up as a model for postwar Bulgarian dress reform.[41] In renouncing the "black partition of the *parandzha* (veil) which separated Muslim women from the white light of all life," the "revolutionary" women of the Soviet East were supposed to undergo their own revolution in consciousness and then set an example for Muslim women elsewhere.[42] The new Bulgarian regime readily consumed the rhetoric and rationale that the Soviets had so eloquently devised.

Under Communism conformity in the realm of everyday material culture was, more than ever, a perceived indicator of social progress. Communism, after all, was a material ideology at its most basic level, one that focused on material conditions and transformations. For this reason ethnography took on a whole new importance because of its keen focus on all of the minutiae of material culture. Ethnographers studied the markers of identity—in particular material markers—and made judgments about the "true" ethnic essence of the populations under consideration. Clothing in particular was a focus of ethnographic study in Bulgaria and elsewhere, as a material indicator of national essence. As Maria Veleva, one of the most prominent Bulgarian ethnographers of folk costume from this period, expressed, "clothes are the strongest document about the origins of a population."[43] Ethnographer Ganka Mikhailova was even more insistent about the "social content of material objects," namely clothing: "An especially telling phenomenon in terms of social life in the realm of material culture is folk clothing, because the connection between it and the person is so close and direct. The dwelling and other aspects of material culture, which also fulfill important needs, are not always present with the person."[44] The ethnographic idea that "clothes make the person" mingled potently with the Marxist assumption that material change brings about a progressive change in consciousness. Hence, if the Muslim women of Bulgaria *dressed* in a modern, Bulgarian way, it was assumed they would become modern and Bulgarian. In spite of the focus on modernity as well as Bulgarianness in dress, the Bulgarian folk costume itself

[39] Shakher Nuriev, *Zhenskii Vopros: Problemi i Resheniia* (Ashkhabad, 1991), 3.

[40] Ibid., 6.; Palvanova, *Emansipatsiia Musulmanki*, 15; and Alimova, *Reshenie Zhenskogo*, 12.

[41] On de-veiling in the Soviet Union see Massell, *The Surrogate Proletariat;* Tohidi, "Soviet in Public"; and Douglas Northrop, "Languages of Loyalty: Gender, Politics, and Party Supervision in Uzbekistan, 1927–1941," *Russian Review* 59 (April 2000): 179–200.

[42] Vera Bilshai, *Reshenie Zhenskogo Voprosa v SSSR* (Moscow, 1956), 146.

[43] Maria Veleva, "Pregled na Prouchvaniiata na Bŭlgarskite Narodni Nosi," *Izvestiia na Etnografskiia Institut i Muzeĭ* 3 (1958): 252.

[44] Ganka Mikhailova, "Sotsialni Aspekti na Narodnoto Obleklo," *Bŭlgarskata Etnografiia* 3–4 (1976): 178.

was not subject to state dress-reform campaigns, on the contrary, ethnographers conceptualized the "egalitarian" Bulgarian peasant woman and her dress as inherently progressive. In fact, ethnographers frantically tried to record and save Bulgarian folk garments as Bulgarians rapidly urbanized and ceased to wear them. Transformations in material culture thus would bring national loss as well as gain.

Gains were predicated on the building of a homogeneous, modern socialist nation without veils or *shalvari*, another garment that was vilified in this period. (see fig. 7) Although the oppressive nature of the veil was questionable in Bulgaria, campaigns against *shalvari* were even more problematic. *Shalvari* had actually been worn by many but not all men and women, Muslim and non-Muslim, in many parts of the Ottoman Empire. But in the nineteenth century and particularly after liberation, *shalvari* were quickly phased out among Bulgarians and gradually among Muslim men who adopted the narrower-legged European–style pants. Muslim women, however, out of habit, practicality, or a sense of tradition continued to wear the baggy pantaloons. Though *shalvari* gradually fell into disfavor in Turkey and perhaps elsewhere, an all-out government assault on the *shalvari* of Muslim women seems to have been unique to Communist Bulgaria.[45] Ironically, the state drive toward progress launched an assault on women in pants at a time when women in the West were beginning to regularly wear pants as a liberating mode of dress. Almost a century earlier emancipationist women in nineteenth-century Britain and the United States had actually initiated an ill-fated movement for women to don "Turkish pants" and shed their burdensome heavy skirts. Amelia Bloomer—after whom the baggy "bloomers" were dubbed—actually took Oriental pantaloons as a model. She justified the new fashion in terms of comfort and practicability as well as noting that even "Oriental women" were allowed to wear such garments.[46] In the West, subversive "modern" changes in dress did not preclude a dabbling in the Oriental, if it suited contemporary visions of comfort, practicality, and style. In Bulgaria, revolutions in dress were to come much later, with much narrower interpretations of what was properly modern and European, that is, suitably Bulgarian. By the 1950s, *shalvari* were unquestionably seen as an affront (along with the veil) to the Bulgarian nation and its socialist future. The transgression of gender lines—that is, women in pants—may have had some bearing on these sustained and persistent campaigns against Turkic pants.[47]

---

[45] *Shalvari* were considered backward and became an object of ridicule by many Westernizing elements in the late Ottoman Empire and in other modernizing Muslim contexts. But I have yet to come across discussions of systematic state-run campaigns against them elsewhere. On the Ottoman context see Palmira Brummett, *Image and Imperialism in the Ottoman Revolutionary Press, 1908–1911* (Albany, 2000), 223; and Nora Seni, "Fashion and Women's Clothing in the Satirical Press of Istanbul at the End of the 19th Century," in *Women in Modern Turkish Society*, ed. S. Tekeli (London, 1995), 28–29.

[46] Dexter Bloomer, *The Life and Writings of Amelia Bloomer* (New York, 1975).

[47] In Bulgarian ethnographic sources, for example, one finds the clearly articulated notion that "pants" were a symbol of manhood and a sign of gender differentiation. In his discussion of the Bulgarian folk costume in a 1914 ethnographic study, Marinov asserts that, "Pants are a man's clothes and as such are the symbol of Manhood. As a woman or a girl has her *prestilka*

But, by and large, campaigns against *shalvari* were an extension of the concerns of anti-veiling campaigns with the "hidden" and Oriental look of draping clothing.

Given the tentative nature of Communist control and Muslim support for the Party the regime undertook such campaigns against Muslim-style dress only after it consolidated power. During the elections of 1945, for example, Party agitators reported on the Muslim mood asserting that, "one part of the Turkish population is worried that veils will be stripped off if the Communists win."[48] In addition, the memory of wartime de-veiling campaigns was fresh and power shifts within the Turkish community in particular made de-veiling seem probable. The Communists had purged many Fascist, conservative elements from the Islamic establishment in favor of the so-called Young Turks who tended to favor de-veiling. But initially Muslims were reassured that the new regime had no intention of forcing Muslim women to remove the veil. At a Fatherland Front conference for new cadres in 1945, Party representatives promised that, "Under Fatherland Front power no one can take the veil off of the Muslim woman."[49]

In the late 1940s, de-veiling began as a strong suggestion rather than an order from on high. Not only did no major campaign occur in the Bulgarian- or Turkish-language Communist-controlled press, but veiled women were occasionally shown in the newspapers as willing participants in Communist society. From early on *Yeni Işık* and other mainstream Communist newspapers depicted Muslim women as de-veiled and liberated examples of idealized socialist women. At the same time, however, these idealized representations of Muslim women were carefully scattered across the pages of Turkish newspapers with a montage of more traditional images of Muslim women with hair covered and in *shalvari*, while fully participating in the building of socialism. (see figs. 5 and 6) Apparently, it was vital not to alienate or exclude Muslim women but rather to mobilize them into the state economy regardless of garment choice. In fact, there is evidence that on one occasion in 1946 in the Southern Bulgarian town of Haskovo, the Fatherland Front actually ordered the provisioning of cloth specifically for the making of *feredzhe* for local Muslim women.[50] The message of de-veiling was temporarily subordinated to the mobilization of Muslim women into the service of the regime. In a kind of aggressive affirmative action the Party sought out women—especially Muslim women—to enter into Party committees and economic endeavors. In order to bring Muslim women into the work of the Party, the regime sent the mostly Bulgarian women in its *zhenotdeli* (women's committees) into

---

(skirt) so should a man preserve his pants . . . pants mean so much that in the absence of a man his fiancée might marry his pants." Dimitŭr Marinov, "Narodna Viara," 146. Along these lines Vakarelski points out that the "main difference between the dress of Bulgarian men and women was that men wore pants and women wore skirts or dresses." Vakarelski, *Etnografiia na Bŭlgariia*, 227.

48 TsIDA (F-1B, O-12, E-222, L-53: 1946).
49 TsIDA (F-1B, O-25, E-67, L-8: 1945).
50 HODA (F-182K, O-1, E-92, L-20: 1946).

Muslim regions to teach courses, hold meetings and working-bees and give lectures such as, "The Turkish Woman: An Active Builder of Socialism."[51]

Even as Muslim women were embraced and welcomed into the Party, suspicions about their true loyalties were never far beneath the surface. Though the Party most often depicted Muslim women as victim and slave to Muslim men, they too, at times, were imagined as part of a hidden threat. One report from the 1947 elections, for example, speculated that Turkish women had been slow in the voting booths because they "hid their opposition ballots in the folds of their *shalvari*."[52] In another case, Muslim women were accused of concealing applications for emigration to Turkey "in veils and *shalvari* . . . in order to hide them from organs of power."[53] Here and elsewhere, it is evident that Muslim women with their hidden faces, bodies, and sentiments heightened the sense of Muslim menace. As a result, by the 1950s the diversity of images of Muslim women in official Turkish-language newspapers faded into a monolith of socialist sameness, with veiled and *shalvari*-clad women appearing only as objects of derision.

By 1956, Bulgarian leader Todor Zhivkov asserted a rapid plan of action for Bulgaria's Muslim populations that had profound implications for Muslim women's dress. Muslim women, and in particular their dress choices, became explicit targets of the Cultural Revolution and the 1958–60 Great Leap Forward. Muslim leaders were instructed to go village-to-village preaching the gospel of de-veiling to their flocks.[54] At the same time, the *zhenotdeli* organized intensive "explanatory sessions" and even door-to-door visits in the Muslim provinces, recruiting Muslim women when possible. Their sessions often included the testimonials of Muslim women who had embraced dresses (that is, shed their *shalvari*) and cast off their veils. As one such re-dressed Muslim women declared, "I've begun to feel like a person . . . in nothing do I differ from my Bulgarian female comrades."[55] Beginning in the late 1950s numerous successes were reported in de-veiling projects and facts and figures on de-veiling were consistently held up as a definitive measure of achievement."[56] When successful, Communists were triumphant and reported back to Sofia with declarations that their Muslim women had broken "the bonds of fanaticism and were wearing beautiful, light, comfortable European clothes."[57] At a conference of Muslim leaders in the aftermath of the Cultural Revolution one delegate proudly declared, "Now wherever you go there is no difference, and you can't even tell who is a Turk and who is a Bulgarian. . . . The Turkish woman is freed from her century-old black veil."[58] Here the Bulgarian-flavor of socialist sameness is laid bare.

[51] HODA (F-675, O-1, E-62, L-31: 1953).
[52] TsIDA (F-214, O-1, E-716, L-19: 1947).
[53] TsIDA (F-1B, O-6, E-5371, L-155: 1968).
[54] TsIDA (F-28, O-16, E-49, L-16: 1960).
[55] TsIDA (F-28, O-16, E-49, L-106: 1960).
[56] TsIDA (F-28, O-16, E-49, L-1: 1960).
[57] TsIDA (F-28, O-16, E-49, L-10: 1959).
[58] TsIDA (F-747, O-1, E-19, L-165: 1965).

But in spite of the euphoria over assumed success, the persistent use of the veil and *shalvari* made it clear that other kinds of approaches were needed, both suggestive and coercive, to bring Muslim women into the fold of Communist modernity. Up to this point the Party generally appealed to Muslim women with abstract notions of progress, civilization, and a bright utopian future. When such appeals rang hollow for many Muslim women, new tactics were employed. One tactic was to assert more control over the distribution of clothing in Muslim districts. By 1960 the increasingly pervasive cooperative farms began to garnish the wages of Muslim members and "advance" dresses against their salaries.[59] Muslim women, who generally sewed their own *shalvari* and veils in this period, had apparently complained that they couldn't afford the more onerous costs of factory-sewn dresses. To avoid such excuses the state simply made the consumer choice for Muslim women; dresses would be supplied in lieu of salaries. Officially, the results were astounding. Reports from the provinces in 1960 touted the 100 percent deveiling and shedding of *shalvari* by Muslim women in certain locales as, "achieved in one week" or in a matter of months.[60] In conjunction with this approach, sewing brigades were sent into Islamic regions to liquidate the problems of veils and *shalvari*. One local report announced that in Razgrad the Great Leap Forward had been achieved with the sewing of 900 dresses in eleven days.[61] To the Communists directing the campaign, coerced supply seemed to solve the issue of lack of demand faster than a revolution in consciousness. In addition to manipulation of supply, by the 1960s and 1970s the Party turned to open appeals to fashion and consumer sensibilities.

This approach was part and parcel of a general, subtle shift toward consumerism in Bulgaria—as elsewhere in the Bloc—in light of the faltering legitimacy of East European regimes. Women, generally, were the primary targets of feeble Party attempts to harness and then redirect consumer desires toward socialist principles. The Communist women's magazine *Zhenata Dnes* (Woman Today) had always featured fashion plates and clothing patterns, albeit buried in the back pages of the paper, presumably to attract a broader readership. By 1959, another women's magazine called *Lada* (Harmony) appeared in Bulgaria's kiosks, devoted solely to fashion and "everyday culture" (*bitova kultura*). *Lada* appealed to women's sense of fashion and beauty, which it linked to the building of socialism: "*Lada* will become your friend. It will help you to choose your clothes—for work, everyday, and holidays . . . *Lada* will endeavor to raise consciousness about all that is beautiful for the builders of a new life."[62] Beauty, in the words of *Lada*, was coterminous with modern Europeanized sensibilities and so was raised to the level of a socialist virtue. But though Bulgarian women were encouraged to look to Europe for aesthetic inspiration, there were clear limits. The Party continued

---

59 TsIDA (F-28, O-16, E-49, L-125: 1960).
60 TsIDA (F-28, O-16, E-49, L-16,23: 1960).
61 TsIDA (F-28, O-16, E-49, L-21: 1960).
62 From inside cover of *Lada* (Sofia), 1959.

to openly condemn miniskirts, jeans, and other fashions reflective of decadent capitalist tastes—and even incarcerated offenders.[63] Still, dress reform among Muslim women was apparently more fastidiously pursued. As an official from a Muslim district pointed out, "Look at the pants that [Bulgarian] girls are wearing! We in the Rhodopes want girls to take them off and in Sofia they wear them, and they are even more motley."[64] Contradictions aside, it seems that women's dress was interpreted as a warning sign, an indicator light of some kind for the onerous influences of both East and West. But although Western influences were only tempered and filtered, the battle against Oriental clothing was gaining momentum.

In fact, the Party employed pseudo-Western capitalist methods in its battle against Eastern dress. By the 1960s and 1970s the Party began to *sell* modern fashion to Muslim women. As early as 1960, lectures and presentations aimed at Turkish and Pomak women contained pleas to discard "out of date, expensive, old clothes" such as the veil and *shalvari* for "cheaper, more hygienic, and practical dresses."[65] Appeals targeting price, comfort, and hygiene—however erroneous they might have been—went beyond past discussions of such clothes as representative of a patriarchal, despotic, foreign past. Instead, in many Muslim districts Party functionaries suggested that local officials organize fashion shows to encourage the Europeanization of Muslim dress.[66] In 1975 an advertisement for one such "fashion revue" in *Yeni Işık* promised displays of "clothes throughout the centuries." Providing a preview of the spectacle, the fashion revue organizers explained that *shalvari* belonged to a past epoch and that, "In our time clothes are light, comfortable, hygienic, and beautiful."[67] The Party also organized competitions, as in one case where, "we carried out a special fashion show-competition . . . to provide our women with work clothes especially for tobacco production. In this way we will work together with our women to free them from the veil and *shalvari*."[68] As a rule, fashion shows were staged in connection with conferences on *bit* or everyday culture that urged the elimination of Turkish remnants in dress, as well the introduction of beds, tables, and chairs into Muslim homes.[69] Party documents remark on the need to work on the "aesthetics" of Muslim women's clothes, hence shifting the focus of their invective from oppression to taste.[70] New "schools of good taste" even appeared, offering courses to Muslim (and Bulgarian) women that preached a standard of modern European style and taste in cooking, sewing, and home

[63] See, for example, Tzvetan Todorov and Robert Zaretsky, eds., *Voices from the Gulag: Life and Death in Communist Bulgaria* (University Park, Pa., 2000).

[64] TsIDA (F-417, O-4, E-58, L-74: 1970).

[65] TsIDA (F-28, O-16, E-49, L-36: 1960).

[66] TsIDA (F-1B, O-509, E-5, L-116: 1962).

[67] *Yeni Işık* (Sofia), 13 December, 1971, 3.

[68] TsIDA (F-417, O-4, E-34, L-6: 1972).

[69] TsIDA (F-417, O-4, E-58, L-12: 1970).

[70] TsIDA (F-417, O-4, E-36, L-65: 1972).

furnishing.[71] Fashion was reshaped as a modernizing Europeanizing force that was therefore an acceptable tool to the Party.

In the name of style, taste, and socialist propriety, Muslim women were also urged to use cosmetics and visit hair salons. Muslim women were expected to make their faces visible and available, by painting on a modern face. As an article from *Lada* explains: "The Pomak woman threw off the veil, but many women still have not thrown off the idea that taking care of one's face, the necessity of a nice complexion and the use of cosmetics is luxurious and vain. Exactly now, when the woman is constantly under everyone's gaze in the factory, in society, in enterprises, she should have a tidy, proper and beautiful appearance."[72] In the Turkish press, too, frequent articles instructed Muslim women on how to dress and preached the necessity of visiting hair salons and using cosmetics.[73] Make-up, it seems, and fancy hairstyles were deemed acceptable for builders of socialism, as long as beauty was couched in socialist terms. Beautifying the woman's face for the sake of the observer and his voyeuristic gaze were deemed paramount.

Whatever the strategy, Party efforts met with varied responses, and the dress of Muslim women became a complex terrain over which the line between resistance and cooperation undulated. Wearing Oriental garb chafed against Party sensibilities and hence was viewed as a form of resistance, but the intent of Muslim women in donning and shedding such attire is murky at best. What is not in doubt is that continued veiling, and what was later dubbed re-veiling, were perceived as resistance by the Bulgarian regime. Notably, a growing literature dealt with veiling as a form of resistance to "foreign" or modernizing regimes in the Muslim world. As Meyda Yeğenoğlu asserts about the French-Algerian context, "In the colonizer's eye, Algerian resistance is condensed in the veil, which is seen as an obstacle to his visual control."[74] Similarly, Fadwa El Guindi explores the persistence of the veil as a symbol of resistance to the State in modernizing Muslim experiments in Egypt, Turkey, and Iran.[75] Finally, numerous sources have explored re-veiling in so-called fundamentalist Muslim movements in the Middle East since the 1970s as a reaction to modernization and Western political/economic encroachment.

The persistence of the veil, and particularly re-veiling, in Bulgaria could likewise be interpreted as a form of resistance to Bulgarianizing, modernizing Communist influence in the countryside. As early as 1951, Party cadres began to speak of the "re-veiling" of de-veiled women as a form of protest by the local Muslim population.[76] After the Cultural Revolution, local officials

---

[71] TsIDA (F-417, O-4, E-36, L-91: 1972).
[72] *Lada* (Sofia), Summer 1959, 13.
[73] *Yeni Işık* (Sofia), 19 July 1975, 3.
[74] Yeğenoğlu, *Colonial Fantasies*, 40.
[75] El Guindi, *Veil*, 1–24.
[76] HODA (F-675, O-1, E-112, L-73: 1951); TsIDA (F-28, O-16, E-49, L-23: 1955).

continued to complain that Muslim women were sporting veils and *shalvari* in their districts. Furthermore, as one Communist cadre reported, in many cases, even when the "transition to dresses" had been made, "*shalvari* were still being worn underneath the dresses of Muslim women in the villages."[77] In particular, Party suspicions were aroused by the failure of de-veiling in Bulgaria given its relative success in neighboring Turkey, "We know that Atatürk banned the veil and in Turkey in general one barely sees it . . . here they continue to wear it. Therefore, this is a demonstration in Bulgaria."[78] While such garments marked the Muslim community more broadly as disloyal, de-veiled Muslim women and their families as well as those who carried out and enforced such measures were, of course, recognized as progressive and loyal. The veil, therefore, continually functioned as a gauge, measuring loyalty or disloyalty to the Communist regime.

But the determination of who was a loyal, modernized Muslim was never easy. The wearing of the veil or *shalvari* by wives, sisters, and daughters of Turkish and Pomak Communist Party members seemed to muddy the waters of their assumed fealty. Concerns about this contradiction were discussed as early as 1951:

> In spite of successes in this area [de-veiling] a large number of our cadres in positions of responsibility still have not decisively broken with the old ways, with religious and everyday cultural anachronisms, or have again made their peace with them. In every Rhodope district there are such cadres. . . . For example, Ahmed Ibraimov is a member of the office of the regional committee of the BCP in Krumovgrad. He holds his family in ignorance, his wife in no way differs in the political and cultural sense from the most backward women in the region. Comrade Yumer Mehmedov, one of the secretaries of the regional BCP in Kirdzhali has done nothing up to this point to bring the new way of life to his family, his wife is illiterate and wears a veil. One would have to say that the bulk of the comrades who work in the committees of the Party, the Youth organization, the Fatherland Front, and in the local committees work very little for the education of their loved ones, they don't include them in political work, most of them are illiterate and their women wear veils.[79]

Here "the bulk" of Muslim cadres were suspected because of their veiled wives. Over time such accusations soften, but nevertheless no shortage of documents question the loyalties of Muslim Communists because the women in their families continue to wear veils and *shalvari*.[80] Party discussions are rife with grievances about how "many of our Turkish leaders say they are for de-veiling but don't set an example . . . their female comrades (*drugarki*), mothers, sisters and close ones don't follow the example of de-veiling." Similarly, the Party took note of the persistence of *shalvari* that were commonly

77 TsIDA (F-28, O-16, E-49, L-16: 1960).
78 TsIDA (F-417, O-4, E-58, L-37: 1970).
79 TsIDA (F-675B, O-1, E-112, L-3: 1951).
80 HODA (F-675, O-1, E-112, L-71: 1951).

worn by the wives of Muslim Communists. A Party report from Razgrad, for example, duly denounced the Turkish president of the agricultural cooperative who reportedly "did not convince his wife to wear a dress," and so raised the question of "how to liquidate the *shalvari* which remain in their [Muslim women's] dressers."[81] The language of this report is revealing of the Party's desire to reach beyond the public realm and into the depths of women's closets to eliminate what lurked there.

The allegiances of all Muslims were called into question given the inherently slippery nature of compliance to dress standards. The veil and shalvari, after all, could be concealed and revealed, taken off and put back on in different places and times, to the great confusion of Bulgarian observers. The ambiguity of the situation is illustrated by the following transcription of a Party discussion concerning dress among Pomak women at a lace factory in the town of Gotse Delchev:

> *Khristo Shopov*: But again they are wearing them. In that factory everyone is wearing the veil.
> *Stoiko Bairamov*: In the factory they work in work clothes and after they finish work they take off their aprons and put on their veils and go out.
> *Khristo Shopov*: Yes, the question is about what they wear when they go outside.
> *Stoiko Bairamov*: Outside! They don't want to take them off inside, and now we want them to take them off outside. From here [Sofia] it is easy to talk about it, but there this work is not easy.[82]

The conversation is indicative of Party consternation in light of Muslim women's selective adherence to official dress codes. Another anecdote about young Pomak girls and a boarding school raises similar concerns:

> On Saturdays and Sundays when they let them go to their homes, you will see how they all pull their *shalvari* and veils from under their pillows and mattresses, they hide somewhere outside the pension, they change clothes and leave dressed in that way. On Monday morning again when they return to school, they change again somewhere near the school and enter the school that way. We were very interested in this because they said the following: "They [the girls' families] will not accept us dressed in these clothes, they will chase us away, and they will beat us." . . . They [the girls] like these [new] clothes, but perhaps conservatism and despotism that exist in the home do not allow them immediately to break with these traditions.[83]

Again, the concern with Muslim dress extends beyond public spaces to the home, the domain controlled by "conservative" and "despotic" Muslim men.

Significantly, Party efforts to re-dress Muslim women intensified as the obligatory Bulgarian content of socialist modernity became increasingly

---

[81] TsIDA (F-28, O-16, E-49, L-21: 1960).
[82] TsIDA (F-417, O-4, E-58, L-20: 1970).
[83] TsIDA (F-417, O-4, E-58, L-37: 1970).

clear. Well before the Party even claimed Turks as Bulgarian, the Party measured the success of dress reform by the appearance of "the beautifully dressed modern Turkish woman, who in no way differs from the Bulgarian woman."[84] For Pomaks this connection was even more apparent, especially by the 1970s, in the midst of the Pomak Rebirth Process, when the dress of Pomak women came under closer supervision along with other vestiges of the Turkish yoke. The irony of the campaigns to finalize the merger of Pomak and Bulgarian was that they actually drove many Pomaks to a closer ethnic identification with Turks. *Rodina's* Petŭr Marinov, recounted an incident from 1975 in his personal diary that illustrated this phenomenon:

> A group of [Pomak] women in veils from the Smolyan district passed me last week on the street in Plovdiv and asked me, "Why should we throw off our *feredzhe?* These are our clothes! The peasant women from the Plovdiv area wear *sukmani* [apron-like garments] and scarves, why doesn't the government want them to exchange those with dresses? Who is offended by our *feredzhe* and *bula?*" And to this I tried to explain: It is true that the peasant women in Bulgaria wear *sukmani* and scarves on their heads. But they do this to protect themselves from the sun and they don't think about anything other than this. . . . But you cover your heads with *yashmaks* and wear the *feredzhe* because you want to separate yourself from Bulgarian women. With that they said: "That is it. Look at us; we don't want to be Bulgarian women! We want to be Turkish women and therefore we wear the *feredzhe* and *bula!* We want to be separate."[85]

The attachment of Muslim women to these garments, I would argue, was above all about the maintenance of ethnic boundaries, primarily between themselves as Muslims and non-Muslim Bulgarians. Although this was not true for at least some Pomaks, who readily modernized and Bulgarianized, for many others the encroaching modernizing programs only deepened the chasm between Bulgarians and themselves.

By 1984 the Bulgarian Communist Party also attempted to completely erase the boundary between Bulgarian and Turk, with important implications for Turkish dress. The so-called Rebirth Process and its famous assimilation decrees targeting the Turkish population are most famous for their provisions on forced name changes. But this assimilation campaign was also accompanied by dress-reform legislation which is lesser known or discussed. For the first time since World War II, state decrees rendered the veil, *shalvari,* and other Turkic articles of clothes officially illegal. As laid out in an order circulated in 1984, "Citizens are prohibited from wearing nontraditional Bulgarian clothes such as *shalvari* and veils."[86] Other documents from the period explicitly prohibit any scarves that are "veil-like" and "nontraditional

---

[84] TsIDA (F-417, O-4, E-34, L-6: 1972).
[85] PODA (F-959k, O-1, E-225, L-7: 1975).
[86] Foreign Policy Institute, *The Tragedy of the Turkish Minority in Bulgaria* (Ankara, 1989), 56.

Fig. 10. "Veiled" Pomak women as shown in the Bulgarian periodical *Sega* (1996).

[meaning non-Bulgarian] clothes."[87] The consequences of ignoring such decrees were severe, namely, persons in such attire could not be served at public establishments or ride public buses, and no jobs were made available to "those who wear baggy pants."[88] To add insult to injury, state officials actually went door to door and confiscated "anything that resembled a Turkish garment," publicly despoiling and destroying them.[89] With the enforcement of dress reform, the "Bulgarian" bodies of Muslim women were thus finally "freed" of their hybridizing Oriental garb.

In the years following the assimilation decrees local administrators issued mixed reports on the successes and failures of the imposition of dress reform. Some Party reports boasted that, "Very quickly the appearance of women has

[87] Ibid., 64.
[88] Ibid., 55.
[89] Eminov, *Turkish and Other Muslim Minorities*, 89.

Fig. 11. "Veiled" Pomak women represented as a political threat in *Sega* (1996). The caption reads "Kornitsa [a village that resisted name changes in the 1970s] again bares its nails at Bulgaria."

changed, the bulk of them now dress in a modern and beautiful fashion."[90] But there are also sources that admit that, "*shalvari* are still worn in the home."[91] In a more detailed elaboration on the progress of the assimilation campaigns in Tetevenska region, clothing is highlighted as a critical issue:

> There is a reduction of the appearance of ethno-differentiating external marks—the wearing of the *shalvari,* circumcision, and peculiarities in tradition. We have worked on the confirmation of Bulgarian elements in the way of life of people. As a whole the old clothes of women and girls have been substituted with the clothes of citizens. This question received a lasting solution at the beginning of 1985, and there are moments of high and low tides. In the beginning of this year there was an increase in the number of women who again put on their old clothes. One could meet them on the main streets of the villages, on the squares, and they made attempts to go into commercial establishments. Unfortunately even young girls, including school girls, have put back on *shalvari*. . . . Party bureaucrats and mayors have stopped dealing with the problem of clothes. . . . These same activists, who loyally and without reserve worked on the clothes issue, now, to avoid trouble with the population, have withdrawn from active work and are not setting an example at home.[92]

90 TsIDA (F-1B, O-3, E-2, L-6: 1987).
91 TsIDA (F-1B, O-3, E-2, L-6: 1987).
92 TsIDA (F-1B, O-63, E-27, L-6–7: 1988).

Fig. 12. An elderly Pomak woman in the village of Shivachevo in the Balkan Mountains, 1998. Author's photograph.

Fig. 13. The author seated between two elderly Pomak women in a village near Rib-novo, 2000. Author's photograph.

Clearly, as in the past, dictates from Sofia were heeded, but only for a short time. Sufficiently far from the gaze of the Sofia establishment even Muslim cadres who had carried out such policies let them slip after a short time. Although after 1985, the official position was that the "Turkish question" had been solved once and for all, in the drapes and folds of women's garments, Muslim difference was still tangible.

Conclusion

Bulgarian national projects in the modern period looked for the future, among other places, behind the so-called veil of Turkish and Pomak women. In the pre-Communist period, Bulgarian governmental policies toward the veil were integral to defining, ordering, containing, or eradicating the markers of difference within and putting Bulgaria on the path to Europe. In the wake of World War II these strategies merged with the imperatives of socialist development and the Soviet model of modernity. There was an even greater need to expose and rule what was behind the veil because women's clothing represented a dimension of society and everyday material culture that was beyond Party control. Both before and during the Communist period, Muslim women were gradually redefined as "Bulgarian" women who had been abducted, raped, veiled, and oppressed by (Ottoman) Muslim men. As a result, miscegenation and the transgression of boundaries were fundamental to the Bulgarian critique of the veil. The "Bulgarian" woman was presumably concealed and hybridized by her veil; only through de-veiling could she, and by extension the nation, look to the future.

Muslim women, through sustained refusal to de-veil or through deliberate re-veiling, transformed the veil (and also *shalvari*) into an "armory" of protest against state-defined emancipation and imposed modernity. At the same time, the boundary between complicity and resistance was porous and shifting, as veils were shed and re-donned with the winds of national and local politics. The assimilation decrees and their attendant legislation on clothes were reversed in 1989 after popular resistance—both Bulgarian and Turk—toppled the Communist regime. Perhaps the persistence of Oriental clothing in Bulgaria played some role in eroding the edifice of Communist legitimacy and hence contributed to its fall. It must be noted, however, that many Muslim women parted with the veil and *shalvari* by the end of the Communist period, and even more so in its aftermath. Others have continued to wear these garments. (see figs. 10–13) In the course of the twentieth century, state pressure hardened the resolve of some to maintain or reinvent tradition, while others jumped on the irresistible bandwagon of modern fashion. Unquestionably, the politics of dress among Muslim women will continue to play a role in negotiations of loyalty and ethnonational belonging in the post-Communist period.

5   A Muslim by Any "Other" Name: The Power of Naming and Renaming

T'is but thy name that is my enemy . . .
What's in a name? That which we call a rose
By any other name would smell as sweet;

—SHAKESPEARE

In a 1996 issue of the Bulgarian periodical *Sega* (*Now*), a reporter related the extraordinary tale of Hasan, a Pomak from the village of Bachkovo, who had experienced numerous name-changing campaigns throughout his life. His saga began during the First Balkan War when Bulgarian troops occupied his village. Hasan, along with his family and all the Pomaks of his village, was forced by the Bulgarian authorities to change his Turco-Arabic name to a Slavic name, in his case "Dragan." A change in politics after the Second Balkan War in 1913 opened the door for Dragan to change his name back to Hasan; so he did. During World War II, however, he was again compelled to change his name to Dragan, in line with the wartime Law on Names. After the Communist takeover in 1944, Dragan was able to change his name back to Hasan when the Fascist policy was reversed. But with the movement toward national integration in the 1960s, Hasan was obliged, yet again, to change his name to Dragan. After the fall of Communism in Bulgaria in November 1989, Dragan was allowed to resume his original name, Hasan.[1] In his one lifetime, Hasan, along with the rest of Bulgaria's Pomak population, changed his name six times, as Muslim names moved in and out of Bulgarian national focus.

---

[1] *Sega* (Sofia), 1–7 February 1996, 27.

Name-changing campaigns, their reversals, and the kinds of resistance they provoked are undoubtedly central to understanding the Bulgaro-Muslim encounter. In the Balkan context, where there is no visible racial/color difference between Christian and Muslim, names are one of the primary indicators of ethno-religious affiliation.[2] Names, like the turban, fez and veil, are obtrusive markers of Muslim belonging—if not generally visible, at least audible and knowable. As with Muslim-style dress, Turco-Arabic names became explicit targets of twentieth-century Bulgarian crusades to control their Muslim provinces and, ultimately, to remake Muslims in their own image. According to Bulgarian formulations names both hybridized and mislabeled essentially Bulgarian populations as Muslim. As a result, in times of war and intense social transformation the Bulgarian state initiated intensive programs, both voluntary and coerced, to replace Muslim names with Bulgarian ones. In turn, Muslim attachment to names ran as deep as the Bulgarian fixation with changing them. Intermittent name-changing campaigns provoked the most sustained and momentous resistance of any such state-run project. This inevitably raises questions. Why were names so important to Muslim notions of self? In turn, why were names such a threat to Bulgarian visions of modernity and progress?

Names have been the subject of philosophical debates and literary musings since well before Shakespeare penned his famous line, What's in a name? His celebrated words cut to the essence of the question posed by men of letters well before Socrates: Does the name determine or reflect the nature of the thing that it signifies? Shakespeare implies that names are independent of their signifiers; that "a rose, by any other name would smell as sweet." This is very much in line with the thinking of John Stuart Mill and other logicians (and linguists) who posited the meaninglessness of names, including proper names, in and of themselves; that is, that they hold no inherent power or meaning. But other thinkers have since recognized that names take on a life of their own, becoming inseparable from that which they signify.[3] In the case of personal names this is especially so. As Johann Goethe recognized: "A man's name is not like a cloak that merely hangs around him, that may be loosened and tightened at will. It's a perfectly fitting garment. It grows over him like his very skin. One cannot scrape and scratch at it without injuring the man himself." This metaphorical reference to clothing is apt, after all, both names and clothes are *worn*, can be altered and shed, and are signifiers of individual and group identities. Names become part of the person, much like dress. So much so, that, as one historian of names ventured, "Erasing a man's name would be tantamount to destroying the bearer of that name."[4] And although the process of taking away someone's name requires a kind of symbolic demolition, renaming also aspires to renovation or reordering.

[2] For a limited discussion of names in the Bosnian context see Tone Bringa, *Being Muslim the Bosnian Way: Identity and Community in a Central Bosnian Village* (Princeton, 1995), 19.
[3] Farhang Zabeeh, *What Is in a Name?* (The Hague, 1968), 8, 11.
[4] Ibid., 5.

Naming has always served the function of ordering or reordering social meanings and configurations. Concerning the representative function of language Foucault reflected, "all words, of whatever kind, are dormant names" and also, that language itself "has always *named*."[5] In a similar vein, Bourdieu recognized that "the act of naming helps to establish the structure of the world."[6] The naming or renaming of people as opposed to things, has its own inherent dynamic, but it is also clearly tied to larger historical processes of social ordering. Since the fourth century BCE in China, personal names have been systematized by the state as a way of population identification and control. As James Scott argues, however, it was early modern European states that first created a system of permanent, inherited surnames for all citizens in order to impose modern "legibility" on unwieldy populations and landscapes. He characterizes the establishment of such name systems as, "the last step in establishing the necessary preconditions of modern statecraft."[7] Surnames were codified as a way of knowing and controlling populations as linked to the development of tax, census, and private property procedures.[8] Government imposition of naming systems was about the extension of citizenship and rights, and the administrative subordination of the lower classes, rural poor, women, and minority populations within Europe and in colonial populations abroad.[9] In the late-eighteenth-century Habsburg Empire, for example, Ashkenazic Jews were forced to either choose or be assigned surnames. In many cases, local officials arbitrarily assigned derogatory names such as Eselkopf (ass head) or Fischbaum (fish tree) to Jews who did not offer them bribes.[10] Notably, after emigration to the United States Jews were the group most likely to shed their fairly recently acquired German or Slavic surnames in favor of unobtrusive Anglicized surnames.[11] Such cases were indicative of the tendency toward voluntary name changes for the purpose of assimilation in the U.S. "melting pot." But at least one example of forced name changes has occurred in the New World context, the renaming of African slaves with English first names and the surnames of their owners.[12] As in Eu-

---

[5] Michel Foucault, *The Order of Things: An Archeology of the Human Sciences* (New York, 1970), 102. Foucault, like John Stuart Mill before him, assumed that all words are "names." On Mill see Zabeeh, *What Is in a Name?*, 11.

[6] Pierre Bourdieu, *Language and Symbolic Power* (Cambridge, U.K., 1977), 105.

[7] Surname systems were introduced into much of Central and Eastern Europe by the late eighteenth and early nineteenth centuries when the Austrian, Prussian, and Russian governments introduced laws requiring the adoption and consistent use of surnames for all citizens. Scott, *Seeing Like a State*, 65–67.

[8] Zabeeh, *What Is in a Name?*, 51.

[9] A notable case of colonial name reform is the Spanish authorities' imposition of Hispanic names on the indigenous Filipino population in 1849. Names were chosen and assigned at random from a catalogue of names, and their use was at times enforced with draconian measures. Scott, *Seeing Like a State*, 69–70.

[10] Anne Bernays and Justin Kaplan, *The Language of Names* (New York, 1997), 58.

[11] This practice was not always without a response from local "bluebloods" who were outraged, for example, in a 1923 Philadelphia case in which Harry Kabotchnik petitioned the court to change his name to "Cabot." Ibid., 56–64.

[12] Ibid., 38.

rope, naming in the United States entailed both "symbolic violence" and "symbolic innovation," and was linked to social ordering or the remaking of identities.[13]

In the European context the importance of names as ethnonational markers eventually began to eclipse their significance as administrative tools. Names were scrutinized and manipulated across Europe, especially in times of war or upheaval. During World War I, for example, the British royal family renounced their German surname, Saxe-Coburg-Gotha, in favor of Windsor, a name that was thereafter retained and passed through the male and female royal lines.[14] In this case even the convention of patrilineal name heredity was abandoned for the sake of the English family name. In other cases, names had far more ominous and far-reaching consequences. In Nazi Germany the "name decrees" of the 1930s entailed the compilation of lists of acceptable Jewish and Gentile names to make Jews distinguishable by the simple mark of their names. Both groups had to make sure that their "race" was clearly recognizable by their names; ultimately a "Jewish" name alone could single out an individual for deportation or execution.[15] Hence, along with other types of social ordering names played a role in the delineation of ethnic boundaries and national meanings.

Renaming campaigns in Bulgaria concerned both the imposition and consolidation of political power and the sorting of native from foreign. Since liberation from the Ottoman Empire in 1878, Bulgarians voluntarily Europeanized their personal names as the state began to gradually rename cities, rivers, and other geographic features. Renaming of both people and places was a critical part of the reclaiming of the Bulgarian lands from foreign occupation and the marking of these territories as their own.[16] The Europeanization of Bulgarian names preceded the more contested process of Bulgarianizing first Pomak and later Turkish names. Bulgarian thinkers gradually reconceptualized names, as with clothes, as illegitimate, impermanent, and removable. Names, therefore, like the fez and veil, could be shed to reveal the essential Bulgarian underneath. But unlike clothes, names were not material; they could not be captured or completely confiscated. Only those things with names written on them—such as documents or gravestones—could be destroyed or modified. Names themselves could be held in the mind, the memory, and on the tongue. Ironically, perhaps because of their ethereality Muslim names had more staying power than clothes.

Ultimately, name changes were difficult to enforce and easy to circumvent;

---

[13] Kertzer, 8.

[14] It was Queen Victoria's prince consort who had brought the later forsaken Saxe-Coburg-Gotha name to the British royal family. Later, Elizabeth II, who married a Mountbatten would retain the Windsor name. Bernays and Kaplan, *Language of Names,* 21.

[15] Scott, *Seeing Like a State,* 373.

[16] McClintock, *Imperial Leather,* 29. McClintock discusses the phenomenon of place naming in the colonial context as an act of establishing control and securing male property and power, a conclusion that could be extended to modern surname systems as well. Though I believe that the practice of naming has important gender dimensions it is not addressed in this chapter.

Muslim names simply would not go away. The Bulgarian state could and did replace documents, alter gravestones, and place restrictions on the public use of names, provoking active and dramatic demonstrations of Muslim resistance that were summarily quelled. But the state could not prevent Muslims from quietly circumventing state policy by holding and using two names—one public and one private. Not all Muslims resisted, however, and many, with the promise of political and economic favor, either partially or completely Bulgarianized their names voluntarily. Naming was always part of the complicated dance of opposition and compliance that characterized the Bulgarian-Muslim encounter, particularly under Communism. As a rule, the choosing or assigning of names was a powerful act in which Bulgarians and Muslims, individuals, groups, or the state assigned meaning and inscribed identity.[17] Bulgarian renamers (and their Muslim coconspirators) clearly acted on the premise that, "T'is but thy name that is my enemy." Significantly, most Muslims did not agree that, "that which we call a rose, by any other name would smell as sweet."

The List of Names

Post-Ottoman Bulgaria inherited a landscape strewn with Turco-Ottoman names. These names, on people and places, not only marked a Muslim presence, but lacked a modern order that was deemed necessary for a European state. During the Ottoman period a system of hereditary first and second names was never established, and Turkey only adopted such a system in the 1930s as an integral part of Atatürk's reform.[18] In Ottoman Bulgaria, as in the rest of Eastern and northern Europe prior to standardization, a two-name nonhereditary patronymic system was standard practice. That is, individuals generally went by a given first name and a patronymic which was based on the father's first name plus "-ev/ov" for males (for example, Borisov) and "-eva/ova" for females (for example, Borisova).[19] With such a system, each generation had a different patronymic; hence there was no transmissible surname. In many cases a surname that corresponded to a person's profession or personal attribute was used instead of or in addition to the patronymic. Usually these third names were neither carried over to the next generation nor even used by the whole family and so were not part of any consistent, standardized surname system.

Though not well documented, a dramatic reconfiguring of personal (and place) names occurred within Bulgaria in the nineteenth century, especially

---

[17] Alhaug and Konstantinov, *Names, Ethnicity*, 18.

[18] Scott, *Seeing Like a State*, 373.

[19] Variations on this theme were present throughout the Slavic and non-Slavic world. In northern Europe, for example, there was no gender-determined ending on patronymics, which were indicated by both prefixes (such as Fitz-, O'-, Mac-) and suffixes (such as -sen, -son, -s). Ibid., 372.

after the 1878 break from Ottoman control. In the nineteenth century at least a portion of Bulgarians began to take surnames and keep them for multiple generations, particularly in urban settings. As Bulgarians became urbanized the importance of surname systems grew because of the increased social complexity of the municipal environment. After the Ottoman period a hereditary naming system coincided with the development of a centralized administrative apparatus and the new naming system slowly spread from new, transforming urban cores to the countryside. The most common surnames were based on the Slavic patronymic of the generation which initiated the practice, for example, Petrov, Nikolov or Eminova. Instances of occupational surname adoption were more problematic, as Turco-Arabic words—commonly used in the Ottoman period and after—often unintentionally were melded into newly formed Bulgarian names. For example, Bulgarians took surnames such as Chobanov (from the Turkish *çoban* or shepherd, and the Bulgarian ending "-ov"). In many cases, Turkisms in occupational names were shed or Bulgarianized. For example, Chobanov became Ovcharov (from Bulgarian for shepherd, *ovchar*).[20] The Bulgarian name system was both internally dehybridized and brought in line with the European standard, though in many rural areas no surname system existed until the twentieth century.[21]

For the Bulgarian population, naming was neither a violent nor hotly contested process. Rather, it followed the general course of cultural Europeanization that characterized the late nineteenth and twentieth centuries. In fact, much later, Communist period scholars concerned with names would admonish the pre-1944 Bulgarian regimes for ignoring the influx of French, German, and English first names and surnames into Bulgarian usage, which caused another abhorrent foreign presence. As one scholar of names, Nikolai Mizov, states: "Old family names at least spoke of labor-industrial activities and the greatness of past Bulgarian generations, even though it was through foreign [Turkish] names, but new 'modern' names have nothing in common with the past or with the future of the laboring Bulgarian nation."[22] The Europeanization of names, as with clothing, was always a process of negotiation between East and West, past and present. Nevertheless traces of the East in the names of Bulgarians and, eventually, even more so Muslim minority names were always the larger concern.

Though Turkish names passed unnoticed until the Communist period, Pomak names were the subject of scrutiny and speculation since the nineteenth century. Travelers, ethnographers, historians, and literati pondered the apparent Turco-Arabic character and Bulgarianisms in Pomak personal names. Through the name, which was often riddled with hybrid forms, they began to determine and untangle the national essence of Pomak populations. On the one hand, these observers assumed that the Turco-Arabic roots form-

[20] Nikolai Mizov, *Taĭnata na Lichnoto Ime* (Sofia, 1987), 45, 55.
[21] Spac Lecov, "Vŭznikvane i Promeni na Niakoĭ Familni Imena v s. Ruzhevo Konare." *Bŭlgarskata Etnografiia* (2) 1980: 28.
[22] Mizov, *Tainata na Lichnoto Ime*, 57.

ing the basis of the bulk of Pomak names were illegitimate. Names—such as Ali, Mustafa, Ahmed, and Mehmed—were characterized as evidence of the presumably forced conversion of Pomaks to Islam in the seventeenth century. On the other hand, the Bulgarian forms that hybridized these surnames allegedly demonstrated the true Bulgarianness of these populations.[23] During his late nineteenth-century travels in the Rhodope Mountains, for example, Ivan Vazov observed and commented on the apparent preponderance of Turco-Arabic names among the local Pomaks. Because of its rarity, he asked his guide about the "pure Bulgarian name" of one of the Pomaks they met. His guide pointed out that the Bulgarian sounding "Moutio" was a nickname for Mustafa which was clearly a Turco-Arabic name, but that local Pomaks also have, "Manchovs and Popovs and Krapchovs—since they were Bulgarians weren't they?" It is unclear at what point the Pomaks or Turks of Bulgaria adopted permanent hereditary surnames, but most likely it was not until the twentieth century. Turks and Pomaks, as with Bulgarians, generally formed second names, whether permanent or not, from patronymics on the regional pattern. But Pomaks apparently tended to use the Slavic –ov/ev instead of the Turkish -oğlu endings on their second name, for example, Mehmedov instead of the Turkish Mehmedoğlu.[24] As a rule, a Slavic or Turkic ending respectively differentiated a Pomak from a Turk, just as a Turkic or Slavic root distinguished a Pomak from a Bulgarian. But name systems were fluid and there was a considerable gray zone, a prevalent hybridity, until name systems were fixed and purged by the twentieth century. As Bulgarian and Muslim names were becoming solidified, Muslim names became the subject of anxiety and debate.

Ethnographic and other studies of Pomak names were only a small part of the impetus for the first name-changing operations that were carried out among Pomaks during the First Balkan War of 1912. As the Bulgarian state moved south, claiming its new territories and populations through the act of forced renaming, it marked Pomak populations with Bulgarian ownership and heredity. Name changes were carried out during the mass forced conversions of Pomaks in the occupied territories, in essence a christening of this population with new Bulgarian names. Conceived as a rectification of past historical injustices, the Bulgarian names of Pomaks were allegedly restored along with their Christian faith.[25] Bulgarian reports from this period detail how Pomak populations gladly and voluntarily embraced the Christian religion and their new Bulgarian names. Initial reports back to the Orthodox Holy Synod and Patriarch Kiril in Plovdiv were positive. In some cases, prophecies and supposed miracles were unearthed. One priest from the village of Kirezli, for example, related the story of a Christian convert from Islam and his divine vision:

---

[23] Ivan Vazov, *Pŭtepisi* (Sofia, 1974), 164.
[24] Mizov, *Taĭnata na Lichnoto Ime*, 141.
[25] Georgiev and Trifinov, *Pokrŭstvaneto*, 8.

We found that the population was gathered and ready for baptism. Their young mayor, who six years ago threw off his Turkish name and replaced it with "Vasil" was in charge. He told the following story, "He had become sick and was in a hopeless situation. In a dream, however, an old man came to him and said that he would get well if he changed his name to 'Vasil,' and also that after six years that [this land] would become Bulgarian and that all the Bulgaro-Mohammedans would become christened . . . [he was told] if he didn't change his name or be converted then he would die." When he woke up, he felt healthy . . . Vasil was intoxicated by his miraculous healing.[26]

Though few and far between, such stories imbued the conversion process with divine legitimacy for the Orthodox observers and participants, and at least a few Muslims.

But the bulk of Muslims were far from amenable to the forced renaming. Non-Bulgarian and even many Bulgarian sources stress the coerced nature of the name changes and the resultant movement of Pomaks across the border into Ottoman-held territories.[27] But perhaps the best indicator of Pomak attitudes toward the policy was the quick reversal by the fall of 1913 after the end of the Second Balkan War, when the new regime announced a policy allowing Muslims to convert back to Islam and reclaim their original names. The Muslim reaction was swift and decisive, Muslim names were quickly reclaimed. Representatives of the Orthodox establishment reported back to the Synod in horror about the spontaneous mass reclaiming of Muslim names. As one priest remarked in disgust, "newly baptized Christians don't go to church, or baptize their children . . . and they call each other by their old [Muslim] first names. . . . I ask them their names and they say their old names."[28] From the priest's point of view the very souls of Pomaks were at stake. Renaming went hand in hand with baptism and the saving of "Bulgarian" souls. In fact, by all indications Muslims saw renaming as exactly that, baptism. But state control over these peoples and territories was also at issue, so much so that political imperatives necessitated a callous reversal of the mass conversions.

Significantly, neither religion nor the church would enter into the renaming equation in the future. Nor would renaming be undertaken without at least some active Muslim participation. Although Bulgarianization would remain a constant, from here on out, the stated rationale for name changes would be "scientific" and linked to modernization. After World War I, ethnographic and other academic studies of Pomaks and their region increased exponentially, providing the "scientific" basis for all future assimilation campaigns, including renaming. The analysis of Pomaks' personal names, as well as studies of ethnonyms and toponyms, set the stage for the emergence of appella-

---

[26] Ibid., 469.
[27] See for example Eminov, *Turks and Other Muslim Minorities*; and Alhaug and Konstantinov, *Names, Ethnicity*.
[28] Georgiev and Trifinov, *Pokrŭstvaneto,* 414.

tions as a critical measure of both Turkification and essential Bulgarianness. Bulgarian social science stood behind interwar geographic place-name changes as Turkish and other "foreign" place names were replaced with old or new Bulgarian ones. In 1925, for example, the newspaper *Rodopa* described the Bulgarianization or christening of thousands of villages in the Rhodope region as a result of the input from, "Bulgarian science, geographers, historians, ethnographers, archeologists, philosophers, and others."[29] By 1934, the state launched a countrywide mass campaign for the change of Turco-Islamic geographic place names, touching about one-third of all villages in Bulgaria; in this way, as one Bulgarian source later proclaimed, the regime erased "the names foreign to the Bulgarian nation, imposed during the five-century yoke."[30]

During this period the term "Pomak" fell out of use in academic writings and the popular press. Detailed academic discussions of the term's origins located its origins in the verb *pomogat* (to help, implying helpers of the Turks) or, alternatively, *pomŭcheni* (those who have suffered).[31] Such controversies revealed the contradictions in Bulgarian attitudes toward Pomaks as both traitors and victims. The term "Pomak" became increasingly politically incorrect and it virtually disappeared from official and academic use, being replaced by "Bulgaro-Mohammedan," which stressed the presumed Bulgarianness of Pomaks. The hope of Bulgarian (and eventually Pomak) enthusiasts was that at some point "Bulgaro-Mohammedan" would be replaced by "Bulgarian" as Pomaks awakened to and embraced Bulgarian national consciousness. It was appropriate therefore, that Father Paisiĭ Khilendarski, the first awakener of Bulgarian national consciousness, would be invoked in discussions of the Pomak ethnonym. In his 1762 *Slavo-Bulgarian History* Paisiĭ had offered the following plea to Bulgarians, "O foolish and disgraceful ones! Why are you ashamed to call yourself Bulgarians?"[32] Paisiĭ's appeal was recycled in a 1937 article in the newspaper *Krasnodar* by one of the founders of *Rodina*, Arif Beĭski, "Oh you, central Rhodope Mohammedans, who are purely Slavs by race, why are you ashamed to call yourselves Bulgarians?"[33] Although it is unclear, even to this day, what ethnonyms Pomaks themselves use or prefer, if any, *Rodina* and its followers adopted the "Bulgaro-Mohammedan" appellation as a transitional measure.

Ethnonyms were always of concern, but Pomak personal names eventually became more critical to the *Rodina* agenda though belated in relation to other *Rodina* projects. By the summer of 1940 members first spoke openly about the need to shed Turco-Arabic names. *Rodina* was clearly sensitive to

---

[29] *Rodopa* (Smolyan), 1 December 1925, 1.

[30] Nikolaĭ Michev and Petŭr Koledarov, *Promenite v Imenata i Statuta na Selishtata v Bŭlgariia: 1878–1972* (Sofia, 1973), 8.

[31] See Marinov, *Bŭlgarite Mokhamedani*, 5–6; Primorski, "Starini Cherti v Bita i Kulturata na Rodopskite Bŭlgari," *Izvestiia na Etnografskiia Institut i Muzeĭ* (8) 1965: 10.

[32] Khilendarski, *Slavianobŭlgarska Istoriia*, 40.

[33] Strasimir Dimitrov, ed., *Rodopski Sbornik*, 228.

the fact that taking Bulgarian names was generally equated with baptism and conversion to Christianity. As a result *Rodina* went out of its way to emphasize that naming was independent of religion. *Rodina* leaders initiated a voluntary movement to give themselves and their children Bulgarian names; Arif Beĭski, for example, became Kamen Boliarov. In addition, in early 1941 Beĭski announced the symbolic naming of his newborn daughter with a Slavic name, Malinka. As *Rodina* writings described it: "With this he wanted to show that the name has nothing in common with faith and that nothing stands in the way of anyone giving their children Bulgarian national names. For God, names make no difference, as long as you fulfill his will. With this Beĭski began the Bulgarianization of names of Bulgaro-Mohammedans."[34] *Rodina* leaders asked the question, "Because we are Bulgarians, and not some other nationality, doesn't it follow that we should adopt Bulgarian names for ourselves and our offspring?"[35] But these spontaneous and voluntary name changes had a limited affect on the Pomak people, most of whom were unwilling to give up their own names or give their children Christian names.[36]

But as Bulgaria entered World War II in 1941, the regime supported the spread of *Rodina* operations into the occupied territories. By the summer of 1942, *Rodina* officials decided that name changes should no longer be voluntary but mandatory. A delegation of *Rodina* functionaries appealed to the Bulgarian government and in July of 1942 a law was passed in the Bulgarian National Assembly for the "Bulgarianization of the Mohammedan names of Bulgaro-Mohammedans."[37] In theory, the law simply provided for easier "voluntary" name changes, but in practice it led to the rapid, forced name changes of a large percentage of the Pomak population.[38] Pomaks were presented with a list of suitable "Bulgarian national names" by local *Rodina* officials and asked to "voluntarily" choose one.[39] Pressure was brought to bear by both *Rodina* members and other local government officials, including, in some cases, threats to withhold wartime food rations.[40]

Yet in spite of the intervention of local police and Muslim officials, many of the name-changing forms distributed to Pomak families were not turned in.[41] Even *Rodina* writings admitted that the 1942 directive had elicited a negative reaction among the local population. One article in a collection of *Rodina* writings described how a Muslim "fanatic" had refused to give a Bulgarian name to his new son. The Pomak in question spoke out in anger against the prospect, threatening to "kill him before I allow him to take a Bulgarian name." Other *Rodina* sources mention certain "fanatic" Pomaks

34 Marinov, ed., *Sbornik Rodina*, 3: 87.
35 Marinov, ed., *Sbornik Rodina*, 4: 2.
36 Ibid., 54.
37 Ibid., 54.
38 Khristo Khristov, *Iz Minoloto*, 136.
39 SODA (F-42K, O-15, E-10, L-319: 1942).
40 PODA (F-959k, O-1, E-225, L-80: 1975).
41 TsIDA (F-142, O-2, E-128, L-85: 1944).

who refused to bear children so they would not have to give them Bulgarian names.[42] In addition, there were complaints of a lack of *Rodina* activists and an excessive amount of "Turkish propaganda" in the districts where the name changing had been unsuccessful.[43] Even the Head Mufti in Sofia, who had lost all jurisdiction over Pomak districts, wrote complaints to the central authorities about the heavy-handed name-changing measures. One such letter to the Ministry of the Interior protested the fact that Muslim clerics had been fired and that rations of bread and wheat were withheld in cases when the name-changing forms were not submitted. According to the Head Mufti, many Pomaks had left their homes and were wandering from village to village or fleeing over the border.[44] Clearly, Pomak opposition to name changing was both present and ongoing.

At the same time *Rodina* officials also expressed satisfaction with good results in many Pomak districts. In some cases, pro-*Rodina* Pomaks allegedly bore children for the sole purpose of giving them Bulgarian names. One Pomak, Salikh Rumetsov from the village of Vievo, was said to have testified, "I thought that I would have no more children . . . but expressly for the sake of taking a Bulgarian name, soon I will have kids and give them the most beautiful [Bulgarian] names."[45] With an outpouring of emotion, the Pomak Mufti of Smolyan, Svetoslav Dukhovnikov (formerly Mehmed Dervishov), expressed, "Congratulations from my heart and soul to all my co-religionists for their new melodious Bulgarian names. We wish they will live long to enjoy and wear these names as a decoration of their belonging to the Bulgarian nation."[46] His sentiments were echoed elsewhere in *Rodina* writings, "We once and for all broke with all that is left of slavery and after throwing off the fez and the veil, personal names were the last mark with which we had to dispense."[47] With such testimonies in hand, *Rodina* celebrated its victories in the Pomak provinces.

As the politics of names heated up in Bulgaria, Turkish names also had an increased significance. Although the state did not intervene in the form or use of Turkish names throughout the prewar and wartime periods, Turks themselves initiated some subtle but important changes. By the twentieth century a standardized Turkish personal name-system had emerged. As with Bulgarians and Pomaks, patronymics seemed to be the primary source for Turkish last names. Although originally these often took the Turkish ending –oğlu (son of), in many cases, Turks started using the Bulgarian endings –ev/ov or -eva/ova and created hybridized Turco-Slavic last names such as Aliev(a), or Ahmedov(a). In most cases such names were donned as a mark of political loyalty to the Bulgarian regime and were most conspicuous, for example,

[42] Marinov, ed., *Sbornik Rodina*, 4: 28.
[43] TsIDA (F-142, O-2, E-128, L-80: 1944).
[44] TsIDA (F-471, O-1, E-1060, L-3: 1942).
[45] Marinov, ed., *Sbornik Rodina*, 4: 28.
[46] PODA (F-685, O-1, E-23, L-9: 1942).
[47] Dimitrov, ed., *Rodopski Sbornik*, 306.

among Turks in positions of power. The Head Muftiship and local Mufti-ships, for example, especially by the 1930s, showed a preponderance of last names ending in –ev/ov. As the Muftiship maintained and spread its power during the Second World War such names were retained and perhaps even grew with the expansion of influence. The phenomenon of Turkish names with Bulgarian endings was carried over and greatly expanded in the early decades of the Communist Period, when such names became the rule. Hence Bulgarian endings (–ev/ov and –eva/ova) were the brand of co-optation and a means of survival for generations of Turks in Bulgaria.

Renamed, Reborn

The Communist period, as it turned out, witnessed the most relentless and long-lasting name-changing campaigns in Bulgarian history. The Communist Party appropriated and employed the power to name and hence to define its citizens as it saw fit. It imbued Bulgarian names with new meaning as modernity and socialist progress became increasingly linked to Bulgarian-ness. Not only did citizens have to look modern and Bulgarian, but they had to wear Bulgarian labels. Non-Bulgarian names, including "bourgeois" West-ern names, came under fire in a milieu where both East and West were seen as anathema to true progress. But the real war was unleashed against Turco-Arabic Muslim names. By the late Communist period, socialist material modernity enjoyed marked, although incomplete success in making Turkish clothes, houses, and property patterns conform to a Bulgarian, all-socialist national standard. Turco-Arabic personal names, therefore, remained the most conspicuous mark of Turkishness—of all that was backwards and bar-baric—a reminder of the Turkish yoke. According to Communist Party offi-cials, these last visible, audible, and knowable markers of the past had to be eradicated in order for "ripe" Communism to arrive.

Nowhere in the Eastern Bloc did names come to mean as much or face such intense programmatic attack as in the Bulgarian context. Elsewhere there were rare cases of mass name changes, some voluntary, some more co-erced. In the Soviet Union in the 1920s and 1930s, for example, it became a common practice to select "revolutionary" names and drop "names with an aura of backwardness," that is, certain political, ethnic, or rural, peasant-sounding names. Unfavorable political names—such as Trotsky, for ex-ample—as well as "Jewish-sounding" names were dropped or wholly Rus-sianized during the Stalinist terror and heightened anti-Semitism of the 1930s. Muslim names, as in the Bulgarian context, were at least partially Russianized as a mark of complicity through the addition of Russian-style patronymics and endings to Turco-Arabic roots.[48] In Communist Albania, state-directed forced name changes occurred in the 1970s when the rogue re-

---

[48] Sheila Fitzpatrick, *Everyday Stalinism*, 83–84.

gime forced all Albanian citizens to eliminate "undesirable" especially religious names for the sake of national unity and official atheism. This did not specifically target Turco-Arabic names, but rather all blatantly religious names, in which God, priest, dervish, or Mohammed was part of the name. Ironically, Enver Hoxha, whose surname is from the Turkish *hoca* or "Muslim teacher," kept his name, in spite of its clear religious connotations. Unfortunately, studies of the Albanian or other name-changing movements in the Bloc, forced or voluntary, are virtually nonexistent. This serves to highlight the uniqueness and importance of the Bulgarian case, where the meaning of names for both the state and its citizens had inordinate power.

But names were not the focus of Communist efforts in the early decades of the period. In fact, in the early postwar period, the Communist party revoked the Law on Names as Fascist and the vast majority of Pomaks resumed use of their Muslim names. As *Rodina* members fell out of official favor the Party made promises to the Muslim community about the sanctity of their names. They were assured that their names would not be assailed by the Communist authorities who were "liberating" them from Fascist oppression, embodied in things such as the renaming practices. These promises were honored at least during the first decades of Communism, when power was being consolidated. Even during the Great Leap Forward and the Cultural Revolution of 1958–60, when clothing reforms hit their first peak of activity, Muslim names were only beginning to attract attention. It was only during the relative quiet of the 1960s and 1970s that names moved to the center of the BCP agenda. Predictably, Pomaks were one of the first targets.[49]

Slowly but surely Pomak names came under scrutiny and attack as academic and political discourse increasingly concerned itself with enforcing the "Bulgarianness" of Pomaks. Interest revived in the rectification of "historical injustices" and the restoring of Bulgarian names to "forcibly" Islamicized Muslims. Name changes would also serve the purpose of national integration and modernization, crucial to progress and building socialism. Not all Communist Party members, however, agreed that name changes were a necessary or expedient method of dealing with Pomak difference and backwardness. Politburo discussions, documents, and memoirs from the period indicated considerable disagreement on the necessity, pace, and approach to Pomak renaming. Such disagreements translated into an occasional lack of conformity in the implementation of name changes. Most sources date the official onslaughts against Pomak names to 1962–64 and again later in 1971–74.[50] Although these were certainly peak times, archival sources reveal that there

---

[49] From 1960–62, name-changing campaigns were initiated among the Roma (Gypsy) population of Bulgaria. Although little research has been done on these campaigns, it is generally assumed that Roma were forced to take Bulgarian names during these years. Official documents, however, suggest that Roma were encouraged to take on either Bulgarian or Turkish names, the latter as a transitional measure for eventual integration into the Bulgarian nation. See, for example, TsIDA (F-1B, O-509, E-5, L-111: 1962).

[50] Alhaug and Konstantinov, *Names, Ethnicity*, 29–31.

were also a series of measures taken in parts of southern Bulgaria as early as 1960 in connection with the tail end of the Cultural Revolution. According to official Bulgarian sources, all phases of the Pomak name-changing campaigns were theoretically "voluntary," regardless of when they occurred. In practice, there were certainly voluntary phases in the campaigns but as a rule, name changes were carried out with considerable force.

In the earliest phases of the program beginning around 1960–61, the Party emphasized persuasion in its approach to Pomak name changes. State publications and recommendations were very clearly directed at the younger generation, born and reared under the new system. A 1961 handbook for elementary school teachers in the Rhodope Mountains, for example, provides information on the role of teachers in the "voluntary changing of Oriental names to Bulgarian names." The text explores the "successes" of campaigns in which students were encouraged to publicly reject their "Mohammedan names" and take on Bulgarian ones. As an example, the handbook cites the case of three Pomak girls in the village of Drenovo who "joyfully and voluntarily" changed their names to "Slavka, Zdravka, and Elka."[51] Reflecting the Party line, the handbook advises that their "Oriental names left the deepest stamp of Mohammedanization" and so "played a harmful role in the formation of Bulgarian national consciousness."[52] As little "Zdravka" and "Slavka" reportedly testified, "Before we changed our names we didn't sleep for two nights. We thought to ourselves, why do we have Turkish names when we are Bulgarian?"[53] To encourage the name changes, Pomak children were even given Bulgarian pen pals, who wrote letters imploring their Pomak counterparts to take Bulgarian names. This letter from the Bulgarian girl Violeta Strakhilova, to the Pomak Rafia Nazirova appears in the handbook as an example: "Aren't you Bulgarian by nationality? Why don't you have a Bulgarian name? Why don't you change it to Snezhanka for example? That is a very beautiful name. I implore you to write me and let me know whether you agree to change your name to Snezhanka. If you don't like it, I'll pick out another for you. Or is someone preventing you—your father, mother, grandmother, or *hoca*? . . . Your name is not a Bulgarian name. In our region only Gypsies have such names; Bulgaro-Mohammedans have already changed their names to Bulgarian ones."[54] In another such letter, a Bulgarian boy, Orlin Mincho, instructs his Pomak pen pal, Mekhmed Akhmedov Deliakhievlev: "Your three names are reminiscent of nothing other than five centuries of the Turkish yoke. . . . We are Bulgarians and our names should be Bulgarian. All other names come from our enemies."[55] According to this handbook Pomak school children were exceptionally amenable to this "revolutionary act," in spite of the fact that their Muslim homes were labeled bas-

[51] Spasov, ed., *Sbornik v Pomosht*, 7.
[52] Ibid., 8.
[53] Ibid., 12.
[54] PODA (F-959k, O-1, E-69, L-5: 1969).
[55] PODA (F-959k, O-1, E-69, L-5: 1969).

tions of "Turcification" and "backwardness." Pomak parents, it was assumed, were the biggest hindrance to the sound social development of Rhodope children because, "they don't know the truth about their national origins and they think they are Turkish."[56]

In light of the general failure of the voluntary approach to name changes, the Communist regime moved increasingly toward coercion to enforce name changing among adults and children. By 1964 the pace of voluntary name changes had touched only a small segment of the Sofia-loyal Pomak population and had slowed to a near standstill. As a result, in the spring of 1964, debates about a more decisive approach to name changes among Pomaks raged in the Central Committee of the Politburo in Sofia. On the one hand, some BCP leaders were afraid that a focus on name changing would only divert attention from the more important task of building socialism. On the other hand, some proponents believed that name changes should be the primary goal in these regions and that it was integral to the larger task of building socialism. Representatives from the districts with compact Pomak populations tended to be more reserved, fearing that local resistance would make any heavy-handed name-changing measures problematic. Ultimately, those in favor of giving name changes high priority won out and, by late March 1964, forced name-changing campaigns commenced.[57] But although the Politburo openly supported these name changes in theory, they offered no blueprint on how to carry out such changes, at what pace, and at what cost.

On the local level, Communist Party officials tended to take matters into their own hands and ignore or push the "priority" according to local circumstances. In 1964, the Communist leadership in southwestern Bulgaria took a particularly proactive approach. Petŭr Diulgerov, the Blagoevgrad Regional Secretary of the Communist Party, led the charge in what came to be known as the Rebirth Process in this region, apparently acting somewhat independently of Sofia. Diulgerov's memoirs published in 1996 focus on the dramatic and often violent events of these years, in which he made some of the most important decisions of his career. His memoirs have been criticized by many because of his convictions that the name changes were historically and politically justified, and that the changes had a fairly widespread base of sincere supporters among Pomaks. Diulgerov assumes that when Pomak communities peacefully accepted the name changes that no duplicity or fear was involved, but rather a sincere desire to return to the truth, that is, Bulgarianness; when Pomaks resisted he assumes that outside—namely Turkish—intervention was the source of this local "fanaticism." Although such suppositions rub his critics the wrong way, Diulgerov's writings do offer a window into the mind of the Communist Party leadership as well as detailing acts of local Pomak defiance.

Diulgerov's story begins in the spring of 1964 when with tacit Politburo

---

[56] Spasov, ed., *Sbornik v Pomosht*, 7.
[57] Diulgerov, *Razpnati Dushi*, 20.

approval he traveled to villages in his district, talking to local elites and testing reactions to the imminent name changes. For the most part he was satis-
fied that most Pomaks were ready for name changes and that little or no opposition would interfere. He does note some dissenting voices in the villages
around the town of Brushten, where older peasants remembered the name
changes of the First Balkan War. In addition, in the neighboring village of
Vulkosel, Diulgerov was met with open hostility: "The last village we went to
was Vulkosel. That was a well-known center of Turcophilia and fanaticism in
the district. . . . Our reason and arguments hit an impenetrable wall. Near
midnight the night watchman in the mayor's office reported that peasants
armed with hunting rifles, axes, and sticks surrounded the building. The inhabitants of Vulkosel had risen up so that we would leave . . . we begged
them to leave us until morning."[58] Diulgerov and company were spared and
they left Vulkosel the following morning, but without the villagers' agreement to the name changes. Although sufficient towns and villages had promised conformity, perhaps out of fear or the desire to avoid confrontation, others were willing to risk the consequences of defiance. Far from being an
anomaly, the Vulkosel incident was indicative of the type of reaction to name
changing that would characterize the remainder of the Rebirth Process
among both Pomaks and later Turks.

In spite of Vulkosel, Diulgerov and regional officials proceeded with vigor
in carrying out name changes in the villages of the region. In only a number
of days, as Diulgerov retells with satisfaction, approximately 80 percent of
Pomaks in the Blagoevgrad region had submitted to the name-changing campaign and chosen new Bulgarian names. Although this process went relatively smoothly at first, rumors of revolt in the village of Ribnovo spread
quickly and the mountain community quickly became the center of regional
protest. As Diulgerov recounted: "The official government of the village was
replaced with a special staff, which created an organization for resistance and
support in the event of name changes. The male part of the population was
mobilized for twenty-four-hour guard duty. They upheld a constant external
blockade and protection of the approaches to the village. The school was
closed, and the Bulgarian teachers were put under house arrest." Not only
did the "rebels" take control of the local government, but they entered into
violent conflict with a government commission and military detachment that
were sent from Gotse Delchev to quell the revolt:

> The Ribnovo inhabitants met them [the regiment] in an organized fashion. Ac-
> cording to command, and without any wavering, they threw whatever they
> could at them [the soldiers]. The commission and the detachment of men were
> surprised and confused. They struck out into panicked flight. A police officer
> was heavily wounded. They disarmed him. A soldier was also caught and they
> also took his weapon. They put fezzes on them and wrapped turbans around

[58] Ibid., 24.

their heads. On the same day they hung a Turkish flag above the mayor's building. They cut telephone lines and they blew up the bridge of the only road into the village.[59]

Unlike Vulkosel, Ribnovo raised an immediate red flag to Diulgerov as well as to the authorities in Sofia. Resistance of this magnitude was not taken lightly.

Far from being an isolated incident, the Ribnovo rebels had sent couriers to neighboring villages and spread the word, creating an immediate chain reaction. As Diulgerov later interpreted it, "Turcophiles and fanatics everywhere organized resistance" and Pomaks who had gone along with the name changes were maligned and ill-treated by the resisters.[60] Most importantly, a delegation from Ribnovo and the surrounding villages went to Sofia and filed a protest at the highest levels, to the Turkish embassy and the central authorities, in that order.[61] In fact, the Central Committee of the Communist Party reportedly first heard of the rebellion directly from the Turkish embassy, which submitted an official complaint. The Communist Party leader, Todor Zhivkov, was compelled to respond in light of the volatility of the situation and the delicacy of Bulgaro-Turkish relations, just beginning to be repaired from Cold War damage. Pomak delegations were received in Sofia, told that the central government had nothing to do with the name-changing campaigns in their districts, and promised that the Party would stop the responsible regional authorities from implementing name changes. Indeed, by the end of March, Zhivkov sent a national commission into the region to reverse name changes, with promises that such measures would not be repeated. He personally sent a telegram to every village that had been affected and sent top generals to enter Ribnovo and negotiate with the rebels.[62] According to Diulgerov, with standing ovations for Zhivkov and toasts of *rakiia* (plum brandy) the Ribnovo inhabitants accepted apologies and promises of future respect for their Turco-Arabic names.[63]

The events of March 1964 put a damper on the name-changing drive that had captured the imagination of BCP officials, especially in the Blagoevgrad region. Although the responsible parties were criticized for their actions that apparently went beyond what Sofia had approved or ordered, no purges of these cadres occurred; they remained in their positions to preside over the next wave of name changes.[64] In the six years between 1964 and 1970, the region did undergo important changes, which, as Diulgerov notes, presumably laid the groundwork for the next phase of integration. Bulgarian education, cultural development, and the expansion of industry and infrastructure

[59] Ibid., 26.
[60] Ibid., 27.
[61] PODA (F-959k, O-1, E-225, L-261: 1974).
[62] Diulgerov, *Razpnati Dushi*, 27.
[63] Ibid., 28–29.
[64] Ibid., 31.

became priorities in this chronically "backward" region.[65] But from the BCP point of view, name changes were ultimately seen as critical to the solution of the Pomak question. As Diulgerov later noted, "The Turco-Arabic name of the Islamic Bulgarians turned out to be a difficult knot, in which political, religious, ethnic, and everyday problems were interwoven."[66] Socialist progress could not proceed, it was assumed, without unraveling this knot.

As a result, by 1970 name changes again moved to the top of the agenda when the Party leadership launched the last, most conclusive phase of the Rebirth Process; they passed a resolution that called for the total, mass name changing of Pomaks. Pressure was brought to bear primarily in the workplace where the failure to reregister with Bulgarian names meant the loss of jobs, pensions or other government benefits. Again, significant unrest ensued, as in the town of Madan in February 1970 where protestors from the surrounding villages gathered after name changes had been instituted. Thousands of men and women assembled for several days to protest the measures and numerous participants in the demonstrations were interned and some killed, their bodies thrown into local rivers or mine shafts.[67] The spirit of protest was apparently contagious, and opposition spread from Madan to Rudozem and then Dospat as name-changing measures spilled into these townships by 1971.[68] According to observers, the Pomaks of Dospat had tried to reason with the enforcing BCP officials by stating, "We've fulfilled labor norms, we've won competitions, and we've done the most difficult physical labor, why now do we have to change our names?"[69] In spite of their questions, the name changes proceeded and, according to one report: "Representatives of the regional administration went there and the people of Dospat—men and women—fell upon them and took matters into their own hands. Rocks were thrown, breaking windows of trucks and cars, and there was even bloodshed. Chaos ensued, creating the need to call for help from the authorities in Devin and the border forces. There was shooting and wounded."[70] These protests were quelled, but only after some twenty four hours of resistance. Pomaks were making their voices heard, and as a result, the confidence of the regime was somewhat shaken.

One aspect of the name changes that provoked particular anger was its focus on newborns, who could be registered only with Bulgarian names. The targeting of newborns in the Rebirth Process contributed to the development of a noteworthy gender dimension to the protest. Pomak women tended to mobilize for protest in significant numbers against the "christening" of their children. In Rudozem, as one observer reported: "Most of them [the protest-

---

[65] Ibid., 36.
[66] Ibid., 50.
[67] PODA (F-959k, O-1, E-226, L-37: 1974).
[68] PODA (F-959k, O-1, E-226, L-37: 1974).
[69] PODA (F-959k, O-1, E-226, L-60: 1974).
[70] PODA (F-959k, O-1, E-226, L-60: 1974).

ers] were women from the villages of the province and neighborhoods [of Rudozem], there were fewer men. All day they spoke out against the authorities, they insulted individual people and threatened the leaders. They wanted the secretary of the village council to come out so they could beat and thrash him, because he was the first to change his name from Fakhri to Zdravko, and now was taking part in registering newborn children with Bulgarian names."[71] Pomak women actively opposed the use of Bulgarian names, even though the Women's Committee of Bulgaria had sent Bulgarian women to prepare Pomak women, holding discussions about the "beauty and meaning of Bulgarian names."[72] These committees encouraged Muslim women to select Bulgarian names for their children and also fought against the secret endowment of Muslim children with second, Turco-Arabic names.[73] This double-naming phenomenon, in which Muslim names continued to be used at home, was so prevalent after the name changes of the 1970s that Petŭr Marinov, an astute observer of this period, would call the Pomak Rebirth Process a "dead revolution."[74] Double naming as a response to name changes began as soon as the name changes themselves and continued until their reversal in 1989–90. Along with this private, quiet type of resistance, more overt resistance would also continue as long as the active name changes were taking place.

Another wave of protest occurred in 1972 in the same region, but centered in the districts around Iakoruda, in the Western Rhodopes. In May of 1972 name changes were administered in Iakoruda with a combination of fanfare and force. Regional Party officials personally made an appearance in the town with "volunteer brigades"—many of them Pomaks with freshly changed-names—to carry out the name changes. In a show of force, the exits to the city were blockaded as an official ceremony began in the town square. Diulgerov himself addressed the crowd with a speech prepared by historians and literati that recounted the "tragic fate" of Pomaks, that is, their forced conversion and Turkification under Ottoman rule. He called for the healing of "the wounds of Turkification" and the return to "our common national roots." The crowd was told that government representatives were poised to visit each and every Pomak family in the village to carry out the "ritual of renaming." They were warned to keep the peace and receive the representatives with hospitality. According to Diulgerov, the process went smoothly for the first several hours until "the Turcophiles and fanatics came to life" and began to "threaten, dissuade, and incite" local Pomaks to oppose the official action. Soon reports came in of barred doors and threats of bloodshed, but the resistors eventually gave in to the pressure of the local authorities.[75] In this case, as in the past, Diulgerov apparently acted without the direct approval of

[71] PODA (F-959k, O-1, E-226, L-40: 1974).
[72] TsIDA (F-417, O-4, E-59, L-19: 1959).
[73] TsIDA (F-417, O-4, E-91, L-4: 1972).
[74] PODA (F-959k, O-1, E-226, L-63: 1974).
[75] Ibid., 52.

Zhivkov, who called him to Sofia on hearing of the incident from the Turkish consulate. Zhivkov admonished Diulgerov, but after a reserved scolding, he raised his *rakiia* glass with a hearty "*nazdrave*" (to your health), congratulating Diulgerov on his success. Hence this time the *rakiia* glass was raised to Party officials for their success in carrying out the name changes—not to Zhivkov for his reversal of them. This round of renaming was not to be reversed while the Communists still held power.

One last notable incident of resistance to name changes occurred in 1972–73 in Kornitsa, another village in southwestern Bulgaria. By the end of 1972 a "pro-Turkish" town government had taken control of the town and refused to implement name changes for the town inhabitants. In essence, the whole town was on strike; children stopped going to school and adults stopped working for official institutions. For two and a half months the Turkish flag was hoisted over the town center. The rebel government even demanded official recognition for the townspeople as Turks, Turkish schools for their children, and the right to keep their Turco-Arabic names. Party operatives watched the situation closely and tried to resolve it without force, but categorically rejected the first two of these demands. On the third point the Party representatives stressed that the name changes were "voluntary" but that the rejection of such changes was clearly indicative of "foreign influence" and that traitorous activity that was a punishable offense.[76] Finally, Sofia authorities took direct action against Kornitsa and sent in police, firemen, and soldiers to quell the revolt. Three locals were killed and numerous people wounded.[77] In this case and others, leaders of the resistance were rounded up and interned, and a number of deaths and internal deportations were reported.[78] Clearly there was some truth to Diulgerov's accusations of "Turcophilia" among Pomaks, as resistance was, at times, accompanied by shows of affinity for Turks, such as flying the Turkish flag or reporting to the Turkish consulate.

In fact many were well aware of the persistence, if not growth, of such affinities behind much of the resistance to Bulgarian integration projects. Petŭr Marinov, although out of official favor, observed and commented in painstaking detail in his personal diaries on the failures of Party name-changing efforts among Pomaks. Marinov conjectured that resistance to name changes had surpassed resistance to clothing reform and other measures because de-veiling was "in the tone of Kemalism, in new Turkey it had happened, and so there was no reason to resist, BUT when the business with the NAMES started, that meant the breaking with the Turkish consciousness."[79] Over the years he wrote detailed letters of advice to the BCP authorities in Sofia and to local officials in the Rhodopes, most of which went unanswered, but not necessarily ignored. Marinov's main criticism of the Communist mea-

---

[76] Ibid., 64.
[77] Ibid., 68.
[78] Poulton, *Balkans*, 112–13.
[79] PODA (F-959k, O-1. E-225, L-245: 1975).

sures was that *Rodina* was not rehabilitated and that most key *Rodina* members like himself were not embraced by the Party or used in the name-changing campaigns. At the same time he expressed satisfaction that the work of *Rodina* was basically being continued and carried out to the letter, although occasionally with excessive force. By 1974—the same year that name changes among Pomaks were finalized—a collection of past *Rodina* writings was even being prepared for republication, a de facto rehabilitation of the organization. Though Pomak names were officially taken by 1974, they remained in unofficial use throughout the period, indicative of Pomak affinities for Islam and their Turkish co-religionists.

Turks and the Rebirth Process

For Turks, a break with Turkish consciousness was even more unthinkable than for Pomaks. Whereas Pomaks had been told they were Bulgarians off and on since 1912, and consistently since 1945, Turks had been mostly granted the inviolability of their Turkishness, albeit within closely proscribed parameters. The Turkish population did view the Bulgarianization of Pomak names with considerable trepidation. For some there was a foreboding that, "we are next," but for most the Rebirth Process of 1984–85 came as a shock. Since about 1980 the possibility of carrying out name changes among Turks was already being discussed, given the growing conviction that most if not all Turks in Bulgaria had Bulgarian origins. But such an approach was opposed by many in the Party leadership due to fear of Turkish resistance or a strong reaction from the West.[80] In spite of these fears, ultimately, the advocates of name changes won out. In 1984 Zhivkov launched the Rebirth Process, centered on the "voluntary" change of Turkish names to Bulgarian forms.[81]

The assumption was that the name changes would integrate the Turkish population once and for all into the Bulgarian nation and hence eliminate the Turco-Muslim threat. After the name changes were carried out, one Politburo discussion advanced: "Perhaps one of the most important motives for the restoration of Bulgarian names is the constant attempt by the Turkish leadership to manipulate this population with pan-Turkic nationalism and their desire to build an antisocialist and pro-NATO "fifth column" in the People's Republic of Bulgaria on the basis of Turkish names. The renewal of the Bulgarian names of Bulgarian Muslims is a blow to these attempts."[82] Here, name-changing campaigns were rationalized by national security, but this was only one of the many justifications for the historical, political, social, and national necessity of the "restoration" of Bulgarian names.

In addition to national security, the rectification of "historical injustice"

[80] TsIDA (F-1B, O-63, E-106, L-16: 1980).
[81] Eminov, *Turkish and Other Muslim Minorities*, 217.
[82] TsIDA (F-1B, O-63, E-4, L-7: 1987).

was the most ubiquitous rationale. The films *Under the Yoke* and *A Time of Parting* were re-released and shown to the public to highlight both the hardships that Bulgarians suffered under the Turkish yoke and the presumed brutality of the Turkification process. At the same time, academics and politicians presented the contemporary campaigns to the public (and each other) as inevitable and natural, part of an ongoing historical process. An article in *Bŭlgarskata Etnografiia* (Bulgarian Ethnography) from 1988, for example, claims that Turks had been "spontaneously" taking Bulgarian names since 1878: "The restoration of Bulgarian names of people, cities, villages, and places in Bulgaria has continued for more than 100 years. This is not a new process. The liberation from the remnants of slavery and the rebirth of all that is Bulgarian—this is a continuous historical process. It has been going on for a whole century throughout various epochs, and has touched various groups of the Bulgarian population that were subjugated in the past to Islamicization and ethnic assimilation."[83] The rebirth through renaming was crucial, according to the article, to the, "healing of one of the most painful wounds remaining from five centuries of barbaric domination." These sentiments were echoed in a Politburo discussion of the following year, "There is no name-changing campaign. It is a hundred-year process that has quickened in the last few years. It is normal and natural . . . part of the creating of a socialist unified nation."[84] The Party interpretation of the Rebirth Process as inevitable and natural starkly contrasted with the regime's interpretation of past conversions and assimilation processes as brutal and unnatural.

The Rebirth Process among Turks followed a pattern similar to the Pomak case, though without reversals and executed more quickly in the course of one year. Beginning in southeastern Bulgaria in December of 1984 and by February of 1985 spreading north to Dobrudzha, old identity cards and official documents were destroyed and new ones issued. The Party applied pressure in the work place, public ceremonies, and door-to-door campaigns. In one procedural innovation, Turkish men were called up for "reserve duty" and then interned. Some were tortured and the safety of their families threatened until they submitted to the changes. Turkish women, left home alone to run the household were also threatened and forced to change their names. Many reportedly resisted until it became evident that without the new Bulgarian-name identity cards that they could neither collect salaries nor receive medical care, and generally would be treated as criminals.[85] A portion of the Turkish elite was directly involved in all phases of the name-changing campaigns, though often in the face of threats. The Head Muftis, Mirian Topchiev and (since 1988) Nedim Gendev, as well as local religious functionaries and secular officials, lent their support and direct aid in the imple-

---

[83] Georgi Iankov, "Niakoĭ Osobenosti na Konsolidatsiia na Bŭlgarskata Natsiia." *Bŭlgarskata Etnografiia* 4 (1986): 13.

[84] TsIDA (F-1B, O-63, E-9, L-6: 1987).

[85] Eminov, *Turkish and Other Muslim Minorities*, 88–89.

mentation of the process.[86] For many, large pay raises and praise from official circles assured their cooperation.[87] At the same time, according to Halil Akhmedov Ibishev, then a member of the Bulgarian National Assembly, the BCP authorities warned that, "Anybody who resists will be killed like a dog."[88]

Nevertheless many Party-loyal Turks defected from their positions to join in the active opposition to the regime that swelled throughout the provinces during and after the campaigns. Voices were raised in protest by the educated Turkish elite, who were attacked and silenced during and after 1984–85. Numerous Turkish students and intellectuals, some of them loyal Party members, were detained, arrested, and interned in pre-emptive strikes in 1984–85, while others were closely watched for the remainder of the period.[89] Even Communist Turks and Muslim clerics protested and joined in local resistance, which sometimes resulted in violent clashes between protestors and authorities, particularly in southeastern Bulgaria. The most dramatic and well-known conflicts took place in Benkovski and Momchilgrad near the Turkish border where thousands of demonstrators were fired upon, many killed and wounded. There were also violent confrontations between Turks and state officials in Haskovo, Gorno Prakhovo, Mlechino, and the northeastern towns of Razgrad and Iablonovo.[90] In all, scores of Turks were killed, beaten, tortured, internally deported, and hundreds or perhaps thousands were arrested as a result of overt opposition.[91] Considerable force was required to overcome this resistance and tanks, military trucks, and fire trucks were deployed to Turkish districts.[92] Tear gas was even used to storm Momchilgrad and other Turkish holdouts. Many protested through emigration; some escaped over the border, and others defected in more public displays of opposition. In one highly publicized case the world-champion weight lifter Naim Suleimanov defected during a competition in Australia. He immediately dropped his "restored" Bulgarian name, Naum Shalamanov, and publicly condemned the Bulgarian name-changing policy. To reinforce his new loyalties to the Turkish government and his Turkish national affiliation Naim even further Turkified his surname from Suleimanov to Suleymanoğlu.[93]

In spite of the potency of public protest, Bulgarian names were decisively, officially imposed by 1985. But the Rebirth Process was far from decisive. Party deliberations and efforts to suppress nonconformity lasted through the remainder of the period. One official from the Leshnitsa district, for example, complained: "In the schools the children in most cases call each other

[86] *Prava i Svobodi* (Sofia), 9 August 1991, 3.
[87] According to Poulton, Islamic clerics who cooperated were given salary raises from 150 to 200 leva per month. Poulton, *Balkans*, 131.
[88] Ibid., 143.
[89] Ibid., 143–44.
[90] Ibid., 139–40.
[91] Eminov, *Turkish and other Muslim Minorities*, 90.
[92] *Prava i Svobodi* (Sofia), 11–17 March, 1991, 3.
[93] Poulton, *Balkans*, 146.

by their old [Turkish] names. This is also true of the factories where one
manager said that if he called them [Turks] by their new names they got
angry. . . . In connection to this, the children being born now, in addition to
their official Bulgarian name, secretly are given an unofficial other [Turkish]
name."[94] Hence, the use of "old" names was not only a private but also a
very public, demonstrative or performative practice that amounted to a kind
of protest. Sometimes such protest was fairly overt, as in Party complaints of,
"hostilely oriented elements . . . morally supported by Turkey" that "have
attempted to demonstratively force meetings in public places with old Turkish names."[95] During one incident in the town of Ruse, local Turks wrote old
Turkish names on gravestones in defiance of government orders.[96] In fact,
graveyards or cemeteries were an important battleground for the name-
change campaigns as BCP officials brazenly crossed out as many Turco-Arabic names on gravestones as possible and replaced them with Bulgarian ones.
Even the dead were not spared the humiliation of being redefined by government dictate. The Party sought to make it abundantly clear to the population
that, "no other kind of names exist except Bulgarian ones and we won't use
Turkish names anywhere for any reason."[97]

The Party policy on names was undergirded by elaborate academic efforts
to illustrate the general importance of names to Bulgarian historical development. In the years following the 1984–85 Rebirth Process a plethora of writings on names was published, including dictionaries that catalogued and
listed the cultural significance of historical and contemporary Bulgarian
names and provided a selection of authentic Bulgarian names that could be
bestowed on newborns, for both the renamed Muslim population and the
Bulgarian population itself.[98] Other works, such as Nikolai Mizov's *Taĭnata
na Lichnoto Ime* (The Secret of the Personal Name) published in 1987, offers
a more thorough discussion of the meaning and social context of names, exploring the functions of names and providing links to the specific Bulgarian
historical context. He discusses, for example, the connection of names to
property patterns, family, kinship, and as markers of gender and status.[99] He
also elaborates the importance of names in determining the place of an individual in society and securing the continuity of that society:

> The name system not only is the basis of the everyday regulation of relationships
> among people, but at the same time, plays a huge role (though it is not always
> noticeable on the surface) of an ideological-educational continuity between his-
> torical epochs and between different generations. It represents an additional
> socio-educational factor for the confirmation of a person as a social being, about

[94] TsIDA (F-1B, O-63, E-9, L-2,3: 1988).
[95] TsIDA (F-1B, O-63, E-2, L-13: 1987).
[96] TsIDA (F-1B, O-63, E-2, L-18: 1987).
[97] TsIDA (F-1B, O-63, E-2, L-47–8: 1987).
[98] Nedialka Ivanova and Penka Radeva, *Ot "A" do "Ia": Imenata na Bŭlgarite* (Sofia, 1985);
and Stefan Ilchev, *Za Khubavi Bŭlgarski Imena za Detsata ni* (Sofia, 1963).
[99] Mizov, *Taĭnata na Lichnoto Ime*, 45.

his formation as a personality, with a place in the progress of his nation and homeland.[100]

In simpler terms, "The name is the solder between the past and the present and at the same time is the stimulus for the future."[101] Hence, Bulgarian academic writings focused on names as significant, if not critical, to the Bulgarian nation and its path toward progress.

Significantly, this path to progress was never directly or unambiguously westward. In fact, in the various writings on names, Bulgarians were also criticized for taking non-Bulgarian "Western" names. Although Mizov predictably embraces "revolutionary" or "Soviet-inspired" names, he hotly critiques "name nihilism, name arbitrariness, and name tastelessness" which he claims, "leads to ethnonational and international name depersonalization, against which we need to conduct a systematic and unwavering . . . struggle."[102] This sentiment is echoed in another book on names, which criticizes the increasingly popular practice of adopting French and German "foreign names," therefore sullying the purity of Bulgarian names.[103] Another source decries the attempts of parents to be original through their selection of "ugly un-Bulgarian names," thus showing "weak patriotic consciousness and lack of taste"[104] Evidently taste resided in the place in between East and West, in the true Bulgarian name.

Ultimately the "restoration" of true Bulgarian names to Muslims proved problematic. Despite its euphoric proclamations of success, the Party continued to discuss problems associated with the goal of "calling people only by Bulgarian names" until the very end of the Communist period. One of the proposed remedies was to put labels or "tablets" with the new Bulgarian names on house or apartment doors and to introduce the wearing of name badges at work.[105] Although it is uncertain whether the name badges were implemented, name plates on dwellings became common practice in Bulgaria, not just for Turks but for all dwellings. The highest Party officials had discussed this question and decided that all houses and not just "those [belonging to] citizens with restored names" should have such identifiers, which would only serve to differentiate them. Part of the goal was also to simply acquaint friends and neighbors with the new names and therefore put them into common usage.[106] Hence the relabeling of Turks as "Bulgarians with restored names" took a very concrete form; the labeling was not only figurative, it was literal.

In spite of the persistence of local problems with the implementation of

[100] Ibid., 183.
[101] Ibid., 84.
[102] Ibid., 159.
[103] Ivanova and Radeva, *Ot "A" do "Ia,"* 11.
[104] Ilchev, *Za Khubavi Bŭlgarski*, 3.
[105] TsIDA (F-1B, O-63, E-2, L-48: 1987).
[106] TsIDA (F-1B, O-63, E-11, L-14?: 1988).

name changes, the Party officially declared itself triumphant as early as 1985. Party officials insisted that, "an essential barrier to the unification of the Bulgarian nation was overcome" and a new era had begun with the recognition of "our common past, present, and future." This, they even declared, was an integral part of the "restructuring of our society" that accompanied Gorbachev's *perestroika* in the Soviet Union in the late 1980s.[107] In reality, the BCP leadership was grasping at straws for legitimacy as faith in the Soviet Empire and Communist rule began to crumble. The imagined approach of ripe Communism and the dénouement of Bulgaro-Turkish unification clearly was grounded in desperation and illusion, not reform. In truth, the Rebirth Process had created a greater fissure between Bulgarian and Turk than had previously existed. If anything it had arrested much of the integration that had taken place as an accompaniment to modernization and drove a gathering storm of resistance among a least a segment of Bulgarians and Muslims alike. As this resistance crystallized in 1989, it played a major role in Bulgaria's velvet revolution of November of that year and the conclusive toppling of the Communist system itself. In fact, under extreme pressure from both Turks and vocal Bulgarian intellectuals, the reversal of the name-changing decrees was one of the first items on the agenda of the first post-Communist regime.

Conclusion

In twentieth-century Bulgaria, the name as an audible and knowable marker of identity served as one of the key objects of both demarcation and negotiation between Bulgarian and Muslim. Through naming, both groups attempted to define themselves and to refine or erase any murky boundaries among their ethnonational groups. For many Bulgarians, first their own hybrid names and then the names of Muslims hindered grander projects of modernization, national amalgamation, and even integration into an imagined cultural concept of Europe. After first redefining Pomaks and then Turks as essentially Bulgarian each group had to be labeled as such and eradication of Turco-Muslim names arose again and again as a critical accessory to progress. For the targeted Muslims, their names became their final distinguishing mark, their last link to the world of Islam or Turkish identity. Since 1990, a large percentage of both Turks and Pomaks have reclaimed their Turco-Arabic names. Some of the fringe nationalist parties in post-Communist Bulgaria have lamented the return of Turco-Arabic names, calling it a renewed Turkification of Bulgaria and Bulgarians. At the same time, many Pomaks and a handful of Turks from the younger generation who have had their Bulgarian names since birth, have kept them as a tool to negotiate the new possibilities of the post-1989 environment. Still others continue to use

[107] TsIDA (F-1B, O-63, E-84, L-2, 3: 1989).

multiple names—Bulgarian names in public, Turkish names in private—as they did in the past.[108] For both the Bulgarian state and its Muslim citizens, naming—bestowing, wearing, changing, and remembering names—was and still is the mode through which identities were performed, negotiated, and continue to be refashioned.

[108] Alhaug and Konstantinov, Names, Ethnicity, 25.

6 On What Grounds the Nation?
Parcels of Land and Meaning

Landscape may indeed be a text on which generations write their recurring obsessions.

—Simon Schama

The migration of Muslims from Bulgaria since 1877 bears a strong resemblance to ebbing oceanic tides. During and after the Russo-Turkish War of 1877–78, the Balkan Wars of 1912–13 and later periodic episodes, large numbers of Turks (and to a lesser extent Pomaks) left Bulgaria for the Ottoman Empire and its successor, Turkey. Some of these waves of emigration were followed by at least partial return. It was never easy for Muslims to leave their mountain hamlets and valleys, their homes and fields, their very sustenance. Attachments to territory and land, long-held or newly forged, were major issues in Muslim willingness and ability to negotiate a place for themselves in modern Bulgaria. But such negotiations took place in eras when Bulgarian bureaucrats, intellectuals, and the Bulgarian population itself were grounding their own national designs in Bulgarian soil. As a result, both Bulgarian and Turco-Muslim identities and relationships were constructed on the shifting and contentious foundations of land and territory, encoded with new meanings in the modern period.

Since the nineteenth century, the process of claiming and elaborating Bulgarian nationhood involved the inscribing of "Bulgarian" territory and lands with cultural significance. The concept of a Bulgarian national claim to the territorial expanse of the so-called Bulgarian lands was born in this period as the parameters of national ownership and belonging were encoded on maps. In the Bulgarian nationalist mind the "occupation" of Bulgarian territories and properties by non-national or traitorous national elements was perceived as a threat to the nation's lifeblood—that is, the Bulgarian peasant and his small plot of land. Nationalist thinkers sought political independence as the most important step toward "liberation" of the peasantry, and by extension the nation, from "foreign" domination. After the autonomy was established in 1878, Bulgarian statesmen looked to territorial expansion as a means of national aggrandizement, reclaiming irredenta, and, eventually, to satiate the growing land needs of the Bulgarian peasant. In addition, intellectuals continued to scrutinize so-called foreign occupation and ownership of the imagined Bulgarian lands, both inside and beyond the 1878 borders. Not just Muslim but also Western ownership was subject to nationalist concern and repossession, especially in the Communist period when all foreign-held properties were "nationalized." Even after 1944, in a time of obvious ruptures from the pre-Communist past, the larger project of creating *obshtonarodno* (all-national) property was in essence conceived and rationalized as the gathering of Bulgarian lands under national control.

For Bulgaria's Muslims, land and territory played critical roles in the construction of identity within Bulgaria and beyond. Migration and subsequent return, or the decision to remain in Bulgaria whatever the circumstance, were perhaps the most dramatic ways that Muslims relinquished, retrieved, or held their claims to pieces of Bulgarian territory. The battle to retain Muslim lands began as early as 1877–78 and has continued into the post-1989 period. Over a span of some hundred years, Muslims battled to maintain control over *vakf* properties which funded Muslim cultural institutions. They continually reconceptualized and redefined their individual properties, as land transformed from a symbol of subsistence to a base of Muslimness or Turkishness. Under Communism, Muslims (like Christians) lost the majority of their rural and urban, personal and communal properties to the Communist centralized economy. But in spite of the fact that everyone incurred such losses, a perception remained among many Muslims that their loss of land and property was predicated on cultural difference. Difficulties in reclaiming Muslim lands after the fall of Communism have prompted an even greater sense of ethnic injustice. Hence Muslim notions of self and community have been intertwined with land and landscape, both in reaction to and concomitant to evolving Bulgarian notions of territory and land.

Generally speaking, property and territory play dynamic roles in the construction of national identities. Nations are most often constructed on the grounds of mythic or real landscapes. As Anthony Smith points out, the nation "domesticates" and historicizes natural sites, while "naturalizing" the built environment—integrating both into national myth-symbol matrices.[1] But these attachments to territory are far from eternal or organic. Rather, such attachments are invented and mapped onto chosen territories, which become dynamic, "politicized space."[2] Significantly, concepts of bounded terri-

---

[1] Anthony Smith, *The Ethnic Origins of Nations* (Cambridge, Mass., 1985), 183.
[2] See, for example, Guntram Herb and David Kaplan, "Introduction: A Question of Identity," in *Nested Identities: Nationalism, Territory and Scale*, ed. G. Herb and D. Kaplan

tory and inalienable property, like "nation," are linked to the proclivity for social and cultural ordering, imbedded in the ideas and practices of modernity.[3] The concept of total, exclusive control over a clearly demarcated territory began to emerge only in the fifteenth century, accompanying the rise of mercantilism, military advances, overseas discoveries, and colonization.[4] Hence national territory is a phenomenon linked both temporally and practically with the spread of nationalism, colonialism, and modern statecraft. As William Connolly asserts, "Territory is . . . land, occupied and bounded by violence" and is therefore critical to modes of modern national and colonial control.[5] Similarly, the simultaneity of the phenomena of "nation" and "property" was no accident of history. As with bounded territory, it is generally recognized that the legal concept of "inalienable private property" was a product of early modern Europe, the same milieu that also produced the first modern nations.[6] Property was a critical nexus of debate for early modern philosophers such as John Locke, Jean-Jacques Rousseau, and David Hume, who all saw property as central to the purpose of a modern state: they concluded that property, for better or for worse, made a political society necessary. Although Locke viewed property as a "natural right" and a building block for civil society; Rousseau, in contrast, became the most influential critic of property with his famous words: "The first person who, having fenced off a plot of ground, took it into his head to say this is mine and found people simple enough to believe him, was the true founder of civil society. What crimes, wars, murders, what miseries and horrors would the human race have been spared by someone who, uprooting the stakes or filling in the ditch, had shouted to his fellow men: Beware of listening to this imposter; you are lost if you forget that the fruits of the earth belong to no one!"[7] For better or for worse, the conditions of modernity demanded a more totalizing concept of ownership in which the nation-state acted as mediator of property rights within the confines of national territory.

As modern East European states emerged during the course of the nineteenth and early twentieth centuries, national control over territory and prop-

(Lanham, Md., 1999), 3; and Jouni Hakli, "Cultures of Demarcation: Territory and National Identity in Finland," in *Nested Identities*, 145.

[3] See, for example, Laura Brace, *The Idea of Property in Seventeenth Century England: Tithes and the Individual* (Manchester, 1998); Tom Bethell, *The Noblest Triumph: Property and Prosperity through the Ages* (New York, 1998); and James Scott, *Seeing Like a State*.

[4] Guntram Herb, "National Identity and Territory," 9–31, in *Nested Identities*, 10.

[5] Connolly's remarks on the origins of the word "territory" are relevant here. "Territory, the *Oxford English Dictionary* says, is presumed by most moderns to derive from *terra*. Terra means land, earth, soil, nourishment, sustenance . . . But the form of the word territory, the OED says, suggests something different from the sustenance of terra. Territory derives from *terrere*, meaning to frighten, to terrorize, to exclude . . . Perhaps a modern territory then is land organized by technical and juridical means." William Connolly, *The Ethos of Pluralization* (Minneapolis, 1995), xxii.

[6] Liah Greenfeld, *Nationalism: Five Roads to Modernity* (Cambridge, Mass., 1993), 27–78.

[7] Jean-Jacques Rousseau, "The Origins of Inequality," in *Property: Mainstream and Critical Positions*, ed. C. B. Macpherson (Toronto, 1978), 31.

erty were central issues. Even after independent states were secured, intellectuals, statesmen, and others expended considerable energy advancing claims to vastly overlapping national territories. In Bulgaria and elsewhere in the region, as territory was gained, lost, and expanded, it became a "holy ground" or reified "altar of the nation," which summoned the need for both "symbolic and material control."[8] This translated into pervasive and large-scale property transfers—before and during the Communist period—that were as dramatic as the radical border changes that brought instability to the region in the modern period. Since the region had been under "foreign" control for much of its recent history, there was a common legacy of foreign feudal lord ruling over native peasants in parts or all of its territories. Across the region, "land reform"—beginning in the Balkans in the nineteenth century, extending to the new states in the north after World War I, and culminating after World War II—served the dual purpose of social and national reclamation. In general, former "masters" of the region—Turks, Germans, Hungarians, Russians, and in some areas Poles—lost ground to new national owners.[9] By extension, property and specifically the distribution of land became a critical base for building alliances, loyalties, and even nations across the region.

In Bulgaria, national projects sought to root or reroot the nation in reclaimed lands, which were purported to have been illegitimately occupied by foreign powers and populations. As Bulgarians began to imagine and map their new political reality, the assertion of national ownership prompted a momentous reordering of domestic properties. The repercussions for local Muslims were immeasurable, as large numbers of Muslims were uprooted through voluntary or coerced emigration, aggravated by loss of property and status. Those who stayed behind faced intermittent assimilation campaigns that targeted the markers of Turkishness and Islam which marked them and the landscape. Once the land itself was recast as essentially Bulgarian, hybrid presences had to be expelled or transformed. As a result, not only did the Muslim presence in Bulgaria become forever precarious, but the fabric of Muslim/non-Muslim relations was inevitably torn.

Uncommon Grounds

Until the nineteenth century, territory and to a lesser extent property had more often entangled rather than divided Christians and Muslims in the Balkans. As Cemal Kafadar argued, the Ottoman polity established itself on Balkan territory, not as a part of a grand "clash of civilizations" but in the midst of a dynamic "frontier ethos."[10] Ottoman sovereignty in these territo-

---

[8] These terms are borrowed from Herb, "National Identity," 22.

[9] See, for example, Wojciech Roszkowski, *Land Reforms in East Central Europe after World War One* (Warsaw, 1995) and Hugh Seton-Watson, *Eastern Europe between the World Wars* (Cambridge, 1946), 78.

[10] Kafadar, *Between Two Worlds*, 12.

ries was assured through various alliances and interactions with local Christians, not solely through violent subjugation as was later imagined.[11] Whatever friction was present, Muslim and Christian coexisted, interacted, and had extensive cultural contact and interchange. As a result co-territoriality bred a degree of commonality, as cultures and political fates were intertwined.

Even in the later Ottoman period, most Bulgarians were still firmly entrenched in Ottoman soil. Though peasant uprisings punctuated the eighteenth and especially early nineteenth centuries, many scholars argue that, in general, Balkan peasant demands were primarily social rather than national. That is, peasants appealed to the Ottoman sultan for relief from local abuses of its authority, not for political independence.[12] At the same time, a large portion of the Bulgarian elite also saw their interests best met within the Ottoman context. The Bulgarian *çorbacı* (local notables), for the most part, were keenly aware that a separate Bulgarian territory would mean a potential loss of status. In addition, many prosperous Bulgarian merchants equated political independence with economic loss because of the necessary territorial truncation of their resources and markets. As a result, a contingency of Bulgarian elite advocated a Turco-Bulgarian "dual monarchy" based on the Austro-Hungarian model.[13] Hence with Christian and Muslim populations mixed and intermingled across Ottoman Bulgaria, the untangling of this duality was not a foregone conclusion.

Tellingly, it was only a small minority of the population that began to raise the issues of territory and land by the nineteenth century. A handful of Bulgarian nationalist thinkers began to discuss and write about political independence as a corrective to Ottoman domination and foreign encroachment on "Bulgarian" soil. These voices justified their cause by highlighting the oppression of the Bulgarian peasant by the Turkish landlord. In his famous poem "The Forest Traveler," Georgi Rakovski, for example, reproached the Turkish occupiers for their violation of the Bulgarian population and land:

> They forcibly Turkified newborn children!
> They completely mastered the land,
> As unlimited power was given to them!
> In the fertile areas they settled![14]

Rakovski's focus on the Turkish occupation of the "most fertile" Bulgarian lands was a common theme in Bulgarian revolutionary writings of this period. The repossession of such lands was seen as a compulsory accompaniment to the future liberation of Bulgarian territory. Rakovski believed that

---

[11] Ibid., 19.
[12] Barbara Jelavich, *History of the Balkans,* 237.
[13] See, for example, *Makedoniia* (Istanbul), 3 December 1868, 2.
[14] Georgi Rakovski, *Bŭlgariio Maĭko Mila,* ed. Georgi Borshukov (Sofia, 1967), 128.

the Bulgarian peasant needed land to inculcate a sense of belonging to a nation. In commenting on Romanian agrarian reform of 1864, for example, he noted the necessity of such reform for the Romanian peasant, "What can enamor him of his birth place if he knows that it belongs to someone else?"[15] Rakovski and other Bulgarian nationalist revolutionaries were ultimately very effective at transforming social grievances into fodder for the national cause. With the peasant as a symbol of national oppression, they managed to attract international attention to their cause and ultimately to secure independence, although territorial dreams were far from realized in the disappointing 1878 Treaty of Berlin.

Beginning in 1878, such dreams were put on the back burner as administrators of the new Bulgarian principality began sculpting the Bulgarian nation out of the post-Ottoman loam. Bulgarian leaders, under the close supervision of the Russian provisional administration from 1878–79, did their utmost to usher in radical change in the local land regime. Bulgarian sources would later describe an "*agrarni prevorat*" (agrarian revolution) following liberation from Ottoman rule, which meant above all the elimination of "Ottoman feudal property."[16] Conveniently, the 1877–78 Russo-Turkish war had caused a large wave of Muslim emigration out of Bulgaria that freed up large tracts of land.[17] It is estimated that at the outbreak of war as many as one half of the population of the future Bulgarian principality were Muslim Turks who held about 70 percent of arable land.[18] The lands of the fleeing Turks were theoretically protected by specific provisions in the Treaty of Berlin, which assured the right of Muslims to return and reclaim their properties within newly autonomous Bulgaria.[19] In practice, however, the property rights provisions of the Treaty of Berlin were largely ignored and the new administration impeded the return of Muslim refugees by granting formerly Muslim lands to Bulgarian peasants or Slavo-Macedonian refugees from Macedonia and Thrace.[20] This was technically a temporary arrangement, but restitution of lands to Muslims was rarely carried out. By 1880, a second wave of Muslim emigration had begun and numerous large and small-scale property transfers reflected the diminishing Muslim presence in Bulgaria.[21] In 1885, the unification of Bulgaria with Eastern Rumelia again

[15] Firkatian, *Forest Traveler*, 135.

[16] Mikhail Andreev, *Istoriia na Bŭlgarskata Burzhoazna Dŭrzhava i Pravo: 1878–1917* (Sofia, 1993), 65.

[17] Richard Crampton, "The Turks in Bulgaria, 1878–1944," in *The Turks of Bulgaria: The History and Fate of a Minority*, ed. K. Karpat (Istanbul, 1990), 45.

[18] Although some Turks maintained larger holdings, an estimated 80 percent were small-scale farmers. Şimşir, *Bulgarian Turks*, 157, 6.

[19] Crampton, "Turks in Bulgaria," 45.

[20] Georgi Todorov, "Deĭnostta na Vremenoto Rusko Upravlenie v Bŭlgariia po Urezhdane na Agrarniia i Bezhanskiia Vŭpros prez 1877–1879 g," *Istoricheski Pregled* 6 (1955): 36.

[21] Many Muslim landholders did not have proper documentation to reclaim their properties due to fluid Ottoman property laws. They were offered some compensation for their lands, which had been sold to Christian peasants under favorable terms. Crampton, "Turks in Bulgaria," 49.

sparked a mass emigration of Muslim populations to Thrace. According to Crampton, by 1900, six million decares (one decare equals approximately one quarter of an acre) of Muslim land had been transferred to local Christians, and 175 Muslim villages had been deserted.[22] At this juncture the emigration of Muslims was politically expedient for the new Bulgarian regime, which now had vast stretches of open territory in which to plant the Bulgarian nation, and, at least theoretically, a means with which to buy peasant loyalty.

In the post-Ottoman period, the peasant clearly remained the focus not only of administrative but also cultural efforts to consolidate a Bulgarian national consciousness. In his famous novel *Under the Yoke*, Ivan Vazov popularized many of the social formulations of Bulgarian revolutionary thinkers. Vazov's Bulgarian characters are represented with various shades of decency in relation to their material gain via collaboration with the occupying Ottoman powers. Although the Ottoman regime and its local representatives were depicted as villains in the larger story, Vazov also depicted the wealthy Bulgarian *çorbacı* as agents of the hated Turkish occupation; "His robbing of the poor, his intimacy with the Turks, had made him hated even when he no longer did any harm."[23] Only a few good *çorbacı* characters—such as Marko and Tsanko, who use their wealth to help the Bulgarian national cause—are atoned of their sins, that is, of acquiring property and position under Turkish occupation. Vazov most highly venerates the Bulgarian national revolutionary, Kralich, a propertyless fugitive and Bulgarian peasant oppressed by Turkish landlords, tax collectors, and Bulgarian collaborators. In Vazov's other writings, he expounds on this same position: "I liked Kamenitsa. It was populated by these Bulgarians who two and a half centuries ago had remained loyal to their faith, had preferred complete ruination and abandonment of their homes to being converted to Islam. Their houses and property in the Chepino villages had been taken over by their converted brethren, while the Turkish sword threatened their heads."[24] Vazov's images of the common Bulgarian peasant and the Ottoman perpetrator permeated the historiography and literature of the new Bulgarian state, as literati and historians alloyed social commentary on the Ottoman past with new national understandings.

The plight of the Bulgarian peasant never left its central place in Bulgarian nationalist discourse. But ironically, the advent of private property in the countryside in the post-Ottoman period brought an unprecedented debt burden to Muslim and non-Muslim peasants alike. Not only was the tax burden higher in the new state, but the peasants were compelled to pay the state for their new properties and often turned to local moneylenders for high-interest

[22] In part this emigration which reduced the percentage of Turks from 26 percent in 1878 to 14 percent in 1900 was a response to offers of land by the Ottoman government in Thrace and Asia Minor. Ibid., 47.

[23] Ivan Vazov, *Under the Yoke (New York, 1971)*, 39.

[24] Vazov, *Pûtepisi*, 201.

property loans. By the turn of the century the percentage of peasants who owned their own land had actually decreased by 21 percent from the status quo in 1878.[25] And as Bulgarian Communist historians would later conclude, peasants had merely replaced one master for another—Oriental despotism for capitalist exploitation.[26] The well-known "Andreshko syndrome" was indicative of the wider cultural awareness of the expanding divide between the peasantry and the modernizing state. The syndrome was named after a peasant coachman "Andreshko," in Elin Pelin's short story by the same name, who chauffeurs a city notable to a small Bulgarian village. In the course of friendly conversation, Andreshko learns that his patron is a tax collector on his way to foreclose on a fellow villager. Unwilling to abet such an injustice, Andreshko drives his coach into the middle of a colossal mud puddle, hops on one of his horses and unties the other, galloping off triumphantly. He leaves the representative of the new Bulgarian bureaucracy to his fate, rejoicing in the poor roads that protected his village from outside penetration. As represented by Pelin, "foreignness" for the Bulgarian peasant was not simply of the Ottoman, Eastern ilk. The Bulgarian city and the new Bulgarian bureaucracy were perceived as vessels of foreign influence by gradually more politicized peasant voices.

Although land was increasingly coveted in the Bulgarian countryside, the urban elite were focused on realizing their own aspirations for Bulgarian territorial expansion, with dire consequences. Expansionist tendencies gained momentum, fueled by growing land hunger and justified by historical and ethnographic claims to Thrace and Macedonia. These tendencies ultimately propelled Bulgaria to enter the First Balkan War in 1912, which began a long period of conflict and devastation, extending through the end of World War I in 1918. The radically shifting borders and jurisdictions of this six-year period caused massive dislocation, casualties, and loss of property, and intensified currents of political radicalization. The Bulgarian state occupied the coveted territories of Thrace and Macedonia during the Balkan Wars and World War I, instituting "land reform" and generally carrying out a program of intensive Bulgarianization. Military defeats in the Second Balkan War and World War I, however, meant the ultimate loss of a good portion of these territories. Though a net gain of territory occurred after the First Balkan War, the losses of the Second Balkan War and World War I would always be remembered in Bulgarian history as "national catastrophes." Muslims too tended to associate these wars with political and cultural catastrophe. The violence and dislocation of the Balkan Wars in particular, caused another wave of Muslim emigration from lands where they had lived for centuries. Although the wars themselves did not always pit Muslim against Christian,

[25] Rothschild, *Communist Party of Bulgaria*, 7.
[26] See, for example, Nikolai Todorov, *Stopanska Istoriia na Bŭlgariia* (Sofia, 1981); and Tseno Petrov, *Agrarnite Reformi v Bŭlgariia: 1880–1944* (Sofia, 1975).

they contributed to growing tensions between Muslim and non-Muslim in Bulgaria, furrowed deep into the Bulgarian soil since 1878.

Plots of Land

In the aftermath of World War I Bulgaria had to seek local answers to national afflictions. As the prominent interwar Bulgarian intellectual Boris Iotsov mused, "Gathered into the crowded borders of its country, surrounded by Balkan hatred, this nation directs its gaze within."[27] In the interwar period, the loss of territory as a result of the wars precipitated a deep crisis among frustrated irredentists, many of whom were former or recent émigrés from Thrace and Macedonia, now landless and radicalized. The flood of refugees, as well as a population surge after World War I, brought a new land scarcity with far reaching consequences for Muslim/non-Muslim relations. From the farthest reaches of the political spectrum, plans and promises for national salvation were rooted in parcels of land and pieces of territory as Bulgarian lands were freshly endowed with national meaning.

In September of 1918 at the close of World War I, peasant unrest erupted into strikes, bread riots, and mutiny and the Bulgarian monarchy turned to Alexander Stamboliski, the leader of the Bulgarian Agrarian National Union (BANU), who was to rule Bulgaria for the next five years. Stamboliski believed that, "no man is truly free unless he owns a plot of land," and he endeavored to rejuvenate the nation by rerooting the peasantry in parcels of land.[28] His 1921 "Law for Labor Property in Land" established a 30 decare maximum for all individual agricultural land holdings with allotments of additional hectares for larger families. The nation would thus be built on small parcels of land. Although he directed his appeals toward the "Bulgarian" peasant, Stamboliski never explicitly excluded Muslims from his national vision so landless Muslims also benefited from Stamboliski's agrarian reorganization. Most historians of the interwar period tend to agree that Stamboliski's tenure in office was a period of tolerance for Muslim minorities. He was, in fact, the primary political beneficiary of the Muslim vote.[29] Between 1919 and 1922, the state treasury allocated some 5,000 decares of land in support of private Muslim Turkish schools.[30] Unfortunately for many, Stamboliski's assassination in 1923 cut short the enactment of his reforms. His downfall was precipitated by his acceptance of the postwar territorial settlement and his refusal to advocate Bulgarian expansion, both actions that

---

[27] Boris Iotsov, "Bŭlgarskata Deĭstvitelnost Tŭrsi Avtor," in *Zashto Sme Takiva? V Tŭrsene na Bŭlgarskata Kulturna Identichnost*, ed. I. Elenkov and R. Daskalov (Sofia: 1994), 478.
[28] Rothschild, *Communist Party of Bulgaria,* 89.
[29] Ibid., 102.
[30] Şimşir, *Bulgarian Turks,* 146.

alienated urban and refugee interests. In the end, territorial dreams won out over peasant land interests; the two were not always compatible.

From 1923 on, national priorities would be established in Sofia (where ruralist Stamboliski had refused to live), although undertaken on the margins of the Bulgarian map. The regimes that followed used land to appease, direct, include, or exclude various forces in Bulgarian society, to consolidate and ground the nation or extricate its foreign threats from national soil. Social tensions and fear of Communist Party influence in the countryside insured that Stamboliski's agrarian reform efforts were never wholly abandoned. Although Alexander Tsankov's coalition—the "Democratic Accord" of 1923–31—repealed Stamboliski's land law, very similar legislation replaced it. In fact, the only real difference in agrarian policy was that now it was possible to have 150 instead of thirty decares for large "scientific and rational" agro-industrial farms and an extra five hectares per person for large families. Ironically more redistribution of land occurred under Tsankov's regime than under Stamboliski.[31] These new agrarian reforms focused on Bulgarian peasants and, in particular, the Bulgarian-speaking refugee populations from Macedonia and Thrace.[32] But unlike in the Stamboliski period, Muslims were directly affected by these reform efforts, which clearly had national as well as social objectives.

It is important to keep in mind that postwar settlements had, in effect, legitimized a total reordering of the Balkan map. As a result of the various population exchange agreements that accompanied the Greco-Turkish Lausanne Treaty of 1922–23, additional Slavic refugees from the Greek and Turkish territories of Thrace poured into the Rhodope region of southern Bulgaria well after the end of World War I.[33] In spite of the almost all-Balkan character of the population transfers, Bulgarians tended to focus on the national tragedy for uprooted Bulgarian nationals. Local newspapers in the Rhodope region, for example, bemoaned the "Greek yoke" in Thrace and how "the Bulgarian population was being driven from their native hearths."[34] In fact, the dislocation of refugee populations caused political and economic dislocation throughout the Balkans, and the new borders were like geographic tourniquets to the economies of natural regions. In the Rhodope region, for example, the loss of the Aegean coast was as detrimental to the local economy as the influx of refugees. Interwar Rhodope newspapers dwelled on the fact that without the summer pastures on the new Greek Aegean coast, the animal husbandry of the mountainous Bulgarian hinterland had been devastated.[35]

To make matters worse, interwar Bulgarian regimes began to impose order out of the perceived chaos of local land organization in the newly acquired

[31] Ts. Petrov, *Agrarnite Reformi*, 81.
[32] Ibid., 83.
[33] *Rodopa (Smolyan)*, 1 February 1925, 1.
[34] *Rodopa (Smolyan)*, 1 May 1923, 1.
[35] TsIDA (F-173, O-4, E-490, L-2: 1927).

(in 1912) districts of the Rhodopes. The Ministry of the Interior expressed concern that these new territories had no system of settling property issues, and that forests, fields, and pastures were in a "chaotic situation" because "even property owners don't know the borders of their own property." Bulgarian officials even assumed that since "properties are a total labyrinth" that this contributed to the "insecurity of borders."[36] In many cases this reordering of local land was ruinous for local peasants and herdsman. Articles in the local paper *Rodopa,* criticized the results of Bulgarian land legislation in the region, complaining that since the Balkan Wars the Bulgarian regime had confiscated as "ownerless" common pasture lands, leaving only the privately owned properties in the villages.[37] They charged that the government had taken over common forestlands, redefined them as state lands, and sold them to speculators and other private owners. This new state of affairs, in many cases, prohibited use of traditionally common lands that had been accessible to local communities "even in Turkish times."[38]

As the regime imposed precise ownership on the Rhodope landscape, they perhaps inadvertently contributed to the emergent discord between Muslim and non-Muslim. Commentary in local presses, refugee organizations, and state documents increasingly referred to local Muslims as foreigners occupying lands that should be owned by Bulgarian peasants and refugees. A *Rodopa* article, for example, complains about the fact that a number of Muslims who had fled their homes had been allowed to return after the war years. Those Muslim lands and homes, the article claims, should have been taken by the government to give to refugees.[39] Radicalized refugee organizations and other nationalist forces soon began to take the law into their own hands and assert their perceived rights to "Bulgarian lands" against the local Muslim presence. Numerous sources reported that nationalist organizations such as the refugee-based Committee for Thrace in the south and *Rodna Zashtita* (Defense of the Homeland) in the north terrorized local Muslim populations in order to provoke migration and open up land for Bulgarian settlement.[40] In *Deliorman,* a local Turkish newspaper, numerous articles reported on the phenomenon:

A sinister organization is continuing its activities in Bulgaria, beating up Turks, injuring and even murdering them in cold blood and insulting their religious feelings by doing such things as smearing pork fat on the village fountain, stoning the imam, and even burning the mosque. It is trying to make the Turks discouraged and terrified in order to force them to run away from this beautiful country. Recently, a second tribulation in the southern regions has been added to this

---

[36] TsIDA (F-264, O-1, E-439, L-5: 1934).
[37] TsIDA (F-173, O-4, E-490, L-2: 1927).
[38] *Rodopa (Smolyan),* 1 March 1924, 3.
[39] *Rodopa (Smolyan),* 1 February 1928, 5.
[40] Şimşir, *Bulgaristan Türkleri,* 163.

tribulation in the northern region . . . there too are some people who want Turks to give up their fields and homes and emigrate.[41]

The land crisis increasingly contributed to the infusion of property with national meaning. As modernity encroached, lines drawn on land contributed to lines drawn between Bulgarian and Muslim.

When economic crisis hit Europe in the 1930s, an even more radical hue of nationalist fervor colored Bulgarian politics, inspiring far-reaching policies aimed at diminishing the Turkish presence. From 1934 until the Bulgarian entry into World War II in 1941, the state directed a pointed campaign to uproot Turkish populations and plant Bulgarian elements on the margins of Bulgarian territory. In 1935, an official from the Ministry of the National Economy asserted that the percentage of peasants without land or with dwarf-holdings was drastically on the rise and that Turkish lands would provide the best solution to this burgeoning social problem.[42] According to the Ministry's report, many Turkish families had already left Bulgaria; 1,043 in 1932–34, 1,800 in 1935, and an estimated 4,000 more families who wanted to leave based on "political, economic, and psychological reasons."[43] Directly provoked or not, waves of Turks and also Pomaks began to either apply for emigration or illegally cross Bulgaria's borders.

The Ministry of Agriculture and other governmental agencies expended considerable energy ensuring that the movement of peoples and transfer of properties would have the desired result in the provinces. They gathered extensive information to locate the largest "compact masses" of Turks who were willing to migrate.[44] In answer to one such request for information, a local official confided that "all the good land was in the hands of foreigners who want to emigrate" and therefore Turkish emigration would help Bulgaria work toward "economic" and "national" goals.[45] In practice, financial obstacles prevented easy transfer of Turkish lands to Bulgarian peasants. The Turkish population, itself in serious debt, was compelled to sell land to various speculators and, consequently, Bulgarian peasants were outbid. This raised a red flag to Bulgarian officials who quickly put a stop to so-called foreign speculation by imposing a state monopoly over all land transactions of emigrating Turks.[46] By 1935 the state-directed *Bŭlgarskata Zemedelska Kasa* (Bulgarian Agricultural Bank) was given priority in buying the land of migrating "foreigners," and passports were withheld from Turks unless they sold their properties through proper channels.[47] By ending speculation, the regime hoped to ensure that Turkish lands were going "into the hands of the

[41] *Deliorman*, March 8, 1930, as cited in ibid., 164.
[42] TsIDA (F-194, O-1, E-2385, L-1: 1935).
[43] TsIDA (F-194, O-1, E-2385, L-2: 1935).
[44] TsIDA (F-194, O-1, E-2428, L-61: 1935).
[45] TsIDA (F-194, O-1, E-2392, L-21: 1939).
[46] TsIDA (F-194, O-1, E-2394, L-26: 1935).
[47] TsIDA (F-194, O-1, E-2386, L-7: 1935).

healthy Bulgarian population."[48] These lands were offered at reduced prices and interest rates to landless families of Bulgarian national affiliation, especially those who were willing to colonize the still heavily Turkish- and Pomak-populated southern borderlands of Bulgaria. As one Bulgarian official explained: "Many Bulgarian families who now have a pitiable existence will become beneficiaries both for themselves and for the nation. They will quickly replace the emigrating Turks, and will form a formidable shield for the protection of native land. From the point of view of healthy national politics, the internal colonization of Bulgarians in this region [the Rhodopes] will result in the strengthening of Bulgarian influence there."[49] The clear assumption is that "native land" needed protection from the Turkish menace.

But although Bulgarian policy encouraged the emigration of Turks, Pomak emigration, in contrast, was increasingly perceived as a national problem. By the 1930s, as large numbers of Pomaks fled over Bulgaria's southern border, Bulgarian bureaucrats lamented that Pomaks had not the slightest trace of Bulgarian national consciousness and even had "Bulgarophobia."[50] Turkish propaganda was blamed in part for Pomak desertions, but insecurity of property was also cited as a reason for Pomak dissatisfaction. In addition to hardships caused by border changes and appropriations of common properties, Pomaks who had fled during the war years and later returned to Bulgaria had to lease their own properties from the government.[51] This was exacerbated by government efforts in the 1930s to transform the region materially and culturally by settling Bulgarians in Pomak districts. Unlike in Turkish districts, colonization projects did not dictate the expulsion of Muslims, but rather introduced mostly radicalized Bulgarian refugee elements without a plan for relieving social pressure. As one Rhodope official complained, the settlement of Bulgarian families into Pomak areas where a scarcity of land already existed had done more harm than good and as a result even more Pomaks were fleeing over the border.[52] In spite of government intentions Pomaks, like Turks, were pressured to emigrate by select nationalist and, especially, refugee organizations. Far from advocating Pomak assimilation, one such organization saw much to gain from Pomak emigration. As reported by a local official: "From such treatment of Pomaks the local Thracianists, without a doubt, receive material rewards as the emigrating Pomaks sell their properties nearly free."[53] Clearly, refugee organizations did not share the enthusiasm of Bulgarian intellectuals and bureaucrats for integrating Pomak populations into Bulgarian national designs. But despite such pressures, a large percentage of Pomaks remained in their native locales.

Similarly, although waves of Turks immigrated into Turkey, a large con-

---

[48] TsIDA (F-194, O-1, E-2385, L-113: 1935).
[49] TsIDA (F-194, O-1, E-2385, L-4: 1935).
[50] TsIDA (F-264, O-1, E-439, L-2: 1934).
[51] TsIDA (F-264, O-1, E-439, L-5: 1934).
[52] TsIDA (F-194, O-1, E-2392, L-38: 1939).
[53] TsIDA (F-264, O-1, E-439, L-7: 1934).

tingency began to renew their claims to local lands based on their "Turkish" birthright. Officials from Turkish districts reported that many Turks had no desire to leave and, instead, harbored a profound fear of losing their land.[54] They even charged that Turks were sabotaging the process of "Bulgarian land reform" in the region by staying put in an effort to keep Bulgarians from settling on their lands.[55] In many cases the "ownerless and abandoned" properties of emigrated Turks were taken over by Turkish neighbors and relatives, provoking complaints that "the Turks are all very organized and won't allow Bulgarians to take over these lands."[56] Some local Turkish-language newspapers discouraged emigration on the basis of the centuries-long presence of Turks in the area, as in this poem from the *Deliorman*:

> Don't flow away like the Kamtchi River,
> Don't destroy your banks,
> Oh, Turk, don't yield your
> Forefather's country to strangers.
>
> Your forefather tilled its soil,
> They suffered much for its sake,
> They shed their blood for it,
> And defended it for centuries.[57]

Along the same lines, an article in *Rehber* echoes the presumed inheritance rights of the Turkish population, "Compatriots and co-religionists, property and a country are not acquired easily. Know the value of the dear lands left to you by your ancestors. They cannot be taken back once they are lost."[58] Thus, though large numbers of Turks left Bulgaria, more stayed behind redefining their plots of land and the territory they occupied as "Turkish lands."

Even conservative Muslims, who rejected most elements of modern Turkish nationalism, began to advance their "Turkish" prerogatives to Muslim *vakf* properties. In exchange for its loyalties to the Bulgarian regime, the Islamic hierarchy had maintained official control over the numerous dispersed *vakf* properties of the Muslim communities of Bulgaria since 1878. In practice, however, *vakfs* were administered on the local level by Muslim Confessional Organizations (MCOs), many of which had lost their hold on their scattered properties. One of the most pressing issues by the interwar period was the Turkish struggle over control of *vakfs* in relation to Muslim Gypsies. Turkish emigration had given Muslim Gypsies a numerical advantage in many Muslim districts and so control over MCOs and their *vakf* properties. In 1925, the Head Mufti complained to the Ministry of Foreign Affairs about Gypsy successes in local elections to *vakf*-control commissions.[59] He was

54 TsIDA (F-194, O-1, E-2428, L-36: 1939).
55 TsIDA (F-194, O-1, E-2392, L-11: 1938), and (KODA (F-14k, O-1, E-97, L-128: 1938).
56 TsIDA (F-194, O-1, E-2392, L-2: 1939).
57 Şimşir, *Bulgaristan Türkleri*, 164.
58 Ibid., 164.
59 TsIDA (F-471, O-1, E-6, L-4: 1925).

alarmed by the concentration of Gypsies in many large traditionally Turkish cities such as Plovdiv, Vidin, and Stara Zagora—three of the most important Turkish cultural centers in Bulgaria with centuries-old *vakf* properties.[60] At a cultural-educational national congress organized by Turks in Bulgaria in 1929, one of the main issues discussed was the "Gypsy infiltration" into *vakf* commissions, which were defined as "solely Turkish national wealth."[61] *Vakfs* also became progressively more imbued with Turkish meaning in relation to Bulgarian claims. Numerous Bulgaro-Turkish disputes arose over the status of individual *vakf* properties, such as the *Demir Baba teke* (the monastery of Demir Baba, a Sufi Muslim leader). In 1937 the MCO of Razgrad filed a complaint about the illegal seizure of the *vakf* lands around the *teke* by Bulgarian officials, with the allegation that, "this is part of a campaign to get Turks to leave Bulgaria."[62] In response to these accusations, a local Bulgarian newspaper, *Razgradsko Slovo*, claimed that the land also held religious meaning for Bulgarians and that its present status "in foreign Turkish hands" was "an unlawful usurpation of a [Bulgarian] national, sacred place and its properties."[63] The article deplored the fact that the "*teke* and its properties are being exploited by foreigners," when the money should go to the village.[64] In response, the Razgrad MCO asserted its own claim to the *teke* based on the fact that, "these properties were bequeathed by our great grandfathers."[65] By the interwar period, growing tensions between Bulgarians and Turks both reflected and drove changes in the definition, distribution, and use of lands within Bulgaria.

Bulgaro-Turkish tensions over individual and communal lands did enjoy at least a partial respite with Bulgaria's entry into World War II in 1941. As a result of its alliance with the Axis, Bulgarian expansion brought a wave of contagious euphoria as nationalist territorial desires were gratified. The Islamic establishment was allowed to expand its jurisdiction over Muslims (excluding Pomaks) into the "newly liberated lands." But in spite of Turkish cooperation with the regime during the war years, Turks, as with other non-Bulgarian elements, were impacted by ambitious wartime nationalist projects, including a massive resettlement and "agrarian reform" program in the new territories. As one official noted: "We need to understand that the agrarian question, the question of owning land, is the most important, not in the agricultural-technical sense but in terms of the national question."[66] In Thrace and Macedonia in particular, dramatic measures were taken to Bulgarianize through settlement, land distribution, and expulsion of foreigners and presumed enemies of the regime. The regime offered land—a maximum of fifty decares per family—in addition to free passage, insurance, and free

[60] TsIDA (F-471, O-1, E-6, L-5: 1925).
[61] Şimşir, *Bulgaristan Türkleri*, 52.
[62] TsIDA (F-471, O-1, E-126, L-7: 1927).
[63] TsIDA (F-471, O-1, E-18, L-2: 1927).
[64] TsIDA (F-471, O-1, E-18, L-2: 1927).
[65] TsIDA (F-471, O-1, E-18, L-4: 1927).
[66] TsIDA (F-194, O-1, E-2185, L-32B: 1941).

medical care—to people of "Bulgarian descent" who were willing to settle in these regions.[67] The fact that many of these Bulgarian settlers were former inhabitants of these regions was used to justify the effective expulsion of Greeks and Turks, who were assumed to be "recent arrivals," products of the massive population transfers of the interwar period.[68] The consulate of neutral Turkey issued complaints throughout the period that the Bulgarian government was forcing the Turkish population to migrate from Thrace; one memorandum demanded an immediate stop to the forced emigration, noting that 3,000 Turks had crossed the border from Ksanti (in Bulgarian-occupied Thrace) into Degedatch, Turkey in only a few days.[69] Even the regime-loyal Muftiship faced wartime incursions upon its *vakfs*, many of which were drawn into the Bulgarianizing agrarian reform efforts in the Muslim provinces. The Muftiship reported numerous incidents of *vakf* agricultural fields being appropriated and distributed to Bulgarian settlers.[70] In addition, the Head Mufti complained incessantly to the central authorities that MCOs were forced to sell *vakf* properties all over Bulgaria as a result of debts resulting from new government taxes.[71] The Muftiship files of this period are rife with protests from across Bulgaria about the demolition and appropriation of mosques by the regime. In 1941, the Sliven MCO, for example, complained that a state commission for public services demolished a mosque because it was deemed "un-hygienic" and "not in use."[72] Thus, the Muftiship's special status by no means protected "Turkish properties" which were in the way of Bulgarian nationalist projects.

This designing of the nation from the ground up was a poignant feature of Bulgarian political life, which intensified from the Balkan Wars until the end of World War II. Territorial aspirations and acute land hunger were important in Bulgarian political and social life and both Bulgarians and Muslims attached national value to parcels of land and swaths of territory. The national dimension of Bulgarian agrarian projects inevitably brought under scrutiny the question of Turco-Muslim lands and the perceived danger of a "foreign" Turkish presence. The regime's efforts to Bulgarianize old and new territories were driven by the belief that the true owners were reclaiming these lands—heretofore illegally occupied by other foreign presences. The land itself was imagined as fundamentally and eternally Bulgarian, in need of reclaiming via the expulsion of illegitimate presences. As Bulgarian regimes

[67] TsIDA (F-194, O-1, E-2193, L-1: 1941); and TsIDA (F-264, O-1, E-176, L-1: 1942).

[68] On Turks see, for example, TsIDA (F-264, O-1, E-497, L-25: 1941); on Greeks see TsIDA (F-264, O-1, E-176, L-25: 1942).

[69] TsIDA (F-264, O-1, E-497, L-53: 1941). In Macedonia, agrarian reform was more focused on Serbian populations who had been settled in the region as part of interwar Yugoslav "land reform" that had "Serbianized" the area at the expense of the local Bulgarian element. TsIDA (F-194, O-1, E-2185, L-60: 1942).

[70] TsIDA (F-471, O-1, E-1321, L-17: 1943).

[71] TsIDA (F-471, O-1, E-1321, L-1, 12, 14, 53, 58, 89: 1943), TsIDA (F-471, O-1, E-1070, L-7, 35, 53, 66, 78: 1942).

[72] TsIDA (F-471, O-1, E-426, L-6: 1939).

imposed national meanings on the scattered Muslim lands of the provinces, Muslim voices also began to chart the "Turkishness" of lands in the kingdom. Turks and Pomaks were active participants in the remaking of Bulgaria, whether through emigration or the refusal to surrender their native hearths. Both Bulgarian and Muslim identities were constituted and reconstituted along with shifting territorial and proprietary borders, a process which only widened the divide between them.

Socialist Lands, All-National Lands

In the post-war period, the Communist regime made a seeming about face in its attitude and approach toward territory and property. The Bulgarian Communist Party (BCP) renounced past territorial ambitions, and launched a war against private property that was, for the most part, ethnically blind. It embarked on a far-reaching undertaking to redistribute property seized from "foreign" economic interests, now primarily defined as bourgeois-Fascist national traitors. The BCP collectivized agriculture by appropriating and consolidating rural lands, which again affected Bulgarians as well as Muslims. And although it is true that both Bulgarians and Muslims were subject to nationalization and collectivization, there is also no doubt that the BCP's economic reorderings were carried out in the name of national ownership. Under the Communist system every parcel of domestic land would be owned by the Bulgarian state in the name of the nation, for protection from foreign exploitation and incursion. At least in theory, the BCP intended to safeguard the nation's disparate properties under the auspices of socialist or *obshtonarodno* (all-national), property. As far as Muslims are concerned, this translated into radically contradictory efforts to either eliminate Muslims or to integrate them into the socialist nation—uprooting or rooting them in Bulgarian soil.

Ultimate goals aside, in the wartime and immediate postwar period, the BCP made a concerted effort to woo Muslim peasants with promises of land and security for their property. Much in line with the Soviet model, the Bulgarian Communist Party initially sought political support on the ticket of land reform, attempting to appeal to all of Bulgaria's rural population. In *Yeni Işık* the wartime government was criticized precisely on the grounds that it violated Turkish property through forced emigration: "Oppression, the creation of economic difficulties, condemning Turks to illiteracy, and forcing them to emigrate were the main elements of the policy that Fascism in Bulgaria pursued against the Turks living in Bulgaria. The goal of this policy was to take from Turks their properties."[73] In the early years of power, the Party pledged that Muslims would live free from such abuses and distribution of land to Muslim peasants became a critical part of Party work in Muslim dis-

---

[73] Şimşir, *Bulgaristan Türkleri*, 133.

tricts.[74] From 1944–47 some 80,000 Muslim families were reportedly given about 1,500,000 decares of land, an average of about 50 decares per family.[75] Though landowners of more than 200 decares were stripped of their private agricultural lands, most Muslim large landowners had long ago emigrated.[76] Yet in spite of Party efforts to use land and supplies to gain Muslim support in the 1946–47 elections, BCP operatives admitted that, "The question of property in these elections played a significant role against us."[77] Neither Party propaganda nor distribution of land to the Muslim masses could stem fears of eventual Communist usurpation of property in the path of socialist development.

But even as the Party attempted to woo Turkish political support, the Turkish place on Bulgarian soil was called into question. In a very telling speech from 1947 by Vladmir Poptomov, the Bulgarian minister of foreign affairs, anti-Turkish nationalism hotly shines through the thin veneer of Party internationalism. Poptomov quotes Party leader Georgi Dimitrov at length: "We the southern Slavs have a historical task; to drive the Turks out of Europe. Their place is not in Europe. They come from Asia Minor, from Anatolia, and they need to go back there. They don't have a place here. The lands, which they rule—Turkish Thrace, that is not their land. This has been Slavic land for centuries . . . our mission is to return it to the Slavs."[78] Hearkening back to the pre-Communist rationale and tone, the Bulgarian task, as Dimitrov defined it, was, "to drive these Turks—Asiatics—to go back where they came from five hundred years ago."[79] Simply put, Turks were remnants of the past on the wrong side of the East-West divide.

But, ironically, the sense of a Turkish threat did not only emanate from the East. As Cold War tensions mounted, Turks represented both a bastion of Eastern backwardness and a tool of NATO-dominated Western imperialism. Given these perceptions, early on an autonomous region or republic for Turks, on the Soviet federal model, was categorically ruled out. This excerpt from the Ministry of War's statement on the "Turkish question" in 1947 clarifies this position:

> The Turkish Minority question here is completely different and much more complex than in the USSR. Above all, the Turkish population here will never forget that a few decades ago it was the master of this land and this nation. Their feelings of hatred and revenge toward Bulgaria and Bulgarians are those of fallen masters now under their power. . . . Here we cannot even consider the autonomy of the Turkish population over a given territory in Bulgaria . . . the danger from hostile Turkey, as a neighbor is much greater for Bulgaria than for the USSR.[80]

[74] TsIDA (F-1B, O-12, E-222, L-53: 1946).
[75] TsIDA (F-28, O-1, E-364, L-5: 1947).
[76] TsIDA (F-28, O-1, E-399, L-69: 1945).
[77] TsIDA (F-1B, O-5, E-11, L-36: 1946).
[78] TsIDA (F-214, O-1, E-189, L-64: 1947).
[79] TsIDA (F-214, O-1, E-189, L-64: 1947).
[80] TsIDA (F-214B, O-1, E-716, L-57: 1947).

Contrary to the Party's official pronouncements about a "brotherhood of nations," it painted an image of the Turk as both embittered fallen master and potential tool of NATO-allied Turkey. As a result, the Ministry of War advanced various proposals to "cleanse" the vulnerable Bulgaro-Turkish border from the "tried and true reserve of Turkey and Imperialism, which is located on our territory."[81] As local Party officials all over Bulgaria reported the apparently growing desire of Muslims—both Turks and Pomaks—to emigrate, it heightened suspicions about Muslim loyalty to the new regime. This rising tide of emigration in the immediate postwar period was considered to be a response to rumors circulating among Muslims that, "the day is not far off when Bulgarians will destroy your mosques and take your properties."[82] And although, initially only selective emigration of Turks (from border areas) had been encouraged, eventually emigration emerged as a viable political alternative for resolving both perceived security problems and domestic policy dilemmas.

Ultimately, emigration and the collectivization of agriculture were inexorably linked. Since its inception, agrarian reform was seen as a temporary measure, a precursor to eventual collectivization. Since 1947, the BCP through collective farms or *Trudovo Kooperativno Zemedelsko Stopansko* (TKZS), had created *obshtonarodno* property in rural areas by rationalizing small-scale backward agriculture.[83] By the end of 1948, the BCP initiated a mass push for "voluntary" collectivization, but by 1949 only 11.3 percent of all arable land had been collectivized.[84] The Bulgarian peasant openly resisted collectivization and began a process of Bulgarian migration into Bulgaria's larger cities and regional capitals that gained momentum over the course of the post-war period. The Muslim population also showed little interest in entering the newly forming TKZSs, but chose to remain in primarily rural areas thereby increasing their social isolation from the Bulgarian mainstream.[85] Muslim resistance to collectivization represented a formidable threat to both Communist economic and cultural programs. The Party assumed that socioeconomic transformation was required to create the material basis for the development of a "socialist consciousness," and by extension the "socialist nation." Intimate links were envisioned between the new agricultural collectives and a web of "social educators" in which teachers would work with the collective farms as pioneers in "the culturally and economically backward regions" where Muslims resided.[86] As a result the continued existence of Muslim private and communal properties was seen as problematic and indicative of Muslim interference with socialist progress.

Both BCP suspicions of Muslim loyalties and problems with the collec-

---

[81] TsIDA (F-214B, O-1, E-716, L-58: 1947).
[82] Misirkova, *Turetskoe Menshinstvo*, 56.
[83] TsIDA (F-142, O-5, E-67, L-6: 1948).
[84] Lampe, *Bulgarian Economy*, 146.
[85] TsIDA (F-28, O-1, E-268, L-9: 1945).
[86] TsIDA (F-142, O-5, E-110, L-48: 1948).

tivization of Muslim populations were responsible for the large scale "expulsion" of some 140,000 Turks from Bulgaria in 1950–51. Large numbers of Pomaks and Turks were ready and willing to emigrate when the government made it known that the border would be opened in 1950. But although encouraging emigration of Turks, the Bulgarian government categorically refused exit visas to Pomaks, because they were considered "Bulgarian."[87] Though Turks were willing participants in the mass exodus, outside sources generally label it an expulsion because of the haste and intent behind the operation. The destabilization of pro-NATO Turkey was one probable objective, but the "expulsion" also coincided with the Party's first big push toward collectivization. A 1950 statute made the transfer of properties from individual to collective ownership the only legal form of property transfer in Bulgaria.[88] Additionally, it was precisely at this time that the BCP outlined the far-reaching Six-Year Plan which entailed the creation of vast collective farms in the Dobrudzha region, home to a large concentration of Turks. Significantly, the greatest annual land increase in the Bulgarian collectivization campaign occurred in 1950—the same year of mass Turkish emigration—when the percentage of arable land collectivized jumped from 11.3 percent to 44.2 percent.[89] Bulgarian collectivization was clearly facilitated by the emigration of large numbers of Turkish peasants out of Dobrudzha in particular, although significant numbers also remained.[90] As a result of both the intensified collectivization campaign and emigration of Turks in this period, 60.5 percent of all arable land in Bulgaria and 65 percent of arable land in Dobrudzha had been collectivized by June of 1952.[91]

Contrary to Communist Party intentions, the displacement and residual tensions of the hurried exodus deepened interethnic tensions in Bulgaria. Property, as in earlier and later episodes of migration, became a divisive issue as select Bulgarian populations saw Turkish emigration as an opportunity for material gain. In most situations Turks were forced to leave their properties virtually uncompensated, save tax amnesty and exit visas.[92] In the aftermath, Bulgarian peasants in this period reportedly expressed interest in whether or not they would obtain the vacated "Turkish lands."[93] Numerous representatives of Bulgarian villages wrote letters requesting better land and houses "abandoned" by emigrating Turks.[94] These expectations contributed to rising tensions between Turks and Bulgarians about the status of these proper-

---

[87] Without proof of "Turkishness"—and how this was proven is unclear—no Pomak was allowed an exit visa from Bulgaria in 1950–51. See TsIDA (F-136, O-1A, E-1558, L-42,: 1950). For more on this issue see TsIDA (F-136, O-1A, E-1557, L-9,14,: 1950); and TsIDA (f-136, O-1A, E-1558, L-15,43,49: 1950).

[88] Richard Crampton, *A Short History of Modern Bulgaria* (Cambridge, U.K., 1987), 144–45.

[89] James Brown, *Bulgaria under Communist Rule* (London, 1970), 201.

[90] Kostanick, *Turkish Resettlement*, 82–84.

[91] N. Tepev, *Tursko Naselenie v Narodno Republika Bŭlgariia* (Sofia, 1954), 69.

[92] TsIDA (F-136, O-1A, E-1558, L-22–23, 39: 1950).

[93] TsIDA (F-1,O-12, E-578, L-2: 1949).

[94] TsIDA (F-136, O-1A, E-1306, L-3–12: 1951).

ties. In one case, ten Bulgarians from the village of Cherna (Shumen district) wrote a letter of complaint to the administration two years after the Turk emigration, stating:

> In 1951 we resettled into this village and bought the properties of Turks who had emigrated. Most of us wanted to form a TKZS and we became founding members of one. Most of the Bulgarian families in our village joined. By 1952 our cooperative was doing comparatively well because we were able to be very productive with these formerly Turkish lands. In spite of the emigration of Turks, there remained about seventy Turkish families in the village. In the beginning of 1953 these Turks began to show hostility toward us and started to launch an offensive against us with the goal of driving us out of the village under the pretense that we took cheap land, practically without money, from the Turks and should leave the lands for them—that these are Turkish properties.[95]

Such disagreements, typical of the consequences of the exodus, reverberated in the period that followed, poisoning Bulgaro-Turkish relations in many locales.

In addition, the loss of *vakf* property was a source of Turkish discontent, even as *vakf* control was used to shore up Turkish loyalties. Since the emigration of entire Turkish communities in 1950–51, collective farms or other state institutions had taken over numerous "abandoned" *vakf* properties.[96] This was in violation of the official property laws of Bulgaria which stipulated that *vakf* properties were supposed to go to the nearest Muslim Communal Organization unless proper compensation was offered to the Islamic establishment. In spite of such laws large numbers of *vakf* properties throughout Bulgaria were gradually scaled down, both through direct appropriation and an intensified tax burden. With the 1947 Party assault on urban landlordism, for example, large numbers of *vakf* stores, cafés, and buildings were nationalized and socialist city planning meant the demolition of many more *vakf* holdings.[97] Still the Party-loyal Muslim establishment did retain nominal control over many *vakf* properties in Bulgaria. As in the past the Muftiship and MCOs continued to assert their "Turkish rights" over Muslim properties at the expense of less-favored Muslim groups, namely Gypsies. In 1948, for example, the Vidin MCO complained in a letter to the Head Mufti that, "It is necessary to note that Gypsies are not Turks, and Turks are not Gypsies" and so Gypsies should be banned from the administration of *vakf* properties. Similarly, a letter from an MCO in Pazardzhik asserted that, "No Gypsy has ever created a *vakf* and only participate illegally by meddling."[98] As a result of these complaints and lobbying by the Head Muftiship, the BCP allowed the Islamic establishment to codify the exclusion of Gypsies from *vakf* commissions in its, "protocols in con-

[95] TsIDA (F-136, O-1A, E-1318A, L-21: 1953).
[96] TsIDA (F-747, O-1, E-16, L-87: 1955).
[97] TsIDA (F-747, O-1, E-30, L-22: 1948).
[98] TsIDA (F-747, O-1, E-12, L-25: 1948).

nection with Gypsy meddling in Turkish Minority *vakfs*."[99] This marked a BCP-sanctioned "Turkification" of the Muftiship and "Turkish" MCOs—hereafter to be called Turkish (instead of Muslim) Communal Organizations (TCOs). By allowing the continued presence of *vakf* properties and by legitimizing them as Turkish, the BCP bought the loyalty of the Muslim establishment, even as it severely curtailed its material base for survival.

As elsewhere in the Soviet Bloc, the BCP pursued its collectivization campaigns with cultural, political, and economic aims. In the Soviet Union from 1929–32 (1941–50 for the territories gained in World War II) and in Eastern Europe from 1955–62, mass collectivization campaigns had served to break the political back of the peasantry and to uproot and disrupt undesirable cultural elements.[100] According to most sources, the collectivization of the rural population of Bulgaria was completed by 1958.[101] This socialist achievement was announced by the Bulgarian Premier, Anton Yugov, at the Seventh Party Congress in June of that year with the qualification that the remainder of arable land was, "mountainous and therefore unsuitable for collectivization."[102] It is safe to assume that this mountainous land consisted mostly of the private smallholdings of Turks and Pomaks in the Rhodope and Balkan Mountains. It was no coincidence that at the same congress a delegate reported that only 70 percent of all rural Turks were collectivized, which compared poorly to the 92 percent average for the population as a whole.[103] At the same time, Party officials lauded the transformation of Turkish villages that had undergone the "agricultural revolution" with the contention that, "in the collective farms it is easier to destroy old traditions and relations."[104] Others noted that the fundamental question regarding the Turks was the "restructuring of agriculture," which became a primary issue in Party discussions in the "Great Leap Forward" period (1958–60).[105] This last leg of the collectivization drive focusing on Turks and Pomaks, was clearly connected to concurrent BCP cultural projects. As articulated at the Party Plenum in 1958: "The socialist restructuring of agriculture is a historic victory for our

[99] TsIDA (F-747, O-1, E-12, L-1: 1947).

[100] Conquest asserts that one of the primary goals of collectivization in the USSR was to crush the will of both the peasantry and the Ukrainian nation. See Robert Conquest, *Harvest of Sorrow: Soviet Collectivization and the Terror-Famine* (Oxford, 1986), 3. Similarly Gribincea stresses the goal of "de-nationalization" in the collectivization of the Moldavian republic. Mihai Gribincea, *Agricultural Collectivization in Moldavia: Basarabia during Stalinism 1949–50* (Boulder, 1996), 14. Fitzpatrick points out that collectivization, carried out in the spirit of the Cultural Revolution, was fueled by contempt for peasant backwardness and focused on eliminating resistance in the village. See Sheila Fitzpatrick, *Stalin's Peasants: Resistance and Survival in the Russian Village after Collectivization* (New York, 1994), 3.

[101] John Bell, *The Bulgarian Communist Party from Blagoev to Zhivkov* (Stanford, 1986), 111; Lampe, *Bulgarian Economy*, 149; Crampton, *Short History*, 145; and Brown, *Bulgaria under Communist Rule*, 203–4. Brown points out that Bulgaria was the first Communist state, after the Soviet Union, to completely collectivize its agriculture.

[102] Brown, *Bulgaria under Communist Rule*, 203.

[103] TsIDA (F-1B, O-5, E-353, L-448: 1958); and TsIDA (F-1B, O-5, E-353, L-457: 1958).

[104] TsIDA (F-1B, O-5, E-353, L-353: 1958).

[105] TsIDA (F-1B, O-5, E-353, L-390: 1958).

people. Out of this, the backward Turkish peasant will soon be transformed . . . because agriculture was the reason for their economic and cultural backwardness. The integration of the Turkish population in the village into cooperative agriculture will become the primary issue in the Party's struggle with reactionary and enemy elements."[106] As another delegate articulated, "Private property is a means of production for divided people, socialist property ties them together."[107] Thus, the economic transformation of Turkish districts was made an explicit part of the continued Party efforts to broker a social, and eventually cultural, merger.

After decades of sustained Muslim resistance to the process, the total collectivization of Muslims theoretically was achieved by 1960.[108] But in spite of eventual Muslim accommodation to the collective farm structure, the resultant cultural change expected by the BCP was not forthcoming. In the years following collectivization and the Cultural Revolution, it became increasingly clear that the transformation of Turkish economic structures did not necessarily dispense with cultural "backwardness." As a result, having mostly resolved the land issue, other aspects of Turkish material and symbolic culture—clothes, names, etc.—came to the forefront of Party campaigns. But land and territory, it seems, remained a subtext for the BCP assimilation campaigns that followed. In the midst of the forced name-changing drive in the Pomak village of Kornitsa, the regional Party representative announced over a loudspeaker, "The government will not allow pure blooded Bulgarians to declare themselves as Turks and so their land as foreign territory."[109] The final and total Bulgarianization of Pomaks in the 1970s was clearly an extension of Party program to "nationalize" and so safeguard Bulgarian territory. In addition, as Bulgarian birth rates dropped, the rural and vital Pomak masses were expected to take their place as a pure receptacle of Bulgarian peasant culture in the countryside. This would eventually extend to Turks.

But until 1984 the BCP continued to pursue a somewhat contradictory approach to dealing with the Turkish presence on Bulgarian soil. Since the mass emigration in 1951, the Party had attempted to inculcate a sense of rootedness in Bulgarian soil for those Turks that remained. This poem in a Turkish-language periodical *Halk Gençliği*, was indicative of the Party approach to keeping Turks in Bulgaria:

> Did you call this a foreign land,
> And the other side "the homeland"?
> It's a lie,
> a lie,
> a lie![110]

---

[106] TsIDA (F-1B, O-5, E-353, L-351: 1958).
[107] TsIDA (F-1B, O-5, E-353, L-364: 1958).
[108] TsIDA (F-28, O-16, E-49, L-11: 1959).
[109] Diulgerov, *Razpnati Dushi*, 67.
[110] Şimşir, *Bulgarian Turks*, 215.

If Party hopes were still alive for a genuine ethno-social brotherhood, they were dashed by the Turks' continued desire to emigrate. In 1969, in direct response to improved Soviet relations with Turkey, a Bulgaro-Turkish agreement was signed, allowing limited voluntary emigration of Turks from Bulgaria—80,000 to 90,000 over a ten-year period. The agreement applied only to "close relatives" of Bulgarian-Turks already in Turkey and so affected only 10 percent of the remaining Turks in Bulgaria. Still, news of the agreement prompted huge numbers of Turks to file for emigration, including many Turkish Party members.[111] The Party considered Turks who registered for emigration to be disloyal and it continued to propagandize against emigration, in both the Turkish-language press and local explanatory sessions.[112] At the same time, apprehensions about the place of Turks on Bulgarian soil were also chronic, especially in light of international events and domestic developments in the 1970s and 1980s. Of these, the Cyprus affair was probably the most important. The fact that a large mass of Turks was compactly settled across Bulgaria's southern border with Turkey had always provoked anxieties about Turkish territorial ambitions. The Turkish invasion of Cyprus in 1974 raised Bulgarian fears of a "Cypriot variation" on their soil and the international spread of Islamic fundamentalism raised BCP fears about Muslim pretensions for rights and autonomy. Finally, the rapid growth of Muslim minorities in relation to the now highly urbanized Bulgarian population heightened perceptions of the potential problem of Muslims as a demographic and territorial threat.

The far-reaching assimilation campaigns leveled at Turks in 1984–85, in theory put an end to all such problems. If all Turks were really Bulgarians then the demographic imbalance, the possibility of Turkish territorial autonomy or of partition were all nullified. With Zhivkov's famous 1985 declaration, "There are no Turks in Bulgaria," all of the land and people of Bulgaria were claimed as inviolable, as essentially Bulgarian. As a result, emigration for Turks was deemed unnecessary and banned. As was declared in *Pirinsko Delo* in March of 1985, for example, "There is and there will be no emigration of Bulgarian citizens to Turkey . . . there is no single section of the Bulgarian people that belongs to another nation."[113] Turks were "encouraged" to publicly embrace Bulgarian blood and soil, as in this 1985 declaration by prominent Turks: "Deeply rooted in the Bulgarian land, the honest and indefatigable toilers—the Bulgarians, converted to Islam and subjected to ethnic assimilation—have never lost their organic link with the historical fortunes of their people. . . . We are all the offspring of the Bulgarian nation, we are the masters of this land, this is our paradise, and there is and there can be no other paradise for us."[114] This connection of "reborn" Bulgarians (former Turks) to the soil presumably cemented their place in Bulgaria, while high-

---

[111] TsIDA (F-1B, O-39, E-522, L-187: 1970).
[112] TsIDA (F-1B, O-39, E-522, L-186: 1970).
[113] Radio Free Europe-Radio Liberty, "Bulgaria Situation Report," 28 March 1985, 4.
[114] Open Society Archive (Radio Free Europe-Radio Liberty): Bulgaria Country File, F-1102, BTA 102, 26 July 1985, 1–3.

lighting their aversion to outside intervention, autonomy, or emigration. The 1984–85 Rebirth Process entailed the eradication of all remaining vestiges of Turco-Arabic cultural difference, including clothes, names, and the Turkish language (although religion, at least in theory, was spared). Still, when such markers were eliminated, it was not just "Bulgarian" bodies, but Bulgarian soil that was cleansed of these vestiges of the "foreign" Ottoman past. In the denouement of over a century of reclaiming it parcel by parcel, the Bulgarian lands were now pronounced as wholly and completely Bulgarian. As one Party source declared in 1989, "Bulgaria is a uni-national state and there is not one inch of foreign land within its borders."[115]

In reality, the achievements of the Rebirth Process among Turks had always been tentative. Since 1984–85 Turkish resistance had persisted, sometimes manifested in violent incidents, in spite of harsh Communist repression. By the spring of 1989, a number of Turks were engaged in hunger strikes and the stand off with authorities had sharpened in a climate of increasing political insecurity. As Communist regimes fell elsewhere in Eastern Europe, Zhivkov took desperate measures to alleviate the Turkish problem at home. The Party quite suddenly and unexpectedly launched a massive campaign to encourage the immediate mass emigration of Turks to Turkey, including a television address by Party Secretary Zhivkov himself, asserting that Bulgarian Muslims (with Turks in mind), "are infidel to the Bulgarian state and should leave forever."[116] Within a few months almost one half of Bulgaria's 900,000 Turks left the country with little more than the clothes on their backs and a few possessions. Since the BCP would only extend the official designation of "tourist" to the population in question, they were only able to take 500 leva in cash (then the equivalent of $450) out of the country. In addition, the hastiness with which the exodus was proposed and carried out meant that most Turks simply abandoned, rented out, or in many cases sold their houses, livestock, and other possessions for next to nothing. In fact, there has been considerable scholarly speculation that the departure of Turks was used in part to alleviate housing shortages in many of the medium-sized provincial capitals where Turks resided. In spite of the trials of emigration, many Pomaks also applied for visas but were denied tourist status. By fall of 1989 large- and small-scale protests, as well as hunger strikes, occurred in Pomak regions over the emigration issue.[117] By this time Bulgarian protest had also taken root and the Bulgarian Communist regime fell by November of that year.

The new Bulgarian regime reversed the assimilation decrees in short order and allowed the organization of various political parties, including a Turkish-led Party with a primarily Turkish and Pomak constituency, called the Movement for Rights and Freedoms (MRF), headed by Ahmed Dogan. But politi-

---

[115] TsIDA (F-1B, O-63, E-84, L-3: 1989).
[116] Vasileva, "Bulgarian Turkish," 349
[117] Radio Free Europe-Radio Liberty, "Bulgaria Situation Report," 1 September 1989, 20.

cal changes wrought by the fall of Communist government also allowed room for divergent strains of extreme Bulgarian nationalism to emerge and cast their shadow on Bulgarian politics. Significantly, the new Bulgarian constitution of 1990 technically banned any political Party that called for territorial autonomy or was organized on an ethnic basis. Bulgarians betrayed fears of territorial mutilation by way of Turkish invasion, Turkish separatism, or the "de-nationalization" or "Turkification" of previously assimilated populations (especially Pomaks). Although the MRF—so-named to avoid any accusation of an "ethnic basis"—had renounced the idea of Turkish territorial autonomy from the day of its inception, this did not preclude accusations by prominent politicians that Dogan was an Islamic fundamentalist who wanted to attach portions of Bulgarian territory to Turkey. Hence Turks and Pomaks continued to be linked to potential territorial threats, a connection that was solidified by the Yugoslav wars and fears that a situation similar to that of Bosnia or Kosovo would replay itself in Bulgaria.[118]

With this in mind the question of the restoration of Turkish properties as part of post-Communist property reform inevitably became charged with ethnonational significance. One of the Turks' most immediate demands following the political change was for the return of properties lost during the exodus of 1989. This was especially acute considering that within four months of their departure, about 42 percent of Turkish emigrants had returned to Bulgaria.[119] In the majority of cases Turkish properties had been taken over by Bulgarians who, along with local authorities, were reluctant to return the land. By 1990, 77 percent of returning Turks were essentially homeless—or whole families were living in temporary situations with friends—and the issue of property return moved to the top of the MRF agenda.[120] After vigorous lobbying by Ahmed Dogan and mass Turkish rallies in Sofia in March 1990, the "Dogan law" was finally passed in July 1992, calling for the return of property to the Turkish "tourists" of 1989. In terms of the restoration of other Muslim rural properties and communal *vakf* properties, the process has been a more complicated one. The 1991 Law on Land aimed at decollectivizing Bulgarian agriculture has tended to favor Bulgarians over Muslims, in spite of the fact that most Bulgarians by this time are urbanized and have no use for such lands. The new law calls for the restoration of lands taken after 1944 to those who have official documentation proving ownership.[121] The problem for Muslims is twofold: many of them had their lands taken prior to 1944, and most have no documents to prove ownership, because all such documents bearing Turco-Arabic names were destroyed during the Pomak and Turkish Rebirth Processes.[122] As one article

---

[118] See, for example, Asenov, *Vŭzroditelniiat Protses: Dŭrzhavna Sigurnost* (Sofia, 1994).
[119] Vasileva, "Bulgarian Turkish," 347.
[120] Ibid., 350.
[121] *Prava i Svobodi* (Sofia), 17 July 1992, 3.
[122] *Prava i Svobodi* (Sofia), 30 October 1992, 2; and *Prava i Svobodi* (Sofia), 25 February 1992, 6.

in the MRF newspaper *Prava i Svobodi* (Rights and Freedoms) claimed, everyone knows which land is theirs but they have no documents to prove it.[123] In another article, the publication makes the plea for land to be returned, "not to its former owners but to those that work it."[124] In fact, decollectivization in the Muslim provinces has only succeeded in wresting from Muslims the rights to local lands and collective farm resources that have become crucial to agricultural production. In terms of *vakf* properties, Bulgarian law calls for their restoration to their proper owners, but again, documentation has been a major problem. In addition, the fact that corrupt pro-government Head Muftiships sold many of these properties has excluded them from the parameters of restitution laws.[125] With or without deeds, most of the MCOs in Bulgaria have submitted requests for the return of their *vakf* properties. Some have been returned but many more were lost forever. For many, *vakf* properties—as with other Turkish properties—have become a locus of local Turkish claims; as one local Mufti recently asserted, "it is known that the *vakf* properties did not fall from the sky, but were earned by our grandfathers and fathers with the sweat of their brows."[126]

In the post-Communist period, the restitution of state-controlled properties has been oriented, to a large degree, toward fortifying the Bulgarian presence on Bulgarian soil. For example, in one discussion of the Law on Land, a commentator reflected on how it had, "returned to Bulgarians the land of their fathers and grandfathers." He went on to posit that, "Because the village is the bulwark of Bulgaria, if we don't return what has been taken by the totalitarian system we simply would be a tree without roots."[127] In contrast, both the restitution of *vakfs* and the return or buying of privatized property by Turks has provoked concern about the alleged role of Turkey buying property on Bulgarian territory. One headline in a 1995 issue of the Bulgarian newspaper *Duma* threatened, "Ankara is preparing for privatization in Bulgaria."[128] This situation is not, of course, unique to the Bulgarian context. As Hilary Appel argues about post-Communist property restitution in the Czech Republic, the return of Czech lands was more connected to "corrective justice to Communist misdeeds" and ethnonational rationale than to liberal economic logic.[129] The return of lands to Czech citizens who were stripped of property in the Communist period offered no means of property reclamation for Jews or Germans, for example, whose lands were taken prior to 1948. Significantly, post-Communist struggles over land in Bulgaria and elsewhere

[123] *Prava i Svobodi* (Sofia), 29 April—5 May 1991, 1.
[124] *Prava i Svobodi* (Sofia), 11–17 March 1991, 6.
[125] *Prava i Svobodi* (Sofia), 24 July 1992, 3.
[126] *Musulmani* (Sofia), July 1992, 1–2.
[127] Open Society Archive (Radio Free Europe-Radio Liberty): Bulgaria Country File, F-1102, "Radio Sofia" transcript, 2 March 1991.
[128] *Duma* (Sofia), 4 December 1995, 1.
[129] Hilary Appel, "Justice and the Reformation of Property Rights in the Czech Republic," *East European Politics and Societies* 9 (1995): 22–40.

have coincided with attempts to recast national and social boundaries in a rapidly changing domestic and international milieu.[130]

Conclusion

In the modern period, Bulgarian territory and the parcels of land that bisected it were the grounds on which both Bulgarians and Muslims constructed or recast local and collective identities. In the nineteenth and twentieth centuries, Bulgarian national projects attempted to define and demarcate every last parcel of Bulgarian countryside. In spite of provisional alliances with their Muslim minorities, these efforts had far-reaching consequences for local Muslim populations, as Muslim ownership was increasingly tentative. In the Communist period, the grounds may have shifted but Muslim presences were still treated as obstacles to state projects of material and cultural integration. Nationalization and the collectivization of agriculture were carried out in the name of the "nation" though ironically Bulgarians too—including the revered peasants—lost their land. But because of their resistance to material change, Turks in particular were intermittently "invited" to leave Bulgarian territory, and so cleanse it of their "Asiatic" presence. But ultimately both Turks and Pomaks were expected to remain and Bulgarianize, to replace the lost Bulgarian peasant endangered by postwar modernization, and to embrace Bulgarian blood and soil. In the post-Communist period, new territorial insecurities and a radically changing property regime only heightened the elaboration of ethnonational meanings on the freshly destabilized Bulgarian terrain. As Muslims left and returned, and as their lands were taken and sometimes restored, land and territory became laden with cultural meaning. In due course, it became an important locus for modern Bulgaro-Muslim conflict.

[130] For an excellent discussion of this process in the Romanian case see Katherine Verdery, "The Elasticity of Land: Problems of Property Restitution in Transylvania," *Slavic Review* 53 (1994): 1073.

Conclusion

It was us, the East Europeans who invented "Europe," constructed it, dreamed about it, called upon it. This Europe is a myth created by us . . . the infantile nations of the continent. Europe was built by those of us living on the edges, because it is only from there that you would have the need to imagine something like "Europe" to save you from your complexes, insecurities and fears.

—SLAVENKA DRAKULIĆ

In the modern period, the impulse to categorize and impose order resulted in the mapping of civilization and barbarity onto the cultural intricacies of the globe. With Western Europe leading the charge, "East" and "West," and the more geographically specific "Europe" and "Asia," were affixed with new meanings that have yet to come unglued. These imagined places and cultural concepts seduced thinkers on every continent, with a special significance on the margins of maps, where conjured worlds meet. The Balkans is one such place. Out of a Balkan reality where Slavic, Turkic, Muslim, and Christian were intermeshed, where boundaries between cultures and ethnicities were shifting and indistinct, modern ideas and methods mitigated a new fixing of borders. By the nineteenth century, Bulgarian intellectuals, insecurely teetering on the edge of the continent, sought cultural mooring for the Bulgarian nation in European soil. Having discovered their own Europeanness, they asserted their cultural superiority via their Asiatic Ottoman overlords. In spite of ambiguities, a new place at the edge of the European map seemed preferable to the margins of the Ottoman one. After gaining autonomy in 1878, Bulgarian statesmen initiated far-reaching efforts to extricate themselves from the Oriental mire, with a marked significance for Muslim minorities left in the Ottoman wake.

In order to claim their place in Europe, Bulgarians needed to build a European façade over their apparent Balkan backwardness. With this in mind, national imperatives demanded a confrontation of the tangible vestiges of the

Ottoman past on what came to be defined as Bulgarian soil and Bulgarian bodies. This required, first and foremost, the reclamation of national territories from foreign presences so that every plot of land could be remodeled in the European image. As the Bulgarian lands—reaching well beyond the 1878 borders—were claimed as essentially Bulgarian, there was a growing tendency to expel or destroy markers of difference on the landscape, material or human. Although much of this proceeded through land reform episodes of coerced migration, ultimately the "liberation" of Bulgarian territory from Ottoman (and other foreign) presences was brokered through transformations of everyday culture. Although Bulgarian culture itself was first cleansed and dehybridized of Ottoman residues, gradually Muslims too were "liberated" from Ottoman occupation. Severely complicated by shifts in domestic politics, wars, and divisions within Muslim communities themselves, Bulgarians viewed and treated Muslims as native and foreign, ally and enemy, self and other. Even as Muslims were intermittently feared and rejected as foreign, backward, and Asiatic "other," they were also brought into provisional and lasting alliances. Significantly, Bulgarian confrontations with the Muslim presence were increasingly rationalized by assumptions about Bulgaro-Muslim sameness as opposed to difference. With claims that first Pomaks (and much later Turks) were racially Bulgarian—forcibly Islamicized and Turkified in the Ottoman period—all visible and audible markers of Muslimness—such as clothes and names—had to be stripped from their "Bulgarian" bodies.

The process of encoding Bulgarian national meanings on the so-defined Bulgarian lands and its populations began in earnest after the Russian victory in the Russo-Turkish war of 1877–78. Post-1878 dreams of territorial expansion were advanced in the name of the Bulgarian peasant, portrayed in the national literature as economically and culturally oppressed for five centuries by their Ottoman masters. In the years leading up to World War II, Bulgarian statesmen used land reform and other measures to rectify these perceived historical injustices, while at the same time Bulgarianizing national territory. Still, Turks and Pomaks had relative tolerance and local autonomy in this period, as Muslim elites cooperated and the Muslim masses were generally loyal citizens of the new state (independent after 1908). But as Bulgarian refugees flooded into the new state and Muslims migrated out, especially after the Balkan Wars of 1912–13, the Muslim presence waned (particularly in the cities) in favor of a Bulgarian one. It was during these wars and after that Bulgarian thinkers and statesmen decidedly turned their efforts to the Muslim periphery as a part of the larger project of territorial expansion and internal political consolidation. With ethnography as inspiration, the First Balkan War (1912–13) brought the first attempts to eradicate hybridity and impose Bulgarian sameness on the Bulgarian-speaking Muslim Pomak population of southern Bulgaria and the occupied territories. Bulgarian troops and a retinue of Orthodox priests entered Pomak villages and forcibly converted the Muslim populations to Christianity, changed Turco-Arabic names to Bulgarian ones, and replaced fezzes, turbans, and "veils" with Bulgarian hats and scarves. Confronted with a measure of Muslim resistance and the political reversals associated with the Second Balkan War in 1913, these measures were summarily overturned. A similar round of name and clothing reform efforts, reemerged in the late 1930s and during World War II, sponsored by a group of modernizing Pomaks themselves. Again Pomaks were expected to shed their markers of Muslim difference and conform to new Bulgarian state, and now elite Pomak, visions of modernity and Bulgarianness.

After 1944 the Bulgarian Communist Party (BCP) visions and the means of attaining them would reach further into all the spheres of life than anything in the prewar period. The Communist period was indeed a new era for Pomaks and Turks, but with important continuities. In the shadow of Red Army occupation and Soviet practice, the BCP advanced the internationalist idea of a Bulgaro-Muslim brotherhood. Muslim populations were needed as allies when newly defined enemies abounded in Bulgarian society and outside the country's borders. Pomaks were not considered a minority population by the new regime, but rather were officially embraced as an integral part of the Bulgarian nation, albeit with special needs because of their "backward" state. In contrast, Turks were extended resources for their own national development and theoretically incited to spread world revolution to their Turkish co-nationals abroad. The BCP employed Turkishness in the provinces because of Soviet demands, but also in hopes of bringing Communism and modernity, in whatever form, to the Turkish-speaking Muslim provinces. But ultimately, the practical attainment of Communism was predicated on Bulgaro-Muslim socialist and later blood-based sameness and, more pointedly, the enforcement of Bulgarian modernization and national integration.

To an extent never before experienced, everyday culture was the arena in which the Communist Party attempted to tame the borderlands and usher in a "bright future" of utopian proportions. After a brief period of power consolidation, the late 1950s marked the beginning of a decisive acceleration in BCP endeavors to completely integrate Pomaks and to a certain extent also Turks into Bulgarian society. Todor Zhivkov—who came to power in 1956 and ruled until 1989—laid the path for the remainder of the Communist period with his optimistic vision of the approach of "ripe communism," in reality fully realized nationalism. In order to eradicate economic and cultural anomalies in the countryside, the BCP collectivized rural properties in Muslim districts and concurrently launched an offensive against Islamic everyday practices on the local level. Campaigns against the fez, turban, veil, *shalvari,* circumcision, and household culture penetrated the most intimate reaches of Muslim homes and bodies. Carried out by co-opted Muslim religious leaders and other local administrators, these campaigns reached a crescendo in the first phase of the Cultural Revolution (1958–60) and, in the face of pervasive resistance, continued throughout the rest of the Communist period. Campaigns for integration of Muslims were intensified in the decades that fol-

lowed, driven, in part, by the perceived threats of Turkish nationalism and Islamic fundamentalism and the growing demographic imbalance between the
more prolific rural Muslims and urban Bulgarians. By the 1960s and 1970s,
Pomak names—as markers of both personal and cultural identity—were
forcibly replaced by Bulgarian ones in the Rebirth Process. A similar Rebirth
Process campaign in 1984–85 replaced the Turco-Arabic names of almost
one million Turks with Bulgarian ones. In both cases, the Party claimed that
Pomaks, and Turks after them, were essentially Bulgarians, forcibly Islamicized and Turkified during the Ottoman period. Hence by 1985, in theory, a
total ethnonational merger had been achieved. In practice the Party continued its battle against these markers of Muslim difference until its fall in 1989.

Since 1878, and especially after 1944, Turks and Pomaks responded to
Bulgarian nationalist endeavors in various ways, from quiet cooperation to
overt compliance, from active protest to milder everyday resistance. In every
period, modernization had pockets of support among Muslim populations,
just as Muslims (like Bulgarians) at times rejected and resisted it. If there
seems to have been a greater tendency among Bulgarians than Muslims to
embrace presocialist and socialist modernity, it was because of the particularly Bulgarian flavor that coated modernization projects. The charms of
modernity had less allure for Muslim minorities as they were constructed in
direct opposition to Muslim culture, or more accurately to what Muslim culture was presumed to be. Still, both before and during the Communist period, a significant number of Muslims entered into the work of the state or
simply conformed on a daily basis. But there were numerous examples of
open and quiet resistance in the interstices of co-optation that reveal the complicated nature of survival for minority populations within nation-states,
particularly under the extreme conditions of Communism. Undoubtedly,
Muslim resistance and compliance had great significance for both the survival and collapse of Bulgaria's Communist system.

The legacy of this period only became clear after the end of Communist
rule in 1989. Under Turkish leadership, a Muslim-supported political party
emerged, the Movement for Rights and Freedoms and Muslims were given a
new voice and place in Bulgarian society. Yet as Turkish voices could now be
heard in Bulgarian society, so too could the most extreme anti-Turkish sentiments. In the uncertainty of post-Communist politics, images of a Turco-
Muslim threat infiltrated Bulgarian identity politics, laced with newly cast
images of historical and contemporary "foreign" threats. The Yugoslav wars
of the 1990s have sparked additional questions about the Muslim presence in
connection with national security and ethnic coexistence. Significantly, these
concerns have been raised just as Muslims have succeeded in reclaiming their
right to use their own names and wear their own "Oriental" attire, and as
they have attempted but only partially succeeded in reclaiming both their private and *vakf* properties from Bulgarian authorities. As in the past, Bulgarian
elite and popular images of the nation have co-opted and confronted salient
categories of Europeanness versus Asianness, West versus East, civility versus

barbarity, in an attempt to untangle Bulgarian from Muslim. The resultant discourse, far from a monolithic anti-Turkish campaign, has revealed the inner complexity of Bulgarian national debates. In a sense, this process has revealed that concepts of "foreignness" are as internally divisive as the supposedly essential cleavages between Bulgarian and Muslim. Furthermore, the relatively functional ethnic politics of post-Communist Bulgaria clarify that even after the extraordinary times of the Communist period, Bulgarians and Muslims still have common ground in Bulgarian soil.

Throughout its modern history, the Bulgarian-Muslim encounter has unfolded in the shadow of European influence. Bulgarians were caught up in the irrepressible current of European ideas, such as nationalism which ultimately drove a wedge between Bulgarian and Muslim. That said, modern ideas and projects spawned new and unexpected bases for intermittent tolerance and practical coexistence. Local conditions and legacies created a multifaceted playing field in which Bulgaro-Muslim conflict was neither inevitable nor constant. Admittedly, Bulgaria's modern cultural and political reorderings have meant persecution for most of the country's Muslim minorities, many of whom sought refuge beyond Bulgaria's borders. At the same time, Bulgaria has remained home to more than a million Muslims. By continually adapting and reinventing themselves, they have negotiated a place in the body politic throughout the many twists and turns of Bulgarian history.

Selected Bibliography

Ahmed, Leila. *Women and Gender in Islam: Historical Roots of a Modern Debate*. New Haven: Yale University Press, 1992.

Alhaug, Gulbrand and Yulian Konstantinov. *Names, Ethnicity and Politics: Islamic Names in Bulgaria 1912–1992*. Oslo: Novus Press, 1995.

Alimova, Dilorom. *Reshenie Zhenskogo Voprosa v Uzbekistane: 1917–1941*. Tashkent: Izdatelstvo "FAN," 1987.

Allcock, John. "Constructing the Balkans." In *Black Lambs and Grey Falcons: Women Travelers in the Balkans*, edited by J. Allcock and A. Young. New York: Bergham Books, 1991.

Alloula, Mark. *The Colonial Harem*. Minneapolis: University of Minnesota Press, 1986.

Anderson, Benedict. *Imagined Communities: Reflections on the Origins and Spread of Nationalism*. New York: Verso, 1983.

Andreev, Mikhail. *Istoriia na Bŭlgarskata Burzhoazna Dŭrzhava i Pravo: 1878–1917*. Sofia: Sofi-P, 1993.

Appel, Hilary. "Justice and the Reformation of Property Rights in the Czech Republic." *East European Politics and Societies* 9 (1995): 22–40.

Aretov, Nikolai. *Bŭlgarskoto Vŭzrazhdane i Evropa*. Sofia: "Kralitsa Mab," 1995.

Asenov, Boncho. *Natsiia, Religiia, Natsionalizŭm*. Sofia: "GEYA-INF," 1994.

———. *Vŭzroditelniiat Protses i Dŭrzhavna Sigurnost*. Sofia: Izdatelstvo "GEYA-INF," 1996.

Averini, Schlomo. "Marxism and Nationalism." *Journal of Contemporary History* 26 (1991): 637–57.

Bakić-Hayden, Milica. "Nesting Orientalismπs: The Case of Former Yugoslavia." *Slavic Review* 54 (1995): 917–31.

Bakić-Hayden, Milica and Robert Hayden. "Orientalist Variations on the Theme 'Balkans': Symbolic Geography in Recent Yugoslav Cultural Politics." *Slavic Review* 51 (1992): 1–16.

Baker, Patricia. "The Fez in Turkey: A Symbol of Modernization?" *Costume: Journal of the Costume Society* 20 (1986): 72–86.

Barker, Elizabeth. *Macedonia: Its Place in Balkan Power Politics*. London: Royal Institute of International Affairs, 1950.

Baron, Beth. "Unveiling in Early Twentieth Century Egypt: Practical and Symbolic Considerations." *Middle Eastern Studies* 25 (1989): 370–86.

Beaglehole, E. "Property." In *The International Encyclopedia of the Social Sciences*, edited by D. Sills. New York: Macmillan, 1968.

Bedermen, Gail. *Manliness and Civilization: A Cultural History of Gender and Race in the United States, 1880–1917*. Chicago: University of Chicago Press, 1995.

Bell, John. *The Bulgarian Communist Party from Blagoev to Zhivkov*. Stanford: Hoover Institute Press, 1986.

——. *Peasants in Power: Alexander Stamboliski and the Bulgarian Agrarian Union, 1899–1923*. Princeton: Princeton University Press, 1977.

Bennigsen, Alexander and Chantal Lemercier-Quelquejay. *Islam in the Soviet Union*. New York: Praeger, 1967.

Bernays, Anne and Justin Kaplan. *The Language of Names*. New York: Simon and Schuster, 1997.

Bethell, Tom. *The Noblest Triumph: Property and Prosperity through the Ages*. New York: St. Martin's Press, 1998.

Bhabha, Hommi. "Dissemination: Time, Narrative, and the Margins of the Nation." In *Nation and Narration*, edited by H. Bhabha. London: Routledge, 1990.

Bilshai, Vera. *Reshenie Zhenskogo Voprosa v SSSR*. Moskva: Gosudarstvennoe Izdatestvo Politicheskoi Literaturi, 1956.

Blackbourn, David and Geoff Eley, eds. *The Peculiarities of German History: Bourgeois Society and Politics in Nineteenth Century Germany*. Oxford, U.K.: Oxford University Press, 1984.

Bloomer, Dexter. *The Life and Writings of Amelia Bloomer*. New York: Schocken Books, 1975.

Bokovoy, Melissa. *Peasants and Communists: Politics and Ideology in the Yugoslav Countryside, 1941–1953*. Pittsburgh: University of Pittsburgh Press, 1998.

Botev, Bobi. "Sŭotnoshenie Mezhdu Pozitivnoto i Negativnoto v Predstavite na Bŭlgariia za Albantsite." In *Vrŭzki na Sŭvmestimost i Nesŭvmestimost Mezhdu Khristiiani i Miusiulmani v Bŭlgariia*, edited by A. Zheliaskova. Sofia: Fondatsiia "Mezhdunaroden Tsentŭr po Problemite na Maltsinstvata i Kulturnite Vzaimodeĭstviia," 1994.

Bourdieu, Pierre. *Language and Symbolic Power*. Cambridge, Mass.: Harvard University Press, 1991.

——. *Outline of a Theory of Practice*. Cambridge, U.K.: Cambridge University Press, 1977.

Brace, Laura. *The Idea of Property in Seventeenth Century England: Tithes and the Individual*. Manchester: Manchester University Press, 1998.

Bracewell, Wendy. "Rape in Kosovo: Masculinity and Serbian Nationalism." *Nations and Nationalism* 6 (2000): 563–90.

——. "Women, Motherhood and Contemporary Serbian Nationalism." *Women's Studies International Forum* 19 (1996): 25–33.

Branchev, Nikolai. *Bŭlgari-Mokhamedani (Pomatsi): Zemepisnite Predeli*. Sofia: Izdaniia na Bŭlgarsko Narodnouchno Druzhestvo, 1948.

Braude, Benjamin. "Foundation Myths of the *Millet* System." In *Christians and Jews in the Ottoman Empire: The Functioning of a Plural Society*. Volume 2, edited by B. Braude and B. Lewis. New York: Holmes and Meier, 1982.

Bringa, Tone. *Being Muslim the Bosnian Way: Identity and Community in a Central Bosnian Village*. Princeton: Princeton University Press, 1995.

Brower, Daniel and Edward Lazzerini, eds. *Russia's Orient: Imperial Borderlands and Peoples, 1700–1917*. Bloomington: Indiana University Press, 1997.

Brown, James. *Bulgaria under Communist Rule*. London: Pall Mall Press, 1970.

Brummett, Palmira. *Image and Imperialism in the Ottoman Revolutionary Press, 1908–1911*. Albany: State University of New York Press, 2000.

Brzezinski, Zbigniew. *The Soviet Bloc*. Cambridge, Mass.: Harvard University Press, 1960.

Brzezinski, Zbigniew and Carl Friedrich. *Totalitarian Dictatorship and Autocracy*. Cambridge, Mass.: Harvard University Press, 1965.

Buchli, Victor. *An Archeology of Socialism*. New York: Berg, 1999.

Butler, Judith, *Gender Trouble: Feminism and the Subversion of Identity*. New York: Routledge, 1990.

Carnegie Endowment for International Peace. *The Other Balkan Wars*. Washington, D.C.: Carnegie Endowment for International Peace, 1993.

Carrier, James, ed. *Occidentalism: Images of the West*. Oxford: Clarendon Press, 1995.

Çavuşoğlu, Halim. *Balkanlar'da Pomak Türkleri: Tarih ve Sosyo-Kültürel Yapı*. Ankara: KOKSAV, 1993.

Chary, Frederick. *The Bulgarian Jews and the Final Solution*. Pittsburgh: University of Pittsburgh Press, 1972.

Chatterjee, Partha. *The Nation and Its Fragments: Colonial and Postcolonial Histories*. Princeton: Princeton University Press, 1993.

Chehabi, Houchang. "Staging the Emperor's New Clothes: Dress Codes and Nation-Building under Reza Shah." *Iranian Studies* 26 (1993): 209–33.

Clay, Catherine. "Russian Ethnographers in the Service of the Empire." *Slavic Review* 54 (1995): 45–62.

Cole, Juan. "Gender, Tradition, and History." In *Reconstructing Gender in the Middle East: Tradition, Identity, Power*, edited by F. Göcek and S. Balaghi. New York: Columbia University Press, 1994.

Conner, Walter. "Europe East and West: Thoughts on History, Culture, and Kosovo." In *Cultures and Nations of Central and Eastern Europe: Essays in Honor of Roman Szporluk*, edited by Z. Gittlemen, L. Hajda, J. Himka, and R. Solchanyk. Cambridge, Mass.: Harvard University Press, 2000.

Connolly, William. *The Ethos of Pluralization*. Minneapolis: University of Minnesota Press, 1995.

Conquest, Robert. *Harvest of Sorrow: Soviet Collectivization and the Terror-Famine*. Oxford: Oxford University Press, 1986.

Constant, Stephen. *Foxy Ferdinand: Tsar of Bulgaria*. New York: Franklin Watts, 1980.

Corrin, Chris. "Introduction." In *Superwomen and the Double Burden*, edited by C. Corrin. London: Scarlet Press, 1992.

Crampton, Richard. *A Short History of Modern Bulgaria*. Cambridge, U.K.: Cambridge University Press, 1987.

———. "The Turks in Bulgaria, 1878–1944." In *The Turks of Bulgaria: The History and Fate of a Minority*, edited by K. Karpat. Istanbul: ISIS Press, 1990.

Creed, Gerald. *Domesticating Revolution: From Socialist Reform to Ambivalent Transition in a Bulgarian Village*. University Park, Pa.: Pennsylvania State University Press, 1998.

Danchenko, S. and E. Viazemskaia. *Rossiia i Balkani: Konets XVII-1918*. Moscow: Akademiia Nauk SSSR, 1990.

Danforth, Loring. *The Macedonian Conflict: Ethnic Nationalism in a Transitional World*. Princeton: Princeton University Press, 1995.

Daskalov, Roumen. "Ideas about and Reactions to Modernization in the Balkans." *East European Quarterly* 31(1997): 141–80.

———. "Modern Bulgarian Society and Culture through the Mirror of Bai Ganio." *Slavic Review* 60 (2001): 530–49.

Davies, Sarah. *Popular Opinion in Stalin's Russia: Terror, Propaganda and Dissent, 1934–1941*. Cambridge, U.K.: Cambridge University Press, 1997.

Davis, Yuval. *Gender and Nation*. London: Sage Publications, 1997.

deSilva, Lalith. "Women's Emancipation under Communism: A Re-Evaluation," *East European Quarterly* 27 (1993): 301–13.

Dimiirjevic-Rufu, Dejan. "The Multiple Identity of Romanians in Melnica (Homolja, Serbia)." In *Name and Social Structure: Examples from Southeastern Europe*, edited by P. Stahl. Boulder, Colo.: East European Monographs, 1998.

Dimitrov, Strasimir, ed. *Rodopski Sbornik*. Vol. 7. Sofia: Izdatelstvo "Prof. Marin Drinov," 1995.

Dimitrova, Blaga. *The Last Rock Eagle: Selected Poems of Blaga Dimitrova*. Translated by Brenda Walker. London: Forest Books, 1992.

——. *Predizvikatlestva: Politicheski Etiudi*. Sofia: Institut po Kultura, 1991.

Diulgerov, Petŭr. *Razpnati Dushi: Moiata Istinata Vŭzroditelniia Protses Sred Bŭlgaro-Mokhamedani*. Sofia: Partizdat, 1996.

Dizdarević, Nijaz. "Forming of Moslem Ethnicon in Bosnia and Herzegovina." In *Moslems in Yugoslavia*, edited by M. Stevanovic. Belgrade: Review of International Affairs, 1985.

Donia, Robert and John Fine. *Bosnia and Hercegovina: A Tradition Betrayed*. New York: Columbia University Press, 1994.

Duraković, Nijaz. "National Question of Moslems in Yugoslavia." In *Moslems in Yugoslavia*, edited by M. Stevanovic. Belgrade: Review of International Affairs, 1985.

Dzhambazov, Ismail. *Religioznite Praznitsi i Obredi v Islama*. Sofia: Profizdat, 1964.

Elenkov, Ivan. "Versii za Bŭlgarskata Identichnost v Modernata Epokha." In *Zashto Sme Takiva? V Tŭrsene na Bŭlgarskata Kŭlturna Identichnost*, edited by I. Elenkov and R. Daskalov. Sofia: Izdatelstvo "Prosveta," 1994.

El Guindi, Fadwa. *Veil: Modesty, Privacy and Resistance*. Oxford: Berg, 1999.

Eminov, Ali. "There Are No Turks in Bulgaria." *International Journal of Turkish Studies* 4 (1989): 203–22.

——. *Turkish and Other Muslim Minorities of Bulgaria*. New York: Routledge, 1997.

Eren, Hasan, ed. *Bulgaristan'da Türk Varlığı*. Ankara: Türk Tarih Kurumu Basimevi, 1985.

Eriksen, Gordon. *The Territorial Experience: Human Ecology as Symbolic Interaction*. Austin: University of Texas Press, 1980.

Fanon, Franz. *A Dying Colonialism*. New York: Grove Press, 1965.

Firkatian, Mari. *The Forest Traveler: Georgi Rakovski and Bulgarian Nationalism*. New York: Peter Lang Publishing, 1996.

Fischer, Bernd. *King Zog and the Struggle for Stability in Albania*. Boulder, Colo.: East European Monographs, 1984.

Fitzpatrick, Sheila. *The Cultural Front: Power and Culture in Revolutionary Russia*. Ithaca, N.Y.: Cornell University Press, 1992.

——. *Everyday Stalinism: Ordinary Life in Extraordinary Times, Soviet Russia in the 1930s*. Oxford: Oxford University Press, 1999.

——. *The Russian Revolution*. Oxford: Oxford University Press, 1982.

——. *Stalin's Peasants: Resistance and Survival in the Russian Village After Collectivization*. Oxford: Oxford University Press, 1994.

Foote, Shelly. "Bloomers." *Dress* 6 (1980): 1–13.

Foucault, Michel. *Discipline and Punishment: The Birth of the Prison*. New York: Verso, 1979.

——. *The Order of Things: An Archeology of the Human Sciences*. New York: Vintage Books, 1970.

Foreign Policy Institute. *The Tragedy of the Turkish Minority in Bulgaria*. Ankara: Foreign Policy Institute, 1989.

Galev, Iliia. *Zdravno-Sotsialnata Deĭnost na Bŭlgarskata Ekzarkhiia v Makedoniia i Trakiia: 1870–1913*. Sofia: Biblioteka "Minalo," 1994.

Gandev, Khristo. "Za Sŭvremena Marksistko-Leninska Metodologiia i Problematika na Bŭlgarskata Etnografiia." *Izvestiia na Etnografskiia Institut i Muzeĭ* 8 (1965): 7–27.

Garton-Ash, Timothy. *The Uses of Adversity: Essays on the Fate of Central Europe*. New York: Vintage Books, 1990.

Gellner, Ernest. *Nations and Nationalism*. Ithaca, N.Y.: Cornell University Press, 1983.

Georgiev, Velichko and Staiko Trifinov. *Pokrŭstvaneto na Bŭlgarite Mokhamedani 1912–1913*. Sofia: Akademichno Izdatelstvo "Prof. Marin Drinov," 1995.

Gilman, Sander. *The Jew's Body*. New York: Routledge, 1991.

Gladstone, William. *Bulgarian Horrors and the Question of the East*. London: John Murray, 1876.

——. *Lessons in Massacre; or, The Conduct of the Turkish Government in and about Bulgaria since May, 1876.* London: John Murray, 1877.

Goffman, Daniel. "Ottoman Millets in the Early Seventeenth Century." *New Perspectives on Turkey* 11 (1994): 135–59.

Goldman, Wendy. *Women, the State and Revolution: Soviet Family Policy and Social Life, 1917–1936.* Cambridge, U.K.: Cambridge University Press, 1993.

Göle, Nilüfer. *The Forbidden Modern: Civilization and Veiling.* Ann Arbor: University of Michigan Press, 1996.

Gollaher, David. *Circumcision: A History of the World's Most Controversial Surgery.* New York: Basic Books, 2000.

Gradeva, Rositsa and Svetlana Ivanova, eds. *Miusiulmanskata Kultura po Bŭlgarskite Zemi.* Sofia: IMIR, 1998.

Greenfeld, Liah. *Nationalism: Five Roads to Modernity.* Cambridge, Mass.: Harvard University Press, 1993.

Gribincea, Mihai. *Agricultural Collectivization in Moldavia: Basarabia during Stalinism 1949–50.* Boulder, Colo.: East European Monographs, 1996.

Gruncharov, Mikhail. *Chorbadzhŭstvoto i Bŭlgarskoto Obshtestvo Prez Vŭzrazhdaneto.* Sofia: Universitetsko Izdatelstvo "Sv. Kliment Okhridski," 1999.

Hadzhinikolov, Veselin. "Etnografskata Nauka v Bŭlgariia pred Seriozni Zadachi," *Bŭlgarskata Etnografiia* (1) 1975.

Hakli, Jouni. "Cultures of Demarcation: Territory and National Identity in Finland." In *Nested Identities: Nationalism, Territory and Scale*, edited by G. Herb and D. Kaplan. Lanham, Md.: Rowman and Littlefield, 1999.

Hallowell, Irving. *Culture and Experience.* New York: Schocken Books, 1967.

Halperin, Charles. *Russia and the Golden Horde: The Mongol Impact on Medieval Russian History.* Bloomington: Indiana University Press, 1987.

Herb, Guntram. "National Identity and Territory." In *Nested Identities: Nationalism, Territory and Scale*, edited by G. Herb and D. Kaplan. Lanham, Md.: Rowman and Littlefield, 1999.

Herb, Guntram and David Kaplan. "Introduction: A Question of Identity." In *Nested Identities: Nationalism, Territory and Scale*, edited by G. Herb and D. Kaplan. Lanham, Md.: Rowman and Littlefield, 1999.

Hollander, Anne. *Sex and Suits.* New York: Alfred Knopf, 1994.

Ianev, Ianko. "Dukhŭt na Natsiata," In *Zasto Sme Takiva? V Tŭrsene na Bŭlgarskata Kulturna Identichnost*, edited by I. Elenkov and R. Daskalov. Sofia: Izdatelstvo "Prosveta," 1994.

——. "Istok ili Zapad?" In *Zasto Sme Takiva? V Tŭrsene na Bŭlgarskata Kŭlturna Identichnost*, edited by I. Elenkov and R. Daskalov. Sofia: Izdatelstvo "Prosveta," 1994.

Iankov, Georgi. "Niakoĭ Osobenosti na Konsolidatsiia na Bŭlgarskata Natsiia." *Bŭlgarskata Etnografiia* 4 (1986): 13.

Ilchev, Stefan. *Za Khubavi Bŭlgarski Imena za Detsata ni.* Sofia: Izdatelstvo na Natsionalniia Sŭvet na Otechestveniia Front, 1963.

Inalcik, Halil. *The Ottoman Empire: the Classical Age 1300–1600.* New York: Praeger, 1973.

——. *Tanzimat ve Bulgar Meselesi.* Ankara: Eren Yaynicik ve Kitapcik, 1992.

Inalcik, Halil and Donald Quataert, eds. *An Economic and Social History of the Ottoman Empire, 1300–1914.* Cambridge, U.K.: Cambridge University Press, 1994.

Indzhiev, Ivan and Stoian Bozhkov, eds. *Publitsistika na Liuben Karavelov: Do Izlizaneto na Vestnik "Svoboda": 1860–1869.* Sofia: Izdanie na Bŭlgarskata Akademiia na Naukite, 1957.

Iotsov, Boris. "Bŭlgarskata Deĭstvitelnost Tŭrsi Avtor." In *Zashto Sme Takiva? V Tŭrsene na Bŭlgarskata Kŭlturna Identichnost*, edited by I. Elenkov and R. Daskalov. Sofia: Izdatelstvo "Prosveta," 1994.

Iovkov, Iordan. *Staroplaninski Legendi.* Sofia: Bulgarski Pisatel, 1980.

Ivanova, Nedialka and Penka Radeva. *Ot "A" do "Ia": Imenata na Bŭlgarite.* Sofia: Narodna Mladezh Izdatelsvo na TsK na DKMS, 1985.

Janos, Andrew. *The Politics of Backwardness in Hungary, 1825–1945.* Princeton: Princeton University Press, 1982.

Jedlicki, Jerzy. *A Suburb of Europe: Nineteenth-Century Approaches to Western Civilization.* Budapest: Central European University Press, 1999.

Jelavich, Barbara. *History of the Balkans: Eighteenth and Nineteenth Centuries.* Cambridge, U.K.: Cambridge University Press, 1983.

Jelavich, Barbara and Charles Jelavich. *The Establishment of the Balkan National States, 1804–1920.* Seattle: University of Washington Press, 1977.

Jirousek, Charlotte. "Dress as Social Policy: Change in Women's Dress in a Southwestern Turkish Village." *Dress* 23 (1996): 47–63.

Kadıoğlu, Ayşe. "Women's Subordination in Turkey: Is Islam Really the Villain?" *Middle East Journal* 48 (1994): 645–60.

Kafadar, Cemal. *Between Two Worlds: The Construction of the Ottoman State.* Berkeley: University of California Press, 1995.

Kahf, Mohja. *Western Representations of the Muslim Woman: From Termagant to Odalisque.* Austin: University of Texas Press, 1998.

Kanitz, Felix. *Donau-Bulgarien und der Balkan: Historisch-Geographisch-Ethnographische Reisestudien aus den Jahren 1860–1879.* Leipzig: Fries, 1879–80.

Karakasidou, Anastasia. *Fields of Wheat, Hills of Blood: Passages to Nationhood in Greek Macedonia, 1870–1990.* Chicago: University of Chicago Press, 1997.

Karpat, Kemal. "Bulgaria's Methods of Nation Building—the Annihilation of Minorities." *International Journal of Turkish Studies* 4 (1989): 1–23.

——. *An Inquiry into the Social Foundations of Nationalism in the Ottoman State: From Social Estates to Classes from Millets to Nations.* Princeton: Center of International Studies, Princeton University Press, 1973.

——. "Introduction: Bulgaria's Methods of Nation Building and the Turkish minority." In *The Turks of Bulgaria: The History, Culture, and Political Fate of a Minority,* edited by K. Karpat. Istanbul: ISIS Press, 1990.

——. *Ottoman Population, 1830–1914: Demographic and Social Characteristics.* Madison: University of Wisconsin Press, 1985.

Kasaba, Reşat. *The Ottoman Empire and the World Economy: The Nineteenth Century.* Albany: State University of New York Press, 1988.

Kenney, Padraic. "The Gender of Resistance in Communist Poland." *American Historical Review* 104 (1999): 349–425.

Kertzer, David. *Politics and Symbols: The Italian Communist Party and the Fall of Communism.* New Haven, Conn.: Yale University Press, 1996.

Khaĭtov, Nikolai. *Poslednite Migove i Grobŭt na Vasil Levski.* Plovdiv: Izdatelstvo "Khristo G. Danov," 1985.

Khilendarski, Paisiĭ. *Slavianobŭlgarska Istoriia.* Sofia: Izdatelstvo Bŭlgarski Pisatel, 1989.

Khristov, Khristo. *Agrarniat Vŭpros v Bŭlgarskata Natsionalna Revolutsiia.* Sofia: Nauka i Izkustvo, 1976.

——. *Iz Minoloto na Bŭlgarite Mokhamedani v Rodopite.* Sofia: Izdatelstvo na Bŭlgarskata Akademiia na Naukite, 1958.

——. *Stranitsi ot Bŭlgarskata Istoriia: Ocherk za Islamiziranite Bŭlgari i Natsionalnovŭzroditelniia Protses.* Sofia: Nauka i Iskustvo, 1989.

Kiliç, Osman. *Kader Kurbanı.* Ankara: Kültür Bakanlığıyayınları, 1989.

Koev, Ivan. "Prinos kŭm Izuchavane na Turskata Narodna Vesbena i Tukanna Ornamentika v Liudogorieto." *Izvestiia na Etnografskiia Institut i Muzeĭ* (3) 1958.

Kohn, Hans. *The Idea of Nationalism.* New York: Krieger, 1967.

——. *Nationalism: Its Meaning and History.* New York: D. Van Nostrand, 1965.

Kondi, Sokol. "Name and Identity in the Region of Dukagjin (Albania)." In *Name and So-*

cial Structure: Examples from Southeastern Europe, edited by P. Stahl. Boulder, Colo.: East European Monographs, 1998.

Kostanick, Huey. *Turkish Resettlement of Bulgarian Turks: 1950–1953*. Berkeley: University of California Press, 1957.

Krasteva, Anna. "The Vision of the Open Cultural Identity: The Idea of Europe in the Mirror of Bulgarian Cultural Identity." In *Bulgaria Facing Cultural Diversity*, edited by G. de Keersmaeker and P. Makeriev. Sofia: International Peace Information Service, 1999.

Kubik, Jan. *The Power of Symbols against the Symbols of Power: The Rise of Solidarity and the Fall of State Socialism in Poland*. University Park, Pa.: Pennsylvania University Press, 1994.

Kunchev, K. "The Path to 1984." *Prava i Svobodi*. February 25–March 3, 1991, 8.

Lafchiov, Stefan. *Spomeni za Bŭlgarskata Ekzarkhiia: 1906–1909*. Sofia: Universitetsko Izdatelstvo "Sv. Kliment Okhridski," 1994.

Lampe, John. *The Bulgarian Economy in the Twentieth Century*. London: Croom and Helm, 1986.

Lapčević, Dragiṣe. *O Naṣim Muslimanima: Sociološke i Etnografske Beleṣke*. Belgrade: Getse Kona, 1925.

Lazzerini, Edward. "Defining the Orient: A Nineteenth Century Russo-Tatar Polemic over Identity and Cultural Representation." In *Muslim Communities Reemerge: Historical Perspectives on Nationality, Politics, and Opposition in the Former Soviet Union and Yugoslavia*, edited by E. Allworth. Durham, N.C.: Duke University Press, 1994.

——. "Ismail Bey Gaprinskii and Muslim Modernism in Russia: 1878–1914." Ph.D. diss., University of Washington, 1974.

Lecov, Spac. "Vŭznikvane i Promeni na Niakoĭ Familni Imena v s. Ruzhevo Konare." *Bŭlgarskata Etnografiia* (2) 1980.

Levintov, N. "Agrarnie Otnoshenie v Bolgarii Nakanune Osvobozhdeniia i Agrarnii Prevorot 1879–1887 Godov." In *Osvobozhdenie Bolgarii ot Turetskogo Iga: Sbornik Stateĭ*, edited by L.Valev, S. Nikitin, and P. Tretiakov. Moscow: Izdatelstvo Akademiĭ Nauk SSSR, 1953.

Lewis, Bernard. *The Emergence of Modern Turkey*. Oxford: Oxford University Press, 1961.

——. *Islam and the West*. Oxford: Oxford University Press, 1993.

Limanoski, Hijazi. *Izlamskata Religija and Izlamiziranite Makedontsi*. Skopje: Makedonska Kniga, 1989.

Liutov, Atanas and Rositsa Gocheva, eds. *Zhenata—Maĭka, Truzhenichka, Obshtestvenichka*. Sofia: Partizdat, 1974.

Lozanova, Margarita, ed. *Bŭlgarite v Tekhnite Istoricheski, Etnografski i Politicheski Granitsi*. Sofia: Izdatelstvo "Spektŭr," 1994.

Macfie, A. L. *The Eastern Question, 1774–1923*. London: Longman, 1996.

Macpherson, C. B. *Property: Mainstream and Critical Positions*. Toronto: University of Toronto Press, 1978.

Marcus, Julie. *A World of Difference: Islam and Gender Hierarchy in Turkey*. London: Allen and Unwin, 1992.

Marinov, Dimitŭr. "Narodna Viara i Religiozni Narodni Obichai." *Sbornik za Narodni Umotvorenie i Narodnopisi* (28) 1914.

Marinov, Petŭr. *Bŭlgarite Mokhamedani v Svoeto Narodnostno Sŭznanie i Vŭzroditelnoto im Dvizhenie*. Sofia: Angelinov and Partniori, 1994.

——, ed. *Sbornik Rodina*. 4 Vols. Smolyan: Izdanie na "Rodina," 1939–1942.

Marinov, Vasil. "Prinos kŭm Izuchavane na Bita i Kulturata na Turtsite i Gagauzite v Severnoiztochna Bŭlgariia." BAN, 1956.

Marinov, Vasil, Zakhari Dimitrov, and Ivan Koev. "Prinos kŭm Izuchavaneto na Bita i Kulturata na Turskoto Naselenie v Severnoiztochna Bŭlgariia." *Izvestiia na Etnografskiia Institut i Muzeĭ* (2) 1955.

Markov, Georgi. *The Truth that Killed*. New York: Ticknor and Fields, 1984.
Massell, Gregory. *The Surrogate Proletariat: Moslem Women and Revolutionary Strate-gies in Soviet Central Asia, 1919–1929*. Princeton, N.J.: Princeton University Press, 1974.
McCarthy, Justin. *Death and Exile: The Ethnic Cleansing of Ottoman Muslims 1821–1922*. Princeton, N.J.: Darwin Press, 1995.
McClintock, Anne. *Imperial Leather: Race, Gender, and Sexuality in the Colonial Contest*. New York: Routledge, 1995.
McCracken, Grant. *Culture and Consumption: New Approaches to the Symbolic Charac-ter of Goods and Activities*. Bloomington: Indiana University Press, 1988.
McGowan, Bruce. *Economic Life in the Ottoman Empire: Taxation Trade and the Strug-gle for Land 1600–1800*. Cambridge, U.K.: Cambridge University Press, 1981.
McIntyre, Robert. *Bulgaria: Politics, Economics and Society*. London: Pinter, 1988.
Memishev, Iusein. *Uchastieto na Bŭlgarskite Turtsi v Borbata Protiv Kapitalizŭm i Fashizŭm: 1919–1944*. Sofia: Partizdat, 1977.
Memişoğlu, Hüseyin. *Pages of the History of Pomac Turks*. Ankara: Safak Maatbasi, 1991.
Mernissa, Fatma. *Beyond the Veil: Male-Female Dynamics in a Modern Muslim Society*. Bloomington: University of Indiana Press, 1987.
Michev, Nikolai and Petŭr Koledarov. *Promenite v Imenata i Statuta na Selishtata v Bŭl-gariia: 1878–1972*. Sofia: Nauka i Iskustvo, 1973.
Mikhailov, Stoian. *Vŭzrozhdenskiiat Protses v Bŭlgariia*. Sofia: "M 8 M," 1992.
Mikhailova, Ganka. "Obleklo." In *Dobrudzha: Etnografski, Folklorni i Ezikovi Prouch-vaniia*. Bŭlgarskata Akademiia na Naukite, 1974..
——. "Sotsialni Aspekti na Narodnoto Obleklo." *Bŭlgarskata Etnografiia* (3–4) 1976.
——. "Vŭznikvane na Vŭzrozhdensko Zhensko Obleklo v Panagiurishte i Panagiursko." *Izvestiia na Etnografskiia Institut i Muzeĭ* (10) 1967
Mileva, Binka. *Zheni ot Rodopi*. Sofia: Izdatelstvo na Natsionalniia Sŭvet na Otechestven Front, 1960.
Miller, Marshall. *Bulgaria During the Second World War*. Stanford: Stanford University Press, 1975.
Misirkova, E. *Turetskoe Menshinstvo v Narodnoe Respublike Bolgarii*. Sofia: "Stopancko Rasvitie," 1951.
Miusliumov, M. *Bŭlgarskata Komunisticheskata Partiia i Turskoto Naselenieto v Bŭl-gariia: 1891–1944*. Sofia: Izdatelstvo na BKP, 1967.
Mizov, Nikolai. *Istinata i Neistinata za Obriazvanieto*. Sofia: Izdatelstvo na Natsionalniia Sŭvet na Otechestveniia Front, 1964.
——. *Izlamŭt i Izlamisatsiata*. Sofia: Voenno Izdatelstvo, 1989.
——. *Taĭnata na Lichnoto Ime*. Sofia: Partizdat, 1987.
Molloy, Maureen. "Imagining (the) Difference: Gender, Ethnicity and Metaphors of Na-tion." *Feminist Review* 51 (1995): 94–112.
Mosse, George. *The Image of Man: The Creation of Modern Masculinity*. Oxford: Oxford University Press, 1996.
——. *Nationalism and Sexuality: Middle Class Morality and Sexual Norms in Modern Eu-rope*. Madison: University of Wisconsin Press, 1985.
Mutefchieva, Vera. "Obrazŭt na Evreite." In *Vrŭzki na Sŭvmestimost i Nesŭvmestimost mezhdu Khrisiiani i Miusiulmani v Bŭlgariia*, edited by A. Zheliaskova. Sofia: Fondat-siia "Mezhdunaroden Tsentŭr po Problemite na Maltsinstvata i Kulturnite Vzaimod-eĭstviia," 1994.
Nabieva, Rohat. *Zhenshchiny Tadzhikistana v Borbe za Sotsializm*. Dushanbe: Izdatelstvo "IRFON," 1975.
Neuburger, Mary. "Bulgaro-Turkish Encounters and the Re-imagining of the Bulgarian Nation." *East European Quarterly* (31) 1997: 1–17.
——. "Difference Unveiled: Bulgarian National Imperatives and the Re-dressing of Mus-

lim Women in the Communist Period: 1945–89." *Nationalities Papers* 25 (1997): 169–81.

———. "Pants, Veils, and Matters of Dress: Unraveling the Fabric of Women's Lives in Communist Bulgaria." In *Style and Socialism: Modernity and Material Culture in Post-War Eastern Europe*, edited by D. Crowley and S. Reid. Oxford: Berg Publishing, 2000.

———. "Pomak Borderlands: Muslims on the Edge of Nations." *Nationalities Papers* 28 (2000): 181–98.

———. "The Russo-Turkish War and the 'Eastern Jewish Question': Encounters between Victims and Victors in Ottoman Bulgaria, 1877–8." *East European Jewish Affairs* 26 (1996): 53–66.

Neumann, Iver. *Russia and the Idea of Europe: A Study in Identity and International Relations*. New York: Routledge, 1996.

Northrop, Douglas. "Languages of Loyalty: Gender, Politics, and Party Supervision in Uzbekistan, 1927–1941." *Russian Review* 59 (2000): 179–200.

Nuriev, Shakher. *Zhenskii Vopros: Problemi i Resheniia*. Ashkhabad: Izdatelstvo "Turkmenistan," 1991.

Oren, Nissan. *Revolution Administered: Agrarianism and Communism in Bulgaria*. Baltimore: Johns Hopkins University Press, 1973.

Palvanova, Bibi. *Emansipatsiia Musulmanki: Opit Paskreposhcheniia Zhenshchini Sovetskogo Vostoka*. Moscow: Izdatelstvo "Nauka," 1982.

Pamuk, Sevket. *The Ottoman Empire and European Capitalism, 1820–1913: Trade, Investment and Production*. Cambridge, U.K.: Cambridge University Press, 1987.

Pechilkov, Andrei. *Istoricheskata Sŭdba na Rodopskite Bŭlgari Mokhamedani*. Smolyan: Dŭrzhaven Arkhiv, 1993.

Peirce, Leslie. *The Imperial Harem: Women and Sovereignty in the Ottoman Empire*. Oxford, U.K.: Oxford University Press, 1993.

Penev, Boian. "Prevrŭshtaniiato na Baĭ Gano." In *Zashto Sme Takiva? V Tŭrsene na Bŭlgarskata Kŭlturna Identichnost*, edited by I. Elenkov and R. Daskalov. Sofia: Izdatelstvo "Prosveta," 1994.

Perry, Duncan. *Stefan Stambolov and the Emergence of Modern Bulgaria, 1870–1895*. Durham, N.C.: Duke University Press, 1996.

Petrov, Khristo, ed. *Nauchna Ekspeditsiia v Makedoniia i Pomoravieto, 1916*. Sofia: Universitetsko Izdatelstvo "Sv. Kliment Okhridski," 1993.

Petrov, Tseno. *Agrarnite Reformi v Bŭlgariia: 1880–1944*. Sofia: Izdatelstvo na Akademite na Naukite, 1975.

Peukert, Detlev. *Inside Nazi Germany: Conformity, Opposition, and Racism in Everyday Life*. New Haven: Yale University Press, 1982.

Pipes, Richard. *The Formation of the Soviet Union: Communism and Nationalism, 1917–1923*. Cambridge, Mass.: Harvard University Press, 1964.

Pletinov, Georgi. *Chorbadzhiite i Bŭlgarskata Natsionalna Revolutsiia*. Veliko Tŭrnovo: IK "Vital," 1993.

———. *Midkhat Pasha i Upravlenieto na Dunavskiia Vilaiet*. Veliko Tŭrnovo: IK "Vital," 1994.

Poiger, Ute. *Jazz, Rock, and Rebels: Cold War Politics and American Culture in a Divided Germany*. Berkeley: University of California Press, 2000.

Poliakov, Sergei. *Everyday Islam: Religion and Tradition in Rural Central Asia*. Armonk, N.Y.: M.E. Sharpe, 1992.

Popovic, Alexander. "The Turks of Bulgaria (1878–1985)." *Central Asian Survey* 5 (1986): 1–32.

Poulton, Hugh. *The Balkans: Minorities and States in Conflict*. London: Minorities Rights Publications, 1991.

Pundeff, Marin. "Bulgarian Nationalism." In *Nationalism in Eastern Europe*, edited by P. Sugar and I. Lederer. Seattle: University of Washington Press, 1994.

Primorski, Anastas. *Bŭlgarite Mokhamedani v Nashata Narodnostha Obshtnost*. Sofia: Pechatnitsa "Pakhvira," 1940.

——. "Starini Cherti v Bita i Kulturata na Rodopskite Bŭlgari." *Izvestiia na Etnografskiia Institut i Muzeĭ* (8) 1965.

Quataert, Donald. "Clothing Laws, State, and Society in the Ottoman Empire, 1720–1829." *International Journal of Middle Eastern Studies* 29 (1997): 403–25.

——. *The Ottoman Empire, 1700–1922.* Cambridge, U.K.: Cambridge University Press, 2000.

Rakovski, Georgi. *Bŭlgariio Maĭko Mila*, edited by Georgi Borshukov. Sofia: Bŭlgarski Pisatel, 1967.

——. *Izbrani Sŭchineniia.* Sofia: Dŭrhavno Izdatelstvo, 1946.

Rakowska-Harmstone, Teresa. *Communism in Eastern Europe.* Bloomington: Indiana University Press, 1989.

Ramet, Pedro. *Nationalism and Federalism in Yugoslavia: 1963–83.* Bloomington: Indiana University Press, 1984.

Ramet, Sabrina. "In Tito's Time." In *Gender Politics in the Western Balkans: Women and Society in Yugoslavia and the Yugoslav Successor States*, edited by S. Ramet. University Park, Pa.: Pennsylvania State University Press, 1999.

Riasanovsky, Nicholas. *Russia and the West in the Teachings of the Slavophiles: A Study of Romantic Ideology.* Cambridge, Mass.: Harvard University Press, 1952.

Rodinson, Maxime. *Europe and the Mystique of Islam.* Seattle: University of Washington Press, 1987.

Roper, Michael and John Tosh, eds. *Manful Assertions: Masculinities in Britain since 1800.* New York: Routledge, 1991.

Roszkowski, Wojciech. *Land Reforms in East Central Europe after World War One.* Warsaw: Institute of Polish Studies, Polish Academy of Sciences, 1995.

Rothschild, Joseph. *The Communist Party of Bulgaria: Origins and Development.* New York: Columbia University Press, 1959.

——. *East Central Europe between the Two World Wars.* Seattle: University of Washington Press, 1974.

Rywkin, Michael. *Moscow's Lost Empire.* New York: M.E. Sharpe, 1994.

Sahmi, Kalpana. *Crucifying the Orient: Russian Orientalism and the Colonization of Caucasus and Central Asia.* Bangkok: White Orchid Press, 1997.

Said, Edward. *Orientalism.* New York: Pantheon Books, 1978.

Saroyan, Mark. *Minorities, Mullahs, and Modernity: Reshaping Community in the Former Soviet Union.* Berkeley: University of California, 1997.

Schama, Simon. *Landscape and Memory.* New York: Vintage Books, 1995.

Scott, James. *Seeing Like a State: How Certain Schemes to Improve the Human Condition Have Failed.* New Haven: Yale University Press, 1998.

——. *Weapons of the Weak: Everyday Forms of Peasant Resistance.* New Haven: Yale University Press, 1985.

Seni, Nora. "Fashion and Women's Clothing in the Satirical Press of Istanbul at the End of the 19th Century." In *Women in Modern Turkish Society*, edited by S. Tekeli. London: Zed Books, 1995.

Seton-Watson, Hugh. *Eastern Europe between the World Wars.* Cambridge, U.K.: Cambridge University Press, 1946.

Sheĭmanov, Naĭden, "Preobrazhenie na Bŭlgariia." In *Zashto Sme Takiva? V Tŭrsene na Bŭlgarskata Kulturna Identichnost*, edited by I. Elenkov and R. Daskalov. Sofia: Izdatelstvo "Prosveta," 1994.

Shishkov, Stoiu. *Bŭlgaro-Mokhamedani: Istoriko-Zemepiseni i Narodouchen Pregled c Obrazi.* Plovdiv: Turgovska Pechatnitsa, 1936.

——. *Pomatsi v Trite Bŭlgarski Oblasti: Trakiia, Makedoniia i Miziia.* Plovdiv: Pechatnitsa "Makedoniia," 1914.

Šiklova, Jiřiná. "The Solidarity of the Culpable." *Social Research* 58 (1991): 765–75.

Şimşir, Bilâl. *Bulgarian Turks: 1878–1985.* London: K. Rustem, 1988.

——. *Bulgaristan Türkleri: 1878–1985.* Ankara: Bilgi Yayınevi, 1986.

——. "The Turkish Minority in Bulgaria: History and Culture." In *The Turks of Bulgaria: The History and Fate of a Minority*, edited by K. Karpat. Istanbul: ISIS Press, 1990.

Singer, Amy. *Palestinian Peasants and Ottoman Officials: Rural Administration around Sixteenth Century Jerusalem*. Cambridge, U.K.: Cambridge University Press, 1994.

Sinha, Mrinalini. *Colonial Masculinity: The "Manly Englishman" and the "Effeminate Bengali" in the Late Nineteenth Century*. Manchester: Manchester University Press, 1995.

Skalon, Dmitrii. *Moi Vospominaniie: 1877–8*. St. Petersburg: Tipografia T-va M.O. Volf, 1913.

Slaveĭkov, Petko. *Izbrani Tvorbi*. Sofia: Bŭlgarski Pisatel, 1989.

——. *Sŭchinenie*. Vol. 7. Sofia: Bŭlgarski Pisatel, 1989.

Slezkine, Yuri. *Arctic Mirrors: Russia and the Small Peoples of the North*. Ithaca, N.Y.: Cornell University Press, 1994.

——. "The USSR as a Communal Apartment, or How a Socialist State Promoted Ethnic Particularism." *Slavic Review* 53 (1994): 414–53.

Smith, Anthony. *The Ethnic Origins of Nations*. Cambridge, Mass.: Blackwell, 1986.

——. *Nationalism and Modernism: A Critical Survey of Recent Theories of Nations and Nationalism*. London: Routledge, 1998.

Spasov, A., ed. *Sbornik v Pomosht na Uchiteli ot Rodopskite Raĭoni*. Sofia: Dŭrhavno Izdatelstvo "Narodna Prosveta," 1961.

Stahl, Henri. "The Onomastic System in the Village of Dragus (Transylvania)." In *Name and Social Structure: Examples from Southeastern Europe*, edited by P. Stahl. Boulder, Colo.: East European Monographs, 1998.

Stahl, Paul. "Classification of Names and Identities." In *Name and Social Structure: Examples from Southeastern Europe*, edited by P. Stahl. Boulder, Colo.: East European Monographs, 1998.

——. "Names of Princes and Peasants in Romania." In *Name and Social Structure: Examples from Southeastern Europe*, edited by P. Stahl. Boulder, Colo.: East European Monographs, 1998.

Stavrianos, Leften. *The Balkans since 1453*. New York: Holt, Rinehart & Winston, 1958.

Stoianov, Valeri. *Turskoto Naselenie v Bŭlgariia Mezhdu Poliusite na Etnicheskata Politika*. Sofia: "LIK," 1998.

Stoianov, Zakhari. *Iz "Zapiski po Bŭlgarskite Vŭstaniia."* Sofia: Bŭlgarski Pisatel, 1972.

Stoianovich, Traian. "The Conquering Balkan Orthodox Merchants." *Journal of Economic History* 20 (1960): 234–13.

Stokes, Gale, ed. *From Stalinism to Pluralism: A Documentary History of Eastern Europe since 1945*. Oxford: Oxford University Press, 1991.

Stoyanov, Zahari. *Extracts from Notes on the Bulgarian Uprisings*. Sofia: Sofia Press, 1976.

Sugar, Peter. *Southeastern Europe under Ottoman Rule 1354–1804*. Seattle: University of Washington Press, 1977.

Suny, Ronald. *Revenge of the Past: Nationalism, Revolution, and the Collapse of the Soviet Union*. Stanford: Stanford University Press, 1993.

Szamuely, Tibor. *The Russian Tradition*. New York: McGraw Hill, 1974.

Takhirov, Shukri. *Bŭlgarskite Turtsi po Pŭtia na Sotsializma*. Sofia: Izdatelstvo na Otechestveniia Front, 1978.

——. *Edinenieto*. Sofia: Izdatelstvo na Otechestveniia Front, 1981.

Talmon, Jacob. *The Myth of the Nation and the Vision of Revolution*. Berkeley: University of California Press, 1981.

Tamir, Vicki. *Bulgaria and Her Jews: The History of a Dubious Symbiosis*. New York: Sepher-Hermon Press for Yeshiva University Press, c. 1979

Tanov, Atanas. *Agrarnata Polititka na BKP na Sŭvremenniia Etap*. Sofia: Zemizdat, 1981.

Tatybekova, Zhanetta. *Velikii Oktiabr i Zhenshchiny Kyrgizistana*. Frunze: Izdatelstvo "Kyrgizstan," 1975.

Tepev, N. *Tursko Naselenie v Narodno Republika Bŭlgariia*. Sofia: Durzhavno Voenno Izdatelstvo, 1954.

Tileva, Viktoria. *Bŭlgarsko Pechatarsko Druzhestvo "Promishleniie" v Tsarigrad: 1870–85*. Sofia: Narodna Biblioteka "Kiril i Metodi," 1985.

Todorov, Delcho. *Bŭlgarskata Etnografiia pres Vŭzrazhdaneto*. Sofia: Izdatelstvo na Bŭlgarskite Akademiia na Naukite, 1989.

——. "Razvitie i Zadachi na Etnografskoto Izuchavane na Nashata Sotsialisticheska Sŭvremenost." *Bŭlgarsksta Etnografiia* (1) 1975.

Todorov, Georgi. "Deĭnostta na Vremenoto Rusko Upravlenie v Bŭlgariia po Urezhdane na Agrarniia i Bezhanskiia Vŭpros prez 1877–1879 g." *Istoricheski Pregled* 6 (1955): 27–59.

Todorov, Nikolai. *Stopanska Istoriia na Bŭlgariia*. Sofia: Dŭrzhavno Izdatelstvo "Nauka i Izkustvo," 1981.

Todorov, Tzvetan and Robert Zaretsky, eds. *Voices from the Gulag: Life and Death in Communist Bulgaria*. University Park, Pa.: Pennsylvania State University Press, 2000.

Todorova, Maria. "The Balkans: From Discovery to Invention." *Slavic Review* 51 (1992): 453–82.

——. "Bulgarian Historical Writing on the Ottoman Empire." *New Perspectives on Turkey* 9 (1995): 97–188.

——. "Ethnicity. Nationalism, and the Communist Legacy in Eastern Europe." In *The Social Legacy of Communism*, edited by S. Wolchik and J. Millar. Cambridge, U.K.: Cambridge University Press, 1994.

——. "Identity (Trans)formation among Pomaks in Bulgaria." In *Beyond Borders: Remaking Cultural Identities in the New East and Central Europe*, edited by L. Kürti and J. Langman. New York: Westview Press, 1997.

——. *Imagining the Balkans*. New York: Oxford University Press, 1997.

——. "Notes and Comments: Ethnicity, Nationalism and the Communist Legacy in Eastern Europe." *East European Politics and Societies* 7 (1993): 131–54.

Tohidi, Nayereh. "Soviet in Public, Azeri in Private: Gender, Islam, and Nationality in Soviet and Post-Soviet Azerbaijan." *Women's Studies International Forum* 19 (1996): 111–23.

Tosh, John. "Imperial Masculinity and the Flight from Domesticity in Britain, 1880–1914." In *Gender and Colonialism*, edited by T. Foley et al. London: Galway, 1995.

——. "What Should Historians Do with Masculinity? Reflections on Nineteenth Century Britain." In *Gender and History in Western Europe*, edited by R. Shoemaker and M. Vincent. London: Arnold, 1998.

Turan, Ömer. *The Turkish Minority in Bulgaria, 1878–1908*. Ankara: Türk Tarih Kurumu Basimevi, 1998.

Udovički, Jasminka and James Ridgeway, eds. *Burn This House: The Making and Unmaking of Yugoslavia*. Durham, N.C.: Duke University Press, 1997.

Vakarelski, Khristo. *Etnografiia na Bŭlgarii*. Sofia: Izdatelstvo Nauka i Izkustvo, 1974.

Vasileva, Darina. "Bulgarian Turkish Emigration and Return." *International Migration Review* 26 (1992): 342–52.

Vazov, Ivan. *Pod Igoto*. Sofia: Dimitŭr Blagoev, 1956.

——. *Pŭtepisi*. Sofia: Bulgarski Pisatel, 1974.

——. *Under the Yoke*. New York: Twayne Publishers, 1971.

——. *Velika Rilska Gora*. Sofia: Dimitŭr Blagoev, 1954.

Velcheva, Nadiia. *Rodopchanka: Shtrikhi ot Etnosotsialniia i Etnopsikhologicheskiia i Portret*. Sofia: Izdatelstvo na Bŭlgarskata Akademiia na Naukite, 1994.

Veleva, Maria. "Pregled na Prouchvaniiata na Bŭlgarskite Narodni Nosi." *Izvestiia na Etnografskiia Institut i Muzeĭ* 3 (1958): 252–64.

——. "Sintez na Etnicheskite Elementi v Bŭlgarskoto Narodno Obleklo." *Izvestiia na Etnografskiia Institut i Muzeĭ* 8 (1965): 65–78.

———. "Za Periodizatsiata v Razvitieto na Bŭlgarskite Narodni Nosii." *Izvestiia na Etno-grafskiia Institut i Muzeĭ* 15 (1974): 5–53.

Verdery, Katherine. "The Elasticity of Land: Problems of Property Restitution in Transylvania." *Slavic Review* 53 (1994): 1071–109.

———. *National Ideology under Socialism: Identity and Cultural Politics in Ceausescu's Romania.* Berkeley: University of California Press, 1991.

Viola, Lynne. *Peasant Rebels under Stalin: Collectivization and the Culture of Peasant Resistance.* New York: Oxford University Press, 1996.

Weizman, Lenore. "Living on the Aryan Side in Poland: Gender, Passing, and the Nature of Resistance." In *Women in the Holocaust,* edited by D. Ofer and L. Weizman. New Haven: Yale University Press, 1998.

White, George. *Nationalism and Territory: Constructing Group Identity in Southeastern Europe.* Lanham, Md.: Rowman and Littlefield, 1999.

Wilkinson, Henry. *Maps and Politics: A Review of the Ethnographic Cartography of Macedonia.* Liverpool: University Press, 1951.

Wilson, Francesca. *Muscovy: Russia through Foreign Eyes 1553–1900.* London: George Allen and Unwin, 1970.

Wolff, Larry. *Inventing Eastern Europe: The Map of Civilization on the Mind of the Enlightenment.* Stanford: Stanford University Press, 1994.

Yeganeh, Nahid. "Women, Nationalism, and Islam in Contemporary Political Discourse in Iran." *Feminist Review* 44 (1993): 3–18.

Yeğenoğlu, Meyda. *Colonial Fantasies: Towards a Feminist Reading of Orientalism.* Cambridge, U.K.: Cambridge University Press, 1998.

Young, Robert. *Colonial Desire: Hybridity in Theory, Culture and Race.* London: Routledge, 1995.

Yuval-Davis, Nira. *Gender and Nation.* London: Sage Publications, 1997.

Zabeeh, Farhang. *What Is in a Name?* The Hague: Martinus Nijhoff, 1968.

Zagorov, Orlin. *Moderniiat Nationalizŭm.* Sofia: Bŭlgarika, 1995.

Zheliaskova, Antonina. "The Problem of the Authenticity of Some Domestic Sources on the Islamization of the Rhodopes, Deeply Rooted in Bulgarian Historiography." *Etudes Balkaniques* 4 (1990): 105–11.

Zlatilov, Vŭlcho. "Istochnorodopskata Oblast v Politikata na Turskiia Natsionalizŭm: 1913–1944 g." *Istoricheski Pregled* 46 (1990): 39–51.

NEWSPAPERS

Balkanlar'da Türk Kültürü
Duma
Halk Gençliği
Makedoniia
Muslumani
Prava i Svobodi
Rodopa
Ruzhitsa
Sega
Turtsiia
Yeni Işık
Zemiic
Zhenata Dnes

Index

Abdülaziz, sultan of Ottoman Empire, 30
Aga, Takhir, 113
agricultural collectivization, 69, 190–91,
    190 n.100
    resistance to, 187–88
Ahmed, Leila, 117, 117 n.5
Albania, 153–54
Albanians, 50–51, 115 n.105
Alexander II, Russian tsar, 34
Alexander of Battenburg, 35, 37 n.53
"Andreshko syndrome", 176
anti-Semitism, 49 n.93, 51–52, 145
Appel, Hilary, 195
April Uprisings (1876), 34, 88, 122
Armenians, 57
Atatürk, Kemal, 85, 104, 134, 146
Austro-German Central Powers, 42, 43

Baĭ Gano, meaning as literary archetype,
    38–39 n.56
Baĭ Gano (Konstantinov), 38–39
Bakić-Hayden, Milica, 5
Balkanism, 5
Balkan Wars (1912–1913), 176
    de-veiling campaigns, 123–24
    fez manifesto, 92–94
    forced conversion of Pomaks, 41–42, 92,
        94
    name-changing campaigns, 148, 149
BANU (Bulgarian Agrarian National Union),
    43
BCP. See Bulgarian Communist Party
Beĭski, Arif, 53, 98, 150, 151
Belene Island prison, 81
berets, 104, 107, 108
Berlin, Treaty of (1878), 35, 174
bit (daily life), 58, 73
blood tax. See devşirme system

Bloomer, Amelia, 128
Boliarov, Kamen, 151
Bourdieu, Pierre, 15, 144
Bracewell, Wendy, 85 n.1
Branchev, Nikolai, 75
Brown, James, 190 n.101
Bulgaria
    Axis alliance, 48, 51, 183
    modernization of, 12–13, 17
    naming systems, 146–47
    national security fears, 37, 60, 66–67,
        71–72, 79, 192, 200
    property restitution, post-communist, 195
    reunification with Eastern Rumelia, 36,
        174–75
    shifting borders of (1878–1945), 20, 178
    Soviet influence on, 9–12
    territorial expansionism of, 176, 183, 198
    Turkish relations, 66–67, 73, 80, 184, 192
    Western European relations, 25–26
    See also Bulgarian principality
Bulgarian Agrarian National Union (BANU),
    43
Bulgarian Communist Party (BCP), 49, 55,
    62, 193, 199
    creation of a secular Muslim elite, 62–63,
        64–66
    demise of, 82–83, 167, 193–94
    emancipation of Muslim women, 101,
        129–30
    fictional repudiation of nationalism, 60, 61
    Kemalist relations, 63–64, 102
    land reform under, 185–86, 188–89
    Muslim collaboration, 12–13, 62–64 (See
        also Kemalists; Rodina movement)
    Muslim manhood, reining in, 100–101
    national security fears, 60, 66–67, 71–72,
        79

Bulgarian Communist Party (*continued*)
  property, nationalization of foreign-held,
    170
  Rodina movement relations, 63, 102–3
  treatment of minorities, 56–57, 57 n.4
  Turkish expulsion, 67–68, 69, 106
  Turkish language and, 64, 72–73, 77
  war on Islam, 64, 70–71, 77–78
  wooing of Muslims support, 56–57,
    63–64, 102–3, 129, 185–86
  See also agricultural collectivization; Great
    Leap Forward; Rebirth Process,
    Pomak; Rebirth Process, Turkish
Bulgarian Communist Party (BCP), Muslim
  assimilation, 58, 102–3, 199–200
  anti-circumcision campaigns, 110–11,
    112–14
  anti-*shalvari* campaigns, 128–29, 128 n.45,
    131, 132–33
  compared to Soviet Union, 11–12, 60,
    81
  de-fezzing and anti-turban campaigns,
    103–4
  de-veiling campaigns, 129–31, 132–33
  dress reform, hypocrisy of members,
    134–35, 138
  dress reform legislation, 136–37
  name-changing campaigns, 58–59, 75,
    77–78, 154–59
  reeducation of women, 69–70
  resistance to, 59, 78, 81–82, 84, 133–35,
    138, 200
Bulgarian Communist Party (BCP), Pomak
  assimilation, 74–75
  name-changing campaigns, 75, 154–59
  See also Rebirth Process, Pomak
Bulgarian Communist Party (BCP), Turkish
  assimilation, 76–84
  motivations for, 79–80
  name-changing campaigns, 77–78
  repercussions of, 80–83
  resistance to, 78, 81–82, 84
  See also Rebirth Process, Turkish
Bulgarian constitution (1990), ban on territorial autonomy, 194
Bulgarianization. *See* Bulgarian nationalism;
  dress reform; land reform; name-
  changing campaigns
Bulgarian Muslims. *See* Turks
Bulgarian nationalism, 6, 13, 19
  anti-Turkish sentiment, 186
  ethnography and, 39–41, 73–74
  gender and, 13–14
  identity crisis of, 3, 18–19, 197–98
  peasant as symbol of, 175, 198
  territory and, 169–70, 172, 173–75,
    179–80, 198
  Western influence on, 7–8, 21–23
  See also nationalism
Bulgarian Orthodox Exarchate, 31–32, 36

Bulgarian principality (1878–1908), 27, 37
  ethnography and, 39–41
  land reform of, 174–75, 174 n.21
  treatment of minorities, 19–20, 19 n.2, 35–36
  Western European relations, 25–26, 35
Bulgaro-Mohammedans. *See* Pomaks
Bŭlgarskata Etnografia/Bulgarian Ethnogra-
  phy, 163
Bŭlgarskata Zemedelska Kasa/Bulgarian
  Agricultural Bank, 180
Butler, Judith, 15 n.36

Chatterjee, Partha, 7
Christianity, 41–42, 92–93, 94, 148–49
circumcision, 14–15, 109–14, 115, 115 n.105
  campaigns against, 110–11, 112–14
  ethnic and cultural dimensions of, 111–12
  sünnetçis, 110–11, 114
Clay, Catherine, 39
collective farms. *See* agricultural collectiviza-
  tion
Communism, 49–50, 127
  name-changing campaigns and, 153–54
  See also Bulgarian Communist Party
Communist Manifesto (Marx and Engels), 61
Connolly, William, 171, 171 n.5
Conquest, Robert, 190 n.100
çorbacı (local elders), 90 n.18
  fez and, 90, 91–92
  support of Ottoman Empire, 33, 173
Crampton, Richard, 175
Cromer, Evelyn Baring, Lord, 117 n.5
Cultural Revolution. *See* Great Leap Forward
Cyprus, 71, 192
Czech Republic, 195

Deliorman (newspaper), 179–80, 182
Demir Baba teke (monastery of Demir Baba),
  183
demographic imbalance, 66
Dervishov, Mehmed, 152
de-veiling campaigns, 48, 123–26, 129–31,
  132–33
  Muslim participation in, 119–20
  resistance to, 124, 133–34
devşirme system, 27, 106
"Diado Ivan" (Grandpa Ivan), 35
Dimitrov, Georgi, 186
Dimitrova, Blaga, 1
Diulgerov, Petŭr, 156–59, 160–61
Dobrudzha, 43, 49, 69, 188
Dogan, Ahmed, 193, 194
"Dogan law" (1992), 194
Donchev, Anton, 106–8
Drakulić, Slavenka, 197
dress, Bulgarian, 122–23
  compared to Muslim, 120–21
  folk, loss of, 127–28
  Western European influence on, 89–90,
    121, 131–32

dress, identity and, 120–22, 122–23, 127, 136
dress, late-Ottoman period, 91
dress, Pomak, 93, 121–22, 137, 138, 139
dress reform
  anti-*shalvari* campaigns, 128–29, 128 n.45, 131, 132–33
  de-fezzing/anti-turban campaigns, 92, 94, 103–4
  fashion and, 131–33
  hypocrisy of BCP members, 134–35, 138
  Law on Clothes (1943), 99–100, 126
  legislation of, 136–37
  resistance to, 133–35, 138
  See also de-veiling campaigns
Dukhovnikov, Svetoslav, 152
Duma (newspaper), 195
Dzhambazov, Ismail, 112

Eastern Europe, as intellectual construct, 55, 55 n.1
"Eastern Question", 26, 34
Eastern Rumelia, 36, 174–75
El Guindi, Fadwa, 133
Elizabeth II, Queen of England, 145 n.14
emigration, Greek, 19, 19 n.2
emigration, Jewish, 19, 19 n.2
emigration, Muslim, 169, 176–77, 192, 193
  land transfers and, 174–75, 174 n.21, 175 n.22, 180–81
emigration, Pomak, 42, 181, 188, 188 n.87, 193
emigration, Turkish, 80, 82–83, 180–81, 187–88, 192
Eminov, Ali, 79
Engels, Friedrich, 61–62
ethnography, 40
  Bulgarian nationalism and, 39–41, 73–74
  dress as identity marker, 120–22, 122–23, 127
  preservation of Bulgarian folk culture, 73

Fakhredinov, Ibrakhim, 101
Fanon, Franz, 116
fashion, tool of dress reform, 131–33
Fatherland Front (FF), 55, 100, 126, 129
Ferdinand of Saxe-Coburg, 37 n.53
fez, 90
  BCP tolerance of, 102–3
  Christianity and, 92–93
  çorbacı and, 90, 91–92
  de-fezzing campaigns, 92, 94, 103–4
  Kemalists and, 95–96
  Pomaks and, 92, 93–94, 94, 100
  rejection of, 90, 91–92, 91 n.19, 94–95, 97–99, 104
  Rodina movement and, 48, 95, 97–99
  symbolism of, 14, 88–89, 96, 105–6
  Turks and, 95, 100, 104
FF (Fatherland Front), 55, 100, 126, 129

Fitzpatrick, Sheila, 190 n.100
folk-Islam, 28
"The Forest Traveler" (Rakovski), 25–26, 173–74
Foucault, Michel, 15, 144

Gandev, Khristo, 73
gender, Bulgarian nationalism and, 13–14
Gendev, Nedim, 78, 163–64
Gladstone, William, 34
Goethe, Johann, 143
Goffman, Daniel, 28
Gorbachev, Mikhail, 80–81
Grand Excursion, 82–83
  See also emigration, Turkish
Great Leap Forward, 69–76, 110–11, 130–31
  See also Bulgarian Communist Party
Great Powers, 34–35, 39
Great Rila Wilderness (Vazov), 120–22
Greek Orthodox Church, 30–31
Greeks, 19, 19 n.2, 57 n.4
  control of Rum *millet*, 30–31
Greek yoke, 178
Gribincea, Mihai, 190 n.100
Gypsies (Roma), 19 n.2, 57 n.4, 154 n.49
  administration of *vakf* properties, 182–83, 189–90

Halk Gençlığı (periodical), 191
Halk Sesi/The People's Voice (newspaper), 46, 95
Hapsburg Empire, 30, 144
harem, 117 n.3
hocas, 71, 103
Hoxha, Enver, 154
Hume, David, 171

Ibishev, Halil Ahmedov, 164
Ibraimov, Ahmed, 134
identity
  dress as marker of, 120–22, 122–23, 127, 136
  land and, 170
  names as marker of, 15, 59, 143, 145
identity, national
  East vs West, 1–2
intermarriage, 51–52, 87
Iotsov, Boris, 177
Iovkov, Iordan, 38
Islam, BCP war against, 64, 70–71, 77–78
Islamic fundamentalism, 71, 79
Istanbul, 32 n.38
Istinata i Neistinata/The Truth and Untruth about Circumcision (Mizov), 111
Italy, 51

janissaries, 106–7
Jews, 57, 109, 144
  anti-Semitism, 49 n.93, 51–52, 145
  emigration of, 19, 19 n.2, 49 n.93

Kadıoğlu, Ayşe, 119
Kafadar, Cemal, 26, 172
kalpaks (sheepskin hats), 88
Karavelov, Liuben, 25
Kasaba, Reşat, 33
Kemalists, 12, 44–46, 95 n.28
  BCP relations, 63–64, 102
  de-veiling campaigns, 124–25
  fez and, 95–96
  persecution of, 46, 49–50, 51
  See also Turks
Kertzer, David, 15
Khilendarski, Paisiĭ, 31, 150
Kiliç, Osman, 96, 102
Konstantinov, Aleko, 38–39
Kostanick, Huey, 106
Krasnodar (newspaper), 150

Lada/Harmony (magazine), 131, 133
land reform
  of BCP, 185–86, 188–89
  Bulgarian nationalism and, 172, 179–80
  of Bulgarian principality, 174–75,
    174 n.21
  Bulgaro-Muslim conflict resulting from,
    179–80, 188–89
  occupied territories, 176
  post-Communist, 194–95
  Rhodope Mountains, 178–79
  under Stamboliski, 177
  under Tsankov, 178
  Turkish resistance to, 182
language
  ethnography and, 40
  Ottoman Empire and, 31–32
  Rodina movement and, 48
language, Turkish, 64, 72–73, 77
Lausanne Treaty (1922–1923), 19 n.2, 178
Law for Labor Property in Land (1921), 177
Law of the Purity of the Nation (1940),
  51–52
Law on Clothes (1943), 99–100, 126
Law on Land (1991), 194, 195
Law on Names (1990), 142, 154
Locke, John, 171

Macedonia, 35, 39, 43, 49
  Bulgarianization of, 41, 176, 183–84,
    184 n.69
Mahmood, Saba, 11
Mahmud II, sultan of Ottoman Empire, 30,
  90
manhood, Bulgarian, 14–15, 89, 128–29 n.47
manhood, Muslim, 89
  BCP reining in of, 100–101
  Bulgarian anxieties over, 85–87
  symbols of, 86 (*See also* berets; circumci-
    sion; fez; turban)
  Western European conception of, 117 n.6
manhood, Western European, 86–87, 89

Marinov, Dimitŭr, 122, 128–29 n.47
Marinov, Petŭr, 47, 110, 136, 160, 161–62
  on fez, 99–100, 102, 103, 104
Markov, Georgi, 55
Marx, Karl, 61–62
Marxism, 57–58, 61–62
masculinity. *See* manhood
material culture, 69–70, 76
McClintock, Anne, 7, 11, 145 n.16
MCOs. *See* Muslim Confessional Organiza-
  tions
Mehmedov, Yumer, 134
Mehmed Sinap (Pomak preparatory school),
  65
Mikhailova, Ganka, 127
Mill, John Stuart, 143
millet system, 28–29, 30–33
Mizov, Nikolai, 111, 113, 147, 165–66
Moldavia, 190 n.100
Mosse, George, 86
Movement for Rights and Freedoms (MRF),
  115, 193–94, 200
Muslim assimilation campaigns. *See* Bulgar-
  ian Communist Party, Muslim assimila-
  tion
Muslim Confessional Organizations (MCOs),
  36
  control of *vakf* properties, 182, 189–90
Muslims
  BCP wooing of, 56–57, 63–64, 102–3,
    129, 185–86
  circumcision and, 109
  population growth rate, 72–73
  See also Bulgarian Communist Party
    (BCP), Muslim assimilation; emigra-
    tion, Muslim; Pomaks; Turks

name-changing campaigns, 142, 144 n.9,
  145–46, 154 n.49
  Albania, 153–54
  BCP, 58–59, 75, 77–78, 154–59
  Christianity and, 148–49
  Communism and, 153–54
  justification for, 59, 162–63
  against Pomaks, 15–16, 53, 148–49,
    154–59
  Pomak resistance to, 105–6, 151–52
  Rodina movement, 53, 150–51, 151–52
  against Turks, 15–16, 77–78, 81
name-changing, United States, 144–45,
  144 n.11
names, 165–66
  as identity markers, 15, 59, 143, 145
names, Bulgarian
  Western Europeanization of, 145, 147
names, Pomak, 147–48
names, Turkish, 148
naming systems, 144–45, 144 n.7
  non-hereditary patronymic system, 146
  surname system, 146–47

national identity, East vs West, 1–2
nationalism, 6–7
  land and, 16, 170–72
  Marxism and, 61–62
  See also Bulgarian nationalism
Nazim Hikmet (secular Turkish gymnasium),
  65
Neuilly, Treaty of (1919), 43
Niuvab (private Muslim seminary), 65
Nova Svetlina (newspaper), 114
  See also Yeni Işık
Nuri Bei, Osman, 45

Old Church Slavonic, 30–31
Ondaatje, Michael, 18
Orientalism, 4–5, 21–22
Orientalism (Said), 4–5, 4 n.7, 4 n.12, 86 n.3
Osmanlılık (Ottomanism), 30
Ottoman Empire, 23–33
  çorbacı support of, 33, 173
  co-territoriality between Muslims and
    Christians, 172–73
  economic system, 29, 32–33
  fall of, 30–33
  language and, 31–32
  millet system, 28–29, 30–33
  religious tolerance, 27–29
  Russian relations, 32
  Turkish yoke, 24–26
  Western European conception of, 23–24
Ottomanism, 30
Ottoman yoke, 24–25, 37–38

Pasha, Midhat, 32
Pelin, Elin, 176
Philippines, 144 n.9
Pirinsko Delo (newspaper), 192
Pod Igoto/Under the Yoke (Vazov), 37–38,
  90 n.18, 92
Pomak, origin of term, 150
Pomaks, 198–99, 200
  BCP wooing of, 56–57, 102
  Bulgarianness of, 2 n.5, 5–6, 12, 40–41,
    46–47
  Christianity, forced conversion to, 41–42,
    92, 94
  circumcision of, 110
  de-veiling campaigns, resistance to, 124
  dress of, 93, 121–22, 137, 138, 139
  emigration of, 42, 181, 188, 188 n.87, 193
  fez and, 92, 93–94, 94, 100
  name-changing campaigns against, 15–16,
    53, 148–49, 154–59
  name-changing campaigns, resistance to,
    75, 105–6, 151–52
  origins of, 20, 20 n.4, 21, 27, 75
  population of, 2–3, 3 n.6, 20, 20 n.3, 22
  See also Muslims; Rebirth Process, Pomak;
    Rodina movement
Poptomov, Vladmir, 186

Poulton, Hugh, 164 n.87
Prava i Svobodi/Rights and Freedoms (newspaper), 195
property, 171
  nationalization of foreign-held, 170
  tax burden of, 175–76
  See also territory
property restitution, 195

Radoslavov, Vasil, 42
Rakovski, Georgi, 25–26, 173–74
Razgradsko Slovo (newspaper), 183
Rebirth Process, Pomak (1968–1975), 58–59,
  156–60, 200
  criticism of, 161–62
  resistance to, 105–6, 157–58, 159–61
  See also Pomaks
Rebirth Process, Turkish (1984–1985),
  58–59, 76–83, 162–67, 192–93, 200
  dress reform, 136–37
  motivations for, 79–80
  name-changing campaigns, 77–78, 81
  repercussions of, 80–83
  resistance to, 78, 81–82, 84, 164–65, 193
Rehber (newspaper), 182
religion
  ethnography and, 40
  Ottoman Empire, 27–29
  Rodina movement and, 52–53
  See also Christianity; Islam
Rhodope Mountains, 41, 112, 178–79
Rodina movement, 12, 44, 46–48, 97, 98
  anti-circumcision campaigns, 110
  BCP relations, 63, 102–3
  de-veiling campaigns, 48, 125–26
  fez, rejection of, 48, 95, 97–99
  name-changing campaigns, 53, 150–51,
    151–52
  religion and, 52–53
  See also Pomaks
Rodopa (newspaper), 150, 179
Roma. *See* Gypsies
Romania, 174
Rothschild, Joseph, 43
Rousseau, Jean-Jacques, 171
Rumetsov, Salikh, 152
Russia, 24, 30, 32, 33, 35
Russo-Turkish War (1877–1878), 33–35

Said, Edward, 4–5, 4 n.7, 4 n.12, 6, 21–22,
  86 n.3
Salveĭkov, Petko, 89–90
Salvianabŭlgarska Istoriia/Slavo-Bulgarian
  History (Khilendarski), 31, 150
San Stefano Treaty (1878), 35
Savaş/War (newspaper), 72
Sbornik Rodina, 47, 97
Schama, Simon, 169
Scott, James, 11 n.28, 13 n.32, 144, 144 n.9
Sega (periodical), 137, 138, 142

Şeriat, 36
Shakespeare, William, 142, 143
shalvari (baggy pants)
    campaigns against, 119, 128–29, 128 n.45,
        131, 132–33
    symbolism of, 14, 128, 128 n.45
Sheimanov, Naiden, 44
Shishkov, Stoiu, 40–41, 123
Singer, Amy, 28
Slaveĭkov, Peiu, 121 n.19
Slavo-Bulgarian History (Khilendarski), 31,
    150
Slezkine, Yuri, 11
Smith, Anthony, 170
Soviet Union, 66, 80–81
    agricultural collectivization, 190 n.100
    emancipation of Muslim women, 126–27
    influence on Bulgaria, 9–12
    Muslim assimilation within, 11–12, 60, 81
    name-changing campaigns, 153
Stamboliski, Alexander, 43–44, 177–78
Stambolov, Stephan, 37 n.53
Stanchev, Sirko, 52
Staroplaninski Legendi/Legends of Stara
    Planet (Iovkov), 38
Stoianov, Zakhari, 88
Stoianovich, Traian, 32 n.40
Suleimanov, Naim, 164
sünnetçis, 110–11, 114
Suny, Ronald, 10, 11

Tainata na Lichnoto Ime/The Secret of the
    Personal Name (Mizov), 165–66
Takhirov, Shukri, 78
Tanzimat proclamation (1839), 30
Tatar yoke, 24
TCOs (Turkish Communal Organizations),
    190
territory, 171 n.5
    Bulgarian nationalism and, 169–70,
        173–75, 179–80, 198
    nationalism and, 16, 170–72
    See also property
Thrace, 35, 43
    Bulgarianization of, 41, 49, 176, 183–84
    population exchanges, 174–75, 178
Time of Parting, A (film), 163
TKZS (Trudovo Kooperativno Zemedelsko
    Stopansko), 187
Todorova, Maria, 5, 23, 31 n.13, 39 n.56,
    55 n1, 87
Topchiev, Mirian, 163–64
Trudovo Kooperativno Zemedelsko Stopan-
    sko (TKZS), 187
Truman Doctrine (1947), 67
Tsankov, Alexander, 178
Turan (Turkish cultural-educational associa-
    tion), 46, 95
turban, 93
    BCP and, 102–3, 103–4

campaigns against, 92, 94, 103–4
symbolism of, 14, 96, 105–6
Turkey
    Bulgarian relations, 66–67, 73, 80, 184,
        192
    modernization of, 45, 96, 134
Turkish Communal Organizations (TCOs),
    190
Turkish language, BCP and, 64, 72–73, 77
"Turkish question", 186–87
Turkish Resettlement of Bulgarian Turks
    (Kostanick), 106
Turkish yoke, 24–25, 37–38
Turks, 200
    BCP wooing of, 56–57, 62–63
    Bulgarianness of, 2 n.5, 5–6, 12, 40
    emigration of, 80, 82–83, 180–81, 187–88,
        192
    expulsion of, 67–68, 69, 106
    fez and, 95, 100, 104
    land reform, resistance to, 182
    name-changing campaigns against, 15–16,
        77–78, 81
    origins of, 3 n.6, 20–21
    personal name-system changes, 152–53
    population of, 2–3, 3 n.6, 20, 20 n.3, 22,
        175 n.22
    state cooperation, 44–46, 50–52
    See also Kemalists; Muslims; Rebirth Pro-
        cess, Turkish

Under the Yoke (film), 163
Under the Yoke (Vazov), 175
Union of Democratic Forces, 83, 115
United Kingdom, 34, 66
    renaming of royal family, 145
United States, 43, 66, 67, 80
    name-changing in, 144–45, 144 n.11
urbanization, 27–28, 73
USSR. See Soviet Union

Vakarelski, Khristo, 129 n.47
vakf properties, 170, 195
    administration of, 182–83, 189–90
    state appropriation of, 184, 189
Vazov, Ivan, 37–38, 90 n.18, 92, 120–22,
    148, 175
veil, 93, 117–18, 134, 137, 138, 139
    as elite urban phenomenon, 118–19
    as symbol of backwardness, 14, 119
    as symbol of oppression, 101, 123
    as symbol of resistance, 120, 120 n.17,
        126, 133–34
    See also de-veiling campaigns
veil, Middle East, 120
Veleva, Maria, 127
Venelin, Iuri, 39
Vidin uprisings (1841, 1850), 32 n.37
Vreme Rasdeleno/A Time of Parting
    (Donchev), 106–8

Western Europe, 43, 109
  Bulgarian dress, influence on, 89–90, 121,
    131–32
  Bulgarian names, influence on, 145, 147
  Bulgarian relations, 25–26, 35
  manhood and, 86–87, 89, 117 n.6
  Ottoman Empire, conception of, 23–24
Wolff, Larry, 55 n.1
womanhood, symbols of, 14–15
women, Muslim
  BCP emancipation of, 101, 129–30
  Rodina movement and, 97
  Soviet emancipation of, 126–27
  as ultimate proletariat, 56, 56 n.2
women, Turkish
  BCP reeducation of, 69–70
World War I, 42–43, 176
World War II, 48–49, 183

yashmak, 123
  See also veil

Yeğenoğlu, Meyda, 116 n.1, 133
Yeni Hayat/New Life (newspaper), 64
Yeni Işık/New Light (newspaper), 64, 103,
    105*i*, 132, 185
  attack on circumcision, 113–14
  promotion of Cultural Revolution, 70,
    104*i*, 129
Young, Robert, 5 n.13
Yugoslavia, 79
Yugov, Anton, 190
Yuval-Davis, Nira, 14 n.33

Zagorov, Orlin, 78
Zheliaskova, Antonina, 21
Zhenata Dnes/Women Today (magazine), 131
zhenotdeli, 130
Zhivkov, Todor, 68, 77, 82, 130, 192, 193,
    199
  Rebirth Processes and, 158, 161, 162
  See also Bulgarian Communist Party
Zlatkov, Atanas, 93